ANTONIA WHITE
Diaries 1926–1957

By Antonia White

Fiction
Frost in May (D. Harmsworth, 1933; Virago, 1978)
The Lost Traveller (Eyre & Spottiswoode, 1950; Virago, 1979)
The Sugar House (Eyre & Spottiswoode, 1952; Virago, 1979)
Beyond the Glass (Eyre & Spottiswoode, 1954; Virago, 1979)
Strangers (Harvill Press, 1954; Virago, 1981)
As Once in May (ed. Susan Chitty and including early Autobiography
and unfinished novels *Julian Tye* and *Clara IV*, Virago, 1983)

Non-fiction
*The Hound and the Falcon: The Story of a Reconversion to the
Catholic faith* (Longmans, 1965; Virago, 1980)

Children's books
Minka and Curdy (Harvill, 1957)
Living with Minka and Curdy (Harvill, 1970)

A play
Three in a Room, a comedy in 3 acts (French's Acting Edition, 1947)

By Susan Chitty

Now to My Mother, A very personal memoir of Antonia White
(Weidenfeld & Nicolson, 1985)

ANTONIA WHITE

Diaries 1926–1957

Volume I

EDITED BY

Susan Chitty

CONSTABLE · LONDON

First published in Great Britain 1991
by Constable and Company Limited
3 The Lanchesters, 162 Fulham Palace Road
London W6 9ER
Copyright © 1991 Susan Chitty
The right of Susan Chitty to be
identified as the author of this work
has been asserted by her in accordance
with the Copyright, Designs and Patents Act 1988
ISBN 0 09 470650 6
Set in Monophoto 12pt Garamond by
Servis Filmsetting Limited, Manchester
Printed in Great Britain by
St Edmundsbury Press Limited
Bury St Edmunds, Suffolk

A CIP catalogue record for this book
is available from the British Library

TO MIRANDA

Contents

Illustrations

Author's note

The diaries have been reproduced, as to spelling and style, as Antonia wrote them except in a very few cases where, for the sake of the sense, I have corrected errors of punctuation. On page 323 there is a list of biographical sketches giving some details of the main characters referred to in the diaries. A † following a name indicates that a biographical sketch is supplied.

S.E.C.

1991

Introduction

Antonia White was born a year before the beginning of the twentieth century, of which she was so much a part. She was the only child of Cecil Botting and his wife Christine White. Her mother always called her Tony, although her real name was Eirene, spelled in the Greek manner. Her father came of a long line of Sussex yeomen but had risen to become head of the classics department of St Paul's School, London, and was co-author of the famous Hillard and Botting Latin and Greek text books. Antonia's early years were spent at 22 Perham Road, West Kensington, where she largely occupied herself by inventing adventures for her rocking horse, Sceptre and her toy poodle, Mr Dash. She was to relive those first four years with increasing affection for the rest of her life and, even when she was in revolt against most of the things her father held dear, she never moved far from West Kensington.

The Sussex background, however, was very much part of her childhood and of her life. Her summer holidays were spent at Binesfield, the cottage standing back from Bines Green where Cecil Botting's maiden aunts, Clara and Agnes Jeffery, lived. Bines Common is between the villages of Ashurst and Partridge Green, near Horsham and the South Downs. Old Stepney, the gardener, used to wheel a handcart four miles to Steyning, at the foot of the Downs, once a week on market day.

When Antonia was nine her father, who had become a convert to Catholicism, sent her as a boarder to the Convent of the Sacred Heart at Roehampton, a southern suburb of London, near Richmond Park and only a bus ride from West Kensington. She worked hard there and won many prizes for work and morals, but disaster struck when she was fifteen. A book she was writing for her father was discovered in somebody else's desk. It was to have been the story of some people with 'unspeakable vices' ('unspeakable' because Antonia did not know what they were) who were ultimately converted. Unfortunately Reverend Mother read it before the young author had had time to write the end. Antonia had always understood that she was expelled from the convent, but she discovered years later that her father had withdrawn her.

She was now sent to St Paul's Girls' School, Kensington. At St Paul's the frivolous side of her nature came to the fore and, from having wanted only to please her father, she now seemed to wish only to annoy him. She failed to work hard enough for the Cambridge Higher Local Examination to win a scholarship, and so to go on to Cambridge in his footsteps. Instead she experimented with clothes and make-up, and, finding by chance that she had a knack for writing advertising copy, she was soon earning £250 a year from Dearborn's Beauty Preparations advertising a product called Mercolized Wax.

Antonia left St Paul's at the age of seventeen, as she had been offered a job by the Lattey family as their governess. During the next three years she supported herself with odd teaching jobs and worked in government offices. Then she did something that must have been still more of a shock to her father: she took a year's course at what is now the Royal Academy of Dramatic Art, and went on to tour the provinces as the *ingénue* in a farce called *The Private Secretary*. She never pretended to be a good actress but she had a fluffy blond charm which saw her through. Even in youth she was attractive rather than beautiful and her looks changed according to her mood.

In 1921, Antonia made a disastrous and incomprehensible marriage to Reggie Green-Wilkinson, a gangling young man of good family whose passions were for driving fast cars and hanging about the theatre. He also drank too much. The only interest the young couple shared was playing toy soldiers in their toy house at 38 Glebe Place, Chelsea.

After three years the marriage was annulled, legally and by the Catholic Church, and Antonia returned to her parents' home. By now she had fallen in love with a handsome officer in the King's Own Scottish Borderers. He was called Robert Legg and he was lucky to have survived the trenches. The two appear to have established telepathic powers of communication when apart. Three weeks later Antonia was certified insane – terrified, she later insisted, by his amorous advances – and spent a year in Bethlem Royal Hospital, often under restraint.

Soon after her sudden and unexpected recovery she returned to her parents' home and spent a night with Jim Dougal, a seedy journalist. He was her first lover, in the physical sense. She conceived a child and underwent an abortion.

The memory of her madness and the fear that it might return did not leave Antonia for the rest of her life. It may explain her second marriage which was not to Robert, who had married somebody else while she was in Bethlem, but to Eric Earnshaw Smith, a Cambridge-educated civil servant whom she had venerated as little less than a seer since she was a drama student at the age of twenty-one. Despite later entanglements, Antonia's veneration for Eric, her closest friend, lasted until his death. Together they moved to 55 Paulton's Square, Chelsea. By now she had a well-paid job as head woman copywriter at W.S. Crawford's advertising agency. It was Eric who persuaded her to abandon her Catholic faith.

During her second marriage, Antonia began to take lovers to compensate for the affairs her husband was having with young soldiers. Her admirers were mostly men whom she met on holiday, and included Yvon from Martinique and Edo from Austria, but one, Bertrand Russell, was far from unknown and not particularly young. Encouraged by Eric, she had introduced herself to Russell after one of his lectures.

In 1928 a tall, handsome young man with a slightly melancholy charm, Rudolph Glossop, known as Silas, crashed into this uneasy household. He was brought there one day by a friend, Frank Freeman, because his motorbike had broken down outside. Silas is my father. He was not the kind of person Antonia was likely to meet at the Chelsea parties she frequented. Although he was well read in French and English literature, he was by profession a mining engineer, often obliged to work abroad. He was undoubtedly attracted to Antonia by her literary powers as well as her charm and became her lover.

Antonia had by now taken on a part-time job, as assistant to Desmond McCarthy, editor of *Life and Letters*, in addition to her work at Crawford's. It was in this review that her first short story appeared. 'The House of Clouds' was based on her experiences in the asylum. She signed it with the pseudonym 'Antonia White', taken from her childhood name, Tony.

In August 1929 I was born and, three months later, Cecil Botting died. Cecil was fifty-nine and had enjoyed only three years of his early retirement, living at Binesfield. To add to the complications of this period of her life, Antonia now fell in love with Tom Hopkinson, a junior copywriter at Crawford's. Tom was one of the four sons of a north country parson. He was recently down from Oxford and was considered a promising novelist.

Antonia was divorced from Eric in the autumn of 1929. She had the greatest difficulty in deciding whether to marry Silas Glossop or Tom Hopkinson, and kept them both in suspense until Silas took a mining post in Canada and went there to await her decision. In 1930 she married Tom and in 1931 my half-sister Lyndall was born. Antonia and Tom moved to 18 Cecil Court in Hollywood Road, Fulham, engaged a nurse for us children and for a few years established a nearly normal home.

Frost in May, Antonia's first and most successful novel, based on her experiences at the convent and published in 1933, was written with Tom's encouragement. He insisted on having a new chapter read aloud to him every weekend. The book was the first and last to be published by a new firm, Desmond Harmsworth (Harmsworth had just set himself up with the money he'd won in a sweepstake) and its dust jacket was designed by Antonia's old friend the painter Joan Souter Robertson. Like her subsequent novels, it was largely autobiographical.

Antonia's celebrity brought her many new friends including the amazing trio of American women, Djuna Barnes, author of *Nightwood*, Emily Coleman, author of *The Shutter of Snow*, and Peggy Guggenheim, the art collector. With them she spent a holiday at Hayford Hall, in Devon (better known as Hangover Hall). Success, however, did not have a good effect on her marriage. Although Tom's short stories were admired, and he was later to achieve fame as the wartime editor of *Picture Post*, none of his novels received the attention accorded to *Frost in May*. It was a cruel turn of fate for Antonia that, just at this moment of recognition, 'The Beast', as she described her madness, returned. This time it came in the form of neurosis rather than insanity and she underwent a Freudian analysis. The same year (1935) she left Tom and moved into a room at 105 Oakley Street, Chelsea, and began a period of almost hectic promiscuity. She had close relationships with the group of young poets of which Dylan Thomas was a member: David Gascoyne, George Barker and Norman Cameron, with the West Indian sculptor Ronald Moody and others in the art and theatre worlds.

In 1938 she divorced Tom Hopkinson and began freelance fashion writing for the *Sunday Pictorial* (Cecil King, its owner, was a friend). For once she had no financial problems and she moved into a handsome two-storey flat in Cornwall Gardens, South Kensington, with my sister and myself, and continued her affair with Ian Henderson, son of her friend Wyn. But with the War her jobs folded, Ian enlisted and the Cornwall Gardens flat was bombed.

Perhaps it was not surprising that Antonia should have chosen this moment to return to the Catholic Church, after a twenty-year absence. She considered that the moment was chosen for her by God and now explored her religion intellectually with a thoroughness she had never done in her youth. She wrote newspaper articles and gave lectures about it and contributed pieces, one on her beloved St Thomas Aquinas, to French and English religious periodicals. She also wrote a series of letters to Peter Thorp, a stranger who had written to her. He had once been a Jesuit. These were published many years later under the title *The Hound and the Falcon*.

During the War Antonia had been obliged to return to fulltime office work. She had a period with the BBC Overseas Department, then moved to SOE (Special Operations Executive). Once the War was over she determined to devote herself to writing novels. She by now had a flat in Kensington at 13 Ashburn Gardens.

It was not until 1950, sixteen years after *Frost in May*, that she produced her second novel, *The Lost Traveller*. It carried Nanda, the child heroine of the first novel, now renamed Clara, through her late adolescence. In a period of rare fertility, Antonia produced two more novels in the next four years, *The Sugar House* (1952) and *Beyond the Glass* (1954). The first was based on Antonia's experiences in the theatre and her marriage to Reggie Green-Wilkinson (renamed Archie Hughes-Follett). The second was about her madness. During the 'forties (more or less) Antonia wrote half a dozen short poems at intervals. They were only squeezed out of her under pressure of strong emotion: thus 'Epitaph' was for a beautiful friend who died a brutal death, and 'The Double Man' was about Ian Henderson. By far the longest, 'Sed Tantum Dic Verbo' concerned the eating of Christ's body.

Now that Antonia no longer received a salary, much of her time had to be devoted to writing for money. She wrote novel reviews for Janet Adam Smith, the literary editor of the *New Statesman*, but relied for serious income on translations. With her first, Maupassant's *A Woman's Life*, she won the Denyse Clairouin prize in 1949. There were thirty-four titles to follow, many of them the novels of Colette, the last translation appearing in 1967.

At this time Antonia also wrote some pieces for such magazines as *Punch* and *Lilliput* (a pocket-sized humorous magazine edited by Tom Hopkinson). Her sense of humour unfortunately could not encompass her relations with Lyndall and myself. I had gone up to Oxford in 1947 and in 1948 Lyndall began a year's stage production course at the Old Vic Theatre School. Antonia's response to any success we had was one of extreme jealousy leading to hostility. I had a severe nervous breakdown on coming down from Oxford and was still recovering from it when she turned me out of her flat on a trivial pretext. I married Thomas Chitty (Hinde) and did not communicate with her for five years. In 1952 I won the Vogue Talent Contest and was rewarded with a job on the magazine which I held until our first child was born. Lyndall moved permanently to Italy. Antonia was not an easy woman to be involved with emotionally. She had at least two intense relationships with women (Benedicta de Bezer, a religious friend, and Dorothy Kingsmill, her friend and analyst) during the post-war period and both ended explosively.

My mother and I were reconciled in 1957, when she met her first grandchildren, Andrew and Cordelia. Lyndall always kept in touch. Antonia later declared that the last twenty-five years of her life were the happiest. Alone in her fourth-floor flat at 42 Courtfield Gardens, to which she moved in 1958 and where her work room looked over the trees and the church in the square, she spent most of the day working at her father's desk surrounded by her books. In the late afternoon she occasionally had a friend in for a glass of sherry (whisky for a priest). Her conversation was anecdotal and often very funny, and she abandoned herself to it with obvious pleasure. She would end a particularly naughty story with a special laugh I can still hear. When I was little more than a child she had kept me up much too late with those stories. I never complained.

As her infirmities increased, the ninety-seven stairs up to the flat became a problem, but she would not move to the ground-floor flat that Lyndall offered. During this period she was threatened with a third nervous breakdown and had weekly consultations with a Dr Ployé.

Luckily, of her surviving friends some were young and strong. A great companion of her last two years was the publisher, Carmen Callil of Virago Press. Besides bringing Antonia's novels back into print, she even did her shopping on the way to work. Antonia was now earning enough to spend her last years without the financial worries, many of them of her own making, that had dogged her all her life. She had usually been in debt to Harrods, Selfridges, or Peter Jones. She was a shameless recipient of handouts, often from people who could ill afford to give ('I know she is hard up,' she said of her friend, Phyllis Jones, 'but it is in her nature to give and I cannot prevent her'). Lyndall provided her with a small income throughout her last years.

Sadly, Antonia did not live to see the *Frost in May* serialization on BBC Television in 1981. She died on 10 April 1980.

Antonia White left behind diaries that spanned more than half a century and filled forty notebooks and ring files. It amounted to a million words, of which I have selected a quarter, and have divided this into two volumes of which this is the first. The first volume of the diary (1926) tells of an aeroplane trip to Paris. The last (1979) records the journey towards her own death. Had it not been for an unfortunate bottle of Pommard 1937, consumed with Benedicta de Bezer, the diary would have gone back to 1921. On that occasion two 'enormous old journals' were burnt and the Office of the Dead was said over them.

Besides the ordinary diaries there are three which differ from the rest. One is 'the Analysis Diary', started in 1935, in which Antonia attempted to record her three-year psychoanalysis with Dr Dennis Carroll. The second is the 'Basil Nicholson Diary' of 1937. On the cover of this separate notebook Antonia wrote 'B.N.' Its more sexual passages were in French. The third is the 'Benedicta Diary', a tiny notebook in which she recorded the events of her tempestuous affair with Benedicta in 1947. In fact none of these (with the exception of the first few pages of the Benedicta Diary and the French passages of the Nicholson Diary) differs greatly in style from the normal diaries, and they have been incorporated chronologically with the rest.

It has been suggested that Antonia's diaries were in fact not diaries but writer's notebooks. She herself referred to them by both names. Certainly they were not diaries in the conventional sense. Sometimes she did not make an entry for many months or even a year. Sometimes, when she was in love or wrestling with a personal or theological problem, she would fill twenty pages at a sitting. External events, even important ones, were by no means always recorded, indeed sometimes they were not recorded *because* they were important. Of her first meeting with her grandchildren she wrote, 'It means too much. I don't need to record it.'

So the diaries, in her small neat hand, were largely an internal affair, 'telling myself about myself', as Julien Green said of his journals. In them, Antonia wrestled with her psychological problems and particularly with the guilt she felt about her father. Many of her dreams were about her father. Dreams form so much a part of the diary that at first it is often hard to tell a dream entry from a real one. During her three periods of psychoanalysis (with Dr Carroll, Dorothy Kingsmill and Dr Ployé) the dreams become exceptionally vivid. Most vivid of all was a dream (recorded elsewhere) in which she was ritually raped by her father and actually felt him penetrate her. It is hard not to suspect that Cecil may have, even if only to a small degree, sexually abused Antonia as a child. Father and daughter had the ground floor of 22 Perham Road to themselves, with a lavatory used only by them (as Antonia always pointed out) between his study and her nursery. It is known that his wife was frigid and he was too devout to have a mistress. If anything did happen, Antonia certainly 'forgot' it. Perhaps she invented her expulsion from the convent as a stick with which to beat her father. So strong were her feelings about him that in the one passage of the diaries where she obscenely abuses him her handwriting deteriorates into a childish scrawl.

Closely connected with her father was the problem of her writer's block, for which she considered him responsible. Diary entries over the whole fifty years refer to her ability to start a new novel and her inability to continue it. She once wrote, 'I have a superb collection of beginnings.' She longed to be able to write novels with the ease with which she wrote the diaries. 'How fast, how comparatively painlessly

I write [these] ... I have sat here for only one hour and a quarter and how many sheets are covered – over ten pages – over 1200 words. If I could do as much each day to my book, I would have the body there to work on in a few weeks.'

The third subject that constantly concerned her was religion, or to be more precise, Catholicism. In the course of the diary we see her slow return to the fold after her long lapse, a period of fervour during the Second World War, and then the equally slow return of doubts, which her painstaking reading of the Old Testament did not allay.

In places, however, the diary *is* a writer's notebook, in the conventional sense. That is to say, it contains sketches of people and places that the writer can call on for use at a later date. There are descriptions of the English countryside in particular, and of Germany and Spain in which she seems to be consciously filling in a card for a card index section entitled, 'Backgrounds, countries, various'. Few of these descriptions were actually used since the events her novels described took place before the start of the surviving diary. According to Antonia, one episode from the lost 1927 diary provided material for a short story. It was entitled 'Mon Pays c'est la Martinique', 1927, and described a holiday love-affair between Sabine, a young English girl, and a boy from Martinique. The setting was the Mediterranean coast of France. Antonia considered the story, her first, a failure, and it was not published in her lifetime. Events in the diary did, however, supply her with material for at least one published short story, 'The Moment of Truth', which is based on a holiday with Tom Hopkinson in Brittany.

Antonia White's diaries are not exclusively for the literary. Life keeps breaking in. A discussion on the literal truth of the Old Testament is cut short by calculations for paying Harrods' bill or planning tea for a burglar. However trivial her subject her pride as a craftsman never allows her to write less than well and her honesty drives her to see the ridiculous in herself as well as others. A critic reading these diaries in manuscript has declared, 'They are more important both as literature and as a record than I had believed possible. They will enlarge humanity.' Most people, on reading the last page, will brush aside a tear for a woman who, though far from perfect, fought a lonely battle against the demons without and within, and never lost her earlier curiosity about this world and the next. Her comment on any particularly unfortunate event was, 'But it was so *interesting*.'

There remains the question of whether the diaries should have been published. Certainly Antonia White constantly read and reread them herself. Not only did she go back over the past year's entries at each year's end, but she often read much further back, frequently amazed to find how little her preoccupations had changed, or, worse still, that she had absolutely no recollection of making certain entries. Occasionally she was pleased by what she read. More often she made remarks like 'They're all alike, the *dreary* things,' or 'It is extra-ordinary glancing through these last pages. They really seem to have been written by someone insane.' During these rereadings she occasionally made corrections or added footnotes. She also gave the diaries to other people to read. She lent Dr Carroll a volume and read extracts aloud to Ian Henderson on one occasion, and to her friends Eric Siepmann and Mary Wesley on another. She once left a volume around for Tom Hopkinson to read during his affair with Frances Grigson (the wife of Geoffrey Grigson), and was surprised that he wasn't nicer to her afterwards.

Antonia did herself consider publishing the diaries. Among her papers is a typed section of the 1937 diary (identified in the text as 'Revised Diary'), describing her holiday with the Group Theatre, sometimes known as the 'Grope Theatre', at Summerhill. It differs significantly from the original diary for the same period. She has added a description of the celebrated educationalist, A.S. Neill, aware that it would interest readers, and cut down on a private adventure.

The question of whether or not Antonia intended her diaries to be published is finally answered by the entry of 24 June 1964. 'I ought perhaps to have put in my will that they should all be burned at my death. On the other hand, if anything of my writing survives, other writers might find things of interest to them in it. And perhaps other Catholics – and people interested in religion. Or in psychology . . . I think the only thing is to tell Sue the whole story and leave her to decide.'

My decision has been that they should be published, believing that, until someone writes a biography of Antonia White (my sister and I only wrote memoirs), these diaries must stand as her memorial.

Chronology

1938   Affair with Ian Henderson
        Moves to Cornwall Gardens with Susan and Lyndall
        Analysis ends
        Divorce from Tom
        Enters nursing home in Devonshire Terrace
        Fashion editor of *Sunday Pictorial*

1939   War.   Stays with friends at South Mimms and Marshfield
        Children evacuated to Tom's parents in Westmorland
        Death of Christine Botting

1940   Return to the Church
        Lyndall to live with Tom and Gerti
        Both children at boarding school
        Return to London to Linden Gardens, Notting Hill
        Job with BBC

1941   Writes 'The Moment of Truth'

1943   Job with SOE (Special Operations Europe)

1944   Moves to 29 Thurloe Square, then to 13 Ashburn Gardens, Kensington
        Three in a Room staged at Oldham

1947   Susan goes to Oxford
        Affair with Benedicta de Bezer. Early diaries destroyed.
        Analysis by Dorothy Kingsmill

1948   Lyndall goes to Old Vic Theatre School, lives at Ashburn Gardens

1949   Denyse Clairouin Prize for translation of *A Woman's Life*

1950   Publication of *The Lost Traveller*

1951   Susan at Maudsley Hospital with depression
        Susan turned out of Ashburn Gardens, marries Thomas Chitty (Hinde)

1952   Publication of *The Sugar House*
        Lyndall goes to Rome
        Four novels translated from the French

1953   Birth of Andrew Chitty, first grandson

1954   Publication of *Beyond the Glass* and *Strangers* (short stories)

1955   Lyndall marries Lionel Birch

1956   Libel action against *The Sugar House*

1957   Publication of *Minka and Curdy* for children
        Reconciled with Susan

1958   Moves to 42 Courtfield Gardens, sells Binesfield
        Translates several Colette novels
        Semester at St Mary's College, South Bend, Indiana

1965   Produces typed versions of first four chapters of two sequels to

Beyond the Glass: *Clara IV* and *Julian Tye*
The Hound and the Falcon published

1966   Lyndall starts relationship with Count Lorenzo Passerini
1970   Publication of *Living with Minka and Curdy*
       Commences writing autobiography
1975   Thomas and Susan walking in Europe – April '75 to Sept '76
1977   Meets Carmen Callil of Virago
1979   Virago edition of *Frost in May*
       Moves to St Raphael's nursing home, Danehill, Sussex
1980   Dies, 10 April

PARIS 1926

Antonia White started to keep a diary in 1921, when she was married to Reggie Green-Wilkinson,[†] but she eventually destroyed the first two 'enormous volumes'. Only the little 1926 diary, printed below, survived. It gave an account of a visit to Paris by aeroplane with an unknown admirer. Antonia was married to Eric Earnshaw Smith,[†] her second husband by this time. They lived in Paulton's Square, Chelsea, and she worked at W.S. Crawford's advertising agency.

Paris 1926 Canaries, wireless, heavy vans, incessant bells, piano with a sharp always recurring in wrong place. Yellow lace, the bronze girl holding up her skirt, curtains like rhubarb striped red and green ... Excessive neatness of the country seen from the air: cemeteries like rows of little white lozenges stuck round a cardboard church. Fields look like stuff, some threadbare, some with a rich pile like velvet, some with a curious cross weave. You can see deep into pools – a lovely pattern of mud and weeds ... Coming down is good wild slanting perspective and all the pigmy trees growing bigger until the plane gets back to its right proportions. In the air our enormous wing covered half a county ...

Armenonville – gravel round a dancing floor. Festoons of paper roses everywhere – the light makes the trees an artificial acid green like the backcloth of a pantomime. The real roses on the tables dashed with water to make them look dewy. Jews, South Americans, loads of jewels. Everywhere the same tired painted faces ...

One beautiful woman with a perfect short oval face, dark eyes, mouth like a red petal, two smooth wings of black hair repeating the long curve of her eyebrows. Very slender, dressed in very perfect black over which she pulled a gold lamé coat with a huge sable collar. Another, her sister, far less beautiful, not beautiful at all, but very *troublante*. The same deliciously slender limbs and polished hands, heavier eyelids, a riper mouth, a darker skin, every line a little carelessly drawn, but infinitely provocative ...

After these enforced gaieties we mercifully go for long drives in the bois. Beautiful these hot starry summer nights ... among trees that seem to spread for miles and do not meet a soul. This soft wind and darkness and the sweet smell of the trees made me quite irresponsible after the dry glare and the intolerable noise of the 'Boeuf sur le Toit' where one goes to look at the Jews and the Lesbians and the fairies. There is a clever little Eton cropped thing called Muriel who plays the piano at the Boeuf. She got up and danced the Charleston among wild applause, hiking up her soft dull rose frock to show a pair of sinewy knees in rolled stockings. She was joined later by a pretty languid little American in chartreuse green. They jigged opposite each other in the exasperating double time of the Charleston while the fairies clapped the tune, until they fell into each others arms kissing frantically from sheer exhaustion . . .

The more I see men the less I understand them. They make the wildest proposals, cry like children, like children drop off to sleep suddenly, offer you the world and refuse to buy you a month's peace of mind . . .   I went with my remarkable Mr Alexander [unknown] on a brisk 'gallery crawl'. We saw . . . a beautiful Renoir, very gay in colour of figures in summer dresses in a green meadow.

I have seen perhaps 30 Renoirs (there are 200 in New York) in the last week and nearly all of them first class . . . the feeling of flesh under the thin crumpled muslins, the stuff must be hot to the touch . . . The glow is all in Renoir's mind . . .

Versailles is a little disappointing. It is my own fault for having made a mental picture. I'm always being had like that and I deserve all I get . . .

. . . there is too much Hampton Court about it – bourgeois families and soldiers everwhere sprawling on the grass, lunching out of paper bags, sewing their undergarments and screeching . . .

But on Sunday night it was transformed. The fountains were playing . . . there were fireworks . . . Once a huge waterfall rained right across the sky and churned up a foam of yellow sparks. And once they raised a great whirling pillar of fire with mad comets trailing their gold manes through the luminous smoke . . .

To-day we saw the Picasso's [sic] again . . .

There were perhaps a dozen sketches of an apple and a glass, each one a sure variation on the theme. This is painting like music and mathematics. You feel that every line is there because there is nowhere else it could be.

ONE

1933-1935

The diary proper starts in 1933. By now, Antonia had given birth to a child, Susan, by Silas Glossop[†] left Eric, and had a second daughter, Lyndall,[†] by Tom Hopkinson,[†] who became her third husband. During intervals from working for Crawford's, she had written her first book, *Frost in May*, and was seeking a publisher. The novel came out in the summer of 1933 to great acclaim, but she makes no mention of this in the diary. Its publication led to a prolonged nervous breakdown which ultimately destroyed her marriage to Tom. Matters were not helped by Tom's affair with Frances,[†] the wife of Geoffrey Grigson.

She wrote freelance pieces for the *Daily Mirror* women's page. Her interest in Thomas Carlyle eventually led to her being commissioned to write a life of Jane Welsh Carlyle, but it was never completed.

1933

20 Jan (Florence MacCunn. *Sir Walter Scott's Friends* Wm. Blackwood 1909) I have just finished this enchanting book which for the time has entirely seduced me from both Lawrence and Carlyle. I read the whole of D.H.L.'s letters last week when in bed with a cold; felt completely in sympathy with him and a passionate desire to be on his side, no matter whom I deserted or decried. Began the whole book again, marking passages, meaning to re-read all his works and try and make him out. All this prompted by an article in L[ife] and L[etters] that annoyed me. J. Soames, comparing him with Rousseau. Probably everything she said was true, but the whole tone was patronising and self-righteous. I wanted to explode a squib under her chair.

Now I want to find if there's any likeness or not between Lawrence and Carlyle. But at the moment I am in revolt against L. Why does one veer about so with him? One day he seems the only right one: the next I turn with disgust from the thought of having to read him again ... I don't really want to live in a model village in the Andes with folk-dancing and handicrafts, yet that old phoenix puts his spell on me every time I open his books. I wish I hadn't a divided nature and could whole heartedly accept the Lawrences or – the aristocrats ...

23 Jan ... Spent week end with Douglas and Kathleen [McClean].[†] Bitterly cold, but the icy winter sunshine was beautiful ... The horses in their long winter coats had a wonderful furry bloom on them in the pale sunshine. Tom [Hopkinson] pointed out the beautiful silvery colour of the dried horse-dung. Twice smelt a fox in the lane.

Heard a record of Maria Iroquine singing a very beautiful old German carol 'Maria auf dem Berg'. I am always so much moved by them; I don't know why. 'Ave Maria Zart' I love; 'In dulce jubilo', 'The Holly and the Ivy'. Much as I love all Wolf's songs, I always particularly want to hear over and over 'Die Leilige drei Königin', 'Nun wandret Maria' and a carol lullaby whose name I forget ... for the duration of the song I accept the whole story without question ...

We spent Christmas at Cockermouth and a bleak Christmas it was, though outwardly they were kind enough. I am very seldom happy and at ease in other people's houses. I feel slovenly and incomplete; can never settle to anything, book or work, and hate the chill discomfort of other people's bedrooms. I wake up a little when we go for walks, for I like walking in the country, but I have some real complex against *living* in the country ... I rebel violently against the idea, strong in Tom's parents and in people like them, that it is somehow more moral to live in the country ... And so, though I had genuinely wanted to see the Lakes and was genuinely impressed by Skiddaw and Helvellyn ... all this was tainted for me by this Christian approval and sanction. Apart from this I could enjoy the extraordinary changing lights, the colour of the hills, the thin waterfalls zig-zagging down dark gulleys and the odd, cold, liquid quality of the air which Tom describes so well in his first book [*A Wise Man Foolish*] ... We walked from Keswick ... over the hills to St John's Church (where we picnicked in a damp graveyard), then on, skirting Helvellyn, to Thirlspot.

25 Jan ... Our Christmas certainly was very gloomy. Apart from the dun walls, the Watts engravings (Sir Galahad (?)) etc and the shelves of semi-religious books (*Road-mending on the King's Highway, Through Palestine with my Camera*), the awful cold, the cheerless meals and untuned piano, the strain was acute. Esther [Tom's sister] hates me; but that is understandable. Having to walk a mile or so we could find nothing safe to talk about but the method of propagation in mosses (they propagate by sperm). But it is Tom's father [the Revd Henry Hopkinson] who is the key to the strain ... I wish he would come out with open hostility instead of this gentle, insulting Christian tolerance ... He will look at nothing straight or on its own merits. Does a book 'do good'? He slides away from every discussion or puts an odd bias on it. Tom said, about suburban buildings 'Why not build them with a decent communal garden instead of these little back yards'. His father said 'Yes, but should we have won the w-w-war with Germany if it had not been for those little b-backyards? ...'

... Yet he can be charming (perhaps a shade deliberately charming) telling stories of saints or even fairy stories in a shy, stammering voice, his head on one side. He lives in an atmosphere of almost adoring admiration ... For his own ends he delayed our wedding on purely worldly grounds of 'not offending the family' etc. His sermon on Christmas day was a wonderful avoidance of issues. A few quotations then a dissertation on the beauties of 's-snow' and how it gave a veil of purity even to ugly objects such as 'dustbins and r-refuse heaps'. I can't manage such thin snow porridge as his form of Christianity ...

Douglas told us of some eminent scientist who died recently. In his obituary it said 'After years of research he brought to a high pitch of perfection the rectal inoculation of lice' ...

I am very sick of waiting for news of my book which Heinemann's have had for nearly 6 weeks. I see that Elizabeth Marbury, who has had my play [now lost] in America since August, is dead. I re-wrote it in full three times and still it is no nearer to production. Jeanne de Casalis borrowed it Nov. 17. to read 'over the week-end'. She still has it ...

27 Jan Spent an hour last night with Eric [Earnshaw Smith] hearing Sibelius I symphony on the gramophone and analysing it. Second

movement particularly lovely. It is amazingly spare, compact, allu-
sive music, difficult to follow until you have got the hang of Sibelius'
idiom.

26 Jan [sic]   I am beginning to toy with the idea of doing a book about
my father. I have always wanted to do a sort of memoir of him . . .

30 Jan   . . . Yesterday I went with Eric to hear Beecham conduct the
philharmonic. Amazing difference since he took them over; they are
now as alive and well drilled as one could wish. Quite gone that
curious limping in the strings and broken bubblings in the horns . . .
   . . . Beecham of course is a performance in himself. He keeps up a
perpetual dance in front of the orchestra; now flogging at them, now
pouncing on one or other group of instruments with his baton . . .
   We went to Geoffrey Grigson's to tea. A silly, amiable, pig-headed
fellow Roy Randall, a pork butcher's son and a Tory who warmed
his great buttocks at the fire and said 'Hungary is the land of my
dreams.' . . . I met Roy Campbell's wife at Wyn [Henderson]'s,[†] a
thin, witch-like girl with snaky black hair hanging over a Roumanian
blouse, singing in a tiny metallic thread of a voice to a guitar. An odd,
parched, haggard look about her.
   I am in rather a tangle about the best way to use my time. At
present I can distinguish three strands.
   (1) The Carlyle-Lawrence chimera
   (2) The 'Period' generally (roughly 1780–1850)
   (3) Vague plans for a new novel. Don't know in what order to
work nor how to make the most of what I read in the matter of notes
etc. . . .

31 Jan   Heinemann, as I expected, have turned down my book. But
Wyn seems hopeful about Desmond Harmsworth's taking it . . .

* * *

Antonia often dreamt about a place called Horsley Towers. This was a
monstrous neo-Gothic mansion, still standing in Surrey, that Antonia
used to visit when she was married to her first husband, Reggie Green-
Wilkinson. It was owned by his aunt Trixie, who was married to Tom
Sopwith, designer of the Sopwith Pup.

* * *

8 Feb ... Dreamt last night as I often do, about Horsley Towers ... I dreamt we were dancing in a big room ... Much gaiety but a feeling it was all put on to hide something. I said to Tom Sop[with] 'Isn't it funny, there are so few couples dancing in this room yet whenever I put out my hand, I touch someone' ... I noticed a little door in the wall. Instead of a name or 'private' it had printed on it MURDER. There was a buffet and the man who was carving the ham looked up at me with the most awful waxen face and bolting eyes and whispered 'I know MURDER' ...

I am reading Carlyle as usual. What a man! ... When I read men like C., I pant along happily at their skirts, thinking myself safe and then, not even knowing I'm there, [they] cuff me with a great fist of a phrase that sends me sprawling ...

... Reading C. one feels that *nothing* is worth writing, least of all own tiny things. No one ever had less *message* than I have and that my 'duty' in times like these is hardly to 'chirrup' on a quiet bough ...

9 Feb I have been in bed 9 days now and still must not get up. My one enjoyment is in reading the letters of Carlyle and Jane Welsh before their marriage ... She begins in the smartest, pertest, Jane Welsh way, but gradually the other Jane begins to break through, passionate, melancholy, impatient, fame-loving – fame-hungry almost – and nervous. But she seems to care for him only as a friend – the idea of marriage is disgusting to her. She is very like me; they had not met for months, had only two hours, and she wasted it all by forcing a quarrel she did not want. And her 'arch enemy' was headache.

12 Feb (?) Still in bed. Have finished the love letters and left my pair on the brink of marriage ... [She] is as lively and hare-brained a rattle as anyone could wish ... She nearly killed herself by going out hatless in an east wind so as not to upset the dressing of her hair; another time she fell off a wall 'trying to hide her ankles' from Dr Fyffe. Yet another time in her zeal for study she sewed the bodices to the skirts of her frocks so that she could dress in ten minutes

... She laments his want of elegance, his Annandale accent. She and her mother are horrified at the notion of his coming to live at

Haddington. No, the marriage must begin somewhere where the flower of Haddington is unknown ...

7 June ... The garden at Binesfield rots slowly away; the lawns covered with 'soldiers' and plantains, the lupins tangled and bedraggled, the walnut tree blighted. I love it still. As soon as I go there I feel contracted to a child again, lazy, restless, half-asleep – waiting for something that never happens. I have been there with husbands and lovers but they too seem to shrink when they are there and I am always thinking of someone else ...

When I am in love I think of the person all the time. I am not happy unless I am in 'a state of grace' with them. But each time I meet them, the deeper I get, the worse I handle them. I take offence at the smallest thing, I stay too long, I become a bore and then suddenly a black curtain of melancholy descends and I feel shut in, cut off – I cannot go away though I know I should have gone an hour ago because I cannot live through tomorrow.

9 June   All well and placid for once. Dined with Ian Black[†] last night. A telegram from Paris about Kurt Weil [sic]. Phone number (say Wagram 1907 but that wasn't it). Ian to his stage manservant 'Sachs – get me Paris – Wagram 1907'. A minute later when the impression had been produced. 'Sachs – don't get Paris ...'

20 June   The usual misery at the thought of writing; even of making notes here. The thought of the second book depresses me terribly yet I want, not to begin it, but to have begun it. I am re-reading *Anna Karenina* with great pleasure and only wish I could attempt a book on a scale like that. So many groups of distinct, yet intertwining lives, all so broad yet so sharp in detail.

I dined with Adrian [Stephen] last night and was happy with him though I have never known a person more nervous and guilty. Lunch with King Bull [unknown] was ineffably tedious. Nothing is more boring than this quicksilver chat about Taoism, Lamaism, Tibetism etc etc ... his wife draws dear little fairies sitting on toadstools so I do not think one need bother about him ...

31 July   ... I have got into the bad habit of starting several

notebooks. Only really need one at home and one at the office ...
Resolved

(1) Not to fuss and fret about clothes. To buy those I need, keep the ones I have in good repair but not waste time, thought and money on them in the absurd way I do now

(2) To read more closely and intelligently, not frittering away my reading as I do now, but reading slowly, reading to the end and taking notes

(3) To get as much time as possible out of each day. If I am slack at the office, make notes, not read magazines

(4) To try and keep things tidy, so as not to have these orgies of getting straight ...

28 Aug ... I am completely paralysed on the new book. Have made two false starts and am horrified at the niggardly mess. Begin to think Eric is right and that I should attack it in quite a different way ...

* * *

Tom and Antonia spent occasional weekends with Tom's uncle, Martin Hopkinson, at Bovingdon, Hertfordshire. Martin had four sons and fielded a cricket team entirely made up of Hopkinsons.

* * *

8 Sept ... For the last two days restless, sleepy and stupid, unable to do any real work or even to thrash down the crop of trivial letters that grow up like nettles nearly every day ...

Bovingdon ... We had a cricket match on Saturday. Jennings [unknown] wrote an alleged humorous account of it in the evening and dissected scores all Sunday morning in the intervals of going to church and playing *The Merry Widow* on the harmonium. Other diversions tennis, shove ha'penny, darts, archery and a toy cinema of a cricket match and a family wedding. Tom electrified the dinner table and actually kept them ten minutes from their coffee by an excellent short discourse on the political situation. They took the splendid line that the rich always take

(a) Poverty is so good for people. It makes them more spiritual

(b) Nearly all the unemployed don't *want* to work. Chris [unknown] said she knew personally that the building trade didn't want to work and couldn't do their jobs if they had them – all 35000, presumably.

(c) How disgraceful it is when the *poor* won't work. Nothing said about the rich.

Greville [unknown] says Cowper was a hermaphrodite. I must read the whole diary this autumn ...

10 Sept   ... Last week an intermittent headache and malaise, probably psychogenic in origin, made excellent 'reasons' [for not writing]. Again I feel 'if only' .... if only I could make up my mind once and for all about religion – if only I had some green typing paper ...

14 Sept   No good, V[ernon] L[ee]'s† plan, but yesterday started again for the 4th or 5th time and really it seemed to go a little better. Trying to dramatise it more instead of making bald statements; the material (only 6 pages) did seem a little more tractable. Shall cut out the mother and focus the interest on N[anda]'s relation with her father [*The Lost Traveller*].

Susan and Lyndall for the last two months (they are 4 and 2 respectively) have been much interested in Death. Yesterday Lyndall found a dead fly. S. said 'Lyndall likes making things killed' and this morning they were both pretending to be dead. Susan lying quite still and Lyndall waving her arms and shouting 'I'm dead too'

18 Sept   Gurdjieff† has sent out an incomprehensible notice of his new establishment to his 'initiates'. One of the attractions is to be a 'retro-rebounding echoraising organ' with 'luminous keyboard'; another 'Thoughtthanbledzoin' ...

* * *

Antonia left Crawford's, and for the next four years worked as a freelance journalist and copywriter. One of her chief customers for advertising copy was Theodora Benson, and her journalistic assignments included reviewing theatre for *Time and Tide*.

* * *

16 Oct   A month gone and no more done to the book but for once I have *not* been lazy. Faced with free-lancing again I am rushed off my feet. Opening connections *Time and Tide*, *Mirror*, Varley and Milliken [an advertising agency] etc. . . .

Propose to read at least 25 vols of Balzac this winter.

1934

1 Jan Well, here we are at another new year . . . For once I will make *no* new year resolutions, however tempting. The Balzac plan deliberately abandoned; as for the next six months nothing can be done but Jane W[elsh] . . .

A week in Edinburgh looking up Carlyle MSS before Christmas. Fog nearly all the time. City smoking away in the valley as one looked down on it from Calton Hill with its unfinished monument and deserted observatory.

How the Scotch hate the English: everything laid at my door, poor teas, prevalence of lipstick, payment of dole, payment of M.Ps. thriftlessness of unemployed, fogginess of London etc. Complacent notion that no town can *possibly* compare with Edinburgh. I met Grierson [Walter Scott authority] who was delightful – and his wife, the kindest, most gracious person imaginable in a blue faded jacket trimmed with lace. Edinburgh mainly hideous. Gothic but Charlotte Square was exquisite, pale yellow stucco, eighteenth century, with a square full of leafless trees and a lawn, all against a clear . . . blue sky – first and only blue sky I saw in Edinburgh.

At present sunk deep in Harriet Martineau: very much attracted in spite of her complacent priggishness and self-righteousness. A very *true* nature there; honest and unflinching and courageous. One gets nourished by the oddest people . . .

* * *

Someone whom Antonia saw often at this time was Alexander Keiller.[†] She used to refer to him, then in his early forties, as the Marmalade King, because that was where his millions came from. He is now remembered for his work on Avebury Ring, but in his day he was also

known as a ski-jumping champion and a driver of fast cars. Antonia
never had an affair with him, and when he tried to bribe her to submit to
sadistic practices she ceased to see him.

* * *

4 Jan   Still very sore in the throat and husky in chest. Children both
have chicken-pox. I was in bed all yesterday: hate the early days of
almost every New Year: usually ill . . .

The more I go into Jane, the more, in a way, she repels me. The
Love-Letters, read for the 3rd time, show *him* in a far better light. She
is maddening with her archness and her flirtations and her sham high-
browism and her 'wee, wee Cicero'. But it's very interesting to see
how awful young girls are; novelists, except Tolstoy, never see it . . .

A[lexander] K[eiller] rang up today

'I don't suppose anyone can move across Europe faster than I can'.

'In the costume of a British ski-jumping champion' . . .

'It's simply wonderful the Christopher Robin birthday book' . . .

A most odd man this: absolutely unscrupulous about other
people's time, tastes or feelings. Reputed a sadist, but the most
sentimental man I know. Yet I enjoy being with him in spite of
egoism, bombast, self-pity, merciless boredom. Full of vitality: has a
definite charm and certainly an element of surprise. *Exaggerated* about
everything – feelings, affections, suspicions. Forces everyone to take
a part in *his* life, whether digging up barrows, collecting cattle or ski-
ing. Very generous, often mean. Not imaginative giver: yet can be
extremely sensitive and shrewd. The most ruthless waster of other
people's time that I know. Yet infects one with enthusiasm and
obviously inspires passionate devotion in people who work for him.

23 Jan   . . . I do not see how to do with less money and the keeping
up of an income on free-lance work is a strain. I am too friendly to
people; too much stung by remorse . . . if I do not answer letters, talk
on the telephone, lunch and ask them to my house. It is no good my
making resolutions. Logan Pearsall Smith[†] says I should take years
over J[ane] [W[elsh] C[arlyle] and make a scholarly job of it. Nothing
I should like better. But how? I am under contract and have no
private income.

Susan said the other day 'I suppose you had Lyndall and Tom had me.'. . . Thank goodness I am free of A[lexander] K[eiller]. There is not time for these violent encroachments on one's time, sympathy, vitality.

* * *

Antonia used to visit her mother, Christine Botting,[†] who now lived alone in the cottage at Bines Green, Sussex. Even before the death of Antonia's father, Cecil,[†] in 1929, Christine had been cut off by the lack of a car. (Cecil had sold his after a fatal accident involving a young woman in a sidecar.) For a time she took a lover called Oswald Norton. She was cared for by a cook, Ludy Dumbrell, and a gardener, Alfred Stepney.

* * *

16 March   . . . Mother (of Oswald N[orton]) 'He's versed in all the arts of Aphrodite – it's amazing the things that man knows about little ways to make one feel naughty'.

19 March   . . . It is incredible to me that it is nearly 12 years since I married Reggie. I remember what a horror I had at 21 of being 30. now I am nearer 40 than I was then near 30. I do resent the physical decay of getting older though in some ways I am no uglier than in those days. One does not notice one is getting older until one sees a really young woman. Even if they are not beautiful there is a bloom on them – a moisture of chin and lip, a sheen on their hair . . .

I am in bed again with a mild attack of tonsillitis and profound depression that always accompanies even a day of illness with me . . . Tom is right when he says I learn nothing from experience. Why is it? I suppose the psychologists are right – that I still react to certain situations in an infantile way . . . I'm not impressed with the results of analysis in any cases I know personally. Whenever I am ill I become morbidly conscious of my looks . . . When I was seventeen I was afraid of marriage because I thought I should look so repulsive in the early morning that a lover would be disgusted. Powder and face-cream have come to acquire a value for me which I cannot explain – it is almost like a lust or a kleptomania. What would happen if I had never been introduced to them? I probably never should have been but for meeting Marion[†] [Abrahams, a schoolfriend from St Paul's] when I was sixteen . . no – fourteen. Would it have developed spontaneously or was it accidental? Marion has influenced me in nothing else – yet after nearly twenty years that little vice or 'tic' she introduced me to persists.

My first thought – on hearing of the revolution – would be 'shall I still be able to get face-powder?'. . .

I was thinking, as I dozed this afternoon, of all the sounds that have soft, languid, ecstatic associations; there are sounds to me that are the quintessence of summer – the tapping of a blind tassel on a window pane, the sound of a distant piano or a girl practising singing, the bright, nicking clip-clop of a horse's hoofs in the early morning – soon those sounds will have disappeared from London.

. . . The London season has always stood for something exquisite and remote the glimpse of a girl in Bond Street in her Ascot muslins, gilt chairs unloading in Berkeley Square, awnings, palms, red carpets, even an ice at Gunter's are all fraught for me with the most exquisite, unattainable beauties. Perhaps Henry James felt like that about London society. I can't help thinking there's some point in being provincial . . .

16 June Aldermaston   Apart from the impulse to write notes about myself . . . I sometimes wonder whether it is of any value to use this as a 'sketch-book'. Looking back I found so many notes rough but with . . . something in them that look as if they might be useful some day yet I have never used any of them in what I have written. On the one or two occasions when I have tried to – eg 'Mon Pays c'est la Martinique' it has been a failure. Yet Logan [Pearsall Smith] tells me to keep a notebook . . .

* * *

In June Antonia went to stay at the Old Mill Guest House, Aldermaston, to be near Bob Gathorne-Hardy,[†] a close friend of Logan Pearsall Smith. When she returned, she discovered that Tom had been seeing Frances Grigson.

Antonia had by now met Emily Coleman[†] (at one of Wyn Henderson's tea-parties) and through Emily she met Peggy Guggenheim.[†] In July, Peggy invited Antonia to a house party at Hayford Hall, Buckfastleigh, Devon. Also invited were Djuna Barnes,[†] author of *Nightwood*, and Phyllis Jones.[†]

* * *

21 June Aldermaston ... Although it is June, the leaves are falling already from the drought. Even the chestnut burrs are falling, unripe like little green gooseberries, their prickles quite soft.

On the Hampshire downs we found lilac-coloured orchids (spotted orchids) with dark brown spots on their leaves and brownish-green tway-blade (?) orchids ...

Bob G. H. showed me how they are fertilised. He thrust a thin blade of grass into them (the bee's proboscis) and brought out a tiny hair like stamen (pistil) with a bag at the end ...

* * *

Towards the end of July, Tom and Antonia set off for a holiday in Brittany. This holiday, later used in Antonia's story, 'The Moment of Truth', was an attempt to escape from the Frances problem.

* * *

25 July, St Germain de Matignon To be in France again after 3 years is both pleasant and disappointing. I am in a very bad state still as I have been for three months – like the worst days of 1921 – and it is hard for me to attach myself to anything for more than a few minutes at a time. In St Malo, on a sunny Sunday morning, I was happy. The town was full of dragoons in their pale blue uniforms; the whole bourgeoisie in extraordinary Sunday clothes ... but ... at St Cast enormous plaster hotels have grown up overnight in every mock-regional style ...

We have found somewhere better – on the Baie de la Fresnaye, an old sea-mill turned into an inn – at high tide the Estuary is flooded up to the walls of the house and to the wood beyond; it recedes leaving a sandy, muddy waste. The furze-covered rocks send out long tongues into the sea; the rocks at the base covered with bladder wrack that shines a bright rusty green in the sun.

Inside, rooms with stone floors, 'lits clos' (cupboard like raised built in beds with sliding panels) copper saucepans, oil cloth table cloths. A sort of raised rostrum by our bed; no curtains but the coarse yellowish crochet ones. Little fish in our cold washing water. Crickets chirp all the time ...

Almost every night Louison brings us a passion flower ...

2 Aug Before every meal Madame brings us out the things we are going to eat – mackerel, stiff and fresh with a mother of pearl bloom

on their bellies – huge knobbed sea-spiders still alive and waving
their great legs and pincers – baskets of pale green beans and fat
yellowish overripe peas. At each we have to exclaim with delight
while she gives us little lectures on their healthfulness and beauty . . .
The black hen she bought for our dinner at the market has slipped its
moorings and flown away. We go out with sticks, beating down the
bracken tearing ourselves on the gorse, cricking our necks gazing up
into the trees, calling, till we are hoarse 'Petite, petite' but no hen
appears . . .

She likes nursing. Nothing too good for the sick . . . nothing too
disgusting for her to do in their interest. Usually her stories run 'I
gave him an injection: two days afterwards he died' . . . 'Poor little
woman. I did everything for her. I laid out her corpse. No one else
would do it' . . .

5 Aug   The black hen, which escaped, was eaten by dogs . . .

Managed with great difficulty to write three letters this morning –
quite long ones – to Eric, Emily [Coleman] and Mamma . . . Tom has
mended my pen and it no longer makes that infuriating noise like the
scratching of a pin, but runs silently.

SANTAYANA ('Reason in Common Sense') . . .

'There may well be intense consciousness in the total absence of
rationality. Such consciousness is suggested in dreams, in madness
and may be found for all we know, in the depths of universal
nature' . . .

* * *

On returning from Brittany Antonia went to stay with Eric Earnshaw
Smith who had rented a bungalow called Ye Olde Cottage, at Shaldon
near Teignmouth, Devon.

* * *

10 Aug, Shaldon   . . . Sitting here alone in the bleak cheerful sitting-
room of this little bungalow with Eric out and the rain driving in
sheets outside the terrible blank depression that has been overwhelm-
ing me at intervals ever since I went to Robb[†] and most of all during
those two bad weeks in Brittany begins to well up again. All the
morning I have sat here writing dismal lists . . . Nothing seems of any
value. I hardly care what I do . . .

Eric The fair scroll of the universe on which God unfortunately scrabbled the history of mankind . . .

Keats (Letter to Geo and Thos Keats Dec 28 1817)

'negative capability, that is, when a man is capable of being in uncertainties, mysteries, doubts without any irritable reaching after fact and reason'.

this quality goes to make 'a man of achievement, especially in literature, and which Shakespeare possessed so enormously'.

I do not think I have any 'creative' genius. Whatever I have, if I have anything, is the capacity to *recognise* things. If I have a 'line' it is this perceptive, interpreting one – not striking out new things, but trying to perceive old or present ones without cant, posturing or accumulations . . .

Eric says one should find one's own morality: make it to measure, not try to fit oneself with a ready-made one.

13 Aug . . . I keep wishing I were a painter especially since I saw those Vuillards. Hideous French rooms all crammed with furniture crimson and blue table-cloths etc: hideous bourgeois families eating their lunch or having a drink in a hideous sitting-room yet all so indescribably lovely. Why *can't* one do the same thing in writing. There *must* be a way.

17 Aug . . . One of the worst things about jealousy is that it creates an entirely false situation between two people. One's impulse is, having been hurt, to hurt oneself still further, to degrade onself to less than human . . .

27 Sept . . . I have not written the history of this summer here because it is not a thing I can write yet. Since this curious change came over me about a fortnight ago I can hardly remember what it felt like. It is less actual to me than the asylum which has now acquired a kind of poetic intelligibility for me . . . I do not think I have ever suffered so sharply and persistently before . . . The Carlyle book is certainly a burden. I feel capable of reading sensibly for it: making notes etc but recoil at the thought of reducing all that to a clear shape and writing anything of my own . . . I rarely take a book about with me now and Keats' letters have lasted me nearly two months . . .

... I feel as if I had lost the power to be in love with anyone. In some ways this is a relief; in others I feel a great hole in my life. I would like to be 'in deep love' with Tom, but this cannot be at the moment ... I feel if only he would be *positive*, assemble himself, decide what he wants and pursue it, I would feel differently again ... It is no good his hoping to find in me a tolerable substitute for F[rances] because I am not F. and don't ever want to be ... Why he wanted to marry me, I can't imagine. I suppose he thinks one part of me corresponds to or stimulates one part of him. But that isn't enough. Only a few weeks ago he could have had me whole and complete (for what that's worth): now every day makes me more independent of him ...

28 Dec ... I feel if someone loved me in the right way I could respond completely. Because I want to *love*, not just be loved. In those odd three weeks in the autumn when I felt cool and clear-eyed, people suddenly began to make love to me, Tom included. And I was pleased, of course. But I couldn't respond ... I know in my bones that by being cool, gay, indifferent, physically passionate with him I can have him if I want to. But I want both to possess myself *and* to love him ... I've been 'loved' over and over again and I've 'loved' too but never, except with Robert [Legg]† and dimly with Tom at the same time ... strong love in him [Tom] seems to be called up by cold or immature people – Pam, Lois, [Tom's girlfriends] F. Not that I'm mature, but I have *something* which a grown-up man could take ... after all it *was* I who first drifted away from Tom. I have not been physically unfaithful to Tom but I have been mentally unfaithful ...

30 Dec
   Likes
   Clean clothes ...
   Being out of debt ...
   Sitting at café tables ...
   Starting a relationship ...
   Decorating rooms ...
   Nice surprises ...
   Sound of crockery when someone is getting tea for me ...
   Receiving love letters

Summer and summer clothes ...
Hates
Feeling fat
Dirt: especially in my clothes ...
My mother's sweetish corruption
Cold and draughts ...
The hours between lunch and tea ...
Meeting people in the street unexpectedly ...
Being pregnant ...
Crossing roads.
Cherry [sic] people
Cold tea ...
People who gush at me and dont really like me ...
Finding people out when I phone them ...
People who automatically ask first 'How are the children?'
Talking politics.
WHAT I WOULD LIKE TO HAPPEN
Tom to fall in love with me ...
To be clear once and for all of the Catholic Church ...

1935

3 Jan   Tired and depressed tonight. What things have made me happy lately?

New hat ...

Party.   In feeling I looked as nice as I can. In coping with a person, not minding if I appeared stupid. Not trying to be bright, clever or up to snuff. Feeling quite at ease and un-anxious ...

In seeing two hens fighting: jumping up in the air, feathers puffed up round their necks ...

Principal discouragements

Just can't get my letters quite finished or mending done
Feel I shall

    (a) never be able to write again
    (b) find anything to write about

Penny pinchings

Never quite enough to pay small odd debts apart from more
serious ones

Life very monotonous

Reading (except the Field book on child psychology ...) too
indigestible. Even H[umphrey] J[ennings]'s innocuous *Little town in
France* began by being sweet but sat heavily on my belly. Disturbs me
with 'shouldn't Is' and the thought of how much I've missed when
I've been in interesting places

Out of my depth with Eric last night over animal faith and
essences. My mind seems of such poor quality ...

6 Jan ... Remember with great pleasure weeks recovering from
abortion in 1924 and for once holding my life in suspension, not
wanting anything, not even concerned with the future, but perfectly
happy reading Proust ...

... I am sick of the high priest attitude of the psychoanalysts.
Perhaps a general hatred of priestcraft and mediators. The artists
don't mediate and say 'come unto me'. They state what they see
and leave you to take it or ignore it. The only thing I dislike about
Jesus is the reiterated 'come unto *ME*' – '*I* am the way and the
truth and the life'. Everything else I accept gladly. It's not that I
won't sit at people's feet: it's one of my favourite attitudes. Or that I
don't want help: goodness knows how I do. But I resent the 'only
way' business ...

Tom saw F[rances] the other day for the first time for months. She
seemed to him, he said, like a person on whom a trick has been
played. To me she seems like a person who always slips away at the
critical moment, leaving her image intact. I don't think she is a
conscious coquette as people say. If she were she would have refused
to see Tom until she had had her child. But I think she is a person of
very little feeling. He attributes to her his own emotions, as one does
when one is in love ...

The book: [*The Lost Traveller*] what is it *about*? The relation of a
father and daughter; the hopeless impossibility of an adjustment
between two people so different when one person will not allow for
differences. The crystallisation about Catholicism. Since one cannot
repeat a situation indefinitely, some incident has got to be found to

(a) consolidate the profound guilt about a fear of sex in the father which reacts on the child

(b) produce the first dislocation in the relationship which makes the light go out for the child.

Therefore we must disentangle the essence of the 'book' incident and transplant it. That, it seems to me, is what 'inventing' incident means. The essences of situations one can only perceive in one's own experience, but, having perceived them clearly, one can embody them in another form. 'Truth' in fiction depends on this. If the thing is rightly perceived, it will convince in whatever actual incident you choose to embody it. The mere recounting of an 'actual' incident will not do it. Hence the failure of the 'actual' episode in *Frost* ...

Something like an early episode with Robin or Jocelyn would do: a kiss in the dark; a fearful scene followed by an almost amorous reconciliation.

Possibly the first part should be entirely devoted to getting *him*. I am sick to death of E[irene] and her convent education. Let that rest. I want *him*. His life is finished: can be examined. I will *not* be afraid of him any more. It is a pure accident that we were father and child. I have a *right* to look at him, yes, sexually too.

7 Jan ... Waitress ... overheard. 'Well, everybody's got their own religion. Pot of tea twice please Olive'.

... fill up odd half hour with writing *some* letters, doing *some* mending: not worried if *all* can't be done ...

Recent pleasures.   Sight of Tom going out to his boat, one lock falling over his forehead (can't think why I like this so much). Getting supper for him (rather unexpected!) Sitting mending while he wrote. No feeling of envy, being neglected, or wanting to do anything else myself. Acute pleasure (tinged with envy) seeing through half-drawn curtains pleasant lamp-lit, bare-walled studio-like room and young man working at a big desk. Always envy people engaged in work, esp. dancers or musicians practising ... Still excited enviously by student life ... Not a good student myself in old days but feel I could be now. Perhaps shirking responsibility: want to be in 'grooming' stage: approbation, advice, competition at hand always ...

Tea-parties intolerable unless someone will talk of what they're really interested in. Pretty woman at Alec's [unknown] yesterday, complete bore as she talked about all her correct feelings about Jugo-Slavia, the Acropolis, Bach, Voltaire, the theatre. Really came to life when she discussed the best way of making chair-covers and getting the webbing taut on settees ... Alick [Schepeler]† less sensitive to offence. Wonder why G.B. [George Barker†] fell in love with her *voice* of all things. She hardly ever *speaks*: sings and screams usually.

Very pleased with Paul [Hopkinson, Tom's brother]'s Persian rug: rich reds and blues and an uneven play of colour: makes the Heal rug pale and self-conscious; don't know why.

9 Jan Spent the afternoon with Georgiana [unknown] ... She makes the business of having children seem so much less terrifying and distorting. I wonder why I have such a fear of having children. I just glimpsed what it *might* mean with Susan. The actual birth my mother always frightened me about. I don't mind that any more. Thought of pregnancy still hateful. Acute discomfort and distortion. One's own friends make it worse still: funny that the people who most embarrassed one and made one feel a member of a lower species, a mere breeding rabbit should be the two who most wanted children themselves, Betty Gill† and Corin [Bernfeld].† I always seem to have had children in an atmosphere of hostility and disapproval. One is forced to earn a living and having children is a handicap. Yet I used to want one so much, in spite of the physical fear. Not children as children though I've even wanted that (e.g. Jim [Dougal]†) but a child by someone I loved. I envied Georgiana so much when I felt V. offered her her happiness so whole and complete, so decidedly. I'm so tired of this ragged piecing together of a relationship. I want a *man*, whatever I mean by that and I can't be a woman or happy as a woman until I have a man, not a boy, however amorous. Very tired and cold. The cold freezes me up. With Georgiana I feel my blood is like vinegar and water: old, tired, spinsterish. So tired, so tired. I am terrified of a 'suppressed desire to have a child' but why? If one has a genuine desire, only happiness can come of fulfilling it. Even the word 'contented' frightens me: a picture of a fat, dowdy placid woman in an old straw hat fiddling in a garden ...

Too much cant about old [William] Brown.† So bloody pleased with himself – Boy Scouts, Girl Guides, parental instinct.

10 Jan ... Perhaps Georgiana crystallised the state. Feelings about breast-feeding aroused by her. Does not seem horrible as *she* is young and beautiful. Otherwise disgust. Feel as Swift did. Why have I become so dependent on cigarettes during the last two years ... Is there a connection ...

Revised diary It's no good. I can't take Brown seriously. I lie on the couch while he murmurs 'Sleep, sleep, think of nothing but sleep' and then, when he thinks I am well under, muttering hastily 'have faith in God; have faith in yourself'. I was flattered but my reasonable self rebelled when he told Tom 'She's worth saving'. I'm sure he's an admirable man but he has too much professional unction. His favourite theme is self-sacrifice. I suppose he knows all about it. Anyhow he makes £5000 a year out of those who don't and lives in a warm steam of approbation.

11 Jan ... I know so well how Anna felt in the train when, reading her 'English novel' she wanted to be living each part. I want to be Vronsky riding Frou-Frou, Anna at the ball, Levin sowing the field and shooting the snipe. I half wish I were a man yet I was meant to be a woman ...

Sunday, 19 Jan(?) ... I was very happy physically with Tom last night. But not deeply happy. This morning I got up early and am writing this in the little coffee shop with a wireless playing

'In Noah's ark they pinched his trunk
So an elephant never forgets' ...

But there is still this something not quite terue in him that I hate. There is something in his relation to Frances that shows it to me. In the middle of her love affair with him, she deliberately has a child by her husband whom she constantly says she hates and despises. Surely a man with a sense of reality would cut it clean off then and there. Instead he still likes to go and sit by her bedside. It sickens me. I understand his having loved her (though I hate the dishonesty with

which he treated me then). Even now he can't *commit* himself finally
to one or the other ...

25 Jan(?)   Last days again very bad: especially yesterday. Yesterday,
feeling Frances as such a terrifying image, I gave way to a violent
impulse to ring her up. I wanted to see her, to reassure myself that,
after all, she was only another human being, like myself, with her
own problems. I spoke to her. She was cool, surprised, quite affable.
Treated the whole thing 'socially' .. would be 'fairly clear' next week.
Obviously did not realise any urgency in my suddenly ringing her up
after six months, or, if she did, did not *want* to. I think it showed a
certain insensitiveness in her. Tom said 'You and I would not have
responded like that.' I was comforted by his saying that. I hope I shall
have the sense and control not to refer to that again.

The feeling of physical inadequacy, of being ugly almost to
repulsiveness, comes up often so strongly. I try to fight it rationally,
tell myself that I am no more repulsive physically than most women
of my age. I have to admit that a great many people have been
attracted to me, people of very different types, some of whom set
physical attractiveness very high and who have yet preferred me to
beautiful women. Yet I feel F.'s beauty has set a standard for Tom
which nothing else can ever equal. Or rather that it can only be
surpassed by someone still more beautiful and possessed of the
qualities he missed in her. I may have those qualities for him, but
allied to the wretched body I have ... He says that I vary so
enormously even in actual physical appearance, that my body actually
looks *more* attractive when my mind 'inhabits' it. But with the
prospect of another year before I can hope for my mind to 'inhabit' at
all securely, I naturally feel alarmed and depressed ...

He tends to prefer the company of his mental inferiors, Paul, Joe
etc [unknown]. Even with Eric he is defensive and behaves like a
schoolboy on guard with a master rather than as a man with a man.
Ten years is a big difference at his age I know, but he should be able to
meet Eric much more as an equal. I think this liking for mental
inferiority tinges his relations with women (cf. Pam, F., the little
girls) ...

It is odd how few friends he has. From Oxford Charles Fenby[†] the
only one with any stuff in him. Sinclair [unknown] is dainty and

shallow. Pocock [unknown] of the coarsest dullest fibre. Very few people accept him unreservedly. The Rugger toughs feel he is superior and 'highbrow'. He can stand a worm like Siddall [unknown] because S. flatters him. Yet he despises people like Silas who have obvious surface faults but are made of much more honourable metal.

29 Jan ... I could not help feeling pleased when R[onald Moody]† said a man said, looking at his head of me, 'How beautiful she must be'.

Analysis diary, 9 March   Analysis began about 3 weeks ago. Difficult to recapture details.

roughly 1st phase – noticing objects in room. Constipation. Trying to get [Dr Dennis] Carroll to advise me. Sensitive to any change in arrangement of objects. Sight of half-opened desk brought up quite forgotten walnut desk of my father's. Attitude towards C. hostile and critical. Thought him undersized, rather stupid: cockney accent. Says I always begin with a question. Extreme depression at week-end.

2nd week.   Attitude to C. more friendly and confident. Nightmare that I was in Maudsley Inst. by his orders; left side of face paralysed and awry: unable to speak plainly. 'I wish I had *five* fountain pens like my father instead of only two'. Intense curiosity about cupboard. Defied my fear and looked in. Only wash basin and what looked like douche cans. Immediately clicking wh. I associated with warning of disapproval started. Curious scene at overcoming of Constip[ation] ... Found click came from outside, not from C.'s chair as I thought ...

3rd week   Great deal about faeces ... Ritual of arriving in taxi ... inability to be punctual except to analysis ... Got through week-end at cottage without swelling up ... Anger at my mother for having sold his books: a part of him ...

Wed.   V. thirsty but did not like to ask for water. Curious noise like hosepipe playing on roof: soon as I looked stopped. Became unconscious of thirst during 2 hour session at Innoxa [brand of cosmetics for which Antonia was writing advertisements]. Often feel thirsty at analysis. Don't want to smoke. Only did so once ...

Thurs   V. ribald about Brown whose bill had come in that

morning. Gave C. cheque at beginning of session. Said 'Now I'll
have a look' (examining desk for stethoscope, blood pressure
machine, fountain pens etc.) ... Woke up cold and gasping with
horror. Cd. not go to lavatory until T[om] came with me. Kept door
open. In bed felt small as a child compared with T. Wished there were
another 'big' person curled at the back of me to keep me warm ...
F[rances] had her baby last night. Felt quite faint when [John]
S[ummerson][†] told me. Seeing Tom bf. dinner and telling him seized
with cold shudders, chattering teeth ...

12 March   Find no desire to write this book [*The Lost Traveller*] since
Tom read it. It produced an effect on him at first but that seemed to
wear off. He asked me to find out when and where F[rances] expected
to have her baby. Summerson told me she had it last Thursday night,
the night I heard of Corin's illness and had the dream about the man
with the deformed face. When I told Tom about it I went cold all
over, my teeth chattered just as they did after the nightmare. (I went
in just now to fetch matches from the dining room. He was writing a
long letter and looked up with such a strange scared look that I felt
sure he was writing to F ...

Take pleasure in my exercises; am remarkably steady in sticking to
my diet. Can control some of my rasher impulses towards extravagance etc. Even when I make a scene and get to the point where I feel
I must dash out into the street, attack Tom or even kill myself, I can
just hold on to the bolting horse and recover my grip ... I think he
will have to see F. again, possibly even make love to her again, before
her image in him is either confirmed or destroyed ...

I amused myself for nearly an hour in the lobby of the H[ouse] of
C[ommons] watching how people self-consciously, yet unconsciously placed their feet in walking. In the tube no face worth looking
at but that of a small, elderly, tired workman in a flat cloth cap, sitting
with closed eyes and his hands clenched together on his knees as if in
prayer.

Analysis diary, Tuesday 12 March   ... trying to talk [to Carroll] about
Tom, felt outraged at having to discuss my intimate affairs and burst
into tears. C. suggested I was reluctant to present myself to him in
light of foolish and unloved woman.

Today ... v. angry and resistant at having to go to C. at all. Whole business of analysis seemed meaningless. Thought I had nothing to say, but ... a lot came up. My father's study, the lavatory between it and my nursery (used almost exclusively by my father and myself) the blue-tiled table in which I used to see ceiling and light reflected ... Thence to looking-glasses; fear and fascination of. Making faces etc. Seeing myself in the organ looking glass at Roehampton. Exhibitionist fantasies and running out naked on the balcony as a child ...

Analysis diary, 13 March Last night dreamt someone gave me a gigantic tube of lanolin-like stuff to rub on my scorched leg ... A great deal came out of tube, rubbed it on burn. Hands covered with it ...

C[arroll] What did tube suggest

T[ony] Oh. I suppose it's a penis ...

To me it seems C. is always suggesting a sexual desire of mine for him. Fearing it, I anticipate and put words into his mouth ... C. says I represent the analysis as a fight. Perhaps I do; anyway it is not a fair fight ...

14 March I have read Tom's [note] book. I had no right to perhaps, without telling him but he has read mine and I did. It gave me a real shock – perhaps because it so confirmed my own picture of what really happened and which he so strenuously denied. I could not have borne it if he had not been honest with me the other night *before* I read it ... Of course it is painful to me to read of all his natural, happy ecstasy over Frances, because it shows me so clearly what I have missed in him – missed in my whole life except for about a week with Silas and those three weeks with Robert ... 'What shall I do without a lover?' I shall become cranky and vinegarish, like Alick Schepeler. I wasted physical love when I could have had it richly because it was a fear and a horror to me. I have lived all my life dominated by fear, but I will try, try, try from now on not to be dominated by it. When I read Tom's book I thought 'My life is over'. But I said to myself 'You are still alive. Do just what you would have done to-day if you had not read it' ... But oh, I have human desires and a human body. Shall I never be happy till I am quit of them? It is such irony that all the years when there were people taking or wanting to take a physical delight in me, I held back, feeling it was wrong and hoping instead for affection, tenderness, respect. And now, when I have the affection and respect, I long for someone who takes physical delight in me and whose body I can give deep pleasure to. Yet even now I cannot accept that just by itself without a feeling of tenderness for the person. Otherwise why do I not take S[iepmann]† as a lover? I have seen enough of him to know that he has physical fire and passion under that peevish, cold, diffident mask. But I genuinely despise his vanity, his cold heart, his fear of responsibility, his unimaginativeness.

It is a cold, dark day, snow or rain threatening. I feel nervous yet almost exalted. Do not want food but force myself to eat. I carry this book from restaurant to restaurant, writing interminably while my coffee gets cold. Has the moment come for me to leave Tom? I thought very seriously of it this morning, of taking my own weekly money and going away – going to live in the same house as Phyllis [Jones] as soon as the children have gone. I *think* it is practical reasons that prevent me and a mistrust of the dramatic. There are technical difficulties; work etc. People would know at once and I do not want anxious inquiries. Then we have asked Phyllis to stay here. She wants to come and [it] means a saving of £2 a week to her. Perhaps with her as a buffer we can preserve the decencies. I think it will be better if Tom has a room to himself. I shall go out as much as possible. Yet perhaps actual separation is what is needed now. I was so afraid of actual physical being alone before. Now I am stronger – but not strong enough to trust myself yet with 11 months more of analysis ahead and my mind still weak and un-dependable. How strange Tom should have wanted me first as a mistress and that such strong physical desire for me should have survived two or three years of marriage. How often he has said to me lately that he saw a real complete relationship possible for us and that it was the hope of that that made him give up Frances. Was that a lie too? Yet there is hardly a word of it in his secret book. Much tenderness and pity: he sees me as a pathetic person. Yet all those pages written only last night are Frances, Frances, Frances. A mention of one week – and one week only at Godfrey St. when he was happy and his mind was only on me. And a hope there that some day Frances' image might recede and that we might become everything to each other. But how frail and precarious it is! The last words are that he saw Frances yesterday . . .

... I have loved other men more, admired them more, had stronger physical feelings for them, a quicker give and take of friendliness and understanding. Yet to no other man have I been faithful for five years, endured things I hate, domesticities, monotony, a dull unvaried life. I have a child by him yet Lyndall, if she means anything to me, means something as an odd little person in her own right, not as the child of the man I love. I wish I loved my children more. Si[las] came back from Mexico loving me like a man and I rejected him. I knew Tom to be at that time cowardly, undecided, unstable, yet I accepted him, believed in him, married him though with a cold exhausted heart ... Surely he can see that she is not *all* romantic. Somewhere inside that poetic body is (I think) a very practical, prosaic, and unpoetic mind. It does not seem to occur to him either that their wonderful times always happened 'round about the 15th'. Presumably the next time it was 'round about the 15th' Geoffrey was there and Tom was not. So much for all-consuming romantic passion. I am sorry for Frances. She is married to a conceited, egotistic fool who is too vain and sure of himself even to mind being cuckolded. But I despise her too for not leaving a man she admits she loathes. Tom despises her a little too. But he forgives her everything for the happiness she gave him ... I wish I had a lover and were not dependent on Tom for physical peace ...

Later same day.

At analysis my self-control broke down and I sobbed myself nearly into convulsions, biting my handkerchief and tearing at the pillow-case – Calmer now, but with dry, hot eyes – I wish in some ways Silas [at this time on the Gold Coast] would come home. There might – I don't know – be something possible for us now which we never had before. But it is bad to live on the memory of past loves – I must learn to get quietly through each day – My strength and my weakness both keep natural love away from me. Men are afraid of me because part of my mind is rough and tough and appalled when they find how ... frightened and unprotected my nature is – Summerson once said to me 'It is the quiet gentle side of you, not the hard, intelligent, amusing one, that has got you all the lovers you have had and will still get you all the lovers you want' ... If I had a body I could trust, lightly and toughly made, I would use it to express so much. But it betrays me: it is heavy and clumsy. It is clothed in very soft skin, but it

is only old men who love with the touch: young men love with the
eye first. R[onald Moody] and Summerson tell me my face is beautiful
but they see me with a sculptor's and an architect's eye. To myself and
the rest of the world I only see the faded remains of mere prettiness
... I must stay anyhow till the children go on Tuesday ... Perhaps I
can never hold a normal man. I have always been terrified of 'normal'
men because I was not good-looking – All the jokes about ugly old
women who want lovers – Why then don't I take a lover while there
are still men who want to have me? ...

... How happy I was going down to Adelaide's [a close friend,
sometimes Addy] because Tom had made love to me the night before
and I thought we were going to be happier. And I know now that the
next day he was miserable and rushed to Frances. And, liar that he is,
he told me he had only gone out as 'an act of faith in us' and was
outraged when I didn't believe him. And how, all that week in
Berkshire, I was longing for him to come down and he seemed
happy, yet his mind was full of Frances (though I didn't know) and he
pretended to be sorry he had to work though in reality he brought the
work so as not to have to talk to me ... Si[las] is vague and childish
and irresponsible, but *he* is honest too ... But for all that she is the
same Frances, yesterday, to-day, and forever. Even her beauty
(though he freely admitted it) did not hold Summerson because he
felt her mind to be dull, cold and commonplace. If that's what Tom
wants, let him have it. But why on earth does he try to persuade
himself he wants me, even as a companion? I don't think I will ever go
on his boat again. Let him keep that for himself and his marvellous
memories ... I wish him no ill but I have wasted five years on him,
have a child by him, and wish I were my own property again. Then, if
he wants me, let him seek me out as if I were a stranger. But then what
am I to do about the children? They love him and he is so good to
them. Emotional disturbances are so bad for them. I suppose it must
come in the end to 'companionship' marriage with all its risks,
frustrations, painted-over miseries.

16 March   It is three o'clock in the morning and I cannot sleep. Tom
sleeps soundly and easily as he always does. He asked me to wake him
if I did not sleep and I know that if I did he would be so good, get me
hot milk, tell me a story and soothe me. But I must get used to dealing

with these things myself. I am thinking very seriously of leaving him soon, at any rate for a time. I think he secretly wants it too though last night he asked me to stay, unless things were intolerable for me. Gradually, inch by inch, I feel a little strength returning. But there is only enough for each day at a time and I must husband it . . . Tonight I nearly knelt down and prayed for strength but I knew that would be false. If my belief in God comes back it comes back (and I must not be afraid of that either) but until then I must get strength from myself only . . . I believe I do love him and I must not be afraid if that is so. Love does not cease to be love if it is not returned but in time it dies. No, it doesn't necessarily die. To love a person wholly, one does wish that person's happiness and not one's own. I have never believed that before . . . All Tom's truth and strength is in his sex. If he had never desired me it would be so much easier. But desire cannot lie and even lately he has desired me and it has been true. It is hard for me to give up completely to him when he makes love to me, even now. Yet I have done sometimes and been rewarded by a very deep happiness though I have often paid for it later with nervous fears and miseries . . . he sleeps there now like a child and does not know I have been gone these last two hours. I think I must be brave and leave him this week. He needs time to himself . . . and I must test for myself what life would be like without him . . .

I feel so tired and sick: I will try and sleep now.

17 March I have definitely decided to leave Tom, anyhow for the present, on Thursday. The room looks grim and bleak but I know I am right to go.

20 March Tomorrow I go. I feel very trembling and frightened but I know this is right . . . To live without hope and without fear is what I have to try and do from now. It must be about five years ago this time that we went for a walk in the country and he said he loved me. I did not ask for it, I did not expect it. He says now that he was never in love with me, or rather, he does not deny it when I say so . . .

I hear she is radiantly happy and absorbed in her child.

* * *

Antonia left Tom Hopkinson on 21 March 1935 and took a room at Shelley House, 105 Oakley Street (the Albert Bridge end). Rooms were let by a sympathetic landlady and Phyllis Jones was a fellow lodger.

* * *

Analysis diary, 31 March   It is very difficult to write up last ten days. I left Tom on March 21st. Since then severe check on writing. V. difficult to work back. Immediate effect of leaving T. relief. Then attack on him last Monday 25th March following bad 2 days. Sunday 26th meant to do [Theodora] Benson article. Paralysis because typewriter was stiff. Came back to 105: actually wrote 1200 words (unspeakably bad) then cd. not go on. Frenzy over trying to make tulle cloak. Eventually to stop crisis lay down. Bad, but recovered, tidied room, wrote 3 essential letters.

Next day Monday bad: did shop-hounding [for an article] but keeping back tears all the time. Analysis bad. Wept convulsively but experienced no relief. Then tea with Corin, straining over her problems. Lay down, but moaning. Forced myself to count 100 etc. Then to do my hair etc. Succumbed to temptation to see Tom: fatal but it brought on a violent attack, a direct personal assault on him followed by appalling depression, tears and the revival of the suicide desire.

We went this week into the work question. How do I do my work? Put it off . . then do it in a rush. If by any chance working continuously as on *Frost* leave over a bit unfinished, so that I have an easy thread to pick up . . .

14 April   It is now over three weeks since I left Tom. Much has happened since then. The strangest thing is that, from the night of my birthday on March 31st Tom suddenly became my passionate lover and for the last fortnight it is on those terms we have met. I saw Frances for the first time last Friday. It was at Summersons. She looked heavy, pale, rather untidy. We talked exactly as if this were not the Frances who has absorbed all my thoughts for nine months but that she and Geoffrey were simply 'the Grigsons'. For a moment we were alone together, putting on our coats. On a genuine impulse I said to her 'I am very glad to see you again, Frances'. I have never seen such an expression of fear and shrinking on any face as she had then . . .

6 May   Jubilee day [25th anniversary of George V's accession] as peaceful as possible in Steyning after a perfunctory little procession. I walked with Helene Cowan† over the fields to Wiston House [local manor house] ... To-day ... the real summer feeling, smell of dust, crushed grass, wallflowers ... dog violets almost as big as pansies ... on the road up to the hills at Petersfield. Yesterday discovered wood sorrel in a valley at Grayshott.

26 May   I am writing sitting at my high open window in Oakley St: the window of which I am sometimes a little afraid. All day until 5.30 I lay in bed in a strange drowsy bemused state, not exactly ill though I have a cold and sore throat, yet not well, so lethargic and thick-blooded that I have not been able even to tidy room and comb my hair. I felt as if I had a low fever but my temperature was normal. For days on and off I have felt like this, following on the climax of the keys [explained p. 51] and the misery, pressure and restlessness preceding. To write is very difficult. Hand moves in a stiff way, very slowly: can only make letters very small. I got up suddenly and dressed wanting to sit at the open window. I am still a little afraid of it knowing how suddenly a mood of weariness, lethargy etc. may turn to a dead-lock inside and convulsive fear. So I have put my three little dahlia plants out on the sill to remind me to keep my head. I feel very remote: have only to walk downstairs to be out in the street, go where I will, meet people. But I cannot do it though I am a little frightened to be alone. Perhaps Tom will pass on his way up from the river and come in. Yet it is pleasant here: this side of the street in shadow, the wind stirring the striped cream and milk-coffee coloured curtains and ruffling (but just bearably) the pages of my notebook, the church bells ringing and the people walking sociably up and down the opposite pavement over which the shadow is beginning to flood. On sunny days a young man in a red shirt, wearing glasses, sits always at the window or on the balcony of the house opposite, reading, writing or typing. In the room behind him are shelves lined with books that look decorative and readable like books in pictures and an open gramophone. He looks self-contained and enviable, a writer presumably, but judging from his taste in gramophone records, one wd. say not a very good writer ... For days I've been trying to copy out that passage – pages from Heseltine [Peter Warlock, the composer]'s letters: the book is on my table: I have the time. Why can't I do it? The young man in the red shirt almost *afflicts* me . . an inhabitant of the same world of sitting at windows writing, yet so complacently at ease in his never pausing to find a word, never looking into the street, never giving one curious glance at my window . . . He is aware of me, I am pretty sure, but resents the intrusion of that monster the 'writing woman'. Yet here am I a creature in distress, only half in my mind, at any moment to be assailed by an impulse to fling myself out of *my* window as he may, for all I know want yet fear to do out of *his*. Yet could I signal to him across the cañon of Oakley St. I think not. Shall I ring up Tom? To find someone not at home in this state of mind is frightening. Yet it is by my own wish that I am to-day cut off, alone . . .

28 May   There followed after that deadlock, crisis and hysteria. The next day Eric saw Carroll and told me the probable 'picture' of my history. In an odd way it is a relief to know that I am really ill, that there *is* a beast in the jungle, that there is more than a possibility that though Carroll can give me some years of complete self possession (the *brain* is not affected) it may pounce in the end permanently and even again (but not fatally) quite soon . . .

1 June   Bad nightmare last night. How cleverly the asylum night-mares keep up to date . . . This time I was an old woman, knowing I was mad, trying to plead with the nurses, explaining to them that things which looked quite normal and harmless to them were terrifying to me. They *seemed* to listen attentively, almost sympatheti-cally, but in the end they giggled, behaved like nurses, and dragged me to the thing. The wire machine and the clippers . . . I had forgotten that strange one [dream] months ago which ended (I was grown up) lying naked on the pavement, mad and knowing myself to be mad, yet peaceful and the little street boys looking at me and touching me, curious and rather frightened, saying 'She's a sleasy lady' . . .

R[onald Moody] said to me the other night 'I love the way your hair leaves your forehead – it does it so *virulently*.'

I am very happy with Ronald feel so at ease, unfolded, understood and deeply cared for and yet also that my best and most are demanded of me, any falseness known.

2 June(?)   To-day, having a slight prescience of 'Sunday neurosis' I have brought my notebook up here to Ronnie's and sit at his table indoors, looking out at the little garden. I can hear the sound of his mallet and chisel as he works ... in the studio that is only a little converted greenhouse ... Yesterday Tom and I walked in St James' Park and looked at the birds. The coots have a white patch on their heads ... Their legs are set very far back, they trail them right behind them in the water as they swim, long separate pale green toes which T. says each carry a little bladder on the top to keep the bird from sinking in marshy ground ... We were walking hand in hand, very gay, and elderly people looked at us kindly as if we were lovers. Strange that my very first writing, when I was only five, should have been of violence; the imaginary storm . . 'the waves are drifting high alas' and the real kitchen-heard anecdote of the cabman who 'had his head bashed in by a lamp post'. On the films I like to see storms, explosions, fires, fiercely running rivers ... a really superb Micky Mouse, all wit and violence . . real genius. Everyone adores Micky Mouse but does not know why. It is at once the most primitive and the most sophisticated thing, a real release of the most violent impulses in pure fantasy ...

4 June (3.45 a.m.)   I will finish the history of Sunday June 2 later on. It was one of the most important days of my life. I feel a real new beginning, such as one has very seldom ...

14 June   ... Last Sunday – no . . June 2 . . R[onald] made love to me. He felt it would be a risk, call up my demons and I knew there was a risk too but wanted to take it. Physically I was cold, terrified and in pain: immediately afterwards my fears came up, anxiety, sense of sin, even the colour bar (but only academically I think: that seems to have disappeared now) and unhappiness over Tom, feeling I had cut myself off from him irrevocably. I was disturbed and wept. But afterwards, as we lay quietly together, listening to 'Deh Vieni' and I heard his breathing so quiet and regular, like the rise and fall of the phrases, I grew calmer. Afterwards, I found I was bleeding, like a virgin. And then a curious peace and happiness came over me. I looked in the glass as I dressed and my face which had been pale, distorted, swollen with tears, looked young and contented and my eyes were bright and cool. We had dinner and I was exquisitely, radiantly happy, looking at pictures of Maillol and the Egyptians and feeling at once new born and yet secure and mature, all my emotions freed and going out towards work and meeting him there. 'Alles', only the head finished yet, is really beautiful. I was moved, could hardly speak and felt tears come into my eyes when I saw it the other day. It is so far beyond anything R. has done yet, much more projected right out of himself than the big head. It really has a life of its own, complete, if he can keep it up through the whole figure.

The next week was difficult. I felt doubt, fear, humiliation, physical desire and misery. It seemed to me that he was treating me with deliberate coldness in order to humiliate me. When I *saw* him it was all right, but when I was alone I could get nothing clear. Now I am glad he made no concessions to me because, for once in my life with a man, I am being honestly treated. He said to me 'No, you may not be young and beautiful, but if you were young you would not be what you are and to me your face is beautiful'. He went all over my face with his hands (which are so much alive, yet so cool and certain) as if he were modelling it, saying how much he liked the shape and adding 'One day I will do a head to express what I feel about this face'. Yesterday I went to lunch with him, arriving in the tired, slowed-down, 'drifting' state but there was so much warmth, gaiety, fearlessness in his physical approach to me that I came away light-hearted and in contact with things again . . . I did not mean at first to tell Tom unless he asked me directly (it is some time since he and I were lovers) but I felt it was too important not to tell. He seemed very understanding but, as far as I could see, it made no emotional impression on him at all. I was half relieved yet perhaps a little disappointed . . .

29 June I begin – very dimly – to see . . . or rather 'entrevoir' something. I have missed all these years the *something* in Catholicism, behind all its terrors, chains, supports, superstitions, denials and 'consolations', which was my deepest life. Anything one longs for so much and with the best part of oneself . . and I have longed for it since I was eleven years old . . must in the end be satisfied. On my First Communion day, November 21st 1914, I felt nothing at the actual receiving of the sacrament but in reading Francis Thompson's poems that day (my mother had bought them for me not knowing what she was giving me) I found something terrible, sweet and transforming which really did make me draw breath and pant after it ... Now I begin to see and hope (yet one must not *hope* yet: one must be content to walk blind, to be in darkness, despised, puzzled, unsure) ... that the source runs pure through the ages and that different religions are but its different incarnations ...

Analysis diary, 6 July   Had about 4 remarkably good weeks, during which I did articles regularly both for *Mirror* and *Everyman* [a magazine], wrote 2 shoe catalogues, did 12,000 words for Theodora Benson .. eventually all in 2 days after having put it off in fear and misery for weeks ...

Most interesting emergencies: the linking up of the click with my father's latchkey. Convulsive horror aroused by C[arroll]'s shaking his bunch of keys ...

* * *

Antonia began to take an interest in the Group Theatre. This progressive theatre company had been founded by two of her close friends, Rupert Doone[†] and his friend Robert, and became famous for its production of Auden and Isherwood's *The Ascent of F.6*. At one point, in 1937, there was a plan for Antonia to edit a magazine for the company.

In 1935, the Group Theatre was holding its summer school at Summerhill – the progressive school at Bilton Hall in Suffolk, founded by A.S. Neill[†] on the liberal principles enunciated in his book, *The Problem Parent*. Antonia attended the school where John Greenwood[†] (whose name she did her best to hide) fell in love with her. Greenwood was the secretary of the Group Theatre and a Quaker. A night spent with him in the garden proved disappointing as, at that time anyway, Greenwood was impotent. He remained something of a rebel (by Quaker standards) all his life.

* * *

Revised diary, 7 Aug   On an impulse I said 'Yes' when Rupert Doone asked me to come down to Summerhill for the Group Theatre Summer School. Nothing could be more unlike my usual way of spending a holiday. Odd to be plunged straight from my solitary bedsitting room life in to communal living with a vengeance. Not

only does one sleep in a dormitory (with the unrepressed scribbles of
Neill's pupils on the wall) but washes in a communal bathroom with
several other women (N[eill] doesn't allow a lock on the door).
Several of the staff are here and many of the children since most of
them prefer to stay for the holidays rather than go home. This is my
first experience of an 'experimental' school in action though of course
Bertrand Russell[†] told me a great deal about Telegraph House.
Everything is cheerfully disorderly; all the furniture ricketty and
damaged. It was a long time before I found a hut with a table firm
enough to write on. I can't help wondering what happens to a child
who has an impulse to work quietly at a desk. The staff is earnest and
enthusiastic; the children seem happy and very much alive though
one newcomer sullenly follows us about with an open penknife and
never speaks. Difficult to judge the experiment till these children
have gone out into a society which still imposes certain rules of
behaviour. Neill obviously inspires immense confidence and affection in them. My impression was that he inspired almost too much,
that in freeing them from their parents (how he loathes parents!) he
attached them too much to himself as a benevolent father figure. One
thing struck me considerably. There is a boy of three who has no feet
but is so fearless and confident that he runs about on his stumps and
joins in everything just as if he were not crippled. A little while ago
N[eill] offered a prize to the child who produced the most original
bedspread. Some of them broke into the Anglican church and stole
the altar frontal. Everyone thought this a very good joke. However,
if the children have an 'impulse' to go to church, he doesn't stop
them.

* * *

In July or August Antonia bought a new pen 'like one of the analyst's'
and began a new book about Tom and Frances. After four chapters her
block returned and she abandoned it.

* * *

7 August, Summerhill   I am worried that I have lost my green
notebook ... Moreover the green one was important to me: the
beginning of it marked the break up of the jam ... I am superstitious
about the green book. I wrote something I didn't understand in it and

took it up to show to Carroll. It is like losing a part of oneself. Here it is hard to get into the mood of the book. Even in a few days one gets so cut off from one's normal life ... There is a young quaker here [John Greenwood], half prig and half poet who for some reason interests me ... there is a real innocence and integrity in him which I like very much. Neill I feel uncertain about. There is so much of the exhibitionist about him, something callow and shallow too, I think. He dances with the careful abandon of an old man showing off. He puts vases of flowers on the piano and one feels he prides himself on insensitiveness to beauty and order of any kind. It's no good; I hate the Scotch. They all smell somewhere. He strikes me as being radically vain ... I slept out last night and the night before. I did not sleep much but it was beautiful. It is light long before the sun rises; a beautiful unshining grey light like the light in Dante's limbo. The sun rose with no clouds, a pale bright disc in a clear sky. There are rufflings and rustlings in the leaves all night ...

Revised diary, 10 Aug This place makes me feel I am utterly out of touch with the modern world. What on earth am I doing here? Someone took me to a Group Theatre show in London and I was struck by the freshness and wit of a kind of *revue*. We arrived late and it was not till the end I discovered it was Auden's *Dance of Death* with Britten's music. They are rehearsing a new Auden show for their Westminster season, *The Dog beneath the Skin*. I can't understand half the allusions. The Group Theatre and its adherents are mainly very young with a sprinkling of my contemporaries and a few earnest older women whom Rupert forces to attend his strenuous dance and exercise classes as a method of breaking down their psychological 'adhesions'. The atmosphere is feverishly progressive. Revolution in politics; revolution in art; revolution in one's way of life. Few actual party members but it is taken for granted that one sympathises with communism. The poets are all becoming propagandists and pamph-leteers. I begin to feel guilty about not being 'politically awakened' and not throwing myself into the movement. 'Writers must come out of their ivory towers' insists Rupert (with Spender, Isherwood, MacNeice, Auden etc. behind him). 'They must become socially conscious, working for the collective good. They must break down their old bourgeois pride and prejudice and individualism'. To

staunch my conscience I type out manifestoes on Revolution in the
Theatre and spend my mornings addressing envelopes to possible
supporters.

Revised diary, 18 Aug   The Catholic Church is definitely the Enemy,
indissolubly linked to fascism, capitalism and the bourgeoisie. None
of these people, all drawn from various sections of the English
middle class, will tell me exactly what they mean by bourgeoisie. To
my surprise I often find myself ardently defending the Church I have
abandoned and sometimes get quite an interested hearing as they
have the vaguest ideas of Catholic belief and practice. I have the
advantage of having read the Communist Manifesto while they
haven't read the Catechism. Quakerism is the form of Christianity to
which they are least unsympathetic. The Secretary is a young and
ardent Quaker who manages to be at once a pacifist and a
revolutionary.

Analysis diary, 26 Aug   ... Most interesting feature of last month ...
the sudden break of the jam for a week during which I write 4
chapters (about 15000) words of a new book.

27 Aug   ... At Bilton Hall in one week summer had changed to
autumn ... I write here before breakfast, tired and stupid, wanting
my tea, at the window. The air is cool and does not smell of summer
any more; people walk up Oakley Street to work with their despatch
cases and their newspapers under their arms. A girl in a thin cotton
dress looks a survivor, like the roses at Bilton ...

28 Aug   ... I wish I had a God to pray for for strength as J[ohn
Greenwood] has. Yet I must behave as if there were one without
demanding sympathy or reassurance. J[ohn] causes me a good deal of
strain, yet I am very grateful for his love and kindness. I believe in
him too, in spite of all his commonness, narrowness, cockiness,
priggishness ... in spite of his usual chetif, undeveloped adolescence,
genuine authority. When this tide of warmth leaves him, it is terrible
to see his face: dead, mean, ugly, almost obscene ... It is strange I
should feel sexual attraction to him when there is so little outwardly
to attract. Yet I feel that it is not only the mad unconscious, in love

with frustration, which turns from the person who can give me real sexual life and satisfaction to this impotent one. Marry I think I never will again, yet this strange and despised, though 'popular' creature may be a real source of life to me . . . Tom, the other day, dropped (by mistake of course) the watch I gave him for a wedding present into the river from his boat. Oddly enough, at the moment, it does not distress me, though I feel it to be a symbol. Something is over between us . . .

2 Sept . . . Read *The Captain's Doll* [D.H. Lawrence] again (about the 8th time I think) and like it better than ever. Odd how again, though, the woman is more real than the man. The man is a mouthpiece for the right ideas but he doesn't quite *exist*. Hannele exists yet the doll is oddly more alive than the Captain.

Revised diary, 3 Sept Back in London, I have had several talks with the young Quaker who is convinced I will find what I am looking for among the Friends. I went with him to Jordans and to a meeting in London. Convinced of their sincerity yet had an impression of joylessness and a certain complacency. Something strained about the silence: tension, rather than recollection. One could imagine getting up to speak simply to break it. On both occasions my young friend felt 'called' to speak and did so eloquently. Each time it struck me as prepared rather than spontaneously inspired and I felt the same with the other speakers. He has made me read Woolman's journal which I found very genuine and moving but not so *bouleversant* as to convert me to the Friends. Can one talk of spirituality as being 'provincial'? Or is that just my old Catholic snobbery?

19 Sept How horrible, how horrible human beings can be. Even when one knows how many actions are prompted by unconscious fears, it is impossible not to be disgusted by them. Even though I know there is something true, warm, incorruptible in J[ohn] G[reenwood] how he stinks of corruption. I feel as if I had been covered with slime even by contact with such a creature. Yet I suppose I should be glad I met him since I have put him in the way of being cured. Proust was right when he said one paid heavily for having to do with someone who is not one's type. There is a real ill-bredness of soul about him yet it does not go all through ... My dream identifying him with Selwyn Jepson[†] may be truer than I know ... My new-found calm is very shaken to-day. I have a horror of this party on Saturday ...

26 Sept   To-day analysis v. bad: one of the worst I have ever known. To-night resting stiff-eyed; half doped with Dial I am suddenly off on a trail. As I left I said 'I don't know where to go: I don't know where to hide'. Carroll said gently 'Perhaps in a day or two you will know where to hide'.

Suddenly to-night I feel I must re-examine my life. This guilt about my writing: distaste for it: guilt at not doing it: fearful anxiety connected with it.

In my youth I wrote naturally and without difficulty. I did not think very much about it. I liked it and it came easily to me and in essays etc. I was almost invariably top and got an exquisite thrill from hearing my work read out to the class. Now my writing, though competent and precocious, was never fresh or original. I think it was almost always imitation of what I had read. I realised the immense difference between Charlotte's work and my own. Charlotte [d'Er-langer],[†] I think was a born writer: forceful, economical and with a real eye. The *quality* of her work showed through all the ignorance of childhood ...

Revised diary, 6 Oct   I have just been reading the record of a dangerous voyage, *Malte Laurids Brigge*. Yet Rilke returned safely. I have seen a photo of him in a black coat and a watch chain standing in the gateway of a German castle. Where have I been from which there was any danger of not returning? Even from insanity I came back to find a name, a latchkey, a home, identifying friends. In writing I hug the shore all the time. Rilke's book has affected me profoundly; given me the sense of being out of my depth, of a dazzling interconnection between two worlds in which one simultaneously moves. It has left me sensitised like a watch that has been too near a magnet. The effect was so violent that I had to lie down at intervals while I was reading it; I was shaking as if in high fever. The telephone was an alarming interruption; I could not collect myself quickly enough to answer coherently

* * *

Probably some time in the early 'thirties Eric Earnshaw Smith moved into a terrace house at 5 Selwood Place, off the Fulham Road. One room there was set aside for Antonia to use as a workroom when she so desired. She was now living in a room at an unknown address.

* * *

6 Oct   It is cheating, I know, to begin a new notebook – But the last one never felt right. And, as I have moved to a new room, I felt it might be excusable ... For hours I have put off beginning to write even in this. I have tidied my room completely ... It is still not quite right: the little tallboy has not come; I must wait till tomorrow for the case for the big magazines that lie flopping clumsily over the shelves. I have even polished all my furniture with white wax and washed cups and glasses ... I enjoyed this domestic work yet felt a little guilty ... Eric has given me a good desk like the one I have at Selwood Place ... I know that tonight I must try to write something, anything. I feel frightened sitting here writing alone in this pleasant, safe cream-coloured room with the clock ticking, the gas fire giving out its continuous even breath, people moving in the room next door. It is as if, sitting here at my desk with the striped curtains, the lamp, the newly polished cigarette box in front of me I were venturing out into an unknown terrifying world from which I might not find my way back. Yet all is safe, friendly, benevolent in the room. Though I sit with my back to it, nothing looks over my shoulder. No mirror is behind me; the only pictures the Chinese fairy with the phoenix and the Buddha head. Beside me a block reminds me to buy kettles, tea, nail polish remover, chamois leather. I wish someone were sitting in the chair behind, absorbed in reading or knitting, yet holding on to me as a child twists the string of a balloon round its wrist, ignores it, yet keeps it safely tethered ... Never in writing, except perhaps occasionally in the notebooks have I felt out of my depth ... In writing, when I can write at all, I hug the shore all the time ... It is strange that in poetry, when I was eleven, I had what I can only call my first revelation from which I emerged dazed, unable to fit the two worlds together. It has happened again now with the Rilke book ... The interruption of the telephone bell was really alarming: I could not collect myself quickly enough to make a voice ... The green one [notebook] was a legitimate new beginning; I cannot help feeling its loss and the consequent break in continuity . . . it was my own fault for wanting to *show* it to anyone, though I think the unconscious was at work making me lose it because I was afraid of what I had written about my father . . . what was in the green notebook was, I think of some value to me. Not only did it break the jam and lead me insensibly to begin the new book during that one astonishing week in June or July, but its pattern . . . had a significance. It was the first time I broke away from the pattern of notebook as much like my father's old ones as I could get . . . Now I begin to be a trifle anxious in case this type of notebook may become obsolete. Should I buy several now and insure continuity of size and shape? . . . What fantastic things I worry about. A disease perhaps, yet I still feel that I may be cheating somewhere in taking steps to be cured of this disease. Carroll says that, without treatment, I should certainly become insane again. It is by no means certain that, even with treatment, . . . I can avoid insanity permanently . . . I think I must accept analysis meekly since it is difficult for me to accept, to blot myself out, become a featureless, a 'case' . . . Yet at intervals after these apparently pointless and painful arguments, these frustrated tears and irrational rages, the pressure is here and there relieved. Even if it is only that one can cross a road or tidy a room with pleasure, it is something. And for a whole week I worked – yes worked ardently, longing to be back with work as with a lover . . . I wish the notebooks seemed to me work: but they do not 'count' for me though I know they have a use, if not for writing, at least for exploring and recording. And how fast, how comparatively painlessly I write to-night; as easily as in those long letters I sometimes surprise myself by writing nowadays to Greenwood, the only person to whom at present I *can* write. I have sat here for only one hour and a quarter and how many sheets are covered – over ten pages – over 1200 words. If I could do as much each day to my book, I would have the body there to work on in a few weeks . . .

*   *   *   *

I saw to-day in a tobacco shop a card 'A man of parts and influence smokes a cigar'.

*   *   *   *

. . . Rilke, after the wonderful passage about the blind man,
    'My God, it struck me with sudden vehamence [sic], thus then act

Thou! There are proofs of Thy existence. I have forgotten them all and have never demanded any, for what a formidable obligation would lie in the certainty of Thy existence! And yet it has just been proved to me. This then, is to Thy liking, in this dost Thou take pleasure: that we should learn to endure all and not judge ...'

* * * *

It is a source of great unhappiness to me that I have no name. I rejected my first name – Eirene Botting – it is the first time for years that I have dared to write it – because it felt so terrible to me, so degrading. Yet I feel one sins in rejecting one's name ... And what is Antonia White? James Stephens [unknown] said the name conveyed nothing to him; it was the blandest name he had ever heard ... It is odd that I take 'Tony', the name by which all my friends know me, from my mother's nickname for me as a child and her own name of White, since all through my childhood and after I hated, despised and rejected all of my mother and would like to have been only my father's child ...

* * * *

If I prayed today ... I would say .... Take away from me the desire to be loved and admired and give me instead the power to love without desiring to possess ...

8 Oct ... Big thimble-shaped drops tremble on the window sash, cling for a moment and are shaken down by the wind; the rain makes a timid scratching noise like a mouse scrabbling in a wastepaper basket ...

I am supposed to be sitting here writing my *Mirror* article. Why do I not begin since it would be good to have the tiresome thing over? I feel raw and humiliated after yesterday's analysis as if everything I did were done from some vile and self-seeking motive ... Now, why will I not get my article done? ... Because I would have a little time left and could get on with my own work? ... The best work I have done and heaven knows it is not much of a best has come when I wanted to work so much that I just *had* to with the same impulse one must buy a new frock, tidy a room, embrace a lover, find food when one is hungry ... Naturally I would like not to have to *work* for money at all; to have it provided for me. But I *am* extravagant. I have ... really lusted at times after £1000 a year ...

14 Oct . . . Trying to manage money: cook own tea and supper. Enjoyed it but waste endless time. This spinster-life pleasant but perhaps very barren for work.

Yesterday the country was so beautiful . . . J[ohn Greenwood] and I found a nest; fine little twigs underneath and above a cup of horsehair and dry grass all netted together and smoothed into a shallow depression. We saw a rat run up a bank: it climbed a tree in the hedge and hid in a cage of twisted stems. It wd. not show itself when J[ohn] gently pushed a straw through the opening; it made not the faintest rustle or stir.

I must go to bed tho' I have a lot to record. This day is filled and must come to an end . . .

29 Oct To-day I came home early, determined to clear up, to finish the *Mirror* article, to face the accumulated mass of letters shut away in a drawer. I made myself tea telling myself there was nothing intrinsically wicked in making tea at 3 instead of 4 in the afternoon. My father hated any departure from the established time of meals: it would have been unthinkable that we should ever have dined at 7 or 8 instead of 7.30, that we should ever have gone into the kitchen and cooked ourselves eggs on a Sunday night instead of sitting down to the same inflexible meal of cold meat and undressed salad. Even if I repeat firmly to myself 'It is NOT a sin to make tea at 3 instead of 4' some part of me is not convinced. Even Eric did not like the upsetting of a ritual. His ritual was less monotonous, but in its own way, equally inflexible. I love to see him, yet it is nearly always he who sets our conversation, decides what we shall talk about and himself does most of the talking . . . He will talk till my head is saturated and swimming, till nothing he says bites anywhere in my mind which has turned to a wet sponge, till my skin is creeping and my eyes sore as if full of smoke and I can feel a sticky film settling all over my body which has become too swollen for its clothes . . .

. . . He *plays* with his world of ideas, plays in the best possible way with deftness and absorption, bringing the whole force of his attention to bear on the scheme he is dealing with at the moment, yet I feel he is all the time only *entertaining* himself with them . . . he makes me feel a barbarian to be so moved by poetry and religion, by moments in which I feel an intuitive knowledge of truth . . .

A few days ago I became uneasy about this room. I feared to go and feared to stay. I thought the landlady was edging me out: the hostile, institutional feeling revived. I searched frantically for rooms, read advertisements, looked at flats though I am not, I know, ready to live alone. Now I am more reconciled to it; willing to settle here a little longer. There is a wide view of sky from the windows in front of my desk. In the half-hour during which I have been writing that sky has changed incessantly now that the wind has been blowing up into a gale. The clouds have drawn almost right across, leaving only one clear space of blue . . . Now and then the wind flings a handful of drops on the pane where they stay splashed in small clusters like a finger print . . .

13 Nov　I am pleased by this last small piece of observation. It is trivial, but it is fresh. Without noting it at the time I should have forgotten it.

D[orothy Holms]† the other night wanted to have a new plate of bread and butter brought because a perfectly clean menu card had fallen on it. Yet she lives in a flat in a workmen's block with no hot water, no bathroom, merely a cold-water tap in a cupboard on the landing and a lavatory shared with the next door tenants. There are patches of damp on the rather dirty walls. 'I should feel it were sordid' she said 'if Cecily [unknown] had not lived here for twenty years before me. And Cecily has had anything but a sordid life. She is the cousin of the Earl of Harrowby'.

A[lexander] K[eiller] has appeared again. He makes the same scenes over the mixing of his gin and vermouth. He perpetually draws attention to his false teeth as if they were a new acquisition though I am sure he had them when I knew him 18 months ago. He complains of having suffered some 'monstrous crash' and only going on lunching at his old haunts to keep a stiff upper lip and not let people know how hard he has been hit. He boasts that he still wears the same suit to the Eton and Harrow match (he is 46) as he wore in his last term at Eton. He tells me . . about the 10/6 pencil he gave me birthday before last . . that he wishes he could have afforded one for himself at the same time. He tells me what effective brooches his mistress (D . . . C . . .) picks up at Woolworths, and what bad luck it is that, having grown out of her last year's evening frocks, she cannot afford a new one.

Soon afterwards he tells me that he is renting, and hopes eventually
to buy, a large 'show' manor house in Wiltshire. That he is working
on his excavations at Avebury sometimes with gangs of 250 men.
That he proposes to move an entire village a whole mile away because
it gets in the way of 'the Avenue'.

Archeology and 'the Avenue' has now become his religion. All the
stones are 'she'. He says the most beautiful music in the world to him
is the sound of the cement-mixer pounding the cement which will fix
the newly unearthed stone in the socket of its stone hole 'to know that
3000 years after I am gone she will still be standing .. and as far as she
can see .. green hills .. not a house or a petrol station'. Every time a
new stone is excavated a flag is flown and the gang lines up. D . . .
C . . . has had no time for her own painting ever since she went to him.
He keeps her busy making drawings of the stones. To find the exact
place of each stone hole the soil has to be sifted and analysed. He has
recovered already 39% of them and is going to dig there for 12 more
years. To raise them up he uses gangs of unskilled men under a skilled
foreman and uses no machinery. He wants to do it under the original
conditions, only substituting steel hawsers for hide ropes. He sent me
some flowers I had never seen before .. Nerings [sic] . . .

* * *

In 1934 when she was drama critic for *Time and Tide* Antonia had praised
the worth of Michel St Denis[†] extravagantly. She particularly admired
the production of *Don Juan* by his revolutionary 'Compagnie des
Quinze'. In 1935 she delivered a series of lectures on Greek drama for
the London Theatre Studio, the drama school which St Denis
established in Islington. She also wrote a play, *Alcibiades*, which is now
lost, for the students.

* * *

20 Nov   I have been in bed for two days with my old low-fever 'flu,
extreme languor and depression . . .

I feel at this moment that everything for the next year hangs on my
being able to work for St Denis. Ever since I first saw the *Compagnie
des Quinze* I longed for some association with them . . . St Denis told
Greenwood he thought well of me . . . For my own selfish ends I need
something to absorb me . . . The stage was my first love and I believe

will be my last. But it has fallen into such lethargy and decay in England . . . He is French and from the south and has more life in him than anyone I have met for years . . .

21 Nov   To-day again it has been worse. Utter exhaustion and a despair which has nothing in the least grand about it – just a weeping, whining infant unable to cope with life. I do not know, literally do not know how to go on living.

TWO

1936–1937

Antonia was to live alone, but not celibate, for the rest of her life. She had affairs with a selection of poets and artists in the late 'thirties, and with the journalist, Basil Nicholson.† She lost her job on the *Daily Mirror*.

1936

4 Jan   It is difficult to cast up one's accounts for the last year. It was a year full of unhappiness, mainly from the tension inside myself, of unproductiveness in *work* . . . If I could only get firmly into my head or rather my solar plexus that all human activities as such are quite neutral in themselves and valuable or dangerous only in so far as they increase or wither the *life* in any individual. At the moment, in a sense, 'art' means nothing whatever to me. I cannot read (except trash) look at pictures, listen to music. I have not even been to the Chinese Exhibition to which I looked forward with such eagerness and which has now been on for several weeks. I suppose all those things will come round again in their turn.

Yet I suppose it has been an 'eventful' year . . . It is hard to say just how analysis has affected me. It will be a year next February since I began with Carroll . . . There have been whole weeks, though not for many months now, when my bosom's Lord *did* sit lightly on his throne . . . The desire to write . . . or rather *to have written*, may be pure vanity and self-display, the passion to give evidence of being a 'remarkable person'. Now, oddly enough, I like evidences of *not* being a remarkable person; of finding other people with the same phobias and difficulties as myself. My only passion at the moment is

for human beings. I like to watch, listen, make guesses about them . . .
I have not time to write much in this book now. I have not even
wanted to for several weeks though vaguely feeling that I 'ought'.
Such small impulse to write as I have has come out in the form of
sudden long letters to Frances, Tom, Emily. I could not keep up the
notes in the other book on the analysis from the patient's point of
view which is a pity . . .

Certainly, even in this curious cramped and mutilated life I have
led this year, things have happened. I brought myself to leave Tom. I
had for a few weeks a satisfactory physical relationship with him. For
a few days in June the same with R[onald]. Since then, with no one.
My physical feeling for G[reenwood] I believe to have been entirely
pathological. Yet it would be dishonest to deny that it existed or that
its necessary lack of fulfilment caused me no distress. But I am fairly
certain I never will be his lover even if he could be mine . . .

In the summer I found that mine was a severe case; that there was
even definite danger of insanity . . . Tom's attitude hurt me very
much; it seemed academic, indifferent. Now he says that for years he
had expected that; it was no news to him . . .

My distaste for woman's page journalism increases and with it my
incompetence. It wd. be funny if after having done reasonably well at
this for 20 years (advertising included) I shd. find myself *unable* to
make a living at it . . .

I have been playing around the theatre a bit ever since Summerhill.
Now I am working (unpaid) as St Denis 'literary adviser' . . .
Something in me obviously fights hard against this attempt to make
some sort of living . . . [by] raving about clothes for typists.

The 'literary world' continues to be kind to me and believe in me
inspite of my having produced nothing (except a short, weak sketch
of theatre life) for 2 years. Logan [Pearsall Smith], Desmond
[McCarthy], [Hugh] Kingsmill,[†] [Cyril] Connolly, Emily etc. It is
astonishing. Of course I am pleased, but have an uncomfortable
feeling that it is not *me* they mean at all!

6 Jan . . . Am I anxious because analysis begins again tomorrow? . . .
I could not believe Tom when he wrote to me the other day that so
much I had said to him in letters had gone right over his head and he
only now began to understand them . . . Perhaps I have a life only of

the understanding before me and must accept that. But the body, the heart, is it over for them? . . . It would be well for me at any rate, to try and find out what other people need and, if possible, give it them. I find it easier to do this for anyone but Tom. Why is that? I suppose I *cannot* get away from the fact that I feel he owes me something, has stolen something from me. I talk as if I were the only one who has suffered. It is evident that he suffers too.

Analysis diary, 7 Jan For months in summer (holiday from anal.) exceedingly well physically. Mentally unstable and flighty but with moments of unexpected insight and even generosity of behaviour. Found myself sexually attracted to someone whom I do not admire at all physically and only to a very limited extent mentally. Discovered that he was impotent wh. he did not know and told him about anal. with result he is now being v. successfully analysed. Discovered Chinese Buddha in S.Ken. Went over and over again (5 times at least) but have not so far gone to Chinese Exhibition. Why? Was Ronald's lover v. successfully 2 or 3 times in June but find complete ban on that relation ever since though I *admire* him, both physically and mentally a great deal. Complain incessantly that I have no lover. Some very distressing scenes with J[ohn Greenwood] who is v. much in love with me but, owing to his psychol. trouble the worst kind of excitant but frustrating lover ... Few days of acute nervous depression and illness in Nov ... from wh. I recovered with dramatic suddenness on discovering the book I really was interested in was not the Tom–Frances one but the one begun in Nov. 1934 about my father – v. patchy but its last bits the best I have done. Uncertainty became almost unbearable. Fearful anxiety about taking the children with Tom to my mother. But during fortnight's break was compara- tively calm and felt great relief at stopping treatment Sunday (last) before due to resume, violent attack of impotent rage on v. slight provocation (restaurant closed: cold wind: no bus etc) after extreme icy depression and self-deprecation ... got rather drunk at night with Siepmann and Tom .. more drunk than I have ever been – practically dissociated from myself yet able to speak quite clearly, cook eggs, etc. all quite mechanically. In early Dec (I think) after a terrific outburst of rage with Carroll, had minor explosions of rage in letters to Joan [Geary, Tom's mistress] and Frances. These worked out quite well in the end; a polite reconciliation with Frances (whom I have never seen alone since the summer of 1934) and a quite warm understanding established with Joan. With Tom . . . nearly always at my very worst . . . Lately reverted to masturbation again, always with stripping fantasy (G[reenwood] usually central figure) angry, ashamed and aggrieved that this shd. be so. To-day at anal. I told him I was continuously putting on weight again. He said some part of me obviously desires to be fat and old . . . He says the ordinary idea of 'middle age' is the middle forties not the middle thirties. I lunched with Tom, began well but became v. bitter and threatened to divorce him . . . Saw trustees about my father's estate. Noted large sums of money he had wasted: lapsed insurance policies; hopeless investments. Absolutely no provision for me until my mother dies; even house will not be my own property.

Came home surly and depressed cd. not settle to work. Suddenly v. sleepy: slept for hour and a half heavily with curious dream. Was with Joan and Tom. Joan had a little car and was going to Watford. Became peevishly jealous of Joan, wished I had a car . . . I felt mad. I was afraid of being found and locked up by police for what I was going to do but I wanted to punish Tom and I knew the act wd. be very exciting and pleasant. I wanted to run about the streets naked. I began to take my clothes off. At first I was interrupted . . . by an old gentleman and 2 women (all half blind and old) . . . Then behind the front door I began to undress v. quickly. When I pulled off my stocking I pulled off half my foot too. It did not hurt . . . as fast as I got my vest off there was another vest underneath . . . Then I woke up, supposing it was night and finding it was late afternoon and I was lying fully dressed on my bed. Felt sexual excitement at memory of dream but did not masturbate . . . and decided to write in this book for first time since August.

Thinking over nakedness question.

Morbid fear of exposure yet secret desire to be exposed . . . Find it hard to do the *writing* of my work for St Denis but quite enjoy the research. Not only feel *incapable* of writing anything original but *do not want to*. Prefer to do this sort of anonymous work and do not seem to worry over the fact that I am not being paid for it and cannot get Michel [St Denis] to suggest any definite terms . . . Do not worry that I cannot pay my outstanding accounts wh. do not amount to more than about £50. Am content to let Eric allow me £15 a month for the next month or two. Probably wd. not refuse work if it were actually offered but am quite relieved that it is *not* offered. Did not dislike writing short comic sketch for Group Theatre but do not want to put my name to it and secretly hope revue will not come off. Must really try now to get my next St Denis lecture finished.

28 Jan About Siepmann there are dangers to be skirted and temptations to be avoided all the time . . . never being able to trust to what had gone before or to forecast even the next day with any security . . . I have learnt to be suspicious of myself when anyone suddenly assumes a violent importance to me . . . I know already that he is in some way mixed up with P.(?) [unknown] in one part of my mind. He is very violent, very destructive, especially of himself, very deeply split, very cold. And, at the same time, tender, simple, honest, sensitive and penetrating . . .

From the front his face is narrow, slightly distorted: the eyes have a peculiar dead look. In profile it is very fine . . . Very vigorous, rather harsh hair . . . the ears, which are very narrow, strike one as mean . . . The two front teeth growing in towards each other give the mouth a very cruel look . . . His body is lean and hard: it feels almost more like metal than flesh . . . You have to be very wary of sudden disarming tenderness: it may be the torturer's hiss . . . He says he want only affection yet his devil drives him to force on something else if only to make him feel his power and to disappoint . . . And you had better be careful [not] to go too near the machine in case you get caught in it. Because it must have something to grind and another human being does very well . . .

16 Feb G[eorge] Devine's† mother suffers from persecution mania. She believes the Prince of Wales is in love with her and the King will not let him marry. She sees spies from the palace everywhere: asks George to hit an ice cream man as he is an enemy etc . . .

Vera [Poliakov, St Denis' mistress] was sulky and tense all through the meeting today. She sat for over an hour in silence, threading her handkerchief through a ring. Suddenly she got up, said she must go. Michel, forgetting the meeting, without a word, snatched his coat and hat and ran after her . . .

[George's] father was a virgin till he was 40; then he married a virgin of 20. She hated the physical relation. When he brought her a present she said 'You are trying to bribe me'. They slept together for 3 months. She left him eventually and he never slept with anyone else. The doctor said that he had a definite physical disease when he died, a disease which you find in priests who have had a sexual fling before becoming celibate for the rest of their lives . . .

George is 25 and unnaturally fat. His mistress looks over 40, a curiously Edwardian looking woman with big faded blue eyes and little veins in her cheeks.

I seem to have promised myself to write a story about Brittany by the end of April and am paralysed.

There is a blind young man I often see about. He sat opposite me in a bus one day. He does not look blind. One eye is shut; the other very wide open; brown, bright, alert. He has an almost idiotically gay smile showing very white, slightly protruding teeth, with gaps between each tooth. He looks as if he were winking . . . at you . . .

Baudelaire when he was paralysed at the end of his life would say nothing but 'cré nom cré nom'. When his friends took him out for the afternoon from the hospital he liked them to wash his hands over and over again. Then he would hold up the clean hands, admiring them, and say 'cré nom' 'cré nom'.

Tom has written to his family telling them that he fell in love with someone else. He could not quite bring himself to say he had slept with Frances.

I think it is over now. They have been seeing each other every week for some time but have not been lovers. Frances wants to marry him, but he says he does not love her enough . . . So she does not want to go on seeing him and I think he is relieved.

About us I do not know. I have a feeling he may within the next months really turn to me. If he does I cannot tell how I shall feel. It may be too late now. In a queer way I love Siepmann. But at the moment all sexual feeling is muted down, probably owing to analysis . . .

John Rodker [unknown] had seen and spoken to Rilke. I touched his right hand because it had touched the hand of Rilke. He said that when Rilke was dying, in great pain, he refused morphine saying 'I prefer to die my own death'.

15 March For the first time for a month the thought of writing this book is bearable to me. It has been a bad month, with Roberta's death [name changed – Ed.], of which I cannot yet bring myself to write ... This is the first death I have completely realised: even my father's death was not so real to me. I was glad at last to be able to weep for someone. I wanted to write a poem about her. I wanted to put on her grave that she was young and beautiful so that people should not remember her as she looked dead with her face swollen and yellow, cotton wool carelessly stuffed in her nostrils, her hair that used to be sleek as a spaniel's ears, dead and dull ... She looked so majestic, so bitter, so disillusioned. Nothing could insult her body any more. She had put off all her beauty; she looked like a penitent in a white sheet ... When I read Rilke I seem to understand her death ... she really had carried it about with her, nourished it, achieved it ...

The Lithopaedion is a child which fails to be born and is petrified into a limestone fossil in the womb where it may remain for half a lifetime. I think that is what has happened to my creative talent, if I have one.

I read voraciously the lives of painters and the journals of poets. I am nourished and nourished but I bring forth nothing ...

I wish I were a painter. I had a mad impulse two days ago: bought tubes of paint, brushes, medium, even a little palette. I felt guilty and excited. I had no right to buy these things. On a canvas board I painted the names of painters, writers and musicians who are my patron saints. Afterwards I felt very foolish and ashamed but I have left the board up ...

Someone told Phyllis [Jones] my lectures were 'brilliant'. Now, in spite of nervousness, I quite enjoy lecturing. I hate and dread the preparation: the reading and predigesting. I feel trapped as if I were being made a schoolmistress in spite of myself: 20 years later finding myself inexorably committed to what my father wanted me to be ...

Tom is very unhappy at the moment, very discontented with himself and his life ...

23 March Last night I wrote a very long letter to Tom, telling him at the end that I thought it better for us not to meet for a time. Already I feel lonely and frightened at what I have done, as if it were irrevocable ...

He left me suddenly last night when I was in a bad state without a word. He did not telephone later on or send a line to me.

I wonder how much one has to suffer to arrive at any knowledge. In my mental confusion I have suffering enough: but that is barren suffering to be endured: one *learns* nothing from it . . .

* * *

Antonia went to Spain to stay with Eric Siepmann at a rented villa called La Felicidad, in what was then the fishing village of Torremolinos. He was covering political events in Spain. Eventually she succumbed to food poisoning and Tom Hopkinson flew out to rescue her.

* * *

26 April?   Torremolinos   I have been in Spain a fortnight and except for a day or two in Gibraltar ill all the time. White houses and red-tiled roofs. Everywhere they are so beautifully arranged and fit so perfectly into their background. The mountains across the bay change in every light. The foothills are usually dust coloured warming to yellow, very definite in outline, veined with dark folds and gullies: sometimes a sharp triangular peak. Sometimes beyond, like a cloud, you can see the pure white snow capped edge of the Sierra Nevada. Everywhere donkeys, mostly brownish grey with huge triangular panniers usually full of fuel or green fodder. The men and women sit up between the heavy loads.

April ?   from E.O.S.[iepmann]'s notebook

   Free spirit liable to possesion or obsession . . .

   Debauchery is the most frozen isolation to which man can condemn himself . . .

28 April   The brown goats being milked on the doorsteps. Brown pigs: quite golden hairs in the sunshine. Round stone fountains. A trough in the village where the women wash. The girl at the farm at her mending throwing her head back and breaking into a howling Flamenco song. Girls at the doorways with flowers in their hair. Balconies. Always a noise: singing, cocks crowing, women calling, children chattering . . . Our house is whitewashed with tile floors and an inlaid carpet of black and grey pebbles. The wooden shutters (inside not outside like French ones) faded through thick layers of cracked paint from a deep blue to lead grey. In the garden roses, hibiscus, marigold, syringa, rosemary, sage, heliotrope, cactus, a plane tree and a cypress tree, a fig tree, all jumbled together ... The 'white' moment in the morning when the sun seems to be silver white, a white mist drifts over the mountains and the sea is calm and like mother of pearl, full of silent lateen-rigged fishing boats lying at anchor with their nets out.

12 May ... I have a feeling that in a year's time a great many things may be clear to me which I now only apprehend in the dimmest, most erratic way. If I can hold on, I really do believe ... that I shall have learnt a new language and that at last I may have a base on which to build ... Every day I become more aware of the extraordinary interpenetration of people's lives. I think of the share Emily had in Djuna's book [*Nightwood*], of the share Emily will have in mine if I can write it, of the small share I have in hers and may have in Siepmann's, of the way I saw something in Tom's drowning story ['I have been Drowned'] of which he was unaware and which Emily brought to flower so that now he has written a quite extraordinary story, beyond anything he has done before and which gave me the same feeling of strangeness, delight, almost awe that Emily's two last poems, 'Melville' and 'The Creation' gave me.

It is Siepmann who is most in my thoughts just now, though he is always straying into my desires from which I must exclude him ... Even the luxury of telling him I love him would be only self-indulgence ... in the long run I have nothing for him or any other man until I know myself ... At the moment all I can safely do is to study him, try to understand him, try to find out what he really needs and give him that instead of thrusting on him what I want to give which is nothing but rape.

... But he is terribly split and divided against himself. Much more naïf and childish than I had supposed, but with a much keener drive of mind and imagination too. He goes pretty deep into anything that really interests him with a real German thoroughness. He is not co-ordinated. His mind strikes here and there like a sharp searchlight, but whole tracts are unilluminated ... He is really fundamentally

honest. [John] Holms† was right when he said that he recognised the
truth when he heard it spoken. But he often wickedly perverts it
when he speaks; a real Judas betraying himself. And yet I believe that
Judas is not his true self but his theatrical mask. Innocent, muddled,
terrified he has built up this swaggering, cynical, Byronic self as a
defence. But his cruelty, his impulse to destroy his own happiness and
that of the people nearest him is very deep indeed . . . A life of *absolute*
evil is as impossible to the human being as a life of absolute good . . .
All my life I shall see things in the Catholic idiom though I shall
probably never again be a practising Catholic . . . A human being
cannot be absolutely pure because animal necessities will not let it be
entirely indifferent to the consequences of its actions. An animal, in
its wild state, is 'pure' in a sense that human beings can never be. The
animals are not reported as having had a 'fall': man's *attitude* to them
changed after the fall: they became . . . creatures to be *named*: as
Santayana would say, essences to be distinguished. But since the fall,
to use S.'s language now, man cannot live entirely in the realm of
essence. Before the fall there was no need for art: in heaven there will
be none either. But here we are 'jostled by irrelevant events'. The
only thing is to make oneself as light, supple and compact as possible
in order to slip through them without being hopelessly crushed.

19 May   Reading the Father Zossima chapter [*The Brothers Karama-
zov*] I felt the confessor-saint fulfilled exactly the same function as the
psycho-analyst. The psycho-analyst cuts a poor and shabby figure
beside the saint but he is the best substitute an age of non-faith can
produce. I see analysis more and more as a therapeutic measure
though even its mythology may be true within its own limits. I do not
believe it can ever *produce* art . . .

Analysis diary, 1 June   Had meant to write in my other 'conscious'
book. Looked at this on an impulse. Did not remember I had made
any recent entries. All my friends now agree that I seem remarkably
better since this 15 months of analysis. I am conscious of this myself;
meaning in a negative way. Bad spells are less severe and shorter. I do
not have days of 'tears behind the eyes' depression, desires to commit
suicide. Agonies of indecision, yes. Terror of committing myself or
giving myself up completely to anything, yes. Inability to [tackle]

things except at the last minute yes. Jam on writing breaks only in occasional very long letters. I resent Siepmann's unresponsiveness for damming up this, my one source of expression. Of creative work not one stroke since this time last year. I cannot bear to be asked 'are you writing anything?' Yet I am furious if people do not know that I am a writer and considered by good judges to have a talent. Physically not well lately. A badly infected cervix for which I have to have an operation which I dread next week. In Spain gastric fever with acute and unnecessary pain ... Headaches now very rare. Only one for many weeks ... Then very acute, accompanied by nausea.

... Masturbation now comparatively rare; accompanied always by fantasies of cruelty, whipping, humiliation. Lost weight in Spain but have put it on rapidly ever since. *Very* rapidly during last week. Am no longer interested in face cream etc: almost indifferent to clothes. Have become greedy again. Yesterday for first time for weeks devoured whole bag of marshmallows and bars of bitter chocolate. Hate my fat; do nothing about it. Hate wholesome food ... Carroll says ... That I will not write a masterpiece because other people would 'devour' it. That I spend money recklessly in a fantasy of unlimited wealth ... Perhaps it is the same with writing. I want the certain consciousness of unlimited talent without the necessity of having to give evidence of any money at all. Now that was quite unconscious – I meant to write 'talent' ... I am just as anxious and embarrassed when anyone asks 'are you writing anything now?' as when my mother or anyone in authority asked if I had been to the lavatory. I have always, since I was about 16–17 written as it were secretly under assumed names ... It is odd I did not change my name at the academy [of Dramatic Art] since I have always been ashamed of it ... How can I have got writing, money, defaecation all mixed up? ... I can only now write freely if I do not get paid at all – letters into which I put myself unreservedly. Probably mine to Siepmann have only now dried up because I fear, being so unreserved, something bad must have got into them and disgusted him. In my photograph where I am laughing my face has an unpleasant mask-like distorted look ... I never use a typewriter now. I like to write directly on paper ... I seem to have a prejudice against getting money by ... writing ... Yet materially I am unable to live without money: I need about £300 a year ... The last work I have done, the little there is of it, was done with no thought of anything but releasing a violent impulse to record something. Immediate stimulus of H[ouse] of C[ommons] desire to display myself to Tom with whom I began to fall in love ... Siepmann if he were not so self-centred and unresponsive might have stimulated me to write again ...

* * *

At the end of June Antonia had a minor operation for an infection of the cervix. Tom Hopkinson was once more supportive.

* * *

9 July   I have been in a very bad mental state for weeks. I expect the operation put me back ... Nothing but the lecture notes (in the weeks before the operation) a letter or two to Siepmann who is in England now and who has become quite unimportant to me suddenly, my two hours attempt at a poem last week and a long letter to Emily last night. I am full of impotence and indecision, guilty about everything, even the things I enjoy. I went to Carroll after a miserable, wasted day in a mood of fury, hatred and despair and came away touched, grateful and affectionate. It shows the violent irrationality of the feelings of a patient ... I do have flashes of clearness occasionally but they last only a few hours; not even a few days as they did last year ... Usually when it is most acute I am too crushed by it to write anything down here ...

   I opened this book today for an odd reason: ... to examine the different attitudes of people I know about money.

My mother   Very avid of it, but quite incapable of saving ...

My father   Very honest yet always hopelessly in debt ...

Tom   Fairly good at managing money. Is hardly worried by debts. Only 2 extravagances ... car and boat. Is not given to bursts of generosity but is very charitable to people in difficulties. Always pays bills in the end. Has no scruples about using his wife's money; expects her to support herself when she has left him though it was because of his behaviour and he refuses to consider her return. Now salves his conscience with £1 a week but feels that is a generosity on his part .. not an obligation. Always pays willingly anything connected with the children. Overpays his present housekeeper who lives in. In giving me presents of money (rare) tends to promise more than he actually gives . . .

Eric Very generous with money. Has often lived above his income but the income usually catches up in the end . . .

* * *

Antonia now returned to 18 Cecil Court, and Tom Hopkinson, who had been in charge of the household, moved into a bedsitter on the other side of the Fulham Road.

* * *

31 Aug It is breaking a resolution though perhaps not an important one to write in this book in pencil. I have moved back into the flat and there is no ink. By reading Frances' letters to Tom I have learnt a great deal about Frances and a great deal about Tom. They are not very agreeable things . . . I doubt now whether, if I met him for the first time, he would ever be more to me than a pleasant acquaintance. He slipped in under my guard . . . Frances has given such an unfair representation of my letters to her to Tom that I shall not write again. I have made my gesture towards her and not for the first time. To do more would be undignified and it is time I learnt a little dignity . . . Sooner or later he [Tom] has got to let something go – either these women or me . . . His making love to me suddenly one night and two days after asking if I minded his having an affair with Joan was something really monstrous and indecent. I was a fool to allow it – that is what 'love' does to one . . . Joan has yet to find out what Tom is like sexually . . . I have given Tom back himself. I must somehow learn to take *myself* back . . . He wrote me a very good letter while I was at Lyme [Regis, with Eric]. I must remind myself through all my resentment justified and unjustified . . .

Interesting thoughts When did Tom first propose to me? When he thought I looked like a child . . .

When was he most centred on me? In hospital when he was ill and depended on me . . .

When did he want me most physically? When I had left him and seemed a stranger . . .

When does he hate me most? When I most needed love and understanding . . .

In life I talk too much, explain too much. In art I explain too much . . .

If I could regard Tom for the time being as an agreeable and interesting friend. I will try.

10 Sept   . . . Tom stares earnestly at me sometimes when I talk like a person conscientiously trying to make out a foreign language . . . I hardly ever feel him there as a real person. Even when he is being harsh and cold I feel him in a sense to be posing as much as when he is being too sweet and tender . . . Frank [Freeman]† says he has a real humility which is very attractive. I think that is true. Frank saw it on the boat: I see it now about his work . . . I was struck by the *vulgarity* of Frances' attacks [on myself], the weightless ineffective spitefulness of them. They are like the children's sudden lapses into silly vulgarity which disgust one and don't really hurt . . .

* * *

Through Emily, Antonia now met a group of poets who included Dylan Thomas, David Gascoyne,† George Barker and Humphrey Jennings.† Under their influence she wrote the surrealist prose poems mentioned below.

* * *

18 Sept   I had the feeling I like best – of flow and communication between people the other night, sitting up till 4.30 a.m. with [Humphrey] Jennings, [David] Gascoyne, Emily and [Samuel] Hoare.† Jennings was amusing about his constant images – the horse, the electric light bulb, the train, Byron, the prism . . . I meant to tackle the Saint Denis lecture . . . and . . . didn't . . . Up to dinner, talking to Emily, practising the piano, playing with the children, reading Hoare's admirable article on Rimbaud the day had gone well . . . Eric has promised me some money for new clothes. Now the planning of them has become a nightmare. I want the clothes very badly. But looking through the pages of *Vogue* has filled me with numb despair. Having them made involves choosing of materials, phoning, fitting etc. and the chance that they will turn out wrong after all. Buying ready made means more expense, endless search, perpetual trying on only to find they don't fit and have to be altered or can't be got in the right colours . . . I cannot control myself. My mind and body seem all flabby and shapeless . . . my mind goes on revolving in a vacuum wearing me out and producing nothing.

28 Sept . . . I love Emily and am too much afraid of hurting her. Her book [*The Tigron* – unpublished] is so very personal to her. She seems to want us and the world to judge it, not as a thing in itself but 'think what this woman must have been through to write it . . .' I love a great deal of the book but I am not happy about it as a whole . . . Her love affairs will always be like that as mine have always been hitherto and still are. She wants to swallow the beloved whole . . . She chooses instinctively the most difficult people and demands from them what is most impossible for them to give: from H[oare] sexual love without guilt and reaction, from B[arker] romantic devotion . . . I know that I can do nothing for her and I care for her most deeply, in some ways more than for anyone I know. She feels that I fail her all the time and in many ways I do . . . When she reads and loves anything she makes it part of her, underlining with a peculiar heaviness . . . If you borrow Emily's Wordsworth you will read not Wordsworth but Emily's Wordsworth. She will fearlessly correct and alter passages. She does not read; she flings herself upon and passionately possesses a work . . . Perhaps we worry too much about Emily's passionate miseries. She seems to be most alive in the element of unhappiness as St Denis works best in an atmosphere of confusion which is misery to his staff . . . The trouble is, in spite of herself, she grinds an axe in this book and explains, or rather protests her particular belief all the time. That Frieda should believe certain things is right. But that the writer should assume certain things are and can be no otherwise is wrong. The novel is not a pulpit. Tolstoy and Lawrence both invalidated their work by preaching . . .

22 Oct In the summer, before I went to Lyme Regis . . . I felt so hopeless – the whole spring had been so bad that I wanted to hide myself. Not in hysterical despair this time but quietly as the only possible solution. I felt I was incurable. Eric begged me to wait for 6 months . . . The autumn, especially Oct–Nov is always a significant time for me. The most important changes in my life happen at this time of year ... I lead a curious life too, like my life at home in my girlhood or in the months after Bethlem, having no regular work except the L[ondon] T[heatre] S[tudio] ... I suddenly, in circumstances wh. I shall not forget, wrote the Roberta poem ['Epitaph']. N[ew] S[tatesman] rejected it 'too violent and emotional'; Jennings has got it into *Contemporary Poetry*. It is amusing to be called too violent and to appear for the first time in poetry among the revolutionary young. I feel much more at ease and stimulated among the young – [George] Barker, Jennings, Gascoyne than among the Connollys, Quennells, Mortimers[†] ... I am surprised to find that though suspicious of surrealist dogma I like some of their work, notably and unexpectedly [André] Breton's *Nadja*. Attracted back to my old adolescent love [of] the magical. If I could combine it with my experience! . . I felt it was good that anyone so difficult as Barker could speak to me so frankly as he did the other night. I love to see other people's faces when they are full of love or completely lost in something outside themselves: Barker's face when he sang and read, Gascoyne's when I told him about Elspeth [Glossop, Silas's sister], Emily's and Jennings' in the first days of their loving each other ...

I am fonder of D[avid] G[ascoyne] than I have been of anyone for a long time. He is in Spain now and I am uneasy about his safety. He looks the type that gets killed. I feel frightened at putting it into words ...

16 Nov ... I am tired and anxious, trying to persuade myself I am not hoping David will ring up since he is due back from Spain to-day. But as Djuna says 'are you a writer or a weeping woman?' I am determined never again to be a weeping woman: no matter how much I care for a man ... I will not let frustration reduce me to pulp ... I have become very deeply attached to Barker whom I have really come to know and perhaps understand a little lately ... Last night he read me Coleridge's 'Ode on Dejection' which is very beautiful in parts. It exactly expresses those bad negative states in which one looks and sees nothing – the 'grief without a pang'. His face is more various than any face I know. It can be quite blank – a mere neat arrangement of features – often quite mean and common – or quite remarkably beautiful ... I find watching this face an endless fascination. The nose is arched, small and pugnacious. The mouth very much curved over rather large teeth and can be either obstinate, negligible or very sweet and humorous. A very characteristic look is with the eyelids dropped and the lips parted ... Sometimes he walks hunched forward and bent as if he had had a severe illness in childhood which had prematurely aged him ... Although he is only 23 I feel him to be in many ways older and more mature than myself though in others he is extraordinarily boyish ... He has a boy's boastfulness, love of teasing, love of preposterous exaggerations, sudden unbounded contempt for 'girls' ... He was born on the anniversary of Keats' death. I find constant parallels to his character in Keats of the letters – 'I always made an awkward bow'. For the first 6 months or so that I knew him he would suddenly break away from any gathering with an abrupt 'Bye bye – I must dash'.

I am so tired: I cannot write any more about Barker to-night though he is so much in my thoughts and I have so much I want to record about him ...

I am demoralised to-night. I sit at a littered desk, smoking endlessly, with itching eyes, feeling oppressed by my clothes. I am trying to behave as if I were not half-hoping for a call from David. I forced myself to spend this evening alone, to write a letter or two, to make an entry here. I kid myself that I am behaving *as if* I were free of preoccupation. I played the piano carelessly and inattentively. I pick up books, any book at hand, and read here and there a paragraph till I am dizzy ... Yes, I am much oppressed to-night – weighed down – the old words mean something. It is like a physical weight in my head and body. For the third time lately I went into the church in Spanish Place and prayed, saying the Our Father over and over again which says all I want to say. Yet do I believe in God? I must behave *as if* I did not trust in any future salvation and yet aim always at that difficult, detached interior life. Yet here I am, involuntarily raising my head to listen to every taxi ... Nature is not squeamish about violence. I cannot read the horrors in Spain without nausea. Yet there are people fighting for beliefs. How many? We are all wild beasts at heart and have raped, tortured and murdered in our imagination. Why should we recoil so to see acted out our own hidden thoughts?

4 Dec   I have thought during the last week of going to Spain [to the Civil War] but on examination find there is too much ... action

rapidly performed 'in the sight of all'. It is better to prepare oneself
coldly, soberly and dully to be of some practical use ...

Tom is very distressed about Frances who does not seem to be
getting on well. I do feel genuinely sorry for him and for once not
with a pang of self-pity that he shows for her all the concern I would
have liked him to show for me. Whether this is because ... I feel that,
having David, I can afford to be generous, I do not yet know.

But in what sense 'have' David? That he has strong feelings of
some kind for me I think I must now believe. Of what kind I do not
know; I shall know better when I see the results of his work: he finds
it extremely hard to express anything directly ... What I do see, of
course, is the often involuntary expression of his *fear* of me ... I do
not realise enough how hard it is for him to express himself and he
does not realise how lost and frustrated I feel when I am not allowed
to express a perfectly natural emotion towards another person ...

What do I find unattractive or irreconcilable in him?

A warm, impulsive quickening towards someone combined with a
cold, rather cruel drawing-back.

A tendency to let other people do everything for him – guilt about
it, but no strong effort to change the situation. Peculiar physical
slovenliness – though he is vain.

A tendency to hero-worship.

He is accused of being a 'climber'. He may be. It is not very
important. Provided he does nothing ugly or dishonest in order to
meet people or keep in with them he is perfectly justified in trying to
meet the people he wants to know.

Laziness – taking the easy way in work. His paper the other night
was full of arrogant and untrue statements ...

I am sure he is physically passionate but suspect it comes out in a
childish narcissistic way.

His mouth can be very bad: obstinate, sulky, peevish and despon-
dent. Forehead is very broad though low: slopes back suddenly and
disconcertingly. The chin too small ... it can look very weak from
certain angles. Imagines his nose is too big (it is not). Dislikes
allusions to his eyes which are singularly beautiful; is very self-
conscious about his hair which is also beautiful though he does
not seem to know it. Quite rightly admires his hands (nails always
dirty) ...

In his written fantasies the image of the explosion, the iceberg, the cave and the subterranean river constantly recur . . .

Talks a great deal about the Marquis de Sade who is one of his heroes . . .

In spite of his youth and freshness, often something dusty and wilted about him . . .

1937

Her state of mind improved by analysis, Antonia took a job at J. Walter Thompson, the American advertising agency. At its recently opened London office, the agency employed only the best copywriters. In 1937 also, Antonia became Basil Nicholson's mistress. She had known Nicholson for a couple of years and probably met him when she was working on the *Daily Mirror*. He had the reputation of being dangerous to women. Silas was on leave from the Gold Coast.

8 Jan   I meant to finish off this notebook carefully with a review of the whole year . . . Reading it through to-night I am struck by the difference in tone . . . between this and any other notebook since I began in 1921. Something positive *has* happened during this last year in spite of the very bad (unrecorded) patches from Feb–Aug. It can be due to nothing but analysis . . .

27 Jan   The end of this book will mark the end of a phase of my life – To-day I have taken a job at Walter Thompson's. I have sworn never to go back to advertising but I am going back to full-time and real drudgery. Carroll thinks it may release me for proper work. We shall see . . . In three months I can pay my debts and get straight. I have got so soft and used to freedom that it will be hard at first. I feel as if I were renouncing the life of an artist . . .

2 May   . . . Ironically enough the end of 3 months finds me exactly as I was as regards debts.

Analysis now pressing hard on the money situation which I resent bitterly and find extremely painful. One part of me knows this is the final test: I must somehow *force* myself to deal rationally with money. The other says money is my own affair: what possible relevance can my dealings with it have for my life either as a woman or as a writer? . . .

15 May . . . What my future with Basil Nicholson may be I do not know. I must guard against my usual trick of beginning to weave projects and anxieties round any nucleus.

Silas the other day caught sight of a reflection in a mirror and thought it was himself. He then saw it was a woman. He then thought what a remarkably good-looking woman she was.

I said to him once 'Can you ever remember having been very happy?' He said 'Yes – driving a dog team alone in Canada'.

He says to me 'You are the only person who understands me and in whose presence I become articulate.'

I shall never have with anyone else the rare moments I have had with Silas. In a sense he is my true love. But there is no possible continuous life for us together. I begin to suspect all romantics . . .

Basil is entirely different in type from any lover I have ever had before. I think that is a good thing. He has deliberately set out to make a success by beating the business people at their own game. I have always thought him cynical, cold-hearted and devoid of any interest in human beings except to use their weaknesses for his own ends. I was very much mistaken . . .

Harsh he certainly is and deliberately ungracious. He accentuates his ugliness. Because he was attracted to me and decided that I might disturb his peace he has been deliberately rude and cold to me for two years . . . if anyone had told me a week ago that he and I would find ourselves strongly attracted physically to each other I should have thought it incredible . . .

23 May I have managed to spend the week-end at home alone, without plans. At first I was secretly hoping Basil would ring up and in that hope probably did not make plans . . .

I admire in Basil his capacity to refrain from explanations and apologies; he merely states and acts . . . I am more physically self-conscious; his self-consciousness is mental; he does not like exposing his mind. We have only been lovers twice, but the second time was not a mere repetition of the first. I felt more physical confidence; he was more frank, warm and simple . . . I was right to take the risk of writing to him. I would do well to write more and talk less . . .

Tom has a remarkably softened *look* these days, but is more simple and decided in action. He is very sure that he loves Joan and wants to marry her . . .

I catch myself weaving myths about Ruth Bowley [Basil Nicholson's mistress], of whom I know nothing. I find myself suspecting, without a shred of evidence that she is silly, vain and shallow. I am probably physically jealous of her because she is younger and a better active physical companion for Basil . . .

Norman [Cameron]† is like a lovable child who has never known hatred. He takes it for granted that everyone will like him and be interested in what he does and says. There is something at once emasculated and cruel about him, in spite of his charm, frankness and amiability. He is a great over-valuer and under-valuer of people, very loyal but not very understanding. Very careless and hit-or-miss in his work and relations, very naïf. Is very vivacious, but has not really much vitality; very lazy. Not the schoolmaster, but the head prefect. I suspect his values are really the public-school ones; you either are or aren't a 'decent chap' . . .

25 May   Again a frustrated and anxious feeling because there was no sign from Basil. I rang him suddenly on an impulse though I had resolved not to. He was out . . .

Last night I had an unexpectedly delightful evening with Djuna, Emily and Silas. Everything was perfect except that Emily, towards the end of the evening became a little bored and sulky and retired into a 'Narcissus clinch' with two of her old letters to me and Djuna who had been inspired for hours became a little drunk, noisy and repetitive. Apart from nervous anxiety that Djuna would be bored by Silas (he was obviously excited and delighted by her) and that Emily would be violent with him, it was an excellent party. I fairly swam in flattery – Djuna said she had never known I could look beautiful before – and far better, she likes the prose poems . . .

Silas hardly took his eyes off me: he was in his dazed admiring mood. But he suddenly became cold and frightened when I showed him the poems. He glanced at them and them put them down in obvious embarrassment.

When I am gay, Silas is strongly drawn to me. When I am unhappy he flies me like the plague. But with Mabel [Lethbridge, Silas's mistress] it is just the opposite. When she is in trouble he feels tender and affectionate towards her. When she is in exuberant spirits, he is glad to get away ... her real hold on him is sheer brute vitality for which he has a superstitious reverence.

He has been very much haunted by his escape-motif again the last few days, though when I last saw him it seemed to have receded into the background. He harps all the time on *the ascent of F6*; not yet realising that F6 is inside oneself. Acting out his dream would not appease him. The camera has been a failure as a magic symbol: for the moment his new car works.

He and Djuna were in complete accord. I was delighted. She smelt death in him ... Emily ... often speaks the truth without knowing it and without realising its implications in her own life and work. She wrote to me a year ago 'Murder and violence come from not having enough imagination to love'. Her imagination is blind and stumbling on earth; free and daring in heaven. She has the awkward beauty, the exasperating clumsiness of the winged creature trying to walk. She is certainly the albatross. She and Djuna both have the same obtuseness of not being interested in anything that is not *immediately* relevant to their concern of the moment.

Djuna said to Silas 'Walk away – I want to see you leaving ... Yes, you've got that gorgon look behind' also 'Take care you don't develop flying buttresses, the infirmity of the Gothic idea.'

To Emily 'You see a man crossing the fiord and you think it's romance, but it's just a get-away' and 'Oh, you've got that *rivetting* look ... it's like our New York skyscrapers – a dead man for every storey and all through that rivetting' and 'You're a rivet inside a cream puff' and 'Cut you and you spurt like a fountain.' ...

She told us about the men rivetting on the skyscrapers: the naked one that wouldn't even wear gloves and toasted his bread at the blaze of the rivetting and how the others began to go naked up on the girders too ... they have to be a little drunk but not too drunk to go up at all ...

... I would say that the real hallmark of genius is to do what seems impossible with apparent ease – anyway with economy of effort. Some people seem to have this by nature: I think Mozart had. Most of his 'taking pains' must have gone in the unconscious which one knows to be tireless and incredibly ingenious. The conscious mind works in fits and starts; the unconscious *never stops* ... Perhaps the function of art is to reveal as much unbearable truth as possible in a bearable form ...

But what *is* this unbearable truth and why is it unbearable? The resistance to Darwin; the resistance to Freud ... Analysis is first scientific attempt to break habits of mind ...

Basil Nicholson diary, 27 May It is rather disconcerting how frequently and irrationally I change my love-object. I fall in love with a schoolgirl rapidity and grown-up intensity ...

I cannot conquer my natural impatience and I seem destined to get mixed up with people who are far more cautious. Jennings, another Keiller, another Siepmann. Heaven knows there is enough infantile cruelty in his [Basil's] book ... I know from experience how rapidly I can change. N[orman Cameron] and D[avid Gascoyne] mean nothing to me now yet not so long ago I was letting them make rain or fine weather for me ...

1 June I shall not see Basil until Thursday, which will be a fortnight since we last met ...

At the moment, thank goodness, I am not in that miserable and familiar state of being between two men ...

I have noticed that women, especially those who have passionate friendships with their own sex and who need constant reassurance in their own relations with the other, tend to humiliate the friends they most care for in their love affairs. Emily, though professing to despise men, will nearly always take the man's side against the woman ...

I am interested to find that, though I have told Emily a good deal about all my other affairs, I do not want to tell her about Basil and take great pains to conceal his identity ...

His very house is secretive – set right back from the street. He tells me very little, but, unless I am completely deluded, what he tells me is true ...

13 June   I am going to try and work to-day. It is 2½ years since I wrote
the 1st chapter [of *The Lost Traveller*]. Tom made a good suggestion:
to cut the asylum part and telescope Robert and Silas, making that the
climax of the Reggie marriage. I think this is right because I do not
want to overweight the thing with pathology.

My father's life is over. I can see it in some sort of perspective. I
want the gradual disintegration of my mother's life through him to
be one of the main things in the book. She takes refuge in a dream
because his own solution does not fit her nature . . .

20 June   I feel very much checked and at a standstill though longing
for action. The job at the office is not sufficiently interesting to hold
my attention. I did do a very little work on the book last Sunday but
very hesitantly, with a feeling of great anxiety and impotence. I
cannot read much, consecutively or well. I am tired of discussing the
minutiae of my friends' psychology and troubles. If I cannot write I
would like to be seeing new people, above all to be *doing* new things
or the old things with new people. This relation with Basil is good as
far as it goes, but like most of my relations, is by no means
satisfactory. I think he is fond of me but he seems perfectly content
only to see me at rare intervals . . . just occasional bursts of sex with a
person aren't what I want. I want some sort of shared life – not
necessarily living with the person – as well. All the intelligent men I
know seem to have this peculiar emotional desiccation if they are not
homosexual. They do not seem to want anything but casual friendship and lust.

I saw the horse show yesterday. I would like to be able to throw
myself into a violent physical activity. Only one horse cleared every
jump . . . the German Alchimist. They curl up their forefeet, fling out
their hindlegs and hurl themselves over the fences in a marvellous
flying rush . . . You feel the huge weight of a horse when it jumps.
Some of them have bright metallic gleams in their hides like the sheen
on a pigeon's neck. I wish I were not too frightened to ride. Their
bodies look so heavy; their feet so fine and delicate, like a dancer's. I
despair of ever being a writer . . .

. . . I will not say that Basil is exactly *mean*, but there is either
something deficient in him or else he distorts his own nature. His
ideal of someone who adapts themselves with quick grace to any

situation is not very well borne out in himself. In his book [*Business is Business*] the graceful spontaneous responses of his hero consist in either shooting or robbing everyone with whom he comes in contact. A man laughs at him and he cuts his eye out with a whip ... Every man I meet is either desiccated and terrified or drips all over me. I am SICK of all these frightened people who daren't take the least risk of getting hurt. Why the hell can't I work? Basil is right – I'm a dangerous character when I'm not working ... Even Basil's vaunted 'ferocity' may be only the little boy playing at tigers. And mere *ferocity* in sex isn't enough, though it's something. If I were more of a woman or more of a man I'd be happier ... I want him to have authority, not just to sneer and bully. I don't make enough allowances for his being very young ...

22 June Susan saw a smashed car to-day. She said it was 'like an empty beetle'

*Basil Nicholson diary, 24 June** I find myself more and more attracted to this curious, and perhaps perverted man. I feel in him a need to be loved and at the same time a childish pride which denies that need. There is in him an almost crazy sensuality ... His cold, hostile manner is deceptive. He appears to despise everything, people above all things, but at the same time one knows he is good, generous and tender at heart ... He has always been a solitary – an observer sitting on the moon ... He says that he wants to know me, to possess me entirely. But he expresses this only in the flesh. He tells me he has never loved or been loved, that he understands only the meaning of desire and friendship, that love is an invention of fools ... He feels for me an unspeakable physical longing; I have never experienced anything like it ... I do not consciously desire him but I will one day. I fear physical dependence, he fears moral servitude ... To me he seems a man too narrow in spirit ... He suppresses all the poetry that exists in his nature, which makes his involuntary remarks so moving. He never declares his love, but stands by my bed stammering 'You', over and over again. Sees me as an animal; a tigress or a doe. He says

* This passage has been translated by the editor. Antonia wrote it in French, presumably for reasons of modesty.

'You wont leave me will you?' After a passionate embrace ... he once
said, with his face in the pillow, 'I can see palm trees, sun, a deep blue
sky ...' Most of all he calls me 'My doe, my own little doe' ... 'You
must love me, I want you to come to me one morning, I want to do
whatever I want with you all day; I want to take you at any time,
whenever I wish.'

26 June   ... I want to record something about tonight because it will
be reassuring another time. Saturdays are usually bad. I keep leaving
the week-end free in the hope that Basil will ring me up which he
never does. I frittered away the afternoon at a cinema ... I came home
about 7, feeling both extreme langour and a nervous desire for action
and company ... I rang up everyone I could think of, whether they
were people I wanted to see or not. I felt the real old rising hysteria
combined with impotence to decide on any action. Out of pure sense
of duty I went to say good-night to Susan. I stayed half an hour. Then
to Lyndall. They were so fresh and sweet and alive. Susan hugged me
which she very seldom does. We laughed and made plans to celebrate
the end of analysis. And somehow that lifted all the dead weight and
relieved the tension ...

27 June   I went to Kew to-day ... It was so wonderful to smell grass,
hay, leaves, broom, roses again ... In one of the hottest tropical
houses there were waterlilies – huge plate shaped leaves, slightly
prickly on the outside, turned up sharply at the rim ... I noted very
carefully the name of the flowers I liked at the Kings [Cecil and
Margaret]† – it slipped again now – I think it is Schizzianthus ...
     To-night I meant to settle down to work but the old langour and
impotence were too strong for me ...
     I wonder if I shall always be like this, hoping to do something
really important, feeling guilty and manquée if I don't, and in actual
practice just drifting along half-heartedly like most people. If I really
have enormous energy somewhere, as Carroll seems to think, why the
hell don't I use it? At the thought of work I become physically tired
and mentally unable to concentrate. The one thing I do consistently is
smoke endless cigarettes which I don't particularly enjoy and
disapprove of ...

I heard from Siepmann the other day. His usual story: quarrels and debts in Budapest; a row with the F[oreign] O[ffice]; walking out of his job ... How I wish he could deal with himself; he is such good material wasted. It seems to me that nine tenths of good human material *is* wasted. Look at Cameron, Silas, nearly everyone I know. The more gifted a nature, the harder it seems for it to realise its own possibilities ...

Everything is relative. A person who is gifted (as I am, I think by nature, for writing, foreign languages, understanding certain things, and for human relationships) is worse off if they cannot use these gifts than a less gifted person who *can* use what gifts they have. Nurse [Mary Hitchcock, Susan and Lyndall's nurse] is a more satisfactory human being than I am. A person who makes £1000 a year and has to pay £900 in debts or blackmail is worse off than one with £200 and no encumbrances. I am somewhere between a thief and a victim of blackmail. Only I myself am the blackmailer!

Basil and I are in a very curious position as regards each other. I think my strongest feeling for him – conscious feeling anyhow – is tenderness. His strongest conscious feeling for me is an almost obsessional lust which expresses itself in strange and violent ways ...

... He is afraid of an emotional awakening; I of a physical awakening. Yet it is what we both need. I have never refused any physical demand of his; I may have found it too much and said so, but I have made an attempt to fulfil it. He has refused, not in word, but in practice, every demand I have made on him . . only small requests about writing and meeting – but things which might strengthen the emotional side and the mental side of our relation ... At all costs I must not, through vanity or mistaken zeal, play the amateur analyst to him as I did with Silas and David ...

Now it seems almost certain that Frances will die [of TB]. How is that going to affect Tom? Perhaps as he once feared it would – he will feel that something in him has died and that something can never be born. What has happened to his feeling for Joan that only a few weeks ago seemed so strong and stable? Was it so strong as his instinctive feeling for Frances? Now he has a new 'distraction'. There is always a woman somewhere in his life. Yet I often feel, and I think he does too, that the children are the strongest and stablest element in his life. Perhaps the one thing of value I gave him was the responsibility for those two . . . Only one 'end' seems in sight . . . the end of Frances' life. Which of us is to blame? None of us: all of us . . .

I used to write as a child for amusement and got great pleasure when my work was praised which to me then was the criterion of whether it was good or bad. But I think I was always interested most of all in people. To have another child to tea was heaven. Reading was a tremendous delight always. But to have someone else to play *with* . . I was willing to put up with a lot for that. Acting was what I liked best; dressing up, inventing stories on the spur of the moment to be *acted* . . .

. . . The trouble is that when you are a child, you actually *do* get some of the things you wish for without having to ask for them or do anything about it. So I suppose you get the notion that they appear *because* you wished for them . . .

28 June   I had a letter from Djuna to-night which pleased me very much. She says about work 'it's getting the awful rust off the spirit that is almost insurmountable, it's why working every day is so important – one may write the most lamentable balls (which nearly kills one) but in the end one has a page or two that no otherwise would have been written.' Also 'There *is* an undoubted gleam of intelligence in your eye; you are going to go right on paying for it.' She ends '*Keep on writing* – it's a woman's only hope – except lace-making; they do say that dulls the eye in about 5 years if persevered in.'

Djuna has genius if anyone I know has genius. What would Djuna's writing have been like had her nature not been what it is? How is anyone to know the best way to work? Djuna arranges herself very carefully, makes up meticulously and prefers to write in bed. Emily scribbles on her knee in an old dressing gown. I feel there is something immoral in not 'sitting up to' a desk as if I were at school – writing in bed wouldn't 'count' . . .

. . . But how the world hates one if one does *not* commit oneself to fixed opinions. With all the present political fever, the fashionable and I think sometimes genuine 'communism' of the intelligentsia, one is made to feel a coward and a traitor if one does not commit oneself blindly and fiercely to a fight against 'the forces of reaction' . . .

The other night Norman [Cameron] was saying he felt there really was a devil and it was incarnate in the Germans. He felt it would be justifiable to stamp them out. Basil believed they should be given everything they wanted in order to restore their self respect. The argument became very heated. Basil said 'You have the mentality that makes fascists' Norman became angry: he first of all hectored Basil in a school prefect way (Basil had certainly been very provoking in *tone* all the evening and had put his case arrogantly and badly) and then threw a glass of soda water in his face. Basil sat quite still . . .

I got Norman out of the house and came back to Basil. He was sitting quite rigid in his chair, his coat all wet. I put my arm round him and he still sat rigid . . . I sat on the floor by him and took his hand and said 'I want to cry'. He stroked my hand very gently and said 'So do I.' . . .

Tom came into the party tonight. I was struck by his handsomeness, his air of gaiety and confidence. I saw that there was something engaging and attractive about him. And yet I prefer Basil, crabbed and harsh and trying to suppress, instead of displaying, any charm. I watched Tom make for the best-dressed and most striking looking woman in the room and felt amused and indulgent. He was such a fine young cock bird strutting . . .

Malinowski[†] [sic] was there to-night. His terrible, destroying vanity. He looks like a dead man with his yellow face. I asked him how he was. He said 'I am suffering from a very common, but very distressing complaint, old age.' For years, every time I have met him he has said the same. Then he made as usual a joking, but embittered reference to the fact that I refused, ten years ago, to be his lover. There is something of Kathleen [McClean] in him, perpetually making himself out to be physically unattractive and then making embittered jokes about no woman wanting to go to bed with him. It is his mortal, corrupting vanity and it is making his body so dead that you can almost smell decay. He has a terrible history of physical illness. And yet one cannot pity him, his self pity is so acute . . .

Basil Nicholson diary, 1 July . . . He is much freer with me; he talks naturally. And I am much freer: I do not need to talk so much.

On a sudden impulse last night I said to him 'I love you'. I had not meant to say it, but it was true. He said nothing but took my hand and held it against him. After a moment I laughed and said 'You are a brave man. I tell you I love you and you do not even flinch.' He said 'No ... because it is you'.

He had made no reference to my last letter. After we had been together for several hours he said 'I do not think your poem ['Epitaph'] was morbid' and that was all I needed him to say for reassurance.

He told me how he lived alone camping for three months on an island watching birds. He had no books and wrote nothing except careful observations of the birds. He said that he gradually came to identify himself with different ones, so that he could know, as he would know of himself, what they would do. One colony lived on the fishing side where work was easy and they had time to become quarrelsome ...

... For the first time last night I was perfectly happy with him as his lover ... I have never yet learnt the language of the body and I think that is why I feel so false and shallow and incomplete. I felt the same thing without quite understanding it with Robert who was like him in many ways, but I was not ready for it and the shock drove me out of my mind. Now I can discover it slowly and quietly and I shall not lose my mind but find it ... I must let it grow for it now seems to me a natural thing with a life of its own which can be left to grow, which has its own heartbeat which must not be hurried.

Basil Nicholson diary, 5 July   The terrible boredom of sitting in the office doing nothing but fritter away time is getting me down. It is a curious way of earning one's living but I am lucky to be able to get so much money easily ...

Basil Nicholson diary, 8 July   ... During the last two days I have become uneasy and depressed about Basil, not seeing him or hearing from him ...

My chief pleasure at the moment is Darwin's *Voyage of the Beagle* ... It is so fresh, so clear, so solid, so modest, so alive. When I read a book like that I am full of admiration yet I feel so humiliated and despairing too ...

I have tried to work lately for an hour or two at the office. The result is terrible – flabby, shapeless, dull. I don't think I have the strength of mind to go on though Djuna says one should write every day no matter how awful it is ... I am not sure whether this is the right way for me ... Usually I work best when there is something I feel very strongly and want to put down. The beginning is sticky and slow; then if it warms up I get quite interested. It is amazing to me that I have ever written even a page worth reading and yet I know from other people that I have.

My life except for Basil seems utterly false and unnatural ...

I feel envious of people, who though obviously self-deluded, are fairly happy in their self-delusion and not being subjected to the remorseless discipline of analysis which, every time one gains a little confidence, tears away that delusion. I feel as if my whole life were based on a lie ... Reading Darwin's [book] I wish I had loved objective things and looked at them when I was a child instead of feeding always on books and fancy ... I feel the only bearable way to write would be never again to write about myself. But in both my projected things I have no alternative but to introduce myself ... I get interested when I write about the other characters and bored and disgusted when I write about myself, partly because there is no play for imagination ...

I am now, in actual fact, happier when I am forgetting about myself and trying to understand other people. But I get tired very often because so many of the people I meet are so very egocentric that they vamp me and give me nothing in exchange ...

Basil Nicholson diary, 12 July ... I notice he started with quite a panicky nervousness twice when he saw me unexpectedly and took several seconds to recover calm. Now he wishes to cut off the sexual relation entirely and that we should get to know each other better by meeting more often and in ordinary casual circumstances. He says ... that he treat him as if he were all sorts of other people, that I distort and exaggerate my feeling for him, that I frequently seem to address remarks not to him but to some one just behind his right shoulder, that it is absurd to say I love him since I know practically nothing about him ... After last night when I managed with some difficulty to fight down hysteria, he said he trusted me more ... Also that my sense of self-preservation is lousy (which Norman also said) in which he is not quite right because somehow or other, battered and dislocated, I am still neither dead nor re-certified . . .

Having rushed the sexual side with great violence, he now renounces it with equal violence . . .

Since I can't fathom his mind yet, I might begin by observing his physical characteristics. He is both alert and cramped in movement. His shoulders are hunched and he pokes his head forward. He damaged his eyesight by using field glasses too much in Guiana – from trying to see too much, in fact. His hair is very thin and he looks older than he is; it is hard to say why – partly his slow, rather inflexible manner as if he were giving evidence in a law court and every word might be used against him, partly a worn look about the head as if he had driven himself too hard. His eyes are very clear, but are often defensive as well as searching. He has a very frank, free laugh and throws his head back when he laughs and a really friendly, impish smile. His clothes are often very oddly assorted and rather ill cared-for but they are characteristic of him, like a bird's plumage. He likes strong clear colours, blues, oranges, reds. He got on very well with the McCleans and understood them well . . . I suspect he envies tall, handsome men, was possibly laughed at as a child for his odd way of speaking and perhaps his appearance. Perhaps acts out his fantasies in the character of a boy as I do mine in the character of a young girl . . .

Basil Nicholson diary, 14 July   I really must stop worrying so much over B . . . Carroll says he is a mass of complexes . . . I know his brief affair with Phyllis gave her a lot of pain (I don't say he was entirely to blame) and had really unpleasant practical consequences. There is something rather ungenerous in his instinctive attitude to people – fear of being done down . . . And, frankly, he is often very disagreeable . . . everyone who has injured him and even everyone whom he dislikes MUST be punished. This is the swaggering aggressive urchin side of him . . . I shall not write or communicate with him again until I hear from him . . . It is practically impossible for him to believe that anyone acts with integrity and how many of us can, even if we want to? To expect complete poise and integrity from a schizoid maniac is asking too much. The girl of integrity in his book, though he admired her, he cheerfully despatched to her death. The bitch, whom he instinctively preferred, betrayed him. I would guess that he was trying to revenge himself on some woman.

15 July I rang Basil about the Group Theatre Magazine this morning, feeling sufficiently cool and in control of myself to do so without risk. His voice was very warm and friendly; he asked twice how I was; said he had twice rung me up at home last night. When we met, he attacked the magazine in question as soon [as] I sat down. Norman joined in . . .

18 July We have been away together for the first time. We walked in the park of Cowdrey Castle. He showed me all the birds. There was a spotted flycatcher hawking for flies for her brood in a nest in the ivy, sandmartens flickering and swooping very high up in the air . . . To-day on the ridge of hills above Cocking we ate wild strawberries and raspberries We saw a mixed flock of birds, tits and finches, moving through the wood. He says they do that when the nesting season is over; forage in flocks. The flies buzzed and bit us all the time, especially the horse flies which have given me a sore arm. We saw a big orange fritillary with dark brown spots, like those orange tiger-lilies. There were flowers like canterbury bells, thyme, harebells and willowherb on the hills . . . the young wheat just beginning to yellow . . .

Basil Nicholson diary, 21 July The clerk who cashes my cheques at the bank is quite a bright, intelligent-looking boy. To-day I had a copy of *Bouvard et Pecuchet* [Flaubert]. He looked at it with curiosity then said 'I expect you think I'm rude, looking like that. But I used to read a lot of those sort of books once' 'What sort of books?' 'Oh, yellow books like that. I picked up a lot in a booksellers. But mine were much bigger than that' 'What were they?' 'Oh I don't remember their names or what they were about' 'Do you remember the authors?' 'Can't say I do. I seem to remember one was some sort of a Japanese story' 'And they were in French?' 'Oh yes, in French of course' . . .

Things have been much better with B. lately: . . . he talks to me more frankly and freely . . .

. . . He believes that in the end, over a long enough period . . . there is such a thing as divine justice, that one has to make oneself into the kind of person needed by the time, that this is not the time for the individual genius (that is the genius who handles men and affairs – the Napoleonic type of genius) but for the competent and incorruptible

man of the Hampden type ... His poetical side seems to be very
simple and concrete, he loves Marvell's poems and Dürer's drawings.
He has a great admiration for Keats but won't read the letters
'because he feels they will probably annoy him'. This fear of being
disturbed, made uncomfortable, is very strong. Usually if I talk at all
about my own subjects he says rudely 'It all sounds very boring' ...
He looks as if he had never allowed himself to weep ... He says there
have been one or two bad things in his life which he has not told me
and anyway he has forgotten them and anyway he is not interested in
himself ...

Basil Nicholson diary, 28 July   I was very happy with him the other
night. We were in complete physical harmony. Afterwards he looked
me very searchingly in the eyes as if asking me a question and, as if I
had answered it, said 'good'. But he had tried to go when Rupert
[Doone] and Robert went. I said 'Stay a minute, there is something I
want to ask you' secretly fearing a refusal. In front of them he said he
could only spare a minute ...

   I said I would like to have a real marriage. He said that he had never
seen one. I said 'Nor have I, yet I still believe there might be such a
thing. Or is it a delusion?' He said 'No, it is not a delusion'

   I said 'I have made such a terrible hash of my life' He said 'So have
I' 'But you are still so young' I told him. He said 'I am so old, I am
nearly dead' and then 'But I'm mad, that's the trouble' ...

   ... His criticism of the Tiger poem [lost poem by Antonia White]
was right. And his judgment of Rupert. He said 'A pansy will always
be more ruthless in getting his own way than a man or a woman'

   Since at the moment I feel there is nothing in the world I want so
much as to marry B. (not that he has ever suggested it!) I had better
think of all the arguments I can against it. Obviously I *can't* because I
am still married to Tom. The children make everything very
confused. I feel a duty to them, often love, but perhaps most often
that they are rather hostile strangers. I feel Tom has all their real
affection, is a much better and more understanding parent yet I feel
it's a bit unfair that he always seems perfect to them (they are too
young to know the whole truth) and I am always the villain of the
piece ... I MUST consider the children though often I feel I would like
to walk right out and start a new life by myself ...

... I have been trying to find whether the new divorce bill makes it in any way easier for Tom and me to get a divorce. It seems that in order to get one there must still be lying.

Legally, the position is this. Tom has 'committed adultery' with four other women. I 'condoned' the adultery with Frances because I stayed with him when he said he had given her up. Now I have also 'committed adultery'. Tom refused to live with me when I still wanted him to: now neither of us wants it. I would be perfectly willing to be divorced but, in order to do that, I should either have to cite Basil as co-respondent which I would certainly not do unless he were willing (and why should he be?) or I would have to give false evidence with someone else ...

3 Aug   Basil had a flower in his coat and I said it was dead. He wrenched it out and threw it away. 'I hate things dying on me ...' ...

After he had decided to give the whole thing up ... he said 'It is rather like having an affair with a mermaid' My old fear of being a monster came up ...

He makes the most savage faces when he is bored and exasperated ...

He said his own face reversed the normal proceeding; that the lower part was strong and the upper incoherent. I do not think there is anything wrong with his face, though the forehead and the top of the head have an odd cramped look, but he makes very curious *uses* of his face ...

Basil Nicholson diary, 5 Aug   Tom took to the idea of a divorce more readily than I would have supposed. I think he really wants it. The difficulties are considerable and this looks like being a very exacting autumn in every way. But I think it had better be gone through with.

About B. it really is no good fretting. I must arrange my life exactly as if he did not exist or had gone away on an expedition ...

* * *

Antonia went to stay with Gerald Reitlinger,[†] a friend who had a house near Northiam in Sussex. She rented a cottage from him and eventually sent Susan and Lyndall to Brickwall, a progressive school in the village.

* * *

9 Aug ... Pleasures since Saturday.

The garden; Gerald's house in the country. Smell of the house; smell of rosemary, sage, peaches, thyme.

Trying to learn to swim.

Unexpected friendliness of Keith Miller Jones [unknown] who looks so like Si. His very comforting and attractive physical presence ...

Making good shots at croquet ...

Basil Nicholson diary, 9 Aug Carroll says of B. that ... he would probably be an impossible husband ...

I am pleased I nearly learnt to swim this week-end. I had to have someone by and I was never out of my depth, but I *did* manage to flounder a few strokes on my own ...

I know that I'm too fat. I don't like being too fat. I know ways of making myself thinner. Yet as soon as I see any nice food I eat it, even if I'm not really hungry. I want people to tell me I'm *not* too fat (I don't believe it when they do!) though they and I know perfectly well that I *am*. Then I often get morbid about it and think that because I am too fat I must be physically repulsive in every way ... But I am not hideous and I've had as much success ... as women with ten times my looks ...

... I feel I could bear things very much better if I felt there were a good God in whose hands one was and whom one could trust, though all one's life seemed to go wrong. If one felt that, in spite of misery and frustration, one were really serving some force that made for good ...

Perhaps nobody punishes one, no one rewards one except oneself.

11 Aug It suddenly struck me to-night whether my ruling passion is not the desire to make money. Is it just the dread of poverty? I don't think it is only that ...

... It was only in reading a book to-night, some remark about a ruling passion ... that made me realise it ...

It was the magic words '£10 a term' that made me leave school and my friends and go and live with strangers. It has made me do jobs that bored me, give up what I knew to be valuable, made me fear to take risks ...

I believe I wouldn't marry Si because he had no money. I believe I married Tom because he had a regular job and a hundred pounds or two ...

The fact that B. now allows me to pay my share may prove that he trusts me more and 'loves' me less.

It may be very unwise to allow myself to become involved with B. over a money-making venture if I hope to continue a 'love' relation with him ...

12 Aug   I cannot deny the fact that I am very sad to have lost Basil ...

... It isn't a sensual ache I feel now he is gone, which is probably what he feels for me if he feels anything at all or allows himself to, but a longing for his presence ... I cannot feel as he does that we have been at cross-purposes all the time. I *know* it is not so ...

15 Aug   ... A visit to my mother is always upsetting. For a few minutes one establishes a contact, then she is back in her endless repetition fantasies. The house grows dirtier and dirtier and she with it. An open sore on her neck, drifts of powder, her cheap clothes crushed and soiled, her hair bright, soft and curly as a young girl's. Her nails half eaten away, patched with nail varnish. The terrible sense of sweet decay. I am sorry for her life, yet exasperated. She is perfectly happy in her dream of loves. She talks of nothing but sex. With a giggle she tells me, in veiled language, that she masturbates.

I feel the seeds of something very much like her in me and am horrified ... She is completely divorced from reality. When she sits up in her shabby bed in a soiled flowered night-dress, with a velvet coat and a moth-eaten fur collar, she thinks she is the Pompadour ...

I am surprised there are so few women artists. I suppose the production of children is a very satisfying thing to a real woman ...

I began to have a new idea of writing novels to-night ... To take characters, put them in certain circumstances, and see what would be likely to happen to them ... This would be a most exciting occupation, giving one a real sense of power ... My first two crude attempts at novels [while at school] were really much more on the right lines because they were imaginative: the trouble was I knew nothing about anything. One could take a known combination, say

my father and mother . . . One then finds out what particular thing in
my mother induced her to marry my father . . .

15 Aug [sic]   I must never allow myself to think bitterly of Basil
because he did set me free from a prison in which I have been for so
long and gave me the power to love, however incompletely, an image
that was not my own. He says it was all unproductive for him . . . But
it was not unproductive for me . . .

17 Aug   . . . I was certainly frightened at first of his fierce physical
possessiveness. I was both flattered and afraid. The physical side was
beginning to come right when he broke things off so violently . . .

I shall always remember Susan's saying 'It doesn't matter loving
another person; it's when you wonder whether they love you that it
gets troublesome' . . .

18 Aug   To-day I really feel for the first time the weight of
preoccupation about B. lifted . . .

I lunched with Jay [unknown] who told me about Basil and M[ary]
B[ell, another of Basil's girls]. It only happened a year ago: it is the
Phyllis story but much worse. She was a young girl and madly in love
with him. She and Ruth Bowley were the rivals.

Somehow this clinched something in my wavering attitude towards Basil . . .

21 Aug   I have spent the whole day indoors tidying up and throwing
away. There is some pleasure in the act of clearing and discarding but
is also depressing. It tells me all too much about what I would like to
ignore in myself . . . Endless beginnings of stories and plays, muddled
and feeble, a possible sentence here and there, but all abandoned in
despair, quantities of things begun, but nothing carried through or
finished. I have not the patience and self control of my own
children . . .

I do feel that in some ways I have more to offer other people than I
had . . . But in spite of good friends I am excessively lonely and I feel
no one wants anything I have to give . . . My existence in other
people's lives bears very little relation to myself except in Eric's
[Earnshaw Smith]. But even to Eric I feel an abstraction and not a

human being. He loves me and I am his ideal companion but I sometimes feel we have no contact at all . . . With Basil too. I am such a terrible failure as a woman; as an artist I have never begun, perhaps never can begin. I cannot bear being an intelligent schoolgirl for ever for I am nothing else but that it seems. *Later*. . . . I think of the times Basil was simple and natural with me, not trying to impress or fit life to any theory and how lovable he was then and how happy we were together and then how cold, contracted, cruel he was when he was treating our relation as a profit-and-loss account . . .

. . . I am amazed at the courage of that little girl Mary Bell. She suffered far more than I did and she could have *known* nothing . . .

My little aunt Clara [Jeffery] lived by love, knew nothing, had nothing and was a radiant figure. If anyone is in heaven she is. I am so defective in love . . .

* * *

Antonia filed for a divorce from Tom as he set off for a summer holiday with Gerti Deutsch,[†] his new girlfriend, in Austria. Gerti, a Viennese photographer, had met Tom at *Weekly Illustrated*. Her father was a Jewish businessman who was beginning to fear the Nazis.

* * *

Basil Nicholson diary, 24 Aug Tom is back from Vienna, is sure he wants to marry his Gerti and wants the divorce to proceed. It gives me a curious 'winded' feeling . . . It is so odd that some part of myself keeps saying still 'But this is all a mistake . . there is a misunderstanding somewhere' . . .

. . . I am going to be stripped of everything and left to myself. Since my one talent is certainly 'lodged with me useless' I feel awfully as if I were being thrown into the sea without a lifebelt . . .

When he married me, he said that he would take all the risks, for by that time I was numbed and dubious. He said he would be responsible for my happiness. I do not think he was insincere; he just didn't know what he was talking about . . . I have *no* emotional relationship with Eric . . . only my original admiring friendship.

Oh, why couldn't I have trusted my original strong instinct when he [Eric] first suggested marriage – a movement as decided as reaching – which said 'This is against nature'. And it was before I knew he was homosexual. Much of value has come from that 'against nature' relation. But the horror to me is that I *know* Eric loves me, though he cannot express it, as a man loves a woman and it is very distressing to me. He is right – it was a kind of sin in him to ask me to marry him and heaven knows he has expiated it by trying to give me back to my own nature. But it is very late, probably too late for me to have a life as a woman. I do not want to be a freak, something against nature, however intelligent or rare. I was born natural and I will not be anything but natural. I am sick of dreamy platonic friendships ... I would rather be an animal with Basil than have the most exquisite 'love' relation ... I do not regret at all that I was Basil's bitch ... I haven't irreparably damaged anyone. Silas, perhaps. I don't know. But he was so damaged already. To have married him in the state I was in could have brought him no happiness. He was incapable of taking any responsibility. I have never loved anyone so naturally except Robert – but what good did it do either of us? There is Susan and she must be saved from this legacy of our own devils. I wish I could have Susan and not Lyndall. I suppose it would be cruel to separate them?

* * *

Antonia now went on holiday to Germany with Norman Cameron. This was her second German holiday with Cameron; the first had been at Easter and is not noted in the diary. Cameron was an elongated poet in his thirties, a Communist. Antonia had met him at J. Walter Thompson and fallen in love with him, but the sentiment was not reciprocated. Cameron did, however, admire Robert Graves's lover, the poet Laura Riding.[†] He and Antonia stayed with a German family called Faust.

* * *

29 Aug, Arras ... . Alex ... the German woman [unknown travelling companion] with us has a plain face with rather fine eyes; a well-knit wide shouldered body, rather rigid. Wears her nails in long points; seems always hungry. Reads P.G. Wodehouse ...

1 Sept, Berncastel   Yesterday very bad. The night before I was drunk for the first time in my life. One part was completely out of control; with the other I managed to perform tremendous feats of self-control, walk and talk. As soon [as] I was in bed I was just flung about on black waves, violently sick. The feeling of being completely at the mercy of my body like nothing I can remember since childbirth.

Headache and weakness the next day only to be expected but in the evening as these got better, a really black hopeless depression like the bad old days set in – I felt a ghost again. I took Dial and have woken up reasonable.

I am interested again in the Laura Riding problem. Both Norman and Alex speak of her as being unique – different in *kind* from any other human being. N. said at first she filled him with violent resentment but that was just 'meanness' on his part. I told him some of the stories I had heard; he was violently indignant. She provokes very violent reactions in people. Norman cannot bear her to be talked about as if she were a human being at all. I remember Greenwood talking about Rupert Doone in exactly the same way . . . Norman says . . . that her association with Graves is for work. That she jumped out of the window because a man who had come to work with them, in whom she believed, turned out to be merely interested in their activities as 'gossip'. Obviously she must have power; she renounces sexual relations for herself but arranges them for others; she arranges them for Graves, but in such a way as to keep him in her power. She seems also to live on other people in a way. She publishes books of letters . . . for which she does not pay anything . . . Norman gave her his house in Majorca. He says . . . He withers when he is away from her . . . She sounds to me uneasy, full of vanity and not really confident in spite of her assertion of uniqueness . . .

1 Sept, Cologne It is curious to be back in the room where a few months ago I was lying in such a frenzy of physical disappointment because Norman did not want to sleep with me. Now I really do not want it. I feel quite peaceful and contented here. I like this town which I have always felt to be friendly and I am very fond of the Faust [unknown] family. To-day for the first time for many days I am not gnawed by the thought of Basil. I do not feel very gay or alive – rather somebody passed over and relegated to a minor place, but not disliked and capable of a quiet amusement on my own. It seems rather an 'elderly' feeling but oddly enough it is very like the feeling in my teens when Marion [Abrahams] was the pretty girl the young men were 'keen on' and I was the tolerated friend and confidante. I felt this very much this afternoon when Norman was devouring Helma [unknown] with his eyes and telling me every time she left us how beautiful she was . . .

I piece together a few more impressions of Laura Riding . . . She completely ignored her existence after she innocently referred to 'the Graveses'. She made Norman pay off the mortgage on the house he had given her. She spends a great deal of time and trouble on her clothes. She is said to have refused to see someone sent by Blakiston [unknown] saying 'You don't believe in me' . . . She has quick nervous movements, very beautiful eyes, a large nose and a pronounced witchlike look . . . She loves to experiment with people and work out combinations. I think she must be like me in many ways, with a consistency I have not got, courage to get what she wants but au fond more away from reality. Her talent I cannot judge, having seen too little. Much of what I have seen seems a nervous and complacent exhibitionism; her criticism shrewd but patronising, some of the poems really deep and fine . . . There may be a good deal of suppressed or unsuppressed Lesbian in her . . . I would like to be much more firmly rooted before I meet her. I feel her work to be partly a *weapon* – perhaps any woman's is. I wonder why all women writers who are any good have been and are sexually very odd . . .

2 Sept I am not stupid but extremely *silly*. Ever since I was seven years old I have put myself in the position of being *patronised*. If a person has *one* quality I admire, say beauty, wit, brains, courage, high intelligence, birth, ease, I tend, because I am inferior to them in *that* quality, to feel inferior on every other ground.

I think I am as dazzled by beauty in a woman as a man is. And I certainly admire something which perhaps I think of as aristocracy – a kind of carelessness, sans gêne – There is a lot of the courtier in me . . .

There was an atmosphere of insane baby worship in the railway carriage yesterday. A mother doting, completely absorbed in an attractive, but perfectly ordinary little boy. The elder child, a plain little girl, obviously had no interest for her at all. By the sheer force of her worship the whole carriage began to participate in her feeling and to see the child through her eyes.

I suppose it is that same insane love one was probably given by *someone* as a child that one goes on looking for as a grown up. *Whatever* the child does is marvellous simply because it does it. What the wretched child does not see is that it is not *itself* the mother loves at all but *herself*. A nurse comes to feel a child *her* child in the same way ...

2 Sept, Cologne   All day I have been wandering about quite happily, looking at pictures etc. In the museum here a great many German primitives, just not very good ...

4 Sept   ... My faults – rigidity, impatience – I find both so difficult to cure. Rigidity is of death. Impatience forbids any real satisfaction ...

Alone, in foreign towns, in hotel bedrooms, I nearly always find a strong sexual desire coming from nowhere which nearly always ends in masturbation ...

All my feeling of being hurt and resentful against Norman – his tactlessness, way of ignoring me, treating me like a ghost which I feel already flared up in a tiny trivial incident when, without asking me, he gave away the sweets Tom gave me which were a touching present from him and a link with my real life ... The next day he went to a lot of trouble to buy me a book of Rilke's poems. It is for things like that – like the episode in the train from Paris – that I have a feeling of real warm affection for him ...

6 Sept   Rothenburg is very lovely but too much of a show tripper place. There are streets of high gabled houses, some stepped some inlaid with wooden beams in patterns. Windows all set flat into the houses, innumerable window boxes (as all over Germany) dripping with geraniums and petunias ... Every street hung with the red swastika banners – aeroplanes passed over in batches, heavy, flying with deadly precision, scattering flocks of birds ...

At Ascherffenburg we stayed at the heaviest, darkest hotel full of plush, antlers, dark furniture. The waiters wore white cotton gloves. A notice in the bedroom said one's bed would be made with wedges, horsehair or feathers to taste ...

Ugliness and gracelessness of people everywhere ...

... At Coblenz the steamers and barges seeming to dance on the stream in time to the waltzes of the café orchestra. The endless bands of people – a band of old men in bright green shiny straw hats; a single file of girls in white hair-ribbons playing on penny whistles; girls walking four abreast in cotton frocks, puff sleeves and aprons; officers walking in fours two in grey green uniforms. People with printed ribbons in their hair announcing they were on a steamer trip. The Germans are a *horde*. Of course endless bands of trippers, of children, of Hitler Jugend in black corduroy shorts. Rude remarks about Jews at the entrance to nearly every town.

Still uneasy and incomplete in mind; a brooding guilt and anxiety. I am sure I understand Kafka's nightmare feeling of something to be guessed under pain of death and no clue given. The fairy tale riddle. In the fairy tales one cheats, overhears the answer by accident or is given it by a witch. Sometimes the fool guesses it.

I begin to range round the idea of writing again since my 'discovery' of the novel. But I cannot decide to do something straight from experience – my parents – Brittany – in which the data are given and imagination is used only in interpretation or whether to launch right out on something new – selecting my set of characters and letting their circumstances grow out of them.

On an impulse I wrote to Basil last night a long letter. I do not know whether it was a good thing to do ...

I feel a curious kinship with, dislike of, yet pity for Katherine Mansfield, whose letters I am reading again. I see all my weaknesses in her, admire her for her frantic attempts to be honest and deal with them. I can now read her, feeling her equal not an awestruck inferior as I used to. I know all she knew.

I remember being so affronted years ago when Jim [Dougal] said all art was unsatisfied sex. What if it *were* true? There still remains good art and bad art ...

7 Sept, Unteraspach (near Nurnberg) ... Nurnberg where I spent a frantic hour this morning was awful because of the Parteitag – the swastika on the long red flag everywhere, (as it has been for miles round on all main roads) Hitler's picture everywhere, the town thronged with brown and green uniforms and ugly women and serious girls, ugly too, in cotton dresses with cameras slung over their shoulders ...

9 Sept . . . I think Basil is very cruel – a *bad* man, if you like – and yet does his cruelty hurt more than the weak cruelty of the average man? . . .

I have been in a pretty bad state all this holiday. Norman, though gentler, is a more nerve-racking companion even than Siepmann and not so stimulating. Laura Riding was penetrating to call him Zero the companionable. I made the mistake of treating him like a human being. He is almost incapable of consecutive thought though he has sudden and illuminating perceptions . . .

Basil Nicholson diary, 15 Sept Although I wish I could make concrete and objective notes to-night, I cannot. I am trying to track something down which keeps eluding me . . . Now the odd thing is that in a sense I *know* the beast in my jungle and have even stated the thing in speech and on paper and *yet*, try as I will, cannot feel it fully and so escape from it. Obviously I am terrified . . . but of what? I *know* that at the back of the whole thing is the delusion of omnipotence . . .

Failure is so terrible to me that I deprive myself of an enormous amount of pleasure and interest rather than expose myself to the risk of it . . . I am a very serious failure . . . because I have no control over my emotions or actions . . .

I feel more and more drawn to the theatre. There is no doubt that the excitement, the compression, the *shorthand* of a play is more thrilling to me than the best novel. And I love the whole atmosphere of a theatre, tawdriness, dust and all – the terrific bursts of work . . . I prefer the revealing of character in dialogue and gesture to the slow unfolding in print . . . Love of the theatre was the one thing Reggie and I had in common. And it is odd how always I come back to *hanging about the theatre* – the Group, St Denis, only fuming with impotence because I'm not *right in*. I don't want to act. I want to write plays, watch rehearsals, and have a say in it all . . . I should like to write really good parts for a young actress with something in her . . . What *seems* to hold me up is a subject . . .

. . . In analysis I fear still more humiliation and suffering than I have yet undergone – some really fearful, rending horror like unanaesthe-tised childbirth which is so awful that I would rather let the child die inside me and die of bloodpoisoning than face it.

Funny how I literally *retained* my second child and was ill for long

after and still bear physical traces. I recovered completely from
Susan. I think I *accepted* the experience of having Susan in a way that I
was unable to accept the experience of having Lyndall . . .

22 Sept   Last night I had a very bad nightmare . . . I came at last to a
place where people were dancing – like a nightclub. Eric was there
too. There were days of drunken orgy, but the dancing went on all
the time – round and round in a circle. I put my finger into the anus of
the person in front of me – a man, I think. Then suddenly an awful
feeling – we had gone too far – nemessis [sic] was coming. Everyone
nervous and frightened – Eric said 'Of course I knew you were
pregnant – suspected it for some time – so did everyone else' I hotly
denied this – said it was impossible. If anything had happened it must
have been during one of the drunken interludes: I had no recollection. But everyone said I must be, I was getting so fat, and I felt with
horror it must be true. And now there would be torture. Hitler, who
ran all this, let the people have their fling up to a point, but every now
and then there was a purge and fearful punishments were inflicted.
These meant tortures so abominable that Eric said there was only one
thing to do, to kill myself. There was no escape. I would be able to do
it on the way to the torture room which was very far away. We were
sitting in a kind of tawdry teashop with very common waitresses.
There were jocular notices from Hitler saying that he would
personally attend to young ladies who had unfortunately got themselves into trouble and convince them that they had been very foolish
and make it easy for them not to get into such scrapes again. The
jocularity was the most horrifying part of it. At last a cheerful,
common nurse beckoned me through a door. We went along a
passage, down some stairs. She was gloating and bullying, but had a
kind of rough kindness. I felt that if I were brave and put a bold front
on it that I might just possibly get through the ordeal which I now
thought of as consisting of extreme humiliation rather than physical
pain. I said to the leering nurse as we parted 'Well, you have been nice
anyway.' I was pushed through a door into the torture room. Here
more nurses seized me and put lipstick crosses all over my face and
forehead to make me ridiculous. In the room which seemed to be
underground and had a stone floor – something like the out-patients'
undressing room in a hospital, very gloomy and dirty looking yet

'institutional', people in rags sat about in apathetic, dejected attitudes, men and women ... An old woman had a child on her knee.
The child wore a boy's cap and she was setting fire to its long straight
hair with a coal. I was standing above the room at the top of some
steps. A brisk-looking Jewish doctor stood up (I do not know if he
was 'The President') and addressed me in a sneering, patronising
voice 'And may I ask what question do you wish to ask?' This
destroyed all my self-possession; I had nerved myself to answer
questions but not to ask them. I was tongue-tied, felt something
unspeakably humiliating and agonisingly painful was going to
happen and suddenly burst out of the nightmare and found myself
panting and sweating in my own bed ...

Basil Nicholson diary, 25 Sept Things are very bad to-day again. I
have had an intermittent headache the entire week; to-day it has
lifted. There are several small concrete tasks I ought to do. I do
nothing ... writing is horror unthinkable. I CANNOT write. Not even
mechanically ...

Basil Nicholson diary, 27 Sept I am feeling aggressive, bitter and
impotent yet know somewhere in myself, though all my 'sources' are
dry that if I give in to bitterness, I am failing. Djuna talked so much
about my potential ruthlessness the other night: I wonder if she was
right. She kept saying that I was marvellous, that the only trouble
was that I hadn't the courage to be ruthless enough. She called me the
last of the Borgias, kept saying 'Look at that wicked little hand – held
straight up'. She said 'You crash right in to other people's lives and
wreck them – look at Silas – you've done for *him* all right – look at
Tom . . I saw him in his boat the other day and that engine just kept
right on stuttering 'Tony . . Tony . . Tony . . Tony . . Tony'. Then she
kept on kissing me and pulling my hair, saying 'But you're wonderful, darling, you're marvellous'. She said 'I can paint you now. I
never thought I would want to. There's something funny and Greek
about the back of your head and I've got to get that into your full
face'. She said 'I would paint Silas as a little bull with those nostrils. I
saw him at Kew, with his face lifted up against a lot of tropical fruits
and flowering vines and suddenly I got it . . 'The White Negro'.

I said 'If I am so wicked, what is my worst vice and wickedness?'
She said 'Giving poison to the wrong man'.

She said 'You're marvellous and I dote on you and I wouldn't have
you any different but I would rather be dead for a row of pins than be
in love with you'.

She said 'there is nothing you couldn't do. You could write
something quite extraordinary. And I feel it very strongly that you
will and quite soon' ...

I said 'I suppose I just haven't the courage to be as bad as I was
meant to be. I've always had this idiotic desire to be good. Perhaps to
get [to] heaven I have got to have the courage to deserve hell'. Emily
said 'Now you've said it. You should have the courage to be the devil
– the devil is a very good thing to be'.

Now this was all flattering and exciting ... But it left me very
uneasy ...

I am resentful that I am to be left with the children – that all my life
now I am to be tied, committed to making money. And yet it is just
possible that I care for those children more than I realise ...

... I would find it very hard to part permanently with Susan in
actual fact, I think. When I went in to say good-night to her, I did feel
a wave of extreme affection for her. I have been selfish about Susan,
shirked my responsibilities, and yet having her was one of the few
genuine things in my life. I loved Si and I wanted Susan, in spite of all
the difficulties.

4 Oct   There was a very odd character at Reitlinger's this weekend –
a dilapidated ex-guardsman of about 50 – Basil Hambro. All his
stories were of men like himself – regimental drunks, gamblers, men
who had run through fortunes. He had got through £5000 in 6 days
(squeezed out of trustees to set him up on a farm in Brazil) ... in Le
Touquet with Sylvia Hawkes [unknown]; most of it went at the
casino.

He had a friend in the guards called Drooky Duncan who had a lot
of medals but was a hopeless drunk. In one bout of DTs he rushed
round Pirbright Camp with a bayonet and a revolver trying to kill
people. The Military Police got after him and he took refuge in an
empty grave in the churchyard, pulled the planks over his head ...
threatening to shoot anyone who came near.

He finally was captured and dismissed from the army and (after forging a cheque) joined the Foreign Legion as a private. Too ill from drink to be able to do anything but be an officer's orderly. Tried to commit suicide by putting his head over a charcoal stove but didn't succeed. Cut an artery in his wrist, but was again rescued. Was given his discharge from the Legion and £12 a month from his family. Borrowed 200 francs from friends in San Raphael. Went to Monte Carlo and lost it. Took room in hotel, ordered enormous dinner and bought a razor. Cut his throat in a public lavatory but not successfully. People saw blood in the street, found him unconscious. Hambro saw him in hospital, all bandaged up, very hoarse. Said hoarsely 'I've buggered it up again. I ought to have got one with a point – you can, I've seen 'em. Then you just run 'em in instead of hacking and sawing the bloody silly way I did. Still I'd have pulled it off if some interfering bastard hadn't come along'.

His father, furious, finally paid the bill at the hotel for the dinner and the champagne. Eventually Drooky *did* bring it off: bought a gun and shot himself ...

* * *

Antonia was sacked by J. Walter Thompson for increasing inattention to work. She had been with them for nine months. This was her last job before the War.

* * *

Basil Nicholson diary, 6 Oct ... Not so much upset because I have lost the job ... but [by] the feeling of panic and emptiness .. what shall I do next? It is very disconcerting the way I get sacked from every job. This makes at least the 10th ...

I seem good at getting jobs: bad at keeping them ... A regular job soon bores me to tears and it shows in my work ...

... I hate not having a lover, not mattering to anyone, but after Basil I am cold and disillusioned ... It is like living in a country where the sun never shines ...

3 Nov Dream. Horsley. The Green-Wilkinsons. Place seemed to have been turned into a museum ... carrying a lighted cigarette all over the house – could not find anywhere to put it out and did not want to drop ash. Thought of stealing Capt. G[reen]-W[ilkinson] [Reggie's father]'s waste-paper basket but did not dare. Think eventually dropped ash on the floor and felt guilty. Then a scene round a table looking at books of pictures with my mother and Auntie Connie [Constance White, Christine Botting's eldest sister]. Rather to my surprise Erna [Antonia's Austrian cook] joined us. Sat beside and put her arm round me. I was rather embarrassed but did not like to resist. I was talking German rather better than usual. My mother praised me for having picked it up so quickly.

Then someone, nurse, I think, pushed a bundle of Rosemary into my mouth, nearly choking me. It tasted very bitter and made my throat dry . . . I woke up panting and gasping, nearly crying; my heart went on beating fast for several minutes and my tongue and mouth were as dry as leather . . .

* * *

Antonia now took as a lover Nigel Henderson,[†] the 'charming boy', son of Wyn. His older brother was Ian,[†] with whom Antonia had a simultaneous affair. Both were handsome young men who had been brought up to do nothing in particular except move in cultured circles.

* * *

Basil Nicholson diary, 30 Nov   My job is finished. I have no new one. Dread empty unsettled days at home, knowing I must write articles, do odds and ends of drudgery, knock at more doors if nothing happens at Brown's and Erwin Wasey [advertising agencies].

I have just tried to create or rather destroy my usual situation. I accept, partly . . . from desire to have some human warmth in my life again, a boy of 20 for a lover. A charming boy of whom I have always been fond, but have always thought of as a child . . . sullen, hysterical, ambivalent, and uncertain. Having been very happy within the limits, I have again on a sudden impulse, done my best to ruin it. I may have spoilt it for ever . . .

He [Carroll] says the same characteristics appear in every man to whom I am attracted – the strong homosexual element, the fear of castration manifesting itself either in impotence or in over violent sexuality, the trait of disappointing women.

And I cannot help noticing that my affairs nearly always run the same course: a violent beginning on one side or the other: reluctance on one side or the other; sexual intercourse in which one or the other is frightened, frigid, or disappointed; a period during which I consciously or compulsively knot all the strings and try to provoke disaster; disaster which brings acute humiliation, sadness, sense of loss and failure and yet, I can see now, has elements of relief, excitement, almost triumph. Then comes an interval during which we do not meet; then follows either total indifference or a warm friendship which the man often values even more than I do and in which my sexual feeling for him never revives though his may ...

... And it is very clear that a great part of my unconscious preoccupation is with the idea of myself as a mutilated man ... Odd that N[igel]'s broken finger has a perverse attraction for me – that I first had intercourse with a mutilated man [Jim Dougal]. Mutilation seems to be a kind of reassurance to me in someone else. In the job at [Erwin] Wasey's, a panic at their satisfaction at my being a woman without a husband – a mutilated woman as it were. Also in serious work, the idea that to be an artist involves suppression of sexual life. Not borne out in fact by male artists. In women you might make out a case for it, narrowing it down to writers. Jane Austen and the Brontes. I *suppose* George Eliot had a sexual life; Georges [sic] Sand certainly did. Interesting all these except Jane Austen took men's names. Jane Austen the only one that wrote *as a woman* .. and was the most perfect *artist*, though by no means the most moving or profound writer. But *she* writes as an *unmarried woman* – the sharpness of the girl, or the wistfulness or shrewishness of the spinster. She makes marriage the climax of all her heroines' careers and I can think of no married couple in her works that she does not gibe at. To fail to get married is to be disastrously humiliated; yet marriage itself is ludicrous ...

4 Dec ... I have not begun to write my *Express* articles nor to finish up the report and I have an exceedingly guilty feeling about this slackness but cannot make the least effort to overcome it.

Djuna told me she had no feeling of guilt whatever about sex, about going to bed with any man or woman she wanted, but that she felt extremely guilty and ashamed about drinking ...

I have no job now. Have tried 8 or 9 different agencies, 2 papers and answered 6 advertisements. I have become more extravagant about money than ever since I knew I was sacked and obviously have grandiose ideas about it; now feel even a thousand is not enough and articles even at 7 or 10 guineas mere chicken feed.

E[ric] thinks I must get an advertising job again and stick to it for a year or two. Half of me wants to; the other half shrinks back appalled at the horror of being engulfed. Carroll says I must like advertising a great deal more than consciously appears. On the whole I loathe it and find it disgusting; sometimes I can regard it simply as a job to be done; occasionally I find it interesting. I do certainly dislike the people in it; not so much the creative personnel as the contact men and the clients . . . I am going all out for the Erwin Wasey job yet shall probably be panic-stricken if I get it. I suppose what I want is the knowledge that I *can* get it, put myself across. Then, having got it, as I got the Carlyle job, I am sick with fear and become impotent at the thought of having to deliver the goods. The difficulties I see if I get the Erwin Wasey job are

(1) I shall prove completely incompetent

(2) I shall have to exhaust myself in doing it and be worn out, unable to have any life or interest apart from the office

(3) I shall become really interested; nothing but a successful advertising woman, lose all interest in art

(4) I shall lose any feminine charm; become harsh, dried up, ugly.

(5) In order to be successful I shall have to be reserved and autocratic; be willing to be disliked.

(6) I shall lose N[igel] . . have no time for him.

Fear of being engulphed prevents me also from being a serious writer. The result is I achieve nothing in any field. I feel always if I give myself wholly to anything I shall lose something of far more value . . God knows what. It sounds very like the man who is afraid to let himself go sexually for fear of castration . . .

Let us try the old wants list again.

(1) To have a decent income . . .

(2) To make something of my relation with N[igel] . . .

(4) Most of all, most of all, to be able to *function* . . .

(5) Not to be such a coward . . . To love truly something outside myself, not my own reflection in a glass – to love what is unlike me . . .

(7) I wish I could pray . . . So that even if my life seemed to me

utterly frustrated and meaningless, I would at least be able to accept it and know that I was not opposing the creator's design.

I cannot tell how much such feelings are genuinely religious or merely morbid. It may be another projection of my father and and my conscience, shelving of responsibility. I so often feel if I try to make my own life I am opposing God's will and shall be punished even in this life by never having a peaceful mind. All the Catholic teaching is the necessity of denying oneself, giving up one's own will to the will of God. Yet I know neither my own will or God's will. I seem to have no true will: only compulsions . . .

THREE

1938–July 1939

The years 1938 and 1939 (until the War started) were a period of rare prosperity for Antonia. She had a new flat in Cornwall Gardens, Kensington, a live-in housekeeper, work as fashion editor of the *Sunday Pictorial*, and Ian Henderson (aged twenty-three) became her live-in lover. In January 1938 she visited David Gascoyne, who was now living in Paris. He introduced her to Henry Miller and Alfred Perlès[†] who, with Lawrence Durrell, edited the bilingual review *Delta* (formerly *Booster*). *Delta* published three of her poems. Pierre Jean Jouve[†] was a fellow contributor. In the autumn of 1938 her marriage to Tom Hopkinson ended in divorce. Her psychoanalysis by Carroll ended at about the same time.

1938

4 Jan, Paris   I have bought myself a great many handsome French notebooks in the hope of luring myself to write.

It seems now that every time I come abroad, I am afflicted with the same langour and malaise. It has not been acute depression this time, thanks to David's company but there has never been a whole day free from extreme tiredness and a muffled feeling of oppression. Also for 3 days I have had inflamed glands down one side of my face which makes one feel abnormal and rather ill.

To-day it has been snowing; a thin icing of snow on pavements, parapets, roofs of taxis and the wooden boxes of books along the quays ...

Most days have been clear, intensely cold and sunny ... the ... pale yellow of the buildings very luminous, the river dark green ... There are booths in the street for New Year; shooting galleries, sweet stalls, chestnut stalls ... Up in the Alisia district where Miller lives there were roundabouts and swing-boats put up in the street and a canvas tank with boats.

There are huge scales of ice in the fountain of the Place St Michel and the gutters are frozen. I am staying in the Rue de la Hachette, just off the B[oulevar]d St M[ichel] by the Seine in a narrow street full of brothels and corset shops.

I am too tired to make proper notes; when I get back I want to write up Jouve, Miller and Perlès. Now I must go back, pick up threads, find a job, reorganise my life ... N[igel] and I[an] are both rather shadowy to me. The person I most want to see is Eric.

* * *

Antonia now started her affair with Nigel's brother, Ian, and this was 'the truth' to which she refers. Ian never moved in with Antonia at 18 Cecil Court, where she had the children and a housekeeper living with her. He spent occasional nights in the flat in Cornwall Gardens to which she moved in October and where she set aside a room as his workroom.

* * *

31 Jan   ... Nigel now knows the truth. I said it in answer to a direct question but I realise now that I could easily have avoided that direct question. I suppose I wanted him to know. I thought it was because I hated deceit between us. Carroll says that it is my impulse to ... hurt anyone who has disappointed me. This is a terrible truth to face, if it is so ... He did not go to Carroll to-day and I have spent weeks trying to persuade him to talk to a psychologist since I do not think anyone else can help him.

Wyn says he is very bitter against me, that he thinks I have knifed him in the back ...

Am I corrupt all through? ... It seems to me we have set up an impossible ideal of what a human being should be and are perpetually torturing ourselves and each other for not living up to it. Where did we get these abstract ideas of truth, love, gentleness, strength, endurance, justice, forbearance? The animals are cruel, aggressive, cunning and cowardly ... How can one change one's *wishes*? One puts up an elaborate defence to prevent knowing what one's real wishes are. Then by the mechanism of analysis one gets an inkling of what they are. One is horrified because they run counter to every ideal that has been set up for one ... Then is it possible to change those wishes? Is man worse than bestial? Is all beauty a hypocritical covering for filth? And yet the fact that a body is full of blood and filth does not alter the fact that the exterior of body may be beautiful or ugly. The fact that a poet was a lecher, a traitor, a liar, a drunkard, does not alter the beauty of a good poem. Nor does a beautiful and well regulated character make a person capable of producing a good poem. Are artists really potential criminals? In a society where all the bad impulses are tamed and regulated, would the artist disappear? ...

14 Feb It is still impossible to work. I tried on Saturday: total impotence. I mean to try again this week, to trick myself by some device into doing something about the Trix story ['The Rich Woman'].

Nigel and I seem to have reached some point of rest. My relation with Ian begins not only to tranquillise my life but to enrich it ...

21 Feb A quarrel with Silas about the arrangements for Susan. He flared up in a rage. So did I ... We both feel we have a grievance. To have heard us speak to-night you would think there had never been anything but hate and graspingness between us ... I made myself write a quiet and reasonable letter, asking him to meet Tom and me and discuss the whole thing practically ...

I feel things to begin to be very good between Ian and me. To the outsider it must seem an incomprehensible relation on both sides. I do not deny that he is not a stimulant to me, but neither is he a soporific drug. I do not feel glowing with any golden light nor great excitement, nor that bruised dreamy sensation I have always associated with 'love'. We talk of and do commonplace things. But every now and then something happens, some fire and release and a sense for both of us, of having acquired a new power, felt a new experience. The only word I can find for this is 'natural' and yet what could be more 'unnatural' by ordinary standards than a love relation between a man of 21 and a woman of 38?

His quietness, evenness, yet deep capacity to feel are something which even a few months ago I might not have appreciated. I am still in a very weak, dim and uncertain state, but if I am becoming ever so little stronger and more stable, he has much to do with it. My role seems to be mainly one of acceptance and yet I feel I have to learn to accept.

I have noticed that people who like to give, in a somewhat headstrong way, find it difficult to accept graciously. Djuna is an example. There are so many kinds of giving. Hitherto I have been one of those for whom giving is an act of self-assertion or of 'buying-off' or of remorse. I hate payments for which there is no kudos, such as paying bills.

It occurred to me this morning that the mere fact of having thought a great deal about something is no warrant that one will come to the right solution ...

... when I live in the 'real' world ... how stale and sterile that seems. Dull jobs, dull streets, dull duties, dull conversations. I begin to think I overvalue art – in the sense that I often think it the *only* thing to live for and do not see it is a flowering of life ... I cannot accept, except with my intellect, the *conditions* of human life ... Very tentatively and clumsily I begin to accept them with Ian. I would like to have a strong *and joyful* spirit instead of only a melancholy and easily-frustrated one ...

I have been trying to write a little. The result was not good ... There is something all wrong in this tortured feeling that one is spinning something out of one's own guts. Yet I mistrust everything I do naturally and without effort ... I am like a man with a glass of brackish and undrinkable water who has only to empty the glass to have it filled with wine. And yet, from fear of loss, I cannot bring myself to empty out the brackish water. I KNOW that Christ said truth when he said that to love oneself was to find oneself ...

27 Feb ... I must make some [money]. What is the best way? In an office I am lucky to make £1000 a year and I hate the irksomeness and boredom of that. Shall I go all out for free-lancing? ... I calculate that to be comfortable, to feed and educate the children to be able to live as I like, how much is required? Say £300 for the children's clothes and school

£200 rent

£100 heat, light, repairs, phone

£200 clothes
£400 general living expenses
£400 wages and housekeeping
£100 travel and holidays
this totals up to £1700 net of which I have at most £500.

With income tax, I need in all about £2000 gross, i.e. I have to set out to make £1500 a year ...

1 March   I have decided for the moment to give up the idea of trying to get an advertising job since it seems hopeless ... and to go all out for free-lancing. I am going to try and do it scientifically; work office hours ... Ian comes and works in Eric's room with me. I find this a help.

This anxious double thing with Nigel and Ian persists. There is some strong link between Nigel and myself which has not been destroyed ... It is Ian I feel now more guilty about, more responsible for. I have gratitude to and a growing affection for him, he can rouse me to a strong physical response, and yet I realise that there is not the same spontaneity about my feeling for him. The two make a remarkable contrast: there is such a strong tie between them and yet such undercurrents of hate and jealousy.

On the surface Nigel is the one more in difficulties. He is excessively nervous and violent, he drinks far too much in a compulsive way, his homosexual side interferes with his relations with both sexes, he ... has black moods of despair, self-hatred and self-destruction. Yet with all this goes a peculiar charm and life, which one feels even when he is under his heaviest clouds ... he is an âme bien née, incapable of cringing ...

Ian has all the qualities Nigel has not got. He has neither fire nor brilliance of imagination, but a clear, steady, logical mind and a fair, consistent critical faculty ... His imagination is in his body. But he has this ... dead numbing weight which paralyses his feelings and his powers of communication. I notice the things for which he has an almost superstitious reverence are articulateness, wit, ability to communicate, creative power ... Apart from sex he is unable to assert himself ... He ... needs to feel he is capable of helping people, is horrified if, having come to rely on him, he lets them down which he does, at unexpected moments, by a complete collapse of himself ... In childhood he was spoilt and over-loved ... He tries to imitate Nigel and cannot ... I am inclined to think homosexuality is a deeper problem, because he is almost unaware of it as a problem for himself, than it is for Nigel who is painfully aware of it ...

And yet at his best he is like a wholesome climate in which someone can expand and feel calm and safe ...

... He [Nigel] is like a better-tempered metal, harder and sharper. He has no vulgarity. Ian has and I have. Something of my feeling for Nigel is my old worship of the aristocrat ... I feel my own vulgarity is too much a part of my nature ever to disappear ... I think it is mainly a kind of greed, a bargaining, shopkeeping instinct ... I believe one of the signs of vulgarity is to wish to be *different* from what one is ... but actually to have different qualities and, lacking them, to pretend and even deceive oneself one has them.

Nothing can be vulgar which simply is what it is ...

23 March   The divorce case is due any day now. Analysis is supposed to end next September. I cannot get a job. I owe £82. o. o., have an overdraft of £50, am owed about £48 which will come in in driblets. I have run my 'factory' for nearly a month but have ... so far averaged only £11 a week.

I have got to bring this up somehow. But how?

10 April   ... Nigel said last night 'Ian would make me a perfect mistress' ...

I am attempting this story about myself and Tom ['The Moment of Truth', 1941]: get panicky and discouraged when it goes off the rails: want to stop and continue it in phantasy. That won't do. Nervous explanatoriness, about circuiting, the bomb going off before its time and so being ineffective all appear as usual. Well I've GOT to learn to handle my material.

What is necessary for this story to turn it from the private case into the universal one?

The shadow of madness is, I think necessary, since it is part of the woman's nature, also part of the fear and pity the man feels towards her. Yet let us eliminate actual case-history madness and see what we have left.

We have two people, married, with a very strong tie between

them. The woman fears jealousy more than anything else since she knows she would disintegrate under it. The flaw in her nature is greed and fear: the flaw in the man's is the desire for universal approval . . .

. . . She is on the verge of disintegration, a spectacle which both appals and fascinates him. She is trying desperately to make him face himself, knowing that he is not what he appeared yet frightened because she knows that in revealing him to himself she must lose him . . .

Could this book be done in two halves?
(1) The woman's part
(2) The man's part.

14 April   I have a new pen – always an important thing for me. And now, to my annoyance it turns out to be very intractable. Possibly it's the pale ink I don't like. The old pen which I have given to Ian seems to me infinitely superior . . .

15 April   Have just completed first twenty-four hours at the cottage. Severe strain. And I can't break this pen in . . . Does this old one of Daddy's write better? Can't do anything till I've settled this pen question . . .

My mother's mind is like a fruit rotten before it ripened. I suppose for years she has not added a new idea or thought to her repetoire. I have never seen her without her referring to my father's isolated act of drunkenness, to the dry birth etc. etc. You can hardly call her 'selfish': she is amiable, hospitable, tractable. But she is simply unaware of other people's existence or of the effect she produces on them. Most maddening of all are her lispings, affectations of voice, all the moues of a privileged pretty woman. That a person who thinks of hardly anything but her looks should be so slovenly, even grotesque in appearance is very alarming. I wonder what she would have been like if she had never been good-looking and had had to make some sort of effort. She is perfectly happy: never has any doubts of her own charms or that everyone is attached to her. I am so frightened of becoming like her that I feel I must have some grounds for fear. You can make no direct contact with her: nothing ever appears to her directly. She deals with shadows at the third remove. The more I see, the more convinced I am that 'nothing is more monotonous than fantasy'.

I do not think my coming closer to Ian is a direct consequence of Nigel's 'revenge' though there is some connection, obviously. I am no less fond of Nigel as a person as a result, but I see that there is no future for us as lovers. He will always recoil and react from any woman; perhaps less from Kathleen [McClean] who, looking more like a man, is more his physical type . . .

18 April   Down here with my mother I feel that nothing can be so preposterous, so undignified as 'love'. I have been reading her ludicrous, pathetic, nauseating diary about herself and Oswald Norton. 'Cleopatra had a famous wriggle last night. Julia ully-ully'.

The sexual act is not indecent but almost any verbal description of it is. Interspersed with all this are prayers, recriminations, schoolgirl ravings, a kind of complacent self reproach.

It is far more strain to be with her than with the children. I sometimes itch to come out with a truth – any truth – but it is useless. Her defence is so complete, ingenious and unconscious that nothing – literally nothing can pierce it . . .

Down here Ian seems very remote: Nigel too for that matter. In a way the Kathleen thing is a relief since it has forced me into a choice . . .

21 April   . . . His [Ian's] feeling of guilt about Nigel is very strong, also his love and admiration for him and his desire to outshine him. There are some people whom one cannot treat too well; their nature rebels against it. I should not be alarmed to see Ian emerge in very different colours from the sweet, kind, apparently frank person he seems. He is very unreliable when frightened and he is easily frightened . . .

Obviously all three of us are working out something by means of each other . . . I talk and analyse far too much . . .

[George] Barker is very happy now. Emily has given him her cottage. I am so mean I find it hard to rejoice whole-heartedly in any friend's good fortune, but I think I do in this.

We were talking about methods of work. He clears his desk completely, tightens his shoe laces, brushes his hair. Looks forward every day to working; is only really unhappy when he has no new work to turn over in his mind.

He has a theory that I shall never get going until I am totally dependent on writing for my living and that then I shall find myself quite incapable of doing my hack work and shall be able to write nothing but serious stuff.

It may be fanciful: I don't know. From Carroll (who is after all not omniscient and whom I may have misunderstood) I do not get that impression. I get the idea rather that

(a) I shall not be able to concentrate on serious work until I have satisfied my passion for money

(b) I shall somehow contrive to break down the demarcation in my own mind between 'good' and 'bad' work and so make money by doing work of which I am not ashamed . . .

Looking for houses yesterday. Ian and I saw two old women. The first, dressed in shabby black, with one rotten tooth and shrewd eyes under wrinkled lids . . . was like something out of Balzac. She looked poverty-stricken but she owns a good deal of house property in the neighbourhood.

The other, in a maisonette cluttered up with furniture and china, was pathetic. Old and stiff, with a pale sheep-like face and glasses, her hands swollen with rheumatism. She wore a faded violet cardigan, a striped blouse with a cameo brooch and a shapeless brown skirt. A kettle was boiling on an oil stove in the kitchen dining room. 'I must have light colours round me' she [said]. 'Sunshine yellow – it looks so gay'. The walls were dingy buffs and apricots, the whole feeling of the place cluttered up and musty. There were enlarged snapshots of dogs, a huge photograph of a man in a cap with a drooping moustache.

They all say the same thing 'The other people in the house are so *quiet*'. People are very quiet in a cemetery.

Susan said of my mother 'She never comes out of her own thoughts. She never even tries to go into yours, does she?'

She is reading *Frost*. She was terrified by the story of the lost child in the cellar.

Her nightly fantasy is that she is an ill-treated horse, forced to drag heavy loads up a hill. She is beaten and the climax is that a spiked club is thrust up her bottom. I said 'Isn't it rather frightening?' She said

'Yes' and added 'But it's *lovely*'.

I asked Lyndall what she thought of in bed. With a sly smile she answered 'Doctor Nelson' [the family doctor].

Lyndall was very motherly, comforting Susan when she had a nightmare. Susan said 'It's very nice to have a sister'.

Bee [Beatrice White, another of Christine's older sisters] and her landlady have competitions in snobbery. 'I was upper housemaid to Lady so and so', 'I taught the daughters of Countess X'. Bee shows the White coat of arms. The landlady says suspiciously 'I shall get my son to look it up. He knows all about heraldry'. Each has a profound contempt for the other.

My mother appeared in six different outfits in 4 days; all tawdry, shabby, stained and dusty.

She says 'I am as slim as when I was a girl. Perhaps even slimmer' (having just told you that she had a 23 inch waist and is now 28).

25 April   Logan's mother [the author, Hannah Pearsall Smith] who was a Quaker 'saint' always advised people to do what they really wanted to do. She said 'People always in the end do what they want to do anyway so they may as well do it with a good conscience'.

He is always very kind, encouraging and flattering to me as a writer. He said 'You and Cyril [Connolly] are the only ones I put sixpence on of the younger ones. You are the only two who have a touch of genius . . no genius is too big a word . . one can never say . . but at any rate a touch of quite extraordinary talent'. I hope to goodness he is right and that we both manage to make use of it.

He advises me very strongly only to write about what really interests me and to go on plugging away at that, in spite of rejections, until finally people come round to it. He is very much against my hack work . . but still one has to live!

I cannot make up my mind whether to press for the Hobson job or go on with these free-lance scraps. Eric keeps saying 'Don't worry – you'll manage all right. Your financial situation isn't nearly as bad as you think.'

I wish I could feel that . . . My debts mount up and things will be far worse in September when Tom reduces my allowance by about £300 . . .

What Logan told me about Lady Ottoline [Morrell] who died the other day makes me feel she would be a very good subject for a novel. The fact I know practically nothing about her would give me scope for invention.

The donnée is a woman, well-born and wealthy, of striking appearance yet without sexual charm. She is kind and 'good' yet produces on some people such an effect of evil that they cannot remain in the same room. She marries a handsome man whom she takes away from his own profession and environment and makes completely dependent on her.

Whatever she wants, she must at any price have. She is a home-breaker, a destroyer of friendships ... She professes a passion for art and literature and hunts in these fields. She will generously help anyone who appeals to her. She takes up people, sucks them dry and drops them. She is all appearances with no core of a real person ...

She has always worn strange clothes, dyed her hair different colours, made up excessively ...

She has had a great many lovers but always refuses to leave the husband. The husband has developed an uncontrollable passion for servant girls and has had children by them. She has been known to lock him up in his room to keep him from getting to a girl. He told Logan once 'I am the unhappiest man alive' ...

I would say she is always trying to buy people yet really wanting to be loved for herself. That she can never participate in anything and is always trying to do so at second-hand ...

She is a vampire, all right, but the victim's blood does not nourish her ...

Analysis diary, 27 April C[arroll] says I put very high value on faeces. From my dream says '35,000 dollars for them' (because I heard someone offering this sum for some information from me to my literary agent while I was giving birth to a bag of faeces) ...

... The act of defaecation is important, pleasurable and highly satisfying to me. I can admit this to Carroll without any shame.

Now, if I really think of my work as faeces, why does the act of writing cause me such distress and misery? ...

Obviously if I really thought writing was shitting, I should be ashamed to admit I enjoyed it, even to myself. I don't of course always 'disenjoy' it: often quite enjoy it. Enjoy most surveying work.

Quantity and quality. Faeces again. Faeces in wrong place, mouth or vagina very horrifying and disgusting. Writing with my mouth – e.g. telling stories. That is enjoyable. Writing with the vagina e.g. masturbatory fantasies. Excitement but shame. Writing no excitement: dreary duty. What to write ABOUT. Obvious free fantasies are mixed up with the cruel inventions leading to masturbation. Now I am sexually freer, should be able to invent more easily. So I can for hack work, not for my own. I define good work as work written to please myself yet it is only in fantasy, except on rare occasions, the *act* of writing pleases me. The *idea* is delightful and thrilling. Perhaps one day can get a stage further. With sex, for 4 years the idea was exciting and delightful; the *act* disappointing, or disgusting or terrifying. Before I always chose the wrong kind of man; now I find the right man quite different to my preconceived ideas … Possibly same applies to subjects. Still need to get my man approved. Relief Eric likes Ian. Trying hard to get C[arroll]'s 'permission'. Obviously really my own. Must SOMEHOW get my own permission about writing and making money …

Presumably sex having cleared should both lighten the load but temporarily drive demon into money and writing. Must be patient, try and co-operate with Carroll and see what happens.

22 May   Went to Hampton Court yesterday. Sun; fountains playing, the dark conical yews on the pale green lawn …

I saw Lady Arabella Stuart (Gheraerts) [sic] again. Since 1921 this picture has always had a peculiar magic for me. She wears a loose embroidered beltless dress all covered with flowers and birds and seems to be pregnant. Her shoes are brilliant blue with pearls sewn all over them. Her headdress is high like a pointed shell, with a long veil hanging over her loose auburn hair. One hand rests on the stag with the garland between its antlers, a tree like a dark chestnut above it and other lighter green trees in the distance. In the branches are latin mottos written in white – *dolor medicina dolori* is one. This is the poem exquisitely written on the shield in the bottom right hand corner.

> The restless swallow fits my restless minde,
> In still revivinge, still renewinge wronges;
> Her juste complaintes of cruelty unkinde

Are all the Musique that my life prolonges.
With pensive thoughtes my weepinge stagg I crowne
Whose Melancholy teares my cares expresse;
Her teares in sylence and my sighes unknowne
Are all the physique that my Larmes redresse,
My onely hope was in this goodly tree
Which I did plant in love, bringe up in care:
But all in Vaine, for now too late I see
The shales be mine, the kernels others are:
My Musique may be plaintes, my physique teares
If this be all the fruite my love tree beares.

27 May ... Meeting a man like [Tom] Beachcroft[†] [writer], obviously a sober and sincere, if not very talented or brilliant writer cannot help feeling his superior on the score of what I haven't written! ...

29 May My approach to writing may be wrong which may be why I find it so very difficult. This morning I thought I would try the 'Field' technique [*Experiment in Leisure* by Joanna Field]; instead of trying in a tense way (I am re-writing a chapter that has gone off the rails badly) I would try to relax, hold myself open as she says, use the will only to hold this gesture of attention. I thought I would try to do without smoking since I know that in analysis I use smoking as a defence against things of which I am afraid to become aware. It gives me a false sense of poise and power and security. I decided I would see if I could manage half a page without a cigarette. It was only a half page of copying out and polishing, a paragraph which had seemed all right before. Now I began to have doubts about it. It was all right from a 'literary' point of view – a quite good bit of description of Tom's eyes. But was it right in that place in the story? I must get the thing an organic whole: not something dead with vivid patches embedded in it. Importance of *movement*. I tried to concentrate on these two people on the deck but they just shredded away to nothing. For though it is a scene that might have taken place, it did not actually take place: it is simply a rearrangement in a different medium of known elements. It is this mixture of 'taken from life' and imaginative construction of something which did not happen in life but might conceivably have happened that is the problem. As yet I feel neither the courage nor the capacity to invent, yet I am hampered by the real facts . . .

I tried the 'I want nothing' trick but it did not work: it was too obvious to myself that I wanted a great many things. A cigarette, in particular . . .

. . . half the time, when I sit down to write, though I may have thought a great deal on the subject and feel it to be significant as I do this one, I feel absolute emptiness, nothing to say. I write words which lead on to other words and they are empty, flat and insincere . . .

Last night I saw Brian Nash [a friend of Robert's]. I asked him if he had heard anything of Robert. He said 'Oh, he is dead. He was killed in a flying accident about three years ago'. The actual shock was very slight. I have always had the idea that Robert would be killed flying. For years I looked at a paper to see the names every time I saw a poster about an R.A.F. crash . . . Now I can never see him again and know the truth. I was glad there was this reason for his not having answered my letter . . . I have felt hurt for years that he never saw me again. The peculiar happiness of those three weeks, though I suppose it was partly the product of my own elated state before madness, still remains for me a standard of human happiness which I had begun to think unattainable . . .

On the way I kept saying urgently 'Robert, give me a sign . . .' I felt that, with the peculiar clairvoyance we had about each other during those three weeks, I should have known when he died. It is as if I felt he had in some way cheated me and I cannot accept it. In bed I was going over times we spent together. I cannot remember anything he said to me except some funny story about a gardener, his saying that he would have liked us to live on a desert island where he could build everything himself, that even if he disappeared for a year or more he would always come back to fetch me, his stopping suddenly in the street and saying 'There is water under here', his telling me how yellow and shrivelled Michael Collins [unknown friend of Robert's] looked in his coffin. I remember places and things we did better: standing on the tower of Westminster Cathedral and dropping down cigarette ends, standing on the seashore at night, driving through Sussex in the sunlight and back in the fog . . . dancing at the Palais, wrestling in my father's study, his promising to send me a jay's feather. I feel superstitious, as if finding a jay's feather would be a sign.

Just as I was getting drowsy I had a very vivid hallucination of a man bending over me. It might have been Robert or Tom. But I had a strong feeling that it was a mocking, even a hostile presence – very much the way I see Robert in dreams . . .

. . . That I should be living in a world in which for three years he has not lived and that I did not know it . . . I would like him to know how much he meant to me and perhaps, too, that I suffered a great deal because of him. Perhaps I have not forgiven him for that though I do not think I have ever felt consciously angry with him. I simply felt that if he had ever understood, if I could have had one more talk to him, it would have been all right. Oh, how I hang on to the past . . .

I showed Tom the picture of Arabella Stuart yesterday. He was very much moved by it and by the poem. He said that the woman was like me and the poem one that I might have written . . .

12 June   . . . Although I have now got it clear that . . . the best thing to do is to get really going on my new book, I still put off from day to day the actual getting to grips with it . . . It will be far better if I do it from the 2 points of view as Ian suggested . . . This morning instead of doing it, meticulously write all possible letters instead . . . Nervous notions too of course that, because I am short of money, ought to do short stories, speculative ads for Drene [the first detergent-based shampoo] etc . . .

I read one of the green volumes of notes [diary] to him [Ian] (Sept to Nov 1937). It interested him very much, said it articulated a great many of his own feelings. At first he was very enthusiastic, then suddenly clouded over and was obviously feeling cold and contemptuous towards me . . . This is certainly not the moment for me to cast any doubts on his civil service plan. Either way it is obviously best for him to take the exam and do his best in it . . . he has no money at all and no one to look after his interests. The more I get to know him and care for him the more I am aware of a quite different kind of person, far more fiery and forceful, under his apparently smooth and gentle exterior. Instead of being distressed when he asserts himself against me, I should be delighted. He has all his life been too meek and ready to please and doubtful that anyone could value him for other qualities.

13 June   I have been trying all the evening to get a little done on the book ... I haven't lost interest in it: it just seems remote. I would like some more action in it. Now of course I feel the subject is wrong ... The first chapter is all right except for minor roughnesses; there is some good stuff there. Better not to yield to the temptation to re-do that all over again ... Should I try treating it as a necessary job to be done? Pray? Force myself? Do it for love of someone? I feel so dried up ... I am so much enjoying and admiring *The Mill on the Floss* but would so much like to earn the right to read it ... The difference between authority, real mastery of one's medium and mere talent so clearly shown in the Rouault pictures and the Paul Nashes. At first sight the Nashes seem full of charm, clarity and poetry: the Rouaults look harsh and forbidding. But after a few moments of looking at them the Nashes seem meagre and faked, the Rouaults are rich and every square inch is alive ... The chorus of praise from critics of all types over *Frost* was a bit too unanimous not to be suspect. I doubt if a book which went deeper would get such unthinking approval ... What would I wish to be happening at this moment? To find a whole story already written without my knowing it – very good of course – as I sometimes discover notebooks I have forgotten. To wake up miraculously very much thinner ...

15 June   I have just finished *The Mill on the Floss*. Reading it and *Adam Bede* have given me the most extraordinary pleasure. I begin to think George Eliot is not only the greatest English woman novelist but perhaps the greatest English novelist. She has not the fiery poetry of Emily Bronte nor the exquisite surface of Jane Austen but she has a richness and sweep and depth that is Shakespearean. The one thing that maims or constrains her a little is some rigid moral sense which goes against her *natural* morality. She is haunted by an impossible ideal of purity and strictness. In *Middlemarch* and *Adam Bede* she incarnates this in two women; one so impossibly good that she is repellent ...

   I am in for a George Eliot bout as a drunkard goes on a jag. Over dinner I raced through a short life of her.

I think I am a bit like George Eliot on a smaller scale. I certainly have not a massive intellect but I *have* an intellect of sorts and am interested in speculation . . . I have not her rich maternal feeling; least of all have I her tremendous staying power . . . A featherweight compared to her, yet there is a likeness. I could have got on with her as I probably could *not* have got on with the Brontes or Jane Austen . . . George Eliot who stresses family ties all through her books, broke away from hers and developed the art of making friends. (It's no good: I can't write with that new pen: this isn't perfect either).

George Eliot suffered from being, in youth, very ugly and so unable to be frivolous. If I had been ugly I certainly should have worked my mind much harder. My looks are variable enough to know both how a pretty woman and an ugly one feels . . .

We only managed a semblance of family life at the cottage [Binesfield]. In London it was conspiracies of twos; my father and mother, myself and my father or myself and my mother. We were not a family . . .

. . . I have got most of my money from cheating – i.e. advertising . . forcing on to people something they did not naturally want and which might even be harmful to them . . .

But the thing people really *do* want from me e.g. books and stories, I won't do. And I find that if I do give people what they want e.g. if I go to bed with Ian instead of forcing conversation on the poor man when he's not in the mood for it, that I get a great deal of satisfaction and happiness too . . .

I DEVOUR books: food too, when I'm alone. I eat twice as much when I'm alone as when I'm with anyone . . .

Do I care for Ian because he is like me or unlike me? A bit of both, I think. The first lover I have had with the same physical appetites. Others may have had but I could neither accept theirs nor realign or express my own . . . Ian and I have the power permanently to enrich each other's lives. This does not mean we shall be permanently together. It is not likely or even desirable that we should be . . .

. . . (I have written about 16 pages to-night – so I *can* write at a stretch if I want to).

16 June   . . . I find it almost impossible to face the fact that I may not be such a very outstanding person after all . . .

... When my father destroyed the beginning of my first silly novel he did not destroy my ability to write ...

* * *

Antonia went to stay with Cecil and Margaret (Margot) King at Culham Court, Oxfordshire. Cecil was related to the Harmsworths and owned the *Sunday Pictorial* and the *Daily Mirror*. Antonia was writing as 'Jane Marshall' on the *Sunday Pictorial* fashion page. The Kings had four children.

* * *

18 June, Culham Court   ... I have been for a very long time aware of this 'mystical' (not the right word but cannot stop to think of another) pull. What frightens me about it is the terror of loss of identity, having to give up something I value, being separated from all pleasant familiar things ...

Particularly difficult in a book by which I want both to achieve a practical result – £200 – and also to do a piece of work as good as I am capable of.

The most striking thing about madness, painful and terrifying as it was was the sense of continued intensity of experience. I was often agonised, miserable and terrified, but I was never bored. Curious that the rich who appear to have all the material of a wonderful life suffer so terribly from boredom. I still cannot help envying the rich – their possessions, their security, their apparent freedom from all petty worries and responsibilities ...

Yet what always terrifies me in the life of the saints is the moment of 'renunciation of the world' even though over and over again they emphasise the fact that the sacrifice itself was easy – no more than disencumbering themselves of something they did not really want ... Just as in money matters, if I curbed myself from spending wildly on things I don't really need, I would have enough to get things I did need without accumulating a burden of debt. I shall *never* manage to hoard against imaginary 'rainy days' – that is where my father's way of trying to make me save as a child was all wrong – he never connected for me the idea of saving with deferred but real satisfaction ...

About writing this book, what I *think* I am worrying about is this question of using my own life as material. It seems too good not to use, I don't feel the power to create something new, yet when I come to try and use it, I find it very hampering and what I write seems either flat and dull or pretentious and and insincere. Then I have vaguely tried to sit down and deliberately construct 'a story' in which characters and situations I know could be embodied, but so far this has never had any result. Perhaps I've not tried hard enough but the feeling of complete impotence and emptiness seems to warn me that is not the right way . . .

D.H Lawrence draws so heavily on his own life – yet how often the best and freest part of his writing is his invention – like the wife in 'The Captain's Doll' . . .

Country houses – spacious – with white walls and mouldings, full of flowers, with an indescribable smell of their own, fragrant yet ever so slightly damp, like an autumnal wood, even in summer have a peculiar fascination for me. I am very fond of Culham with its yew-tree hedges and gardens, the rows of clean, orderly greenhouses. The pleasure and faint repugnance of sharing, but not belonging to, the life of a family living an entirely different way from one's own. The servant turning my stockings inside out. Yet that amusing episode about the peaches – in spite of all this wealth and plenty, it's impossible to have some small thing you want 'out of hours'. There only seems to be one tiny ashtray in the whole house and I am so afraid of disturbing the church-like orderliness of the place that I don't like to leave it cluttered up with ashes so every few hours [I] climb up to my bedroom to empty it into the wastepaper basket . . .

I suppose the Harmsworth fortune has been built on contempt for human beings. The younger ones are curiously sapless; they have a timid respect for or even dabble themselves in the arts – like Desmond. They tend to marry women with far more force and vitality than themselves. The brilliance and vitality of the King children is remarkable . . .

. . . In a well-ordered or in a disordered home I feel equally an outsider . . .

Dresses very simple, beautifully cut, beautiful fabrics . . . The *working-clothes* of any profession – chorus girl's practice dress, workman's clothes, sailors. One thing I'd like . . in being a nun, wearing a habit. But I'd want a feastday one as well! . . .

19 June ... King saying 'I don't like pets I can't eat.' He likes Doughty, Arabian Knights [sic], Froissart. Seems to have amassed so much knowledge; talks very intelligently and yet one feels he cannot use it, cannot get it out of himself ...

20 June ... He is with Margot a complete baby: can hardly bear her out of his sight. Margot's plan to stay back at Culham with me could not come off because Cecil refused to go to a tennis party a few miles away without her, although she had no wish to play and didn't. Out of the question, of course, that Cecil should be upset. I suppose she is absolutely the only person with whom he has any real contact. And she enjoys that: it is her power. Peculiar ruthlessness of the woman with a mate and cubs. There is ... gleam in her eye when she is thwarting someone's wishes. Her pleasure in cutting every single one of the sweetpeas – I almost feel *because* it distresses the old gardener so much. The ardour with which she agreed with me that it is better to go to a hanging than to be titillated by constantly reading accounts of one. I wish Margot weren't quite so *moral*, she is so convinced that whatever she does is right and always *for the best of reasons*. She makes a great show of liking people, wanting them to enjoy themselves but nearly always it is *her* will which is imposed on the others. She rules Cecil by apparently obeying him in everything. Like all rich women she likes little economies, sells the surplus peaches from the green-house which cannot bring her in more than £20 a season. They have four gardeners and at least seven indoor servants.

24 June ... I waste a great deal of time every day. Not all is wasted: I know that I need a certain amount for reading and rumination, but a good deal is frittered. If I have not a definite job to get done, I drift. Yet I know that I cannot be hard and efficient all the time. If I undertake too much, I get a fearful sense of oppression ...

25 June ... What is it in me that both kicks against a 'useful' or 'successful' life and yet desires one? Rimbaud deliberately cut off his talent at the moment when he had offered it to the world and it had been rejected; he never achieved any satisfaction for himself, as far as one can see, and died a painful, unnecessary death ...

... I had a shock in childhood which paralysed me emotionally. Now if I were to have another shock, would that release me? Something in my nature craves for violent surprises .. an unexpected happening, even if it is painful, sharpens my sense of life. Interesting the modern craving for 'thrills' when the ordinary person's daily life provides so few. Accounts of murders, speed racing, fatal accidents may be an absolute necessity to people and the papers may be perfectly justified in providing them. Interesting too, the more safe and peaceable people's lives become, the more violent and destructive their forms of warfare .. and the more released from personal responsibility ...

I didn't feel the tremendous excitement and satisfaction in having a baby that most women seem to feel. I half felt it with Susan, but it was clouded by all the difficult circumstances, Si's not being there, not having it as a proper married woman, and above all the disappointment of her not being a boy. I suppose I want a book in some funny way to be a male child, something powerful, able to fertilise other people. I can understand the extraordinary satisfaction of producing a son. A woman has not a penis but she can produce a being with a real penis. I did once, anyhow, conceive a son. I wonder if the realisation of that was what made me so extraordinarily happy and peaceful after that abortion [1924] which was in so many ways a very distressing experience. It was as if after that I really recovered from insanity and collected my wits again ... My impulse to write a novel began in the year following the beginning of menstruation. My father, as it were, killed the child. He thought of it as *having been conceived in sin*. Just about ten years later, I conceived a real child, about the same time of year, this time definitely 'in sin' and to my father's horrified disapproval. This time my father wishes me to go on and have the child, in very distressing circumstances, *as a punishment* ... I suddenly remember something I had forgotten – I cheated him over the money, told him the injections cost £1 each time instead of 10/– ... He was very kind to me when I was in pain and had to go to the nursing home ... I borrowed £30 from him (he was reluctant) in connection with Susan's birth ... He was more willing to lend money for the abortion than for the birth of a child. If Susan had been a boy, he told me he would have found it far easier to overlook the circumstances of her birth. It was a great distress to him that all his children were girls ... I think he felt it in some ways to be a punishment ...

My difficulty is not in beginning books but in finishing them. Since I was fifteen I have begun, since the first fatal one, six books. The only one I finished was *Frost* . . about 17 years after I had begun it and then because Tom told me to and it had all the feeling of a boring, disagreeable imposed task, the only pleasure being in reading it chapter by chapter to Tom and finding he approved of it ...

I did not begin to write notebooks until just before I married Reggie: my writing went underground as it were. The only form of writing I have persistently kept up, yet I never use anything from them ...

The only thing I really work hard at nowadays ... is finding out things about myself ...

28 June   I suppose by this time Carroll knows what I really want but *I* don't. I long for him to tell me ...

Now if as it seems clear from several indications I want my father's penis or a child by him e.g. a work engendered with his loving approval. What am I fussing about?

I can't have his loving approval because he is DEAD

I couldn't have had intercourse with him anyway because presumably apart from morals

(a) he didn't want it

(b) I couldn't have endured it without mutilation ...

... Yes I will write backhand in spite of my father I WILL WILL WILL. Couldn't even write – filthy dirty beastly old man the way I WANTED TO – Well I will. You'll see. I spit on your corpse. You're dead and I'm alive. So I'm one up on you now. I hope you've been punished. You punished me enough. I've forced myself to be sorry for you and admire you. You've ruined my life. I don't honour you and I don't honour my mother. I'd like to fight and kill you both, trample on you, take your money away. I'm sick of justice. A lot of justice you both showed me. You never loved me for a second and I'm damned if I'm going to go on loving you. The letters you wrote me. I was hurt and wanted your approval. THAT would have hurt you all right to know your standards meant nothing to me. I'd like to have you both dependent on MY charity. You only gave me what *you* wanted, never what I wanted ...*

5 July ... A woman with any life and intelligence has got to be extremely clever and disciplined to make a success of marriage. Each side is constantly demanding reassurance in their own way and usually cutting at the other's pride to get it. Men's terror of women is a very real thing and they are driven to great cruelty by it ... I made a mistake in taking him [Ian] down to Reitlinger's. He did not know that I had to force him on R. against his will. Oh, my vanity needs correcting all right ... Ian's vanity may for some reason be in a very inflamed state, and goodness knows, I am tactless ... For so long he has been forced into a position of apparent dependence on me by having no money ...

6 July What is my real feeling about this holiday [at Wyn Henderson's cottage]? Apart from grievances I might feel or think myself entitled to feel? For myself I would like to go away with Ian: somewhere where we could be alone together – say for a fortnight. It would have been nice to go to France, but if he goes with Nigel he won't be able to afford his share. All the Hendersons live on dream money a good deal, but Ian, as far as I see, does in the end pay up ...

I wonder what is behind Nigel's sudden insistence on Ian's going to France with him. Is it sudden renewed affection for Ian or is it, consciously or unconsciously, an effort to carry out his old threat that he could break us up? Is Ian under Nigel's thumb still? ... Ian obviously has very strongly the desire both to hurt and to hurt himself. The same mean look comes into his face as G[reenwood]'s when he feels uneasy. His account of his interview with the [civil service] examiners shows how he half went out after approval ... half gave spontaneous ... answers ... But his attitude is much less defeated than it was. Sometimes I am too indulgent to him for fear of losing him. This is quite different from making a real effort to understand him and make allowances for him. And it is all wrong ...

... The mania for increase of possessions *is* decreasing with me. I suppose any sense of loss of prestige or satisfaction makes people

* This entry is in a handwriting quite alien to Antonia's usual small neat style.

desire to increase their possessions. Often these take the form of actual robberies – getting things on account that you can't pay for, taking someone else's man when you have lost your own, etc. No wonder people are *themselves* so rarely – they're cluttered up with a lot of stolen or borrowed feelings or possessions or ideas . . . Wherever *did* we get the idea of *consistency* in a character? Sometimes I think the nearest one can get to defining 'character' is to say that it is the sum of a person's reactions to different stimuli. And people by no means react invariably to the same stimulus . . . I know my own very slow and tentative development consists in not always *automatically* responding in the same way to the same type of situation or at least in becoming aware that the response is automatic and so trying to be conscious of it and be able to try another.

7 July   Oh dear, I wish I were not so peppery and quick to take offence. Ian . . . tends to get sullen and frightened when he suspects he is being attacked . . . I often bring it on by over anxiety when there is no real danger. I REALLY must try and behave rationally over all this because I *know* Ian is very fond of me and I of him though we each find the other peculiarly exasperating at times especially when we're both under a strain for other reasons. The exam certainly is a danger point and brings up all his conflicts. Obviously he both wants to pass *and* to fail. He loses the pen he writes best with (which I gave him) assumes someone has stolen it, forgets he has a paper on Saturday, asks both Nigel and myself down for the week-end . . . You can convince Ian of almost anything and yet he remains at heart unconvinced . . or rather you can make him acquiesce in anything. I suppose I must allow him to be very assertive at the moment and a bit of a bully but I don't a bit like his manner of asserting himself – cold and sneering – and I can't help asking myself 'Why put up with this?' It's funny how I'll go on being obsessed by a person as long as they have any power to hurt me. I used when I was young to define love as giving someone the power to hurt me. The best thing about my relation with Ian is that I can sometimes allow myself to be dull and happy with him. Boredom with him is an active state: he is bored with someone or something. I have a more vicious kind of boredom that I easily fall into if nothing special is happening . . . I am always trying to wake him up when he's asleep. I really am awful – I just can't bear to think of people existing when I'm not there. But then so often I don't feel as if *I* existed unless I'm the object of someone's concern ... There is NO happiness possible for me or for people closely connected with me unless I'm doing work that really interests me. Hack work isn't enough ...

8 July ... I do not know at all whether he will get through this exam ... But I think whether he passes or not is a psychological thing. Quite apart from our being lovers, as his friend I want the best for him just now. And I don't know whether my own weakness will let me ... Try and keep personal feelings in the background. But can I? Our confidence in each other is shaken ...

10 July I wish I could shake off this bruised, leaden feeling. I don't think it's really to do with Ian though obviously that accentuates it. And there is no real 'situation' there – we parted very sweetly. Why should I be so surprised at ambivalent feelings in him when my own are so ambivalent? ... It was a mistake our meeting yesterday. He suggested it but I should have had the wits to make an excuse and wait for Saturday. I am such a fool, always allowing myself to be rushed into something for a momentary gratification against my better judgement. The trivial cause of our quarrel was the business about the holiday ...

... The funny thing is that, though I have a more satisfactory physical relationship with him than I have ever had with anyone, it looks as if he were more dependent on me sexually than I on him ... I believe a feeling of inadequacy is one of the strongest motives of promiscuity. His sudden isolated homosexual venture came, I remember, at a time when he was feeling inadequate. So all the exam fever which may rouse his feelings of inadequacy may be predisposing him to a physical experiment ... Is there something in me which will cause any man to fly from me however strongly they are or have been attracted to me? Eric says 'Treat people as things' It sounds such bleak advice, yet I know there is something in it. Yet I am so made that I cannot help loving, hating, and entangling myself with people ...

... What I value in Ian far more than sexual passion is that he really loves me as a human being ... The whole question of sexual

intercourse is so complicated since one act can signify so many things
– love, hate, union, defeat, victory, destruction, revenge, curiosity,
consolation and far more as well . . . Now if Ian is acting out a kind of
symbolic annihilation of me, which I suspect he is, he will be almost
certainly bound . . . to return at intervals to see that I have not actually
been annihilated. His tears have always come at moments when,
expecting to have destroyed me, he finds he hasn't . . . I am unlucky in
not being able to put my superfluous nervous force into anything but
it's no good complaining about that. The thing is to see if I can't *for
once* do something I've always failed in . . . Well, Ian is going through
the ordeal of the exam . . . After it is over we can either have a
patched-up relationship which will inevitably end in humiliation for
one or both of us or we can make a real jump forward into something
as yet only guessed at by either of us. But I have GOT TO PAY IN
ADVANCE instead of in remorse afterwards. I am faced with the thing I
find hardest to bear – apparent coldness in the person most important
to me at the moment and the possibility of a rival . . . The Spanish
have a verb, an active verb, for doing nothing . . 'holgar' . . .

Analysis diary, 12 July   This must be the briefest account of three
years ever written. I do not know on what principle I write in this
book and not in the other. Came across this by accident to-day.
Interested to find I'd written even as much as this. No idea that there
was such a recent entry. See I dated 1st entry 1934: actually it was
1935. Closing date has now been set for analysis: end of September. I
have brought a divorce action against Tom: expect the decree
absolute at end of Sept. when he is to marry Gerti Deutsch. March
1934 must have been about when I started with Robb. Connections
with Wyn [Henderson]. Wyn is a fat woman, sexually successful on
the surface. First she helps me procure an abortion (reduces fat)
Second she encourages me to write and publish a book (secondary
result of book, I lose weight). At a party of hers Tom meets Frances.
Through her, via Robb and Adrian Stephen, I get on the way to
being analysed. I have an affair with both her sons. The second affair
with the eldest turns out to be the most satisfactory sexual relationship I have ever had. During it both he and I put on weight rapidly. I
produce a short poem as a result of my relation with Nigel. No poems
with Ian but two pieces of prose – both beginnings only which jam

up. Interesting how original preconceptions of analysis crop up again and again and at the end we are still revolving round the old themes which I see as music which will be finally gathered up and resolved. I am getting very fat very fast again but believe it is psychological and that physical measures even if I could stick to them, won't be much good. Once again, Carroll says I feel it safer to have things *inside*. Have reverted to fashion writing again [in *Sunday Pictorial*] for a living: can do it without undue anxiety. Feel panicky and oppressed over one job: doing a catalogue for a Jew who wants me to take full responsibility. Impotence, fear of failure, also very likely guilt that I am asking too much money for it ...

... Feel a great need for a husband. *If* I had a husband would like to live in the country .. a good part of the time anyway. But feel panicky at the thought of living in the country alone or with children only ...

Carroll said 'Do you *want* a husband?'

I said 'Yes'

'Any particular husband?'

'No'

'Can you imagine what he would be like?'

'Someone like you' ...

A dream about Cambridge last night: visiting girl students as a *persona grata* and enjoying a lot of fun and prestige with them. Very sorry I had never gone to Cambridge – the next best thing to be a schoolmistress. 'Of course – that is what I have always wanted to be'. Now consciously I have always hated *the idea* of being a schoolmistress, having a picture of a schoolmistress as a grotesque, unloved spinster. In practice, have always enjoyed teaching and been very fond of my class. Like teaching a lot of people more than one ... These fashion articles are a kind of indirect teaching. Advertisements, my most successful, always where I was *teaching* the public. Those who *can't*, teach. Haunted by that. But liked doing pure nonsense 'without the selling stuff' for Jaeger. All my advertising, even the best, an improved crib of someone else. Doing what a lot of people could do: doing it a shade better. No great selling schemes. Clever adaptations. My poetry more like something original, peculiar to me.

In the dream Eric kept performing feats of physical strength. Running with me up and down stairs. I was afraid of banging my head on low ceilings. A meal at which he kept forcing me to eat things I didn't want to eat. I got angry. Someone dropped a plate of food on his knee. I said 'serve you right' then saw him pale and wincing in agony. He was badly hurt in the groin: I tried to comfort him, was distressed and apprehensive. He moaned 'I shall never be able to do it again'. I knew he was very badly hurt. Repulsion strongly mixed with my pity. I woke up panting and upset.

The thought of any physical or married relation with Eric horrifying to me though I am so fond of him. I cannot bear it when he is hurt or ill – a sort of indecency in him, I feel it. I remember how I used to torture myself with fear as to how I would behave if my father was ill or in pain: my own instinct would have been to rush away and not see it. It seems unbelievable I lived in a state of complete happiness with Eric for 2 years – as happy as if with someone I was sexually in love with too and for many more years shared a room with him and only chafed when I was in love with someone else . . . It isn't his homosexuality – its a kind of helplessness in him. Just as he, touchingly, wants to look like other men, so do I want him to . . . There are times when I *want* to run down and be dirty, coarse, greedy, disorderly even to smell bad, be disgusting in my habits. If Eric were just occasionally a bit untidy or dirty. He couldn't be if he tried. Yet he will fart with the greatest enjoyment, talk about shit and vomit till I feel sick . . . I understand why Ian likes to see me grubby and untidy sometimes. There *is* something repellent about these too immaculate people. Eric is a man of catchwords. For frivolity I don't know anyone to equal him for charm. It was his gaiety, lack of pretentiousness that first attracted me. I should think Carroll probably has execrable taste in art. But it's probably a sincere taste. I've never contemplated or not for a long time having anything to do with a man who had execrable taste in art. There's snobbery for you. Heaven knows my father's was pretty poor in places. Funny how I seem to rule out or never even to meet men with my father's virtues. Uprightness, devotion to what he believed the truth, capacity for hard work etc. I am sure unsuitability or even impossibility wouldn't stop me from falling in love with Carroll in the ordinary way. No good to pretend I am squeamish about sex now. I adore giving pleasure to and receiving pleasure from a man and feeling myself in communication with another human being in the most intimate possible way. Perhaps analysts really do sleep with all their patients after a certain stage and neither patient nor analyst tells. This is obviously wild fantasy!!! Yet I really do feel as if at some point there would be a ... burst of friendship. In all my old dreams of the end of analysis I got the idea of a physical annihilation followed by an exhilarated resurrection – still tied and haltered but complete security. 'I have come through. Whatever happens it's all right now' ...

... Is my 'after September' fear not just loss of income and Tom but loss of Carroll?

* * *

Antonia and Ian Henderson spent a holiday alone at his mother Wyn's cottage at Summer's Heath, near Henley-on-Thames.

* * *

31 July   No .. 'holgar' only means 'to do nothing' in the sense of to be idle, waste time etc. Looking through this notebook, see how long-winded and stammering my writing has become. Probably from writing so much privately – nothing publicly.

This is being written in bed before breakfast at Summer's Heath.

3 August   I had a crisis of panic last night. I took Dial but it had no effect and I had to fight the whole thing out with Ian as I had hoped not to do. He was very good indeed. It was a strain for him but he did not lose his head and I managed to get back into focus again ... I feel an absolute lust for a house, possessions, a place of my own. I can hardly bear it that I am only a guest here, that the cottage does not belong to Ian and me ... an artist has to learn to live as a guest everywhere and to possess only in loving and contemplating ... And there is so often this rising tension of hysteria to be fought down since I can find no safe outlet for it. I only know the relief of tears in sleep and sometimes at analysis. For so long I have not dared to weep that now I cannot. Much too late I have the desire to make a home for a man and share a life with him. With no other man have I truly wanted this – I have only wanted to want it and in reality have hated losing the illusion of freedom. What I should be doing is making a home for my children and without the impulse of love I cannot see it as anything but a mutilated and dreary life to centre my life round

them, least of all be left to look after children without a man . . . I am
so weak that I doubt if I can behave as an ordinarily decent human
being without the support of a religion. And all my pride revolts
against admitting this . . . It may be an illusion to rely on God, yet it
makes it more possible not to lean on human beings . . . I would like,
and sometimes am able to, accept as Eric does the chaos and
contradiction in the external world and in himself but I have this
craving to find order in it . . . Yet can I ever again accept the
restrictions and superstitions of an organised religion? I feel the
Catholic religion to be the only possible one for me but I can only
accept it in a new way . . .

4 August The physical difficulties here are pretty exhausting to cope
with. Food will not keep in this hot weather. Meat turns maggoty in
24 hours, the butter melts, the milk turns sour. Ian is laid up today
with painful sunburn. The cottage is full of flies and wasps by day and
moths by night: the window sills littered with dead ones. I seem
always to be doing odd jobs in the house yet it never seems clean and
orderly.

27 August Our holiday together is over. I do not think I shall go
back to Summer's Heath. With Wyn in possession . . very much in
possession . . it is simply another house to be visited. I am glad we
made the experiment of living together like that. It was certainly a
crisis in our relationship. I am very uncertain about the future of it.
We had some of our best moments and some of our worst. At the
moment, I feel very angry with Ian. I have heard not a word since I
left. He must have known how very much I should have appreciated
a letter, however short. Yet nothing is any good from him that is not
spontaneous. There is something about the Hendersons way of life
which shocks and disgusts me: this eternal living on credit, or other
people. They are all in their way spongers, Ian less than the others,
but tainted with it. Sometimes one wonders if any of them care for
anything for its own sake. Wyn, I think at last, is really a *bad* woman . .
what Djuna would call 'unimportantly wicked'. There is something
false even about her apparent generosity. The fact is, she has nothing
to give except dope. No doubt she cannot be blamed for this and she
has genuine impulses to generosity but they seldom go further. She is

a born procuress; she will procure you any drug or distraction you want .. at a price. The motto of the whole family is 'Someone else will pay' ... he [Ian] is spoilt in so many ways – very largely Wyn's fault. She has brought them both up as if they were little princes to inherit the earth. And because they are young and charming plenty of other people have fallen into the conspiracy. I consider that Wyn has *debauched* her children .. she has tried to make them as much like herself as possible and now she wrings her hands over them. I am amused – sometimes disconcerted – to see how much she hates me under her purring softness. Well, let her hate me. She can do me no harm. If Ian lets her break us up, it means he is so weak I don't want him ...

... I hate to see him show off and pander to men. No, there is no pity for him in my heart at the moment. I am sick of being sorry for people ...

... She [Wyn] does not *want* to be bad .. She just cannot deny herself *anything*, no matter how humiliating and painful the consequences ...

I have been reading again the notes I made this time last year about myself and Basil. Somehow more truth and less distortion gets into these notebooks than into anything else. They are only a half-way house and a prop, I know. I think they will stop in their present subjective form when analysis is over and I eventually get going on work. It is significant that I began them just when I began to crack up – the year before I married Reggie. That was really the time when I went underground. Now there is very much less divergence between them and my actual behaviour. They are still a sign of my distrust of myself: I look at them when I feel confused or lose my sense of identity. They are like a photograph of myself to which I refer. It is curious how, the more vain people are, the less they have a sense of identity and pore over photographs and mirrors. One should be like an animal and be able to keep oneself clean without a looking-glass. 'They do not lie awake in the night and weep for their sins' Supposing the tiger had become 'human' instead of the ape. Or the albatross or the horse.

It is as if I kept my identity in these books. I become more anxious to show them to people – though still apprehensive ...

I should demand less of Ian because the whole thing is far less important to me than Basil was. Ian is too young, too undeveloped,

perhaps too slight in himself to be able to absorb me in the same way
... I would rather lay my bones with Basil than with any other man
even than with Robert who was the lover of my youth. I failed Basil
as much as he failed me and yet I feel we parted with honour ... I
think he's probably made the right marriage. But it would only be my
bones I laid with Basil after neither of us had any flesh or blood left to
damage ... I am losing my taste for the unhappy and unsuccessful and
misunderstood ... Yet, as Djuna says with perfect truth 'No man can
stand an ailing woman'. One's most loving friends would prefer one
to die rather than to be perpetually ill and *not* only for one's own sake!
Yet Djuna saying this, knowing it to be true, in love with Silas and
feeling she is losing him, miserable and cursing her own illness,
refuses to take steps to be cured ...

28 Aug   I have just begun Forster's Life of Dickens again. I did not
finish it before. I think that will start me off for the autumn. I want a
fact book not a fiction book. There are some wonderful things in it.
When Dickens finally left the blacking factory he so much hated, he
wept. 'With a relief so strange that it was like oppression, I went
home.'

I begin to think it a good thing Ian and I should have this short
separation ... I wish he did anything absolutely on his own, even
collected stamps! ... It is not that he is unintelligent but he is
curiously slow and uneven. He seems to understand a thing one day
and not the next ...

29 Aug   Rationally or not, I feel outraged at Ian's not having written
to me all this week ... there is something so ungenerous in this
behaviour. Probably I made a mistake in treating him as an equal ...
There is nothing to be done but wait at the moment and see whether
all the good things I have seen in him are my own imagination or ...
whether they justify my going on.

I am pretty sure the Henderson family is having a nice little klatsch
on their own. Nigel ought to have been hard at work to-day and he
has not come up. So Wyn must have repented of her moral mother
mood. And Ian has probably relapsed on the maternal bosom. Well,
let them have their fun. We shall see. They're all so tangled up
together they can't really disentangle themselves. Susan [Henderson,

Wyn's daughter] shows a lot of sense in having got away ... [Wyn will] do her best to separate Ian from me and I shall be interested to see whether she does it or not. Because I am more important to Ian than the others have been, she'll make a real move to break us up. It remains to be seen whether she will have the self-control to make the right one ...

I think if I really want to be Ian's friend, I must stand by him now in spite of being hurt and resentful of his treatment of me. If I throw him over nothing would please Wyn more than to comfort him and dope him with women chosen by herself ... Wyn has always weaned him from everything he was likely to care about on his own – such as politics. All her talk about the cottage being 'his'. *He* has paid for everything. I know she does try not to be possessive about him but it is too hard for her. It is remarkable the way that she tries always to part people from their money or their possessions on the grounds that it is to their advantage and to offer them substitutes of her own choosing ...

I wonder if being fat is taking up more room in the world than one is entitled to as a compensation for feeling deprived of power? Eunuchs become fat, so frequently do women after the menopause and after childbirth. The last I have noticed very much when they have some resistance to having the child. Women who really want childen and feel a sense of power in having them, usually regain their figures. Eric wants to be fat: his thinness seems to be pathological . . as if he deliberately took up *less* room than he was entitled to. I think part of my fat is due to lack of recognition. When I feel I am being neglected or ignored or deprived of my rights, I put on weight quickly. It was very remarkable how very quickly I lost it during the few weeks I was with Robert. It is notable that both Ian and I have got fatter since we were together ...

I wish I could stop smoking ... I simply cannot believe I could do any work without them. Yet perhaps if I could break myself of this compulsive habit, I might progress in work instead of sticking always at the same point ...

Carroll assures me that he is the man I want . . not a man like him but himself. And that I think I cannot possibly attract him because I am too bad ... That seems to work out in my relations with other men. Having attracted someone by wit, gaiety, or apparent independence, I usually take great pains to lose all semblance of these qualities and become dull, melancholy and abjectly dependent. So I must feel there is something unbelievably shameful in the *desire* to attract . . . Djuna has done the same thing with Silas. And she goes on clinging to him although she *knows* it is the wrong thing to do.

I think this 'protective' idea about men is very largely a fiction. I have not found men protective except in very short spells . . . Women are far more protective than men, both to men and to each other. Certainly a man likes to feel protective now and then. But I think he likes best hurting you and – *if you don't complain* – being sorry afterwards . . .

3 Sept   The last bout of analysis which I have so much dreaded is now on. Actually, though I am being driven hard, I am in far better spirits and less inclined to melancholy and depression than during the break.

He says I have spent nearly all my time in analysis in endeavouring to hide my true nature from him and have only succeeded in hiding it from myself.

He says that my impulses are exceedingly cruel, that any anger or cruelty I have expressed are mild compared to what I really feel and that it all centres round money which is my real passion and preoccupation. Not at all the sort of person I would like to think myself . . . I can never grasp *in feeling* the fact that if I became aware of such violent impulses, I should be impelled to *act* on them. Yet I can become aware of an impulse to destroy my mother without the least likelihood of actually killing her! . . .

. . . It is an exquisite pleasure to me to comfort someone *I* have hurt. Much more ready to do this than comfort those injured by others. Yes. I *have* a torturer's nature . . .

The strongest emotions I feel are rage, terror and desire to possess. I am very nervous of *asking* directly for anything I want. I prefer to get it by force or cunning. I love getting presents but think I am suspicious of them as putting me under an obligation to the giver.

I have passionately wanted money ever since I was little, yet again and again I have thrown away opportunities of making it and have always used it to get myself into difficulties when I have had it.

It occurred to me to-day that it would be an ideal profession to be a fan dancer: to do something which gave one a guilty pleasure and the onlookers a guilty pleasure and to be well paid for it . . .

I want both to be the only person benefited by psycho-analysis and also to drag everyone else to be analysed in order that they may go through as much humiliation as I have . . . I seem to look on myself as sub-human or super-human, never as just 'human' and I would prefer to be called a devil to an ordinary human being. I am like Susan, I can't bear not to be best at everything. While admiring Tom's book [*The Man Below* (1939)] I have great pleasure in finding its weaknesses and though I cannot help admitting there are passages in it far beyond my own powers, I feel resentful of this and that in some way such passages must be due to my influence or to Tom's having stolen them from me. Yet even in his earliest, crudest work . . . there are indications of such descriptive powers . . .

I see now the question is not is there a God, but if there is, is he necessarily of the kind official Christianity states? . . .

I can see why people who may be passionate lovers in private may disown each other in public. They are ashamed of what draws them together.

What sort of things make me instinctively annoyed if my attention is drawn to them

(1) Suggestions that my illness is 'all imagination'. In a sense that is perfectly true. Well, what an imagination . . why not use it for something more interesting?

(2) Queries 'How do you spend your money?'

(3) References to the name of 'Botting' (much better lately: still wish I had had another name but feel awfully sheepish about 'Antonia White'. Such a transparent affectation!)

(4) References to my being fat. Well, if I really hate being fat, why not diet or take more exercise?

(5) 'Have you written anything lately?' or 'When are you going to write another book?' Often feel as if I *had* written several masterpieces and they ought to know about them. Or that it should be obvious to them that in my own time I *shall* write masterpieces . . .

(6) Suggestions that I don't understand what people are like (Feel I am so superior that *of course* I must understand what inferior people are like) . . .

Note The last 2 of these books have been filled between June 13 and

Sept 3 – a period of only 7 weeks. They have been done at odd times as I felt inclined and except for 14 days holiday (when I wrote practically nothing) during a fairly full working time. If I could turn this on to outside work, I could get quite a lot done without 'making' time. This represents roughly . . . 21,000 words . . . say between ¼ and ⅓ of a full length novel . . .

11 Sept   The beginning of the last week of analysis (anal lusis). This diary rapidly becoming as unprintable as the present sessions. War suspense everywhere. Irony if just as I am through with analysis, war breaks out. Impossible, of course, for the megalomaniac unconscious not to think the two connected. Practically as unlucky for me if there's a war as for everyone else and lucky that I shall have finished treatment for the present and so be more able to deal with difficult situations. Have decided that the best Dennis [Carroll] can do for me is – *literally* – to 'make an honest woman of me'. No easy task. He is pressing very hard on the sorest spots but, though I find the sessions trying and get no quarter from him and have very restless and nightmarish nights, I am not, so far, depressed. I must be tougher, or he could not turn the screw like this. He tells me I have the nature of a torturer, that my ruling passion is money, that my voice is powerful and aggressive, frequently rising to a scream and that I tend literally to talk people to death. Whereas I would *like* to write them to life!

* * *

Wallace and Maud Hurnall invited Lyndall and Susan to stay at their cottage in the country this summer. The Hurnalls were friends, possibly relatives, of Oswald Norton, Christine Botting's former lover.

* * *

I have been staying for a day at the Hurnalls. Very curious, these women who 'only live for others'. On paper Maud is running over with motherly sympathy: in conversation she is malicious. Neither she nor Wallace give the impression of having the least interest outside their own affairs. Every name she mentions – all people unknown to me – leads her rambling on to disconnected facts about them and their relatives. She delights specially in retailing every kind of accident, illness and financial disaster. Says she cannot bear even to *mention* money but it is always in her conversation and she hinted very broadly that she expected me to pay for the children though nothing was said of this in her 'invitation' to them. Her face fell when I suggested paying what I pay at the cottage: she would not *name* any sum but I know she will feel she has not been paid enough. I gave her 30/–, considerably more than I pay at Binesfield and I am sure mother does not lose on that. I don't think she much liked their asking for second helpings! . . .

Jack was her favourite son. But she said what [bad] luck his dying when he might have contributed some money to the family and 'Of course, if he'd lived, we should have had heavy doctor's bills. As it was, they were less than they might have been because he was a Scientist'. . . She has some very beautiful old china and furniture which she obviously appreciates and cares for very much. Susan unfortunately trod on and chipped a rare old plate of 'Old Rose' willow pattern (a simpler willow pattern with roses round the edge) which Wallace had carelessly put down for the dog. It was not the child's fault but I am sure she will hold it against her and me for life. She is very bitter . . . against my mother – a story which may be true of her 'defiling' their bathroom – repeated often and with horrified gusto . . .

Oswald has now got a tobacconist's shop, acquired very characteristically. A man was willing to pay for it outright, but Claudine nipped in and paid a deposit and Oswald is to pay the balance 'out of profits' which, of course, he and the Hurnalls are convinced will be handsome! . . .

My children certainly *are* a responsibility but one that I am becoming inured to gradually. I do want (faintly) to do the best for them . . . and of course for myself too . . . I am . . . a little frightened of them . . . I expected them to be . . . more interested in me . . . I know my first lesson is the one people have tried to din into me all my life; the necessity of managing money sensibly . . . I see Susan daily dissipating her quite remarkable powers of understanding in dull, monotonous fantasies. She leads a complete other life as a horse. 'Susan on four legs' . . the horse that can run faster than any other horse but is always cruelly treated. Both children really *feel the need* of harsh treatment sometimes. I want Susan to have every opportunity of *real* achievement; that is why I want her to go to a school where she will have rivals worthy of her . . .

... If I could make Susan see that the wasp stings her because it's *frightened* of her ...

* * *

Antonia went into a nursing home for two weeks, ostensibly to lose weight. Lyndall has suggested that she underwent an abortion and sterilisation at the same time but no written proof has been produced, and it would be surprising, bearing in mind her frequent references to her earlier abortion, that she should have made no references to this one.

Antonia does, however, refer to a 'severe operation' when looking back over her diary for the following year (1939), and although there are gaps in the 1939 diary during which such an operation might have occurred, it is possible that she was referring to what had in fact happened in October 1938.

* * *

23 Oct, Nursing Home, 3 Devonshire Terrace   Nurses on night duty – 2 free nights a month. Often stay out during morning on night duty: sleep 5–6 hours in afternoon ...

25 Oct   Have been extremely languid and depressed ever since I came here. It is not the very low diet but the old unconscious trying to frighten me off getting rid of my fat. I have decided to stick out the second week in spite of it. I had hoped to have a clear head here – to get on with German, Italian etc. and to read some history. But I have been so heavy and tired all the time that I can only manage snatches of *War and Peace* and *Sherlock Holmes*. I am supposed to have done a detailed criticism of Emily's book – I have skimmed through it but that is all.

The end of this year really ought to bring me some kind of new beginning. I have got a new place to live [Cornwall Gardens] – the first time I have ever rented somewhere on my own. Then analysis is, temporarily, anyway, over. This stabilisation of the glands ought to settle the fat question satisfactorily ...

I begin to think it is best to try hard to send the children to a country school. Money is the great difficulty ... What they both long for is a school in the country. Can only write a few words at a time ... Before I came in I was in a state of feverish energy over the house. I have known this sort of state suddenly yield and a violent impulse of energy come over me to pursue some new line – as when I suddenly got work out of St Denis ...

I must somehow feel safer and more powerful fat ... Certainly this compulsory loss of weight is accompanied by extreme mental and physical fatigue, anxiety, lack of interest and sense of impotence. *Later* This state seems to get worse instead of better. A thick cloud has settled over everything – complete accidia [sic]. I do not even want anything – yet as always I am afraid of drifting – of giving myself up to the bad state and accepting it. Everything is without savour, like my food here. To continue in such a state really would be [sentence unfinished].

26 Oct There is just a bit of time in the morning – about 7 when nurse brings me tea when I wake up for a little. My eyes are still tired but I feel more alive – like this early tea in a room with the lamps on, a feeling of a midnight feast – outside it is not quite light and people are going to work.

I think I am not *serious* enough! Sometimes when I look through the *New Statesman* ... I see all the lists of books on social, economic, ethical, historical, philosophical subjects I feel ... that I am a useless frivolous creature ...

Oh this fear, fear, fear, fear, fear. This terror of making a mistake ... fear of other people's opinions – fear of damnation – fear of not making the best of oneself – fear of sin, dishonour, God knows what.

Particularly the fear of making a mistake. Certainly mistakes can be fatal. I always feel if I can't do a thing perfectly the first time I shall never do it at all and it's not worth trying. I feel the most extraordinary shame when it is pointed out that I have made a mistake ...

To write a play would satisfy all my ambitions. It would make me widely known, it would bring me in considerable money and I should really enjoy the process once I got started. It would free me from the drudgery of Fleet St. articles, put up my prices on them, leave me free for months at a time. And it is a nice compact piece of work, unlike a novel; it could be done in a few weeks ...

... of course I take it for granted I *could* write a play 'if only I had a plot'. Eric constantly screams at me 'any old plot ... no plot'.

Well, who do I know who would make good characters on the stage?

My mother

Auntie Bee

Sir William [Crawford]

Peggy [Guggenheim]

Siepmann

Reggie

Something might be made of the vamp – the sexual dazzler at home . . .

2 nurses making a bed. Looking at everything

It *is* a bit better today. Have got on a little with my patchwork . . .

Lot of domestic problems to solve – children – school – May [Antonia's housekeeper]. All these could be solved with money . . . Again I can track down my vague fears to a common base – fear of loss. What are the things I have been fearing to lose –

the new house and things for it such as stove . . .

my children's affection

services of a maid . . .

help from Silas . . .

Old Logan talking about the dedication of the artist – a bachelor with a comfortable income.

29 Oct   . . . The first 3 times I made money –

(1) round about 15 or 16   Government office – this was *not* patriotism but excitement of pay envelope plus doing what other people approved of

(2) going as governess,   again lure of money – £10 + being independent, getting away from home, feeling grown-up

(3) finding a way to make money by my own work not just doing an employee's set task – impulse to this *desire to give a present*.

Result . . . far more profitable!

1st salary as governess = £30 a year

1st salary in advertising = £150 a year

13 Dec   A year since Ian and I were first lovers. Several weeks since I have stopped to think at all. I am caught up in a whirl of writing articles, furnishing houses, spending quantities of money in advance and hoping I shall make enough to catch up. I feel a little guilty and frightened at the thought of this new material expansion: have I a *right* to a flat *and* a cottage ... I seem to have a tremendous lust for *objects* .. not clothes now but furniture ...

It is very hard to economise with Ian around. He goes on spending my money and his as if he *were* earning money himself.

He suddenly seemed a new person when the camera idea came up. Now I wonder if it was not largely relief at not having to cram any more for the C[ivil] S[ervice]. I do wish he weren't quite so vague ... He certainly takes a lot more out of the world than he contributes to it. But we all spoil him and so I suppose it's our fault. There is something so lovable and honest about him ... But greedy! He is getting much too fat ...

... I saw Charlotte [d'Erlanger] today in a shop. I did not recognise her at first. I merely thought 'There is a woman who looks a little like Charlotte but she is far too old to *be* Charlotte'. Her beauty was gone, yet it was hard to say how. Her cheeks hollower, more lined; her skin sallower, her nose looking gaunt. But her voice, figure, everything else the same. No doubt I could have rediscovered her beauty, knowing where to look. Which is, I suppose, why we long for people who have known us when we were young and *who know where to look*.

Just now again I am acutely conscious of the difference in age between Ian and myself. It is almost always I myself who take a perverse pleasure in bringing it up. Yet he is aware of it all the time – and discounts or accepts it as one of the *facts* in our lives. I suppose I *can't* accept it and that's why I harp on it ... Just now I so awfully want a man for the rest of my life and it seems to me that only a very young woman can hope for that. I am terribly envious of Gerti – not because she has Tom in particular but because she has a husband. I feel fearfully humiliated not having one myself ... In actual practice I would hate to be married to Ian as we both are.

A month or two ago I was saying to Nigel 'Wait and see. I cannot bear very much more of this. There will come a time when the sheer boredom of it will get me down'. Now lately I have felt firm and deep with Ian again ... Sometimes I feel he is all I shall ever want again from a man. I feel tender to him, passionate, full of hope for him. And then comes the inevitable reaction – what *is* he? Vain, greedy, lazy, colourless ... If he hadn't got this ... pathetic slowness of a creature hampered in some way ... I would long ago have given him up ...

1939

13 Feb　Chaos is come again so I must see where I've gone wrong ...
(1) Too much occupied with self ...
(2) Book is so painful and terrifying I can barely even think about it ...
(3) Pleasure in reading even spoilt because I am so envious of the characters whose love ends happily ...

I wish to heaven I were single minded – but I go in crazes like a child – now this thing, now that, seems the most important and I drop it before I have attained any real mastery of it. I am *always* the amateur.

War menace *is* real to me now: makes me feel terribly frightened and insecure but anxious to acquit myself well ...

I am very much interested in the change in Ian since his overdraft stopped. His very appearance has changed. He is once more frank, sweet, warm and modest instead of being peevish, lazy, touchy and vindictive ...

A true belief in God would be the strongest spring of action and happiness ...

One can call 'God' *the nature of things* perhaps. It is confusing to say 'God' because of all the church associations. This 'God' must be something outside oneself, immensely transcending oneself and yet something of which one feels a part.

I have been struck by finding the same thought within a few days in two very different places – in George Eliot and in an American magazine. That is the idea of a person's horror at a crime coming not from the crime but from the fact that *they* have committed it ...

Christ said 'bear ye one another's burdens' which is certainly much easier than bearing one's own ... Two people flying madly from something and colliding with each other may seem to have been rushing into each other's arms – perhaps this is the explanation of much 'falling in love' When their pursuing terrors catch up with them they will run with the same speed *away* from each other.

I remember my headlong flight to Silas after Tom's rejection of me . . .

I just wonder about Tom and Gerti. Things aren't altogether right with them . . they may be one day. But Tom must have been badly needing action of a benevolent kind to appease his guilt over me and Frances and she was flying from other fears — insecurity, political troubles, etc. Why, if she wants a child so much, does she not have one now? Tom's position would justify it, even though he has to pay me £200 a year. But she says she will not until she can have a nurse etc. . . .

17 Feb   I don't know if notes will help the book jam . . .

I think I tried rather feebly to *invent* a subject. Then with relief, also with guilt, fell back on the old autobiographical subject. I talked about this with Ian, even got enthusiastic, saw various scenes and possibilities very vividly, but as soon as I began to try the first chapter, it began to split and dissolve . . .

1 March   The shock last night when Ian was cold and unenthusiastic about the first bit of the book which I'd managed to write. I burnt it. I . . . hoped he would stop me . . . He explained how tired he was and unreceptive . . that there were good things and it was only too short-circuited. He was right too. I want to start again today but I am stuck . . . I wrote to please him and he wasn't pleased . . . Such *shame* when a person who is not themselves a writer criticises me. Is there a hint here? I feel no shame when someone who *is* a writer points out faults . . . Is that because other writers accept me as one of themselves and so the awful doubt '*Am* I a writer?' does not arise . . .

I must not forget that my father was not at all unsympathetic about my 2nd book and I read it to him with no misgivings. But obviously he judged me by too high standards and felt that if I weren't George Meredith full grown . . . I was no good. He didn't really feel easy about anything I'd done until someone else had praised it . . .

. . . I always feel that, unless I produce a good piece of writing I shall cease to be loved . . .

I suppose that I can do journalism because I don't look on it as a means of gaining love but only as a means of gaining money . . .

I know writing too is a way of 'putting myself across'. I *want* to do that . . . I feel my own life is all I know yet the mere fact that it is my life distorts it. But I cannot invent . . .

When I am writing well, I am so happy. Everything falls into place.

My father is dead. I feel I shall never be at peace with his ghost until I have shown the full force of my love and my hatred of him, neither of which I showed in his life. Yet I feel too that he would never forgive me if I wrote about him – that it is the unforgivable sin to expose his nakedness to the world . . .

I could not live by the rule of the Catholic Church. But the morality of which Carroll made me conscious is one that I can at least attempt to live up to . . .

. . . [Discussing the plot of *The Lost Traveller*] *Subjects* have always been my difficulty . . . They very rarely occur to me spontaneously . . . I need always to have something suggested to me. Is that hangover of schooldays where the subject was always set?

I don't agree plot not important. It is half the novelist's job to create situations. The plot is often the most characteristic thing of a writer. H[enry] James' subjects are very much more revealing than his style.

Before theory of unconscious all motives had to be explicable. The fact that we now know that most people are ignorant of their own motives or give entirely wrong reasons for them . . .

Weddings and funerals

The effects of my grandfather [Frederick Botting]'s death?

He [her father] had about 10 years before he retired, during [which] most of his trouble came from me and from money worries . . .

He treated his wife like a child, his daughter like a wife. . . .

To understand is a way of loving those to whom love is difficult. Do we try to root out of our children our own faults, not appreciating their virtues?

In fact, can we see in our children nothing more than our own faults . . .

I think I am a reporter, not an inventor . . .

The revelation of the interaction of 3 characters on each other.

With my grandfather's death one phase of my father's life ended and perhaps my own childhood came to an end . . .

26 March ... Reading George Sand's and Flaubert's letters. Her warmth, geniality, tolerance compared to his anxiety, narrowness, fear of life. They really cared for each other. She is like the man, he like the woman. If Sand was a Lesbian she has the strong maternal feeling so typical of the Lesbian ...

... Flaubert says the great thing for a novelist is to be able to go out into his characters instead of drawing them into himself. The effort of *imagining* people and scenes was so tremendous for him that he dared not interrupt it by any new stimulus from life and real people. He dared not go and stay with George Sand while he was writing *L'Education* for fear of this ... He seems to write books such as *Bovary* and *L'Education* as a penance ...

4 April ... Ian brought himself to go for me last night. He said among other things that I was smug, vinegarish, a grievance monger, bourgeois and unresilient. That I was rigid, unable to let myself go or live by my instincts, unaware of other people's feelings and frequently bludgeoning and indelicate. All this is true ...

He praises and loves my body. It is always strange to me when any man has a strong feeling about my body ...

Why is it I can't be 'natural'. And what *is* 'natural' to me? To be alternately gay and sad, lazy and energetic ... The silly thing is I'm always even now trying to be 'good' .. whatever I mean by that ...

It's a queer thing that I've so much oftener been loved for my body than for my character ... I think I know almost nothing at all about love: I am so greedy of *admiration*, so resentful if I don't get it.

I have turned 40 now. Is there *nothing* I won't do for money and admiration?

It is true I was systematically educated to mistrust and check every natural impulse. Yet the nuns were by no means bad judges of character ...

I think the happiest time of my life, when I was least afraid of public opinion, was at St Paul's ...

Did Christ really show us how to live? There is something repellent in the idea of Christian meekness, loving all men equally. It is not natural – perhaps it is supernatural. If nature were the only thing, there would be no such thing as art. So to be a Christian may be to be an artist with one's nature – composing and disciplining its elements . . . A life spent in trying hopelessly to conform to this quite arbitrary pattern would obviously be miserable and frustrated . . .

22 July   . . . The things which seem so clear, definite and desirable by day, change at night exactly as light and sound change. I was idly looking at *Jacob's Room* to-night. It exasperated yet charmed me. Here was an attempt to relate day and night. She [Virginia Woolf] lays her little strands side by side instead of working them into a pattern. But perhaps it is because there is no solid structure underneath that it leaves me with this curious empty and dissatisfied feeling. In the last book it is beaten out so thin that it is threadbare.

Life may be entirely meaningless and yet I feel that in art you must impose a form on it. The most beautiful reproduction of sounds and colours and atmospheres is somehow unsatisfactory . . .

Something tells me I have got to a critical point in my life where I must either go forward or back but cannot stand still . . . Some of my activities for the next few months, are already decided for me . . provided there isn't a war. But there is plenty of free time in which to do all sorts of other things . . . At the moment idling and frittering do not matter so much: I have the excuse of recent illness for 'going slow' and have not very much energy . . .

The point is that I do not from *any* view want to spend the rest of my life doing nothing but fashion articles and scraps of journalism. And merely reading or looking at other people's work isn't good enough. I want a *working* centre of my own. Good resolutions to do this aren't enough. I've tried them for 20 years and I invariably break them. I don't any more bitterly resent having to make a living. I get quite a lot of satisfaction out of it. The more completely mechanical the work, the better I like it. Thus I prefer doing fashion articles to the borderline articles for *Picture Post*. I get neither the mechanical pleasure of a definite job competently done nor the pleasure of running free from the latter. And in life, emotional complications and tearing up by the roots bore me. Those people seem to be in a hopeless pathological state and I know now that I can do nothing about them . . . I am very happy in my relationship with Ian and we both feel that is alive and growing . . . But to swell it in my imagination till it filled my whole life would be to destroy it . . . it is vital for me to find my own centre and live from it . . . But how to find it? I can only do it negatively at the moment, saying 'This or that is not necessary to me' . . .

. . . With Tom married to another woman and absorbed by a difficult job and new interests, only a kind of shorthand is possible between us. In struggling to preserve what we had we are likely to wreck his marriage and perhaps to destroy something between us. But these necessary renunciations leave me with a great many blank spaces in my life and the emotional force that went into the relationship unused. I feel like someone with a lot of spare capital to invest and not knowing the best place to invest it. The way I always come back to money metaphors! I certainly am preoccupied with money . . there is not a day when I do not dwell on it or talk about it in some way. Only I don't feel so guilty about it as I did . . rather the other way . . a sort of swaggering defiance . . . Uncomfortably like the typical 1920s attitude towards sex. I still can't make it very successfully, however. Perhaps the 1920s deliberately played sex small and made it seem a kind of parlour game just because they dared not acknowledge to themselves that they wanted it badly and wanted a great deal of it. They frittered it away in small sums . . .

Yet when I am honest, I don't feel that I have the power or the originality of a writer like Joyce or Gerald Brennan or Djuna . . . I like success . . . I am pleased when I sell 4000 coats from a *Sunday Pic[torial]* article and I am pleased when poets genuinely like a poem of mine . . . But I like to do it all off my own bat. I just *cannot* immerse myself in impersonal 'service' or subscribe to a doctrine or go in for organised charity or co-operative work . . . It requires constant discipline for me even to recognise other people's needs and rights but that's something I *am* willing to do now. Only I can't make a whole life just out of remembering to hold back and make allowances . . .

One thing about getting older is that one's choice inevitably narrows. When you are young, if you have any life and power, you feel there is *nothing* you couldn't do if only you concentrated on it. The only fear that faces me now is does that power contract until one can only do what one has been in the habit of doing? I do not think it has quite reached that point with me but there *is* a danger, I think, if I do not very soon find a new direction. I definitely don't think I am working to 'capacity' yet. The last few years have shown me that I have a good deal of nervous energy. And since some of that must have been released by analysis I should be 'in funds' there . . .

FOUR

November 1939–1950

The War brought with it Antonia's return to the Catholic Church. It also brought the collapse of most of the outlets for her freelance writing. In the earlier months of 1939, however, she had written a play based on her nursing-home experiences, entitled *Three in a Room*, which she was now trying to place. It was eventually staged at the Oldham Repertory Theatre in 1944, and was published in a French's acting edition. Other war casualties were the flat at Cornwall Gardens and the affair with Ian Henderson – who joined the RAF.

Antonia went to stay first with Douglas and Kathleen McClean at Rabley Willows, near South Mimms, in 1939, with John and Clement Davenport† at Marshfield, Wiltshire, in 1940, and finally with Ian Black at Linden Gardens, Notting Hill, in 1941. Lyndall went to live with Tom and Gerti in the cottage next to Wyn Henderson's at Summer's Heath near Henley on Thames, Oxfordshire. In 1942 Antonia moved to a flat in Thurloe Street and then to one at 13 Ashburn Gardens. Both these flats were shared with Ronald Moody and his wife Hélène.† Lyndall was sent to a boarding school at Headington, Oxford, Susan to the Godolphin School, Salisbury.

During the War Antonia had jobs at the BBC (1940) and at the SOE (Special Operations Executive) (1943). After the War she was asked by Hamish Hamilton to translate Maupassant's *A Woman's Life* (1948). She won the Prix Clairouin with her version. It was to be the first of more than thirty translations from the French. She also completed her second novel, *The Lost Traveller* (1950) and started to work on her third, *The Sugar House* (1952).

The first entry of 1939, mentions 'the Brittany book'. Antonia had evidently planned to extend 'The Moment of Truth' into a novel, but this proved only another of her 'famous beginnings', as did *Crosshanger Court* (presumably based on Hangover Hall), and a book on George Sand.

1939

Analysis diary, Nov   Still waiting for revelation: key to unlock. Setback and disappointment over play has caused old trouble ... Great deal of money trouble lately between self and Tom. Cutting down of alimony ... Extreme resentment at feeling forced by Tom to pay insurances ...

I still hate being asked exactly how much money I have ... If I let Eric help me over money, I ought to do some work ... Do I or do I not seriously want to write? ... Nothing else seems really satisfactory since I can't see anything else at which I would get beyond a certain point. Languages, yes, but they are too passive as an end in themselves ...

Put it this way. You may not want to *write*, but you want to tell someone something. You love writing letters. You also want to display yourself to people. But you are afraid that this telling and displaying may expose you to contempt. Also that in some way it may impoverish you. That what you give will be no longer yours – you will be depleted. And yet you want to get rid of it. I believe the book should be about my father. If some of the trouble comes from having my father inside me, I should get him out. Tom is a very good ... audience for my book. The Brittany book [unfinished novel] feels too much like an attack on him ...

... It is mainly as humiliation that I feel the divorce. That it rebounds on me. 'There goes a woman who couldn't keep her husband. Look at her. It's not surprising, is it?' ...

... Why am I so frightened of the word 'impersonal' when in practice I *know* that impersonal contemplation brings the greatest happiness and release, far more than sex or 'pleasure' and that it is not conditional on outward things. How seldom I am satisfied with something as it is and therefore cannot wholly give myself up to it. When I am writing, I must always be smoking or nibbling. I *feel* that it helps me to concentrate. Actually I am pretty sure that it *prevents* me from concentrating. I put into smoke what I should put into words. Something to hold on to: something to protect myself ...

For the first time it is *possible* for me to live honestly as regards money if I try. If I get into debt now, it is from pure perversity. I get extravagant and anxious when I go to London. Extravagance is I am sure a symptom of anxiety with me. I was managing very well until this business about the play [*Three in a Room*]. I obviously thought it a better job in its own line than it is. It isn't a work of art, but I thought it quite good of its kind. I am reluctant to make alterations though I feel it needs some that I wouldn't mind making. But this coldness of reception was obviously a great disappointment to me. Maybe I haven't the patience and toughness a playwright needs ...

... Is the craving for a cigarette expression of horror of the void? Daren't experience *emptiness* . . like annihilation. Starvation diet produced complete numbness of mind and extreme depression. I am always so busy stuffing something into my mind or my mouth that I very seldom experience real hunger ...

See 18 months ago reduced my wants to 3.

Ian or a man like him

money situation clear

work clear

Well, I have 1, and 2 now. Both are compromises in a way. The money situation clear does not mean that I have everything I want but it does mean that, for the moment, I need have no anxiety about money. In many ways my relationship with Ian is meagre and incomplete yet it is *something*.

2 Dec, Rabley Having made no entries for months it is no good trying to recapitulate.

Until the November gales stripped the trees almost in one night the leaves were wonderful in colouring. I have not seen an autumn 'through' in the country since the last war when I was at the Latteys. My situation is curiously like that of 1916–17. I am living in someone else's house, have very little money ...

In a fog the safest guide is a blind man. This a '*sortes*' from Julien Green[†] to whose journal I turn for some light ... he always used to begin his books 'blind': simply writing a page and then letting another come. In his later books he says that will no longer do for him. His mind is like a horse that knows its way back to its own stable. Since I feel so much sympathy with Julien Green and so many resemblances I feel he might be useful in my present uncertainty and inability to work. Carroll also suggested it might be my best way to work at the moment . . simply let go and make no plan. Hitherto I have always found this method leads to a dead end. But I have not seriously tried it since analysis. In a sense I tried it in the play and it was not unsuccessful. I did however have a vague idea of the principal characters . . .

4 Dec   Julien Green says that he got rid of his sadness 'en la faisant passer dans ses livres'. I discovered in analysis that the main cause of my own melancholy and paralysis was . . . repressed rage . . . what I feel when I begin to write anything is a complete *lack* of power. My mind seems to go to pieces. Or else I find I have come to some point which frightens me . . like the 'free' story which led to my father's corpse. I have got very fat during the last few weeks: quite marked since the check over the play. I can see I'm frightened at parting with anything. Yet I like to give out of affection but cannot bear having anything *forced out* of me or taken from me. This money situation with Tom has stirred up a great deal of hostility and I feel I could do real violence to the whole Hopkinson family. I can't forgive them for not loving me . . . I'm sulking in my tent and don't want to pit myself against the world.

It seems to give me a perverse satisfaction to have something to hate. I find myself getting excited even at the clashes between Douglas and Kathleen. This appals me and I know that love would be far more satisfactory. But something in me delights in violence.

9 Dec   I began 'Crosshanger Court' [working title of unfinished novel] a few days ago. I find it slow and difficult and am not sure whether to treat it realistically or from an angle. But I have a feeling about it that I have not had so far about anything else I have tried to write that the book *exists somewhere* and that it is just a question of searching it out.

The other day there was a heavy white mist. All the hedges were beaded with water-drops and occasionally a little shower pattered down from the trees. It was so silent that you could here [sic] the noise of the streams running in the ditches . . . In the churchyard at Ridge a square tomb with a stone cushion and an open book on it. 'There shall be no more condemnation to them that are now in Christ Jesus for they walk not in the flesh but in the spirit' . . .

31 Dec Frosty mornings . . . Spiders webs covered in frost. Snow . . .
Today last day of year. It has been full of 'events'. A severe operation, the war, my mother's death on Dec 17th. One can only plan one's life in a very general way for next year. Concrete things I want to do are to finish play. If I get it put on, I want to put Binesfield in order and get on to a book.

. . . To try as he [Spinosa] says to convert passive emotions into active ones. To get more control of myself and to *understand* more of the outside world . . . To make something much stronger and more definite of my relation to the children . . .

1940

4 Jan, Culham [Court] Suppose a play in which every character was by accident deprived of the thing they most valued . . money, beauty etc.

14 Jan With any luck my income for next year (1941) should be about £500.

17 Jan . . . I *MUST* get the play finished and out of the way and get going on a book . . .

15 March Second draft of play was finished on March 1st. Binesfield now completely furnished, redecorated and repaired. I take the children away for a month on Monday. After that, in the middle of April I mean to start straight in on the book [*Crosshanger Court*] and keep to a schedule of 7,500 words a week . . .

13 May I have begun the book and hope to keep up at any rate 5000 words a week . . .
At the end of March at the cottage the daffodils and hyacinths were just coming out . . . and kingcups in the meadows.
When I got back to Rabley in the latter part of April the white plum . . . blossom was out . . .

... On May 1st I dismantled the flat [Cornwall Gardens] and did it without sadness, though I still feel as if it existed, with all its furniture somewhere. It was the pleasantest place I ever had to live in and the most doomed to ill-luck.

... The war is in full swing now since the invasion of Norway, Holland and Belgium and it can hardly be long before England feels the pinch. Air raids are what we are all waiting for ... I suppose one always feel[s] as long as they are only a possibility that one will be one of the survivors ... I don't in the least want to die yet for I feel I've only just begun to get any control of myself or my life.

I think I have changed during the last year more than at any other time of my life. When I look back and remember how I used to fall violently in love and become entirely preoccupied with one person and the impression I was making on them, I can hardly recapture the feeling.

People have far less power over me than they did ...

28 May   The Belgians have surrendered ... It is England and France now against Germany. If we win it is at the cost of the most terrible sacrifice ever known. Shall we forget and settle down to our old ways?

... a woman in love will lose overnight every sense of values she had before and become almost unrecognisable. The same thing does not seem to happen to a man. However violent his passion, it does not invade his whole nature and change it ...

* * *

Lyndall and Susan had been evacuated to Tom's parents in Westmorland, but Antonia now took them to the Malting House, Marshfield, near Chippenham, where John and Clement Davenport kept open house for artists during the War. Other members of the house party were Dylan and Caitlin Thomas and William Glock,[†] who was conducting an affair with Clement in the basement.

* * *

8 Jun, Chippenham ... The last fortnight I have been intensely restless, partly the war, partly the two egoisms of Rabley between which I am feeling more crushed than usual. This invitation from the Davenports came just when I felt I could bear no more and is just what I want. To be able to talk freely, read, hear music . . I had forgotten what it was like. I feel like one of the shades in Homer who has just had a good draught of blood. Lovely 18th century house of grey Cotswold stone with arched niches full of books and beautiful doors. A walled garden: cornflowers, sweet williams, guelder roses ... and plenty of vast waste space in the old Malting House. everything I can't have at the cottage. Future more unplannable than ever. We may be invaded at any time. Impossible to realise one may *stop* completely at any moment. Here there is such a strong sense of continuity that the war seems much farther away than at Rabley. A composer, Lennox Berkeley, with a face I like very much, is sharing here; also a fantastic Anglican clergyman, Cyril Tomkinson, who gesticulates, minces, plays with a silk handkerchief while he talks ... of the love of God.

12 June   Italy came into the war last night. The Germans are 30 miles from Paris ... In a few weeks perhaps everything one has been accustomed to ... care for may have been destroyed and one will be a prisoner in an invaded country waiting to be destroyed oneself.

Yesterday after weeks of brilliant clear weather the sky clouded over – at 10 a.m. . . . . The grey stone houses were almost white against the muffled sky, standing out sharply as if in limelight.

I walked out in morning along the roads bordered by stone walls that intersect everywhere ... the grasses along the road with tall plumes white, green, purple, yellow, all fine and distinct on tall stems. I had never seen such grasses before though they must be common enough. I brought home a few to look out, each one so delicate and perfect and *coloured*. The sorrel, like a miniature tree ...

1941

12 May   It was interesting finding the above [entries of 13 and 17 Feb, 4 April and 22 July 1939] today when for the first time for about 10 months I felt the need to make some notes. I also find myself in exactly the same confused and impotent mental state described in Feb 1939 ...

The beginning of the war meant a complete upheaval. Loss of jobs, money, the flat and the children. For 13 months, I lived in other people's houses, having to adapt my life to theirs. During that time my mother died, causing me a great deal more of natural grief than I should have expected (and certainly more than my father's did which I could only feel as a relief) . . . I even feel less terror at the prospect of seeing my father again, if that were possible. I think I could now talk to him without fear, even naturally and with pleasure. Yet even now I do very occasionally dream that he is alive and wake with fear. This dream is, I think, always connected with fear of his discovering me in the sexual act.

Obviously the most important thing that has happened to me is my reconciliation with the Catholic Church last Christmas and my efforts to practise my religion again. This is now the central point round which everything revolves, with the eternal conflict between love and hatred, fear and desire, acceptance or rejection. It was quite an unexpected step for me and, looking at it as a 'natural' phenomenon, it is probably significant that it happened at Christmas and in the Carmelite church to which I had gone so often as a child and had a special affection for. It occurs to me now that this church was one to which I went more often with my mother than with my father . . . I was always painfully aware of his presence and, as it were, of seeing him do something which should have been done in private. When the three of us went together, this feeling was neutralised: my mother was a protection. Also her much looser attitude towards religion, though I priggishly despised it, was a great relief to me. At the end of her life, when her religion became important to her, she never became intolerant towards my extraordinary goings on but always sympathetic and affectionate. When she was alive her vagueness and her irritating ways made it very difficult for me to be with her. But now she is dead, I can see what a lot of remarkable qualities she had . . real sweetness of disposition, an extraordinary capacity for forgiveness, a kind of independence in judging and, in the last months of her life, a really amazing courage and unselfishness. She made absolutely no demands on me, showed no self-pity but was quiet, humorous, patient and quite unafraid.

Again, from the 'natural' point of view I have every sort of qualm about this return of mine. I anticipate every criticism of 'escapism' 'reversion to childhood' mental dishonesty and laziness, or the result of getting older or the result of the war. This anticipation of criticism may be pure snobbishness, inability to admit that one is weak and needs a guide or that one should return to anything so discredited as the Catholic Church or any organised religion with supernatural beliefs is in the eyes of the kind of people I mostly know. Yet, recording the facts of how 'intelligent' people have received it, I do not find they tally with my fantasy. I am naturally curious to know what Carroll thinks. Eric is actually pleased and considers it a sign of my cure; urges me to continue practising it when I am tempted to give it up. Ian Black is also extremely sympathetic and says it has produced a remarkable external change in me of which I am quite unaware myself. Wyn, of course, takes the attitude one would expect her to take but only the most perverse vanity could be wounded by Wyn's opinion. Ian [Henderson] is on the whole not unsympathetic and loyally defended me to Wyn.

But ... there does remain a nucleus of real doubt. Eric would undoubtedly say that the dogmas of the Church are poetry and symbolism and cannot possibly be *literally* true. And so often I feel this to be so. Yet the Church demands that they be believed in as truth, or at least as the articulation of truth and without this genuine faith I do not see how one's practise [*sic*] can be anything but a kind of make-believe ...

Let me try from another angle. These beliefs, irrational or not, have been accepted not only by vast numbers of intelligent men in the past and are certainly still held by many intelligent people today. Therefore the assumption that only idiots could possibly hold such views does not hold. This does not prove the beliefs either true or false; it merely disposes of the argument that to subscribe to them *necessarily* means that a man is a fool.

Up to 22 I don't think I ever had doubts about my faith. I certainly found it hampering and often tiresome to practise but I ... defended it stoutly against all comers, even those whom I most loved and admired e.g. Robin [unknown], Wilfred [McVicker, early boyfriend] etc. It was not till I met [Eliot] Seabrooke[†] that I began to have any real doubts ... With Robert I seemed to have dropped straight back into unquestioning faith and acceptance ...

After the asylum I certainly remained a Catholic ... The end of the

Dougal episode seems to have left me perfectly serene and unguilty. I certainly practised again afterwards but in a much cooler and more formal way. It was not till I married Eric that I did not so much deliberately leave it as let it drop away gradually, bit by bit, as I become more and more in sympathy with Eric's way of looking . . . at things. I suppose I gave up finally about 1926 or 27 – probably when I began to go in for promiscuous love affairs. And I must record the fact that I returned in a period of sexual calm when I was quite ready to face the fact I should have no more sexual life. Certainly my chief difficulties about the Church centre round her attitude to sex. So a case could evidently be made out for the Church being an alternative to sexual life. Whatever the truth is, it is certainly a fact in my own life that I have always had an either/or attitude about sex and the spiritual life. For years I felt I would not be able to write if I had a happy sexual life. Both the Church and Freud are right about the profound importance of the sex instinct – probably the Church's extreme attitude about sex which so often seems unreasonable is due to the fact that, indulged for its own sake, it takes away spiritual force . . .

13 July   Last night I woke up with a feeling of extreme depression. I realised . . . how completely I have lost control of my own life. This is on the surface due to money, as well as, of course, to the war. Although officially I have charge of the children, in practice I can do next to nothing about their lives. Entirely through the force of money Tom has been able to dictate their lives and I can do nothing but acquiesce. I do a meaningless job at a small salary and spend what I make entirely irresponsibly. I want my children back. I want a home. But do I want them back enough to make . . . any effort when the future is so uncertain. I wonder if I was wrong not to take the children to S.Africa when I had the chance . . .

29 July   Tomorrow Ian goes to India. It may be years before we see each other again. I am sitting up waiting in case he manages to get away from Woolwich for one last night as he is trying to do. We have been very happy and very close to each other these last few weeks and even if we can only get letters at very long intervals I believe that the feeling of closeness will persist. Even if it gets dim from separation and all the things that may happen to us both, I feel we are firmly established again . . more than we have ever been . . and when we meet we shan't have been estranged. The house is quieter tonight than I have ever known it so that the trains which I usually hardly notice seem to thunder past and shake the walls almost like bombs. It is more than possible he may not be able to get away; there is a farewell dinner in the mess for the draft yet I feel quite calm and patient though I know I am sad underneath. We have had to say our final goodbye so often that perhaps I don't quite realise that he goes tomorrow.

I still cannot rest peacefully in Catholicism but keep searching, rather wildly and fitfully, for ways to reconcile what I feel to be true in it with what seems true from other experience. There is a peculiar flavour about Catholic writings which I still find repellent. [George] Tyrrell† is the only modern one with whom I feel in sympathy and he was condemned by the Church. Moreover I find something forced, hollow and uneasy about the few Catholics I know ... The Church sticks in my throat: I can neither swallow it nor reject it. The elaborations of theology, as I was taught them as literal truth, seem to me meaningless yet the spiritual discipline which amounts, I suppose to Santayana's 'disintoxication' seems to be profound and true. Yet *that* attitude is to be found in the Chinese, the Hindus, probably in the Greeks and perhaps anywhere where people have tried to organise a life of the spirit. There still remains the riddle of the 'experience of Christ'. Is that a delusion? ...

18 August   About a week ago, after months of hesitation and doubt, I felt I reached firm ground. I do not pretend to explain it: in fact I can't explain it anyhow except by 'grace'. It is not as if I had had any miraculous revelation or had arrived at a satisfactory reconciliation of all the problems. All that I know is that an eye seemed to open somewhere inside me, an eye very filmed and feeble, seeing nothing definite but yet knowing that there *was* something to see. This is the nearest to 'faith' I have ever come in my life ... I am only trying to write it down so that when the inevitable doubts and reactions begin again I shall have on record that I did have a period of real, deep conviction ...

1942

Analysis diary, 22 Feb   After a long time, I felt impelled to read through this book again in the hopes of finding some clues. What made me do it was an unexpected dislocation . . . a very old one! For the first time for two years I was stirred up and emotionally excited by a new person. I had really thought I had become immune – Ian is different . . he seems in a special category and whenever he reappears in my life, our old relation comes back spontaneously. But for months now, any new man I meet arouses no more than friendly interest. Then suddenly I meet a stray young man at a party who devotes the whole evening to me and shows, or pretends to show, an interest in me and very much to my surprise I find myself immediately responsive. He is going away for a week. I am half sorry, half relieved. Perhaps it's only a flutter of excitement and months of a rather monotonous life have made it absurdly important . . . But it's shaken me in what seemed a settled calm . . . I try to hold on to my religion in spite of it but the religion seems suddenly much less real . . . When I was having a very intense sexual life with Ian last summer, my religion certainly did not become meaningless. But this has brought home to me how much I need human warmth and tenderness and how much I want to give it too. The more I try to practise 'charity', the more irritable, aggressive and contemptuous I *feel* though up to a point I can *act* with forbearance. The young man is either a good guesser or a good psychologist and he said things that got under my skin . . .

The work situation is no better. I can't bring myself to plunge either into the [George] Sand book or the father one. I strongly suspect that the 'reading up' on Sand which is so interesting is one more of those defences to give me a respectable reason for not doing what I should be doing.

I still have not exercised free choice in anything. I went to the BBC simply because it opened a way of escape from the Davenports. It is extremely unsatisfactory as a job: it simply provides an income and a way of filling up the days . . . Practically, religion has been of great value to me, giving me a centre, helping me to deal a little with my immense egotism – but all the time curbing and calming rather than giving me incentive – It helps me to *endure* but not to take action. I am still frozen, lazy, unproductive ...

... There is something I have *got* to do but what is it? ... It certainly looks like the book about my father which seems much too difficult to undertake. But then so has every bit of work I've ever tried to do – *Frost*, the Brittany story etc. The things that *look* easy, like the play, never come out right ...

It's the old thing which came up so clearly in analysis as I see reading through those notes – the *keeping something inside*. Now I know in my head and from experience that the only way to get any real satisfaction is to abandon oneself to a thing. And it is this nervous holding-back which is not self-control that is my real bugbear ...

Have there been positive results from analysis? Some, yes. I suffer much less from morbid terrors and anxieties: my headaches have gone during the last few months and were less frequent and severe before: I can bear to be alone much better; I am on the whole more reasonable about money ... and my relation with the children is enormously improved. But it's only a beginning ... I waste enormous mental energy on people who aren't really benefitted by it .. e.g. Thorp [Peter].† It is much better for me to write for *people in general* ...

Carroll once said to me that I arranged my life so as to disappoint and to be disappointed. How horribly true that is. Yet up to my 15th birthday I did not disappoint my father. I think I must still want his approval. Oh, the Church, the Church: There is only one thing that matters and that is love. Christ says it. But ... I fear the love of God because I think of it as destructive ...

If I stay in the Church it *must* be from love and not from fear. Fear is the worst possible motive for me. Awe is not fear ...

Why is religion acceptable in one age and not in another? Has it anything to do with 'science' and 'knowledge'? 'Science' now commands the same awed respect that religion once did. But are people more thoughtful, more educated, more intelligent than they were in the 'ages of faith'? ...

Analysis diary, Sept I had quite forgotten this last entry. No recollection of even having such thoughts ... To work is perhaps for me to pray. The point I come naturally back to always is the

Santayanan one. I love the Church: it is almost a physical love. Sometimes it is compulsive. My intellect does not love it. I can only be a very childish Catholic. I feel older than the monks and nuns I know. I love them in proportion to their holiness . . . Any art I have is inextricably rooted in Catholicism . . .

 . . . Dreamy and compulsive lately: cram myself with reading, put off all activities. R[onald Moody] notices one side of me dead. In my mind aggressive, irritable, prejudiced, contemptuous in spite of all efforts to be charitable. The doubts begin again: an almost steady rhythm of faith and doubt ever since I came back. Terror of failure in the spiritual life . . of my last state being worse than my first . . .

Since the turning-down of my *Horizon* article ['Smoking Flax' about her return to the Church] driven back on myself . . . Dissipating time and money: tired, without initiative. Can neither take religion or leave it . . . Equally repelled by the fanaticism of . . . the Catholics and the Communists. Critical of everyone except Eric whom I value more and more . . . I keep saying 'Thy will be done' but I really want mine. And yet I have no will . . .

1943

4 *June*   I have not made notes for a very long time – But I have arrived at another of those critical periods when it seems necessary to do a little stocktaking. This is one of those old familiar situations in which everything has boiled up together – losing job, physical illness, religious uncertainty, angst, apathy and depression.

Outward signs: maniacal reading, either pure escapism or . . . the search for the magic word . . . complete jam in writing again after a tolerably steady period . . . desire to eat, drink, smoke. Loss of fountain pen . . . irresponsibility, touchiness . . . eternal gnawing question, is Cath[olic] religion *true*? . . . reading mania but do not read slowly and intelligently. Try and swallow books whole . . . No one to whom I can go for advice, who knows *all* the circumstances. Would I trust them if I did? I try to make acts of love and submission to God but they don't convince me . . .

... Everywhere conflicting creeds, opinions. Church offers security but do I really believe in the Church? Still *odi et amo* as much as ever ...

I was brought up a Catholic. I responded to it. I left it and never quite found anything to take its place ... Question the most devout Catholics and you will find very different opinions combined with deep loyalty. But I suppose the core would boil down to always the divinity of Christ, the teaching authority of the Church. But oh how difficult all that side is. One is driven back to the Gospels and one does not know how to interpret them ...

1944

5 August [written on sick leave from SOE]   Cannot find any entry since June 1943. Have not looked at notebooks for a very long time. Once again have had a prolonged bout of the usual state. The same symptoms (except there were many fits of weeping and in the end I broke down in the office). Inertia, paralysis, depression, extreme sleepiness, maniacal reading, the eternal book trouble. As regards religion, I practise it with joy, and adhere to it. Nervous and overwhelmed at the thought of all I *ought* to do . . Catholic action, study etc. The more I read of theology, Church history, apologetics, philosophy, scripture interpretation, the more hopelessly at sea I find myself. I feel on firm ground with Walter H[ylton] and Dame Julian [of Norwich] and in the prayers of the Church. I do not find it easy to get on with Catholics or to be really intimate with them. I am struck by their difference rather than by their uniformity. Fr. Kehoe,[†] Fr. White,[†] Fr. Pius[†] . . all v. impressive in their different ways. I truly respect them. If one could only talk to them informally. With Eric I can make no headway at all. He knocks down every statement I make yet he likes me to be a Catholic ...

But why, just now, should I have 'panicked' again? Certain frustrations in the last 6 months went home badly. K.J.R [Kathleen Raine[†]]'s violent attack on me. Rejection of my French article by air ministry (but I feel McMillan[†] [Brigadier at SOE] agreed with them).

[George] Orwell's ignoring my letter about Catholicism . . . Getting fat again . . . People continue to believe in me but only those who know me pretty well. Don't think I would impress any new person. I live entirely on past reputation.

I have wasted this sick-leave, neither really resting nor achieving anything . . . I dream that I would like to belong to an order, to have my life planned and my activities regulated but this is not 'vocation' but a desire to give up responsibility for myself. It is not impossible that I ought to have been a nun . . or tried, anyway. But the test would have been really giving up something I wanted. Now it would be giving up what I don't want . . .

There is so much hatred and contempt in me . . . As a Christian one tries to down these feelings of hatred. But that is not the same thing as unconscious repression . . . If one is angry inside it's as bad as being angry outside . . . I am certainly ill-tempered and irritable enough . . .

Analysis brought I think incontestable evidence that money is very important to me . . . We never hear of Our Lord having any money transactions: we know He was very poor. Still they did have a purse and they did have something to eat and drink and wear.

The primitive church lived on the pooled contributions of the faithful but there had to be something to contribute. So we needn't be guilty about earning money. I don't *seem* to be awfully extravagant yet I never have any money to spare. I suppose household expenses are about £225; cigarettes, lunches, hairdressing, clothes about £200, Susan and Lyndall about £200, books about £60, charity, entertaining etc. about £100. It all goes anyway . . .

. . . I long to simplify my life and it seems the hardest thing in the world to do.

1945

5 August   I saw Father Pius tonight for perhaps the fourth time in about 10 months. I wish I had always written down what he said. To-night I told him about my obsession with K.J.R.'s 'case', how I could not get her out of my mind, was extremely critical of her attitude, also

Antonia's mother, Christine Botting, in 1898

Cecil G. Botting, Antonia's father

Antonia and her mother,
photographed in 1906
when Antonia was seven

Antonia, with fashionably shingled hair,
at the age of seventeen

Antonia and Reggie Green-Wilkinson
after their marriage in 1921

Tom Hopkinson with Susan and Lyndall at a fair in 1936

Antonia with Lyndall and Susan in 1945, on the occasion of Susan's first communion

Susan aged seventeen, in her first ball dress, preparing to visit the Cecil King family in Aberdeenshire

Antonia, photographed in 1947

full of feelings which are certainly resentful and pharisaical etc. He said 'You should *look through* such things. Lift up your heart and mind to God'. . . .

As to K[athleen] he said, 'There is a good deal of cattiness on your part'. I said 'Yes, I know' . . . Obviously I do feel resentful and would like to see her 'put in her place' . . .

I said, 'What am I to do about her?' 'Do nothing whatsoever. Don't discuss it with people.' 'But suppose she brings it up herself?' 'Refuse to talk about it' . . .

He is very pleased about Sue [under instruction with a nun]. He said 'You have been given a very great grace and you should be very thankful to Almighty God.' I said 'Yes, I know. I'm afraid my gratitude takes the form of asking for another favour' I meant L[yndall] of course. He said 'That's quite all right. Go on asking.'

17 August It is very difficult to realise that God loves people entirely different from ourselves . . .

Oct The old troubles persist: the old symptoms. I have had them now for 24 years. Lately the one human thing I have thought of as stable has been threatened. Eric [who had suffered a nervous breakdown]. Yet in one thing I do know where I stand: my religion. That is my centre. One's neurosis can get into one's religion, too . . .

It is the great root of my pride I have to pull up . . . I have to learn to live *without the good opinion of myself or others* . . . I do not attract people to Christ *because I have no joy. Only the humble have joy* . . .

1947

In January 1947 Benedicta de Bezer[†] fell in love with Antonia. Benedicta was a dark, mannish woman who had exchanged playing jazz on the piano in a Chelsea club for painting sombre and enormous religious pictures in her room in Belsize Park. Sometimes she dressed as a monk.

The Benedicta diary differs from most of the others in that it fills a very small notebook and its early pages were written in note form, at a sitting. It almost certainly replaces a diary that Benedicta persuaded

Antonia to destroy. From Friday 14 March, however, its detail suggests
that it was kept more or less daily. (It is certain that on 21 March 1947
Benedicta ordered the destruction of the two large volumes of the early
diaries, 1921–1933.)

Benedicta was a notorious Lesbian, and there is no doubt that Antonia
was strongly attracted to her physically. She was also attracted by
Benedicta's passionate Catholicism. Benedicta now church-crawled with
the passion that she had once pub-crawled. (She got locked into St Mary
of the Angels several times.) Under her influence Antonia began to show
signs of a similar religious mania. She now headed diary entries with the
name of the saint whose day it was. She even volunteered to clean the
chancel of St Mary of the Angels although she could hardly handle a
broom. With Benedicta she attended lectures by learned Dominicans and
exchanged holy medals, particularly the Miraculous Medal (dedicated to
Our Lady and said to have amazing properties). Under Benedicta's
influence Antonia became a lay member of the Dominican Order, and
together they said the special daily prayers required by the Office.

When Holy Week came round, they attended all the services that lead
up to Easter. On Maundy Thursday they went to the office of Tenebrae
and saw the candles go out one by one: on Good Friday they walked
round Eric Gill's carved stations of the cross in Westminster Cathedral,
contemplating each event in Christ's passion; on Easter Sunday they
were back in the Cathedral for High Mass, followed by wine and song
round the piano at Ashburn Gardens. As Susan was home from school
for the vacation she was included in these last observances.

Fri 14 Feb   the poem

Mon 24 Feb St Mathias
   Mass at the Cathedral
   St Dominic at Our Lady's altar.
   We have a feast
   She [Benedicta] gives me the lamp
   She discovers that Robert looks like Dudley [probably Benedicta's
brother to whom she was close]

Thur 27 Feb   She has a terrible day
   Fr. Cantwell's blessing

Sun 2 March   I have a terrible day
   She takes it over the phone for $3\frac{3}{4}$ hours and I am cured

Tues 4 March   Dorothy [Kingsmill]† sings Mozart

Wed 5 March   Fr. Gervase Mathew.
Contemplation

Fri 7 March St Thomas Aquinas
Mass at the Priory.
I send her the Greek alphabet
She sends me her Gethsemane picture

Sat 8 March   First attempt to see the Prior [of the Dominican Priory,
Haverstock Hill]
Confession Fr Gumbley†
De Profundis.
She has *Adoro Te*

Sun 9 March   We have a strange day. She talks: a moment comes
when I am frightened and bewildered. I think it is that night I have
the dream about us in Carmel [i.e. as Carmelite nuns]

Mon 10 March   I think I tell her the dream

Tues 11 March   A strange day connected with the dream. I tell her
what I think is the truth

Wed 12 March   She arrives here in a terrible state. She gives me the
Samurai sword. Père Henry dines with us and gives us his blessing.

13 March   Chelsea. Crane. Servites [Catholic church and community, Fulham Road] – We dine on chicken.

Fri 14 March   I spend all day with her and take her the Apocalypse.
We talk of movement: then we go through one of Kehoe's lectures,
looking up references.
   We say rosary and litanies. In the evening we try again to see the
Prior. We make the stations. At Simon of Cyrene, the sad woman
Lilli comes in. We take her for coffee and do not see the Prior. I go
back to Benedicta in a fearful mood. Sex and the fingernail. I think I
have wrecked everything.

15 March   I have a crisis and decide to go for 3rd time to Priory. I do not know if she will be there but pray she may. She finds me crying by the crucifix. (She has found her voice to say she will be there just as I am going). Through her persistence the Prior does come just as I have finished the Resurrection decade. I go to confession to him: am received as a postulant. We are deliriously happy: go to a café; separate for rest of day.

Lecture 16 March   Everything goes mysteriously right for us in morning. We have untasted breakfast in a café: go to Cathedral: say office: find Fr. Gervase Matthew [sic] preaching. Every word seems meant for us: our Rule. We have lunch at Dorothy [Kingsmill]'s. Tom is there: difficult. We go back: rest peacefully. We have a misunderstanding about Office. She thinks I don't want it. I force her to say it with me. But things have gone wrong: she is overwrought and has a crise. We have 3 minutes for reconciliation.

17 March   (I *think*) She gives me my medal

18 March   She meets Fr. Victor [White] for first time ...

19 March, St Joseph   she gets locked in again at St Mary of the Angels. She finds St Joan ... The instruments of the Passion. The Immaculate Conception. Fr. Victor's Mass.

National Gallery, 20 March, St Michael   We find the Miraculous Medal. We find a train for tomorrow which will not disturb her. Kehoe gives a wonderful lecture: he blesses the medal which is on her *left* hand. She meets Kathleen [unknown], Dorothy and Leila [unknown]. I have the Oakley Street dream.

21 March, St Benedict   We stay here: it is raining. She brings Pommard '37 and daffodils. We are very happy. We talk again of the hesychast prayer. We talk about her family and restoring her name. She tells me about the woman in the kitchen when she was a child. I burn my notebooks. Something goes wrong. I am lost and bewildered again. We say part of the Office of the Dead together: rest on our own. She needs desperately to be alone. I have an intimate experience at Holy Communion. I ask something special for her but do not tell her what.

23 March   I go to St Mary of the Angels. I find a charing job. a 3rd book on Angels and a blessing.

24 March, St Gabriel   ... I ask B. to Chaplet of Five Wounds for her annunciation.

25 March   We do not meet or communicate. I type 'Sacrifice of Praise' Our Lady suddenly overwhelms me with joy.

28 March, Seven Dolores.   Sue comes home [from the Godolphin School, Salisbury].

31 March   I sweep the sanctuary at St Mary of the Angels: the children.
   She sends me the Dominican medal and rosary – on Palm Sunday we met Benedicta at the Cathedral ...

2 April   Benedicta here. I give her St Michael. Sue comes under the spell. We say Office together. Afterwards Benedicta says it was 'impossible'.

3 April, Maundy Thursday   We are all at High Mass at the Cathedral. We spend the rest of the day with Benedicta in her room and at the Priory. Tenebrae. Sue is in tears. Sue tells me how things are with her. I go to Confession to F. Gumbley: told to pray for strength.

4 April, Good Friday   The three of us are all day together. The Cathedral in the morning: Stations and Fr. Victor's sermon in the afternoon. Sue is profoundly unhappy.

5 April, Holy Saturday   We go to Mass at the Priory. Benedicta does not come back to our bench after Communion. In the afternoon I am very sad and worried. Benedicta suddenly appears with bunch of primroses from Our Lady of Sorrows. She is all compassion and warmth. She asks me if I will trust her with S[ue] ... Atmosphere not quite right.

6 April, Easter Sunday   We go to High Mass at the Cathedral all 3.
Very happy 'family' feeling . . . Party. Lyndall sings – Benedicta plays
heroically. Last part is not good. Benedicta venemous [sic] against
Leiler [Leila] . . .

7 April, Easter Monday   We spend the day here all three – Benedicta
arrives very early. The children sing with her. Afterwards the
atmosphere becomes progressively uneasy . . . She is 'getting at' me.
The Order and the Eton crop. Sue is very uneasy.

8 and 9 April   Sue becomes aware of sense of evil. We find same
things disconcert us about Benedicta . . . Sue . . . has 'lost Our Lady':
is suffering very much. She forced herself to face what seemed an
actual evil presence. Something said to her 'Do not fear evil: love
good'

10 April   Things come to a crisis. Sue was in a fearful state all day.
Benedicta did not grasp the full implications: how could she? In the
end Sue lay down. Everything was far away: religion obscured by
this dark cloud. She could not pray: Could not even hold her rosary.
At last I gave her her crucifix: she held on to that. Benedicta said her
Office for Sue. Still she did not understand and became quite
confused, almost childish. Sue recovered complete calm. Benedicta
was still at a loss. Fr. Victor came: we 3 asked for his blessing. He
blessed the house. Sue had been very insistent that he should bless the
bathroom. During dinner Sue and I were feeling perfectly calm:
Benedicta was still uneasy. Dorothy Kingsmill came: her talk was
remarkable and Fr. Victor was truly impressed . . . When the others
had gone (Benedicta in saying goodnight to Sue had suggested she
could always come to her for refuge) I told Fr. Victor at his request
the experiences Sue had been having. He took it all quite seriously . . .
He says whatever it is Sue and I have she is evidently rejecting . . . He
agreed about the real terror about her feminine side and its
repression.

11 April   Fr. Victor said Mass at Our Lady's altar . . . and I answered
. . . She [Sue] told me that she had woken in the night afraid again . . .
Then she very clearly heard me call and went up to my room but I was

asleep and did not wake even when she knocked. She was then convinced it was Our Lady who called her ... We decided it was necessary for us both to see Fr. Pius.

I wrote to Benedicta, showing it to Sue.

13 April We saw Fr. Pius. Sue told him she had experienced love and evil together. He told her to keep inner peace. He said how delighted he was with Sue. I came out with the events of the last days. He asked if there were 'manifestations'. I said in Sue's case yes. He said also that in attained sanctity there was not strain but peace. He talked of how careful lay apostles should be ... He also said there are dangers of presumption: priests are given special grace for the ministry and even so must exercise extreme prudence. His last words to me 'Do not be dominated'. Sue decided, after much hesitation, to see Benedicta alone and rang her up. Benedicta referred to my letter: said she could not understand it.

14 April I spoke to Benedicta on the phone. She was in a state of furious condemnation of nuns, materialism in the church, lethargy etc. the suppression of individual enterprise.

When Sue was with her I prayed. I went down to Reparatrice and prayed. Suddenly while I was cooking I felt an atmosphere of danger (about 7.45): fell on my knees and said 'Memorare' ... found that things had begun to take a wrong turn at that time. By time I phoned (about $\frac{1}{2}$ hr) later she [Sue] had already put on her things to go. Her first words were 'Well that is finished I know where I am and don't want to see her again ...' Benedicta had spoken of me with 'mildly affectionate contempt', as Sue said, 'a nice aunt who had got hold of the wrong end of the stick'. She said that from the very first I had been quite deluded in the idea that there was anything special between us, that she had only had one friend in her life (who was dead) etc. But I was a brilliant writer but saw things all distorted by a dramatic sense ... B. then referred to my last letter. Asked Sue if she could explain it. Sue said 'You only want to know in order to mock'. For a moment B. said 'how wonderful' ... But she reverted almost at once to the other line and they parted in extreme coldness. Benedicta seems most definitely to have implied that she wanted to ally Sue with her against me. Immediately after, while Sue was on the way home,

Benedicta rang me up with the most gay voluble friendliness. She sounded as natural as in the old days before February.

* * *

Antonia decided to be received as a Dominican tertiary in Paris. This caused great offence to Benedicta, who had made a scapular (a small square of the cloth of a religious habit, worn suspended from the neck) for her. Accompanied by Susan, Antonia went to the Dominican Friary, in the rue La Tour-Maubourg to meet Père Maydieu† and after the ceremony they travelled to Alsace, where they stayed with Lexi and Antoinette Grunelius†. The family were firm believers in the apparition of Our Lady weeping at La Salette in the Alps, and were passionate admirers of the works of Jacques Maritain† and Léon Bloy.† When Antonia left, Susan stayed on to teach English to two of the six Grunelius children.

* * *

15 April   ... I went and saw Fr. Pius ... I am to be 'hard headed': at all costs not let Sue lose confidence in me. I am to put Sue's welfare absolutely first and she is not to be involved. He said spiritual friendships are tricky 'and you are both very young in such things' He very much approved of my receiving the Scapular in Paris not at the Priory ... Sue said we had both gone ... She is on the defensive even against Dorothy Kingsmill. Burnt her prospectus.

I wrote to Benedicta trying to make it sound natural, rather light. I told her why I had decided on Paris (the truth) thanked her for all she had done about the Tertiary thing. By same post, I wrote asking for Mass to be said for Ian [Black] on 22nd ...

16 April   ... I cannot tell how she will react to Paris. In her present variable state she may take it as a relief or a betrayal ... I am praying all the time for us and that we may find God's will in all this. I have got to purify my heart. I pray for true love. A dream showed me there was more flesh in my love than I knew ...

17 April   Benedicta rang up to say she *had* made my scapular ... She insisted that I was staying on at Kolbsheim for my own convenience – *therefore* wanted to be received in Paris and took what was the absolute truth for 'a slap in the face' for her to cover my own convenience. My letter had made her furious; she felt it monstrous after 'putting up for 3 months with your impossible temperament'. She said 'everyone attacks me' 'Sue and you say you love me but reproach me' that she had prayed not to answer my letter in the way she felt like doing. I kept as calm as I could, trying to convince her that I *was* only being received in Paris because of my very strong impression about her attitude of contempt and mistrust and wanting to dissociate herself. Then she said she wanted me to have back the black book. I said 'I don't take back what I give.' She said it was a special book. I said 'Yes. That was why I gave it you and I would give it you again tomorrow' Suddenly her voice softened: she said 'God bless you' in her old way and rang off.

18 April I was increasingly unhappy after yesterday's conversation. In the morning my heart was like lead. I *had* to find a church. I had meant to go to Warwick St. On a strong impulse I went instead to Maiden Lane. Exposition, Litany of the Sacred Heart; benediction. I knelt where we knelt that day, imploring help for us both, and felt more peaceful. I lit a candle for her and me to St Joseph: 2 for her and Sue to Our Lady. I rang up to tell her what I had done. She was completely different: like her old self: warm and friendly. We decided to meet at the Oratory tomorrow and both ask for forgiveness. I was overjoyed: I could not bear to have my scapular feeling we were not in charity with each other. Sue had bought me daffodils, seeing how unhappy I was ... When she came in with them, I told her the good news. She could not take it in. She said 'I can't *believe* she could change so quickly' Her own last impression was still so strong. She had sat up late trying to write to B. telling her she loved her more than anyone but that she felt this evil in her and could not condone it: she *had* to be sincere just because she cared so much for B. . . . I could only say the Magnificat and lie down and rest from exhaustion. It has been a strain.

19 April We met at 2. We went and talked a little, but not *really*. She looked tired but 'natural' ... She said a terrible thing: that if God condemned her to hell, she had made a pact that all her efforts should not be wasted but applied to the Holy Souls. It was awful, as if she had had moments of despair. What had distressed Sue most in the haunting face was not evil but ... despair ... We tried to go to Confession at the Oratory but no priest came ... While we waited she grew very restless: her face became bitter again. She said she felt for weeks as if bewitched, under a curse. She gave me one look which might have suggested it was I who cursed her. She seemed to want to repudiate the past months altogether, as if everything had been evil, not God's will. When we got to the Servites we did get confession ... When she came out she was much shaken but I felt that at last there was hope. In the taxi, I could not speak. She said 'at last it seems possible to look at the future'. I took her hand and she clutched mine like a child. She said 'Do you think one day I may have a friend?' I said 'Yes'. We were quiet. I had never felt more love for her: it was peaceful. I saw that she was crying. In the evening ... She took away her black habit ...

20 April I had an extraordinary dream last night, recorded elsewhere. A kind of holy 'thriller' in which B. played the part of leader of persecuted Catholics. In one part of the dream she was ill: insisted on making a lotion for herself on scientific principles ... She snuffed it up her nostrils too hot and was in great pain. Sue and I had only vaseline to offer. I was afraid to hurt her; my fingers seemed too coarse. Her fingers in dream were even smaller than in life. She applied it herself. I told her the whole dream. Her explanations seemed too slick. This part she saw only as ... sexual ...

21 April ... There was a letter from Fr. V[ictor] W[hite] ... He said we must leave her to the Lord and that I must get away: that he hoped I would 'pray and dream it out' She rang up to say she had thrown away the Harukiri sword.

22 April She rang up very sweetly to say goodbye ...

24 April I answered Mass at Tour Maubourg [*sic*]. Went to Confession to Père Louvet ... My reception took place in the afternoon with the complete wonderful ceremony. My scapulars and belt were on the altar and I was given the lighted candle from the altar: Père Maydieu gave me a discourse. I asked for the conversion of Lyndall and for the gift of charity. Susan found at N[otre] D[ame] the

Crown of Thorns said one for me and one for B. . . . I wished B. could have been there. But I would have felt mean when she had had such a miserable reception . . .

30 April, St Catherine of Siena I want to know about her. She is one of B.'s . . . saints. Mme G. loves her too. We sat up late, the G.'s and I, talking about La Salette. Mme G. feels much that B. does: the importance of Contemplatives, a tendency against the supernatural in the church, a fear of it, even among priests. Too much action: a new kind of rationalism. Mme G. says how subtle the devil is. Also how he seems to be working very hard to blind even good men to the implications of Salette. She and I agree that we need to revive devotion to the *angels* today. Many currents are in the air which B. picks up as Bloy does: the apocalyptic, the sense of the supernatural in every day life, awareness of the dangers of pettiness in religion. This house (Kolbsheim) is consecrated to Our Lady of La Salette. I think B. and I should go to Salette. We prepared the altar at midnight.

1 May We had mass in the chapel. I prayed very much not to leave Our Lady's tears unheeded. And I prayed that B. and I should be allowed to serve God together in some way. She is a noble soul. I am too ready to see faults and to forget her great love of God . . .

* * *

On her return to London, Antonia almost immediately became involved with Dorothy Kingsmill, a 'psychiatric consultant' whose influence over her was as strong as that of Benedicta had been. There was, however, no sexual element in this relationship.

Dorothy was the wife of Hugh Kingsmill, the author, and had four children, Tony, Edmée, Brook and 'Little Dorothy'. A follower of Meher Baba,[†] an Indian holy man who communicated with his disciples by thought-waves, Dorothy was, and still is, a prominent member of his London Circle. She was also involved with followers of Gurdjieff, the Theosophists, the Buddhists and the Arcane Society.

Dorothy was a woman of some beauty and style, with blue eyes that could compel respect. She spoke with a slight North Country accent. Before she was married, she had a relationship with a well-born young man called John, whose intentions were honourable. He took her down to a family stately home to meet his uncle, who appeared to be charmed

by her, but when Dorothy left he said, 'Never bring that w... here
again.'

In places, Antonia addresses Dorothy in her diary as 'you'.

* * *

21 June   Following her own 'intuitions' and mine, D[orothy
Kingsmill] feels that the three of us were involved before. Also, as I
feel too, that she was the 'successful rival'. She thinks that she and
I have something to work out together, to forgive each other for.
We have hurt each other in the past. After praying, she opened the
N[ew] T[estament] for the three of us.
For B[enedicta]. Paul on the road to Damascus ...
For D[orothy]. The miracle of the water into wine at Cana
For me The grain of mustard seed ...

1948

16 Feb   Now that it is all over I can see how wonderfully the texts we
found fitted ...

There still remains Benedicta ...

I wrote to tell her I had been cured. I wanted to make quite clear to
her what Dorothy had done. Also that, as a Catholic, she need have
no misgivings. I thought I would get no reply or a scornful one. I got
however a strange little note.

'Dear Phoenix

May the last embers be extinguished by the draught of your
brave wings. love. Benedicta'.

She [Sue] and a Catholic friend at Somerville want to start a
Catholic group for 'promoting' Catholicism to the non-Catholics,
answering difficulties 'intellectually and logically'.

I am a trifle uneasy about this particularly as she said in her letter
'It would make one's religion so much more real to oneself if one
were doing something active to promote it' ...

... It is obvious that for the last few months religion has seemed
'unreal' to Sue. And that seems to me just the moment when one

should *not* set about trying to convince other people . . .

Everyone says how wonderful Sue is. And she is – or could be – wonderful. But she has a very impressive façade which, as she frankly admits herself, is only one side of the picture . . .

18 Feb Last night I dreamt about Benedicta again but cannot remember what. But I had a rather odd dream about a small house that Eric and I nearly took when we were first married. It was in Hill Street, Knightsbridge and we had paid a deposit of £80 on it which we lost when we decided in the end not to take the house. We did not take it because we thought after all it would be expensive to run and so stayed on in Eric's furnished rooms.

In the dream, I went back to this house and looked out. It was unfurnished but was still decorated as it had been for our going in . . . I was amazed to find it all looking so fresh and new though this redecorating must have been done in 1925 . . .

I seemed to be going over the house with some people. It is possible you were one of them . . .

Before I went to bed I was very conscious of what I can only call 'emanations' from Benedicta and not very pleasant ones . . . I had to summon up 'good influence' as it were and tell myself there was nothing to be afraid of.

* * *

Antonia resumed going to the meetings of 'The Children of Mary' (sometimes 'Enfants de Marie'). These were for the old girls of the Convent of the Sacred Heart at Roehampton.

* * *

19 Feb I overslept heavily though I had gone to bed early. I had a dream which I thought I had pinned down most carefully and now cannot get a single clue to it. Only thing I can be pretty sure of is that Dorothy came into it. It is annoying how completely it has gone as I ran over the main points when I was fully conscious to 'fix' it . . . Did an umbrella come into it? Or have I got the word 'umbrella' in my head having just read in the paper of a woman who kept one always open in her room to ward off evil spirits? Also I left mine . . . at the Sacred Heart convent when I last went there for Children of Mary meeting.

Now I see 22 Perham Road – my address as a child . . . That *must* be from the dream. I saw it written on a sheet of paper and thought how odd . . .

I was struck by what you said last night about 80% of your childhood mystical experiences turning out to be 'escapism' under analysis. But 20% remained authentic . . .

I think this process works everywhere and is especially clear in the spiritual life and in art. But it is fatal to *stop* the growth even though it produces all sorts of excrescences . . . That is why I think we must be careful in judging writers like Bloy who is full of glaringly repulsive qualities but marvellous ones too. To me Jane Austen's 'perfection' is highly suspect and though I *enjoy* her (who wouldn't) I don't really admire her.

I think she is the most bourgeois of all writers. She has certain ethical standards which are not always reducible to mere good breeding, but of all writers she must be one of the least 'spiritual'. Her whole mainspring is materialistic. She is really the last of the 18th century writers with their terror of 'enthusiasm' . . .

Perhaps that is why Christ is being constantly accused of consorting with drunkards and harlots. The drunkard's love of drink may not be admirable but at least he loves it enough to risk the hangover. And something can be made of such love or lust. But nothing can be made of the mild preference which says 'Let's get married when we can afford a car'.

19 Feb [sic]   . . . I must be exceedingly careful about this Sue business: as detached as possible and keep my 'natural' feelings as much in abeyance as possible – especially the whole question of whether Sue 'loves' me or not. I must concentrate on the fact that I have a very great responsibility to Sue and my 'emotions' do not matter. I must trust D[orothy] and give her every possible support and co-operation since I think she is the only *human* person who can help . . .

It looks as if things were serious with Sue . . . All my maternal instinct of course cries out 'The poor child . . it can't be as bad as that' But, of course, from one point of view Sue is not a child. She was, in a queer way, mature when she was three.

It does not mean Sue is 'bad'. But it does mean she is in danger. In danger from some falseness within. Thank God she does know it herself. But something very powerful in her is fighting to make her think 'it doesn't matter'

When Sue first wanted to have a religion (she was about 15) . . . she said she wanted to feel there was a centre in her life. Later she said to me that she felt as if her heart were shrivelled and that she was incapable of love. It was about then that she said she wanted to be instructed as a Catholic: before that she had thought she would prefer to be an Anglican.

She told Father Pius about the Benedicta thing that she 'had discovered love and evil simultaneously'.

Sue has always been a 'disturbing' influence in any school. She fascinates and puzzles people. No one has ever had any real power over her. (I come nearer to it than anyone. There was Benedicta of course but even Benedicta came up against something she could not break down). In the end Sue is always left to go her own way. She has what I would call tremendous negative force. As a small child she was aggressive and bullying. But Sue has a peculiar way of not identifying herself with her own actions. She seems to stand quite aloof from them.

Yet she is very sensitive, very kind. At one time all her feeling went to animals. It was very strong feeling. She really *entered into* all the animal's needs and would take endless trouble over it . . . Most children take a fancy to an animal, adore it for a few days and then get bored with looking after it.

Though she pretends that small children are tiresome, she is actually very fond of them and quite remarkably good with them. I am convinced she would make an absolutely first-class mother.

But she hates being a woman; *really* hates it. And as she is now, sex would be an absolute nightmare to her.

She appears calm but is very far from being so. I do not know anyone who gets into worse nervous panics and states of depression. But it is impossible to get her to take any steps which would prevent the situation which creates the panic.

You cannot exactly call her 'selfish' or even 'self-centred'. She often complains that she *has* no self. All the same, if she wants something, she goes all out till she gets it even if it gives her and other people a lot of trouble. But very, very often when she gets it she no longer cares for it . . .

Last holidays, when she really was in rather a state ... she said again that she had no central interest in her life, nothing she felt was worth living for. She did not even mention religion ... it has been obvious to me for some months that religion has ceased to be 'real' for her.

It was certainly real to her last summer, during the first part of her stay in Alsace. But something went wrong there. I don't know exactly at what point. I could tell from the tone of her letters that *something* had happened to disturb her ...

Older people fall a little in love with her . . men and women. Particularly religious people. She is so like one's dream of what a young girl should be ...

It would be possible for Sue to be 'wicked' on a really grand scale. I do not believe that Benedicta is anything like a match for Sue ... [She] has a cold powerful intelligence ... She is capable of being completely impersonal ... Flattery hardly touches her. She is so ruthlessly critical of herself and sets herself such impossibly high standards that outside praise or criticism means very little to her ...

She needs most desperately to love someone and knows this ...

She does love me, I know (and of course hates me too) ... We have an exceedingly strong sympathy with each other and an identical sense of humour. When things are going well between us I think we enjoy each other's company as much as we do anyone's. But Lyndall, Sue and I don't make a very good trio. We all become self-conscious and L. complains that Sue and I always quarrel when she is there. If the three of us do something together Sue is rather apt to behave ... childishly and 'spoil the party'. I think she likes to keep me and Lyndall in separate compartments ...

As mother and baby, we somehow got off on the wrong foot ... (... I made the fatal mistake of wanting her to be a boy) but I've been a mother to her really. Not a mother at all when she was a baby ...

I've got to 'earn' Sue. I've had her 'on account' as you might say. Now the bill has come in.

I was thinking in that first odd dream about the church how you were kneeling near me and seemed 'so much at home' and how Edmée [Kingsmill] was kneeling some distance away and was rather heavily made up.

In real life Edmée makes up too much and Sue not at all. But perhaps Sue 'makes up' her character.

It is rather interesting about those two. They obviously had plenty to say to each other the only time they met.

And both Edmée and Sue at various times have vaguely suggested arranging to do something together. But neither of them has done a thing about it . . .

21 Feb . . . I am again much preoccupied with Benedicta. I suppose because it is obvious that Sue has been so much affected by it all . . .

. . . If the whole thing meant nothing to her [Benedicta], why did she behave as she did? It would have been so easy for her to get out of it. Yet the way she wrote to me, the way she spoke, the fact that she was incessantly ringing me up and inviting herself to see me (and she would arrive early and spend the entire day) were not at all the behaviour of someone who had got involved in something they don't want to . . .

But, looking back, it really seems impossible to know whether she ever told the exact truth about anything. Even in the most trivial details where there was no advantage to be gained by lying, she would lie . . .

. . . I think she believes that, at great personal sacrifice, she tried to help someone else who then betrayed her and threw her over . . . She told Sue she had only had one friend in her life and the person was dead. (I think she meant her brother) and that after eight years of absolute unquestioning devotion from Dorothy Truman Taylor [actress who shared Benedicta's flat in Belsize Park]. If she hasn't a friend in Dorothy, then I don't know what a friend is.

And all this falseness is mixed up with something wonderful. I have never known good and evil so inextricably tangled up in a person . . . And I think that is why 'her' Dorothy succeeds where everyone else has failed because though, on the surface she is completely artificial, she is fundamentally innocent and humble . . .

I am trying to find what is wrong in my attitude to Sue. I can't change her, but I can try to change myself.

I suppose what I *suffer* from most in Sue is the feeling that she despises me and is ashamed of me . . . Sue *could* not despise a person who was altogether admirable. So instead of being hurt and angry . . . I must accept it as useful . . . criticism.

Where I have failed my children most is in a morbid terror of their annihilating me ... it is hard for me not to see them as enemies out to take away everything I have.

For the last few years I have been, I suppose, what could be called a reasonably 'good' mother to Sue ... And she tries, bless her, to be a 'good' daughter to me ... But it is a strain on her and we both break down frequently at crucial moments ...

Prolonged being together is always a great strain on both of us. We do best when we are apart and writing to each other (which we can do with great freedom) ... It is a delight for us to meet but, unless the stay together has been a short one, a relief to part ...

I do not know how 'jealous' I am of Sue. My friends are certainly always conspiring to make me so! I am always hearing, on all sides 'How wonderful it must be to have such a beautiful and brilliant daughter' ...

And of course I *am* very proud of Sue. Maybe I don't think she's as perfect as some of her many admirers do: on the other hand I think I appreciate something very remarkable in her (more remarkable than her looks or talents) which most people don't recognise. But I don't, I am afraid, see in her the end and justification of whole life.

I have to admit I frequently find the financial 'obligation' of being a parent very trying ...

Sue is sometimes very good about that side of things and puts up uncomplainingly with old things and tries to save me money.

On the other hand she often runs me into unnecessarily heavy expenses: expensive holidays, riding etc. And I do like her to have such things: I like to see her enjoying things and feel that she's had rather a rotten life and deserves some treats. Also it's hard on her if Lyndall has them and she doesn't.

But ... she has a way of getting back on me which costs me more than the economy saves. This is by losing things. She is absolutely notorious everywhere for this and the list of things I have had to replace is very long. Also she is terribly careless of her clothes so that they are always having to be cleaned. However now she has to pay all this out of the allowance Silas gives her. This started in October. She is also inclined to borrow my things, lose them or leave them at places ... All this causes friction in the home as also does her habit of *never* doing anything till she has been reminded over and over and over again and her total lack of time sense.

When she first comes home, I make great efforts to be patient. But of course sooner or later I do break down and nag and then say too much. I wouldn't say so much if she did not incessantly argue and make excuses and, what is far more irritating, relapse into a stony, superior faintly smiling silence . . . a trick she has had since she was a child . . .

In the last year or two she has taken to being rather ungrateful . . . to other people . . . Her attitude is a little 'Well, *I* didn't ask them to. I suppose they wouldn't have done it if they hadn't wanted to' or 'I suppose they felt they ought to'. But she is nearly always very sweet and appreciative if I give her something . . .

I'm afraid I'm not one of those mothers who sink themselves in their children. I want Sue to have her rights but I'm much too egotistical not to want mine too. I feel I've got a life and a job to do as well as being Sue's mother. And Sue . . . is occasionally inclined to think that my 'job' is mainly earning money. Actually, when she wants to, she understands the writing side very well and is an admirable critic of my work. I think she may be a tiny bit jealous . . .

Owing to not having a husband and also having had rather an isolated life the last ten years I have talked to Sue too much as if she were a grown-up. She is so intelligent and mature in some ways that it is tempting. And as she very seldom seems to have much she wants to talk about herself . . . I have done too much of the talking . . .

But it has had a very bad result for which I blame myself now very much. She finds most of her contemporaries 'raw' and insipid and says she herself feels as if she knew a great deal about life without having *experienced* it and so doesn't know how to 'be her age' . . .

Yet she has an admirable social sense, always takes trouble at parties, even with people who don't interest her and is a charming hostess and a charming guest. But *before* a party she is always in a state of panic . . .

I think it is rather difficult for a short mother to have a very tall daughter. They are always bending down their swan like necks to you or putting things on shelves you can't reach and taking such long strides you can't keep up with them. I think it is almost impossible not to develop an inferiority complex and to become a bit of a tyrant by way of compensation. You can neither effectively cuddle or scold a creature a head taller than yourself who seems to be almost out of earshot. I feel like a hen who's hatched a crane . . .

* * *

During the War, Eric Earnshaw Smith had married Georgina Horley,[†] a writer. The name was a pseudonym and anyway she was always known as Georgie. She had been in love with Tom Hopkinson during the early days of *Picture Post*. At about the same time Silas Glossop had married Sheila Felton, a widow, who was working in SOE (Special Operations Executive).

* * *

21 March, Palm Sunday   A year ago today, at B[enedicta]'s instigation I burnt my first two notebooks. In this year the whole axis of my life has changed. I have found the 'one thing necessary'.

Meanwhile on the outside, everything has changed. The people nearest me are estranged. Eric is married; Emily [Coleman] quite incapable of understanding what has been going on: Benedicta completely gone . . and hostile too: Susan, the last to go, hating me coldly. I see what it is all for and try not to complain too much inwardly. And even in the outside world there are compensations: new warmth and kindness from people who were not much more than acquaintances before and friends I feel I can trust . . Barbara [Ward],[†] Kathleen [Raine], Joan [Cochemé],[†] Enid [Starkie],[†] Margot, and above all Dorothy. And Sheila [Glossop].

* * *

Early in 1948 Susan returned from Oxford half-way through her second term with a nervous breakdown, brought on by the approach of an examination called Sections. Dr Carroll suggested that she should go and stay with friends, and Hubert and Margaret Waley, the parents of a school friend Isabel Waley (now Ide) put her up.

* * *

But there is still the sense of something unresolved . . Susan above all, but Benedicta too for the two are closely associated. Now that it is Holy Week again, I feel that the events of Holy Week and Easter last year will have an echo. That story is not finished yet. Now I have the two of them against me – S. and B. Last year Sue had a new awakening: now she is like a dead shell of a person. I do not know if they have met yet: I think it almost inevitable that they will very soon. Sue is more untruthful than I had supposed. How consciously untruthful, I don't know. And she is treacherous: again how consciously, I don't know. She hates D[orothy]. That will be a bond with Benedicta. But she does not KNOW that she loves or hates anyone. I have trusted her and it is by no means all her fault if she had been 'disloyal'. What frightens me is her apparent total unawareness of what she has done and does ... She will look like shining truth and lie, just as when she was little ... She looks awfully pleased with herself like a clever, naughty child who has 'got away' with something. I suppose Carroll can handle her ... She sits slumped forward ... pretends not to know what on earth I'm talking about. She says she only wants to be left alone, not to have to be amiable to anyone. She sees to it that I fetch and carry for her and is superbly 'above' practical details. She has the same lofty attitude to all of us; Si, Sheila, Tom ... She is like a creature poisoned at the source ... It is as if my getting better has brought out all *her* dark side ... There is no *order* in Sue's life. Either everything is swept utterly blank and bare or · it is in utter chaos. Her room never looks as if it were *lived in* by a normal person. Either it is bare, blank, utterly uncared for though 'tidy' or a hopeless mess. None of her possessions look cherished or cared for ... If it is not a trail of positive disorder, it is little tracks of ugliness and contempt ... there is something indefinably old, grey and dusty about her. I used to notice the same with David Gascoyne.

She said to me the other day 'I haven't lived since I was five years old' ...

Life absolutely terrifies her. You can watch her trying hard to escape into illness ... She is always trying to score off me, make me look a fool. She doesn't want to be with me yet she is always coming round here or ringing up on some pretext or another ... Like B[enedicta] Sue intuitively knows profound truths without being 'true' herself ...

... She has complained for years of her stomach trouble yet she becomes angry and defensive as soon as anyone tries to probe into it ... She proved very clearly she didn't *want* to get rid of it by not even trying to co-operate with 'Uncle Lock' [an expert on relaxation]. She is trying the game my mother played on my father, getting money out

of him for doctor's bills ... And since she has had her allowance she
has become markedly less generous. Lyndall, who has far less, takes
infinitely more trouble over presents etc. and shows real thought and
imagination ... On the surface, the 'Tartan horse' was a rather
shabby let-out for a Christmas present. Underneath it was a desperate
appeal ... She loses what *does* belong to her and 'borrows' what
doesn't ...

1949

There is a gap in the diary from March 1948 to June 1949. Antonia had
let Binesfield to Hugh and Dorothy Kingsmill. Hugh died while they
were there. Antonia had entered a state of negative transference with her
tenant-cum-analyst and given her notice to quit. During this year she
finished *The Lost Traveller* and began *Julian Tye* (published incomplete in
As Once in May) and then *The Sugar House*.

2 June   Small things worth noticing with D[orothy] K[ingsmill].
    1. Her admission that she did not ask me to the cottage, though
always saying I must come, because I was so 'emotional' that she kept
putting me off.
    2. Not sending me the letter about the electricity for a fortnight
(perhaps not worth mentioning)
    3. I suggested several times that I should come down and do the
inventory with no results. In her letter to me after H[ugh]
K[ingsmill]'s death she says 'You never came down to do inventory'
and writes as if I were unwilling to take her word as to what is hers
and what is mine ...
    She also kept assuring me that there was no self-interest in her
suggestion that it would be a good thing for me to go to the cottage.
And fundamentally I am sure this is so. BUT the moment I said I
would be lonely, she suggested coming down herself every week-end
... Then she told me how sorry Little Dorothy was to leave the
cottage. Naturally I felt a brute ... The fact remains that the cottage
belongs to me ...
    ... It was her idea that Hugh should go to the cottage, cut

connections with his London friends and write. He went there, he promptly became ill and in a year he was dead. Nor do I think she helped the situation by ... coming up for longer and longer stays in London every week and filling the house ... with ... her patients, during their holidays ... I don't think D. is quite as capable as she believes herself to be of taking responsibility for other people's lives.

Why, I wonder, is she identifying me with Georgie, the patient whom she most dislikes? ... Georgie is avaricious ... Georgie is married to Eric, Dorothy's instinctive first choice of a husband in the event of H[ugh]'s death ... This month she will for the first time be having to pay *me* money for the rent of the cottage. And I think, unconsciously, she will resent this because I did not pay her for analysis ...

I think there is no doubt that there are certain parallels between the Georgie-Eric, Dorothy-Hugh situation as regards marriage. Dorothy married Hugh after a bad 'let-down' and humiliation. She married a man, older than herself, whom she admired intellectually ... She has often said to me that Tom broke with Georgie because of 'snobbery': as John [see pp 193–4] did with herself. Georgie's emotions dried up because of Tom: her own, as she said the other night, dried up because of John. G[eorgie] ends each session in tears, saying 'I never finished my affair with Tom' ...

Dorothy's attitude to Gerti ... probably affects the situation. She naturally likes Tom and doesn't like Gerti, she has quarrelled with Gerti's analyst, she probably slightly resents (especially since H[ugh]'s death) Gerti's comfortable worldly situation ...

I have just rung up D. to tell her about the rent ...

... I was very glad Dorothy accepted the rent: at first she ... smelt a psychological rat – and she was right! – but possibly not the rat *I* smelt. Some day she will be able to have friends, not patients ... there's a danger in turning friends into patients. For one thing it isolates D. too much ... It is perhaps the awful lack of love in her own childhood that makes it so hard for her, like Benedicta, to be the recipient and not the giver.

5 June Tomorrow is Pentecost. A special feeling of its importance this year ... I went to part of a 'day of recollection' at the Spanish nuns [a local Kensington convent]. A Jesuit spoke: nothing flowery or sensational but solid. The thing I don't find among these theosophical types is humility and the practical effort to live what one believes ... a tremendous amount of talk and emotion ... but something very ... puffed-up. The fierceness with which they go for each other ...

D. is, I know, a genuinely religious person. But I think she is rash in assuming she is a kind of saint. Potentially, yes: actually no. The people from whom I have had that sense of extraordinary radiance and love – *calm* too – have all been Catholics and all been humble ... Fr. Victor, for example: in other words the light goes on and off. I get strong feeling of it from that Hindu's book .. more even than from the Baba books but that may be because they are not written by Baba. I don't profess to the Baba thing. Yet ... I feel myself to be influenced and guided by him ...

... The very dangers in my relation with Benedicta I now find threatening with Dorothy. I let myself be dominated by B. because I loved her intensely but, as I now see, in an impure and disordered way. With Dorothy it has not been so much love, as fear ...

I wonder why B. thought D. took drugs and gave them to others. I myself should have thought that was the very last thing D. would do. I have very little experience of drug takers. B. of course has a lot. But to see them together, I am sure B. looks far more like the usual idea of a drug addict than D. She is always talking about them too. Benedicta certainly implies that at one time she did experiment with them but I have not the slightest reason to suppose that D. ever did.

Tomorrow will be the anniversary of that strange Whit Sunday at the cottage last year. Going to Mass with D. and Little Dorothy. The child's wonderful quiet in the church ... Then Dorothy's announcement that she thought she would become a Catholic and abandoning the idea because Edmée suggested she wouldn't be free to lecture. Then my awful nightmare ... The other day she told me she had a 'dreadful time' with me after that. It was the following Sunday I went up to see Fr. Richard [Kehoe] ... Not long after she told me she had had a letter from him 'very complimentary to me' (i.e. Dorothy) She repeatedly said she would bring up this letter which she told me I should find very reassuring, but she never did.

After that I had a really bad time, the worst of all, culminating in the Baba experience. I don't profess to understand it all ...

6 June, Whit Monday   Pentecost was very important as I felt it would be. I spent the evening with B. Gradually I begin to piece things together, how she, I and D. are using each other and I also believe being used to work out certain things by and through each other . . .

I see that my next problem to work out is Sue . . . How much unthinking love, care and the money which symbolises these things have gone to people who were not my first natural care and my children have only had the pickings and leavings . . . Why did my feeling for B[enedicta] bring Sue and me together and my relations with D[orothy] drive us apart? There was love, real love . . . for B. That I never had for D. Admiration, fear . . . but never for a moment 'being in love' as I was with B. There is no doubt that Sue and Dorothy, while admiring certain qualities in each other, hated each other . . .

. . . Her [Dorothy's] relations with Edmée are remarkably like mine with Sue . . uncomfortably like. Both our daughters 'steal' from us (stealing the love we could not give freely) and neither of us can accept, I think, *the father's share in the child* . . .

13 June   In the first book I didn't do justice to my mother. In the second (and in the first too) I was not really fair to my father. I tried to be: maybe I didn't see him quite right. Obviously one can never *really* see a person. In the new one [*The Sugar House*] I have somehow got to try and see them both as clearly as possible . . . The money thing, never properly worked out after Carroll has got to be worked out now. I was going all right on the earning side (except insane spending on I[an]) till war interrupted everything. But I could not get going properly on the book. I am perfectly sure D. cannot help me analytically at the moment . . . as she did not finish her own analysis, she is not ripe to deal with them . . .

. . . Her attitude to money is in some ways even more unrealistic than mine as she has never had to manage and control it . . .

24 June   Rather edgy all day and slight headache. Feast of the Sacred Heart, last day of my novena for Dorothy. Fr. Victor was here. I answered his Mass at the Oratory . . . They must have forgotten to give him a host for me and he gave me a particle of the big one. He becomes a different person when he is saying Mass . . .

This evening I suddenly wanted to read the 15 page dream of '47 again. I did so, seeing much in the dream which now seems clearly to apply to Dorothy . . .

We never got out 'Margaret' in my analysis. She says she never got out 'Flower Song' in hers. Lately my hunch is that 'Flower Song' is connected with her painful experience with John's uncle (see pp 193–4) which is connected with a flower garden. Her case is very like my own: the 'light woman' episode must have been the counterpart of my Roehampton experience. Damming up of the love nature, like my damming up of writing. 'Margaret' is obviously the 'dominating' woman of a certain type . . . 'good' type in a way but not understanding a certain side of me: Margaret Thornton,[†] Havinden,[†] King. Highly capable women. Margaret King on her 'good works' side, not her odd one. Dorothy in her scolding 'housewife' mood . . . coming out now in my extreme annoyance with Dorothy's neglect of the cottage . . . Why can't I look at the other side . . . and say 'It's Dorothy's Russian side' instead of being so sore about it . . .

Hugh's death *must* have a profound effect on her unconsciously. . . . Suspect she feels, not so much a widow as an orphan . . .

26 June   . . . Sometimes I think St Thomas was the greatest human being who ever lived. If I have a real patron, it is St Thomas . . . His prayers – I've loved them since I was a child – seem to me just simply the best prayers ever written. Why shouldn't he be the patron saint of artists as well as of intellectuals? Because he *was* one. Look at his poems . . . The sanest of the saints . . . He just rings dead true right through. He had a wild, passionate love of God expressed with the utmost sobriety . . .

My main worry at the moment is money . . . I would so like to . . . be able to give up Tom's £20 a month: quite impossible at the moment . . . Other people seem to be asked to do things but I don't. It seems the only hope to go and see Morley [Antonia's bank manager].

30 June   I did go to see Morley . . . and he was exceedingly nice so I can get through the immediate crisis of rent etc. Yesterday I had a long and extremely frank talk with Benedicta . . . there is no doubt that this Dorothy business has been very much more dangerous than I had realised . . . The fury with which she has turned on me because I refused to let her dictate my life (though it was she herself who told me my analysis was finished) proves that she was using analysis as a weapon: what she is doing now amounts to psychological blackmail. From the first part there is no doubt I got a great deal of benefit. Things began to go wrong from the moment she took the cottage and Hugh became ill, improved for a time . . . and took a serious bad turn this time last year . . . she is not nearly 'integrated' enough . . . to be safe in wielding the enormous power analysis gives one . . . There is no doubt that she still has enough psychological hold over me to cause me considerable disturbance. When after thinking and praying about it during 24 hours, I wrote her a calm, but firm letter my hands trembled so violently that I could hardly form the letters. And even today, when writing to her lawyer to say that I waived all claims for damages, neglect etc my hand at once became unsteady again . . .

1 July   . . . D. substituted herself for B. *but* she didn't know where to stop and couldn't let me go. She wanted the influence acquired during a 'positive transference' to go on when it was over . . .

Now D. and B. both say the same thing about each other . . . Like Emily saying how ridiculous for me and B. to go from church to church together when she and I had done precisely the same thing and she had thought it wonderful . . .

Interesting, incidentally, that though it was D.'s first idea . . . that this was a two-way experiment between us equally useful and equally risky to both, I have actually given her a little money . . . besides being indirectly responsible for her receiving money from Tom and Eric. And D. wants money even more than I do . . . This is natural, having suffered far more bitter poverty in childhood than I ever did. Mine was just cramp and insufficiency which I wouldn't even have felt if my father hadn't sent me to school with wealthy girls. It isn't the diamonds and mink coat sort of wealth I want but the Roehampton kind where there was no question of ostentation; money was there and one didn't have to think about it. Of course there one was up against 'inherited money' and also against the idea of 'making money' even by earning it was a sign of social inferiority. Dorothy, bless her, would be blissfully happy as a 'nouveau riche' or rather with the actress's diamonds and champagne – her desire for the *audience*: mannequin . . . as well as dressmaker . . . current mania for displaying herself with guitar. *Almost* slight irritation with Hugh for 'stealing the show' by his amazing death. She cut off *his* audience by fixing up the cottage and got her own back on him for shutting her away in Swiss hotels. The tragi-comedy of their life together, so superb at the end in spite of everything. Hugh's heavenly sense of humour which persisted after death. Hers too. I wonder if anything unites people more than a shared laugh at their own expense . . .

D. and the cottage. She loves it and . . . wants it to be hers. Her neglect of my furniture: in the garden only what she has planted is cared for . . . the cottage isn't *mine*. I have a life interest in it: it is in trust for my children. All that *belongs* to me is the furniture and, if I sold it, the interest on the capital . . . Almost her first remark after Hugh's death 'It is time I learnt something about the law.' A true remark . . .

4 July   I've been a fool: no doubt about that. What I can't quite make out is how it all started. Trouble is, there's so much truth mixed up in it all. For about 25 years now this business of 'masters' has been in the air . . . I think there's something phony there at once . . . I won't accept his idea of the church. For years, [Ronald] Moody tries to put Ouspensky over on me. I'm not having it . . but . . there are moments when I'm uneasy . . . I live 4 years with the Moodys and study them at very close quarters. I like them both. But once that 'I know' look appears . . . I find them very difficult. They exploit me . . . give me all the dirty work to do while incessantly lecturing me on my irresponsibility. The emphasis is always on *power*. The thing really begins with Benedicta. I let her dominate me . . .

There is so much that is ludicrous in this whole business: . . . Van Ryswick, Collostrom, Arcane Society (Robb a member) . . . All these rivalries, backbitings, jealousies among the 'masters'. Such a phony set up . . .

My own unsolved mystery is Baba . . . Should I have 'contacted' him if it hadn't been for D.? . . . She certainly talked about him a good deal, quoted letters etc. And she did say she had asked him to 'contact' me. This was about 18 months ago . . . Many of his words affect me deeply . . . Of course now that I know Dorothy plays rather wildly with truth, many of the things she has told me – such as his 'connection' with Padre Pio [Italian priest with stigmata] may be quite untrue. Frankly I am more impressed by some of his other 'disciples', those who have actually met him ... than I am by Dorothy. They are much humbler ... What I don't understand is the connection between Baba and Christianity ... I've told both Fr. Richard [Kehoe] and Fr. Victor [White] about it; neither of them seem to show alarm ... Yet some recent reports made me a little uneasy. Jean [unknown] said the love was now much less apparent than the power. And this money question which seems inseparable from these people crops up again. I know that Baba uses the money for his work: he cares for the sick, builds schools etc. These tremendous and apparently capricious journeys are more difficult to understand. He is always sending people off to raise large sums. Yet all that can be interpreted in a special way. But Christ's way of working seems so much simpler ...

This cottage business I don't understand. D[orothy] is evidently putting it over as Baba's idea as much as her own. When I went down and saw Hugh's death mask, I was very much aware of Baba's picture looking at me ...

One thing I definitely mistrust in D. is her evident dislike of my going to the sacraments. Very often this has been the occasion for sneers. I know ... she sometimes ... goes to communion at ... Van Ryswick's catholic [church] ... But she's no real understanding of the *sacraments* ...

5 July No communication either from D. or from her solicitors to whom I sent a formal letter ... waiving my right to go through the inventory.

I am trying to see how Dorothy felt when she wrote the letter. Savage and unjust as it is, she must have felt really aggrieved ... I'm sure she's convinced that she had my best interests at heart in trying to force me to go and live alone at the cottage ... it was very petty of me even to mention such details as nettles and neglected furniture ... I would certainly have considered letting her take it on unfurnished if she hadn't proved that she really isn't capable of looking after that garden properly. It isn't just a cash question: the place will go to rack and ruin if it isn't properly looked after and it's a full time job for someone who understands gardening and does not have their own work to do as I have ... I'm sure one reason (she probably doesn't know it) for keeping us all apart is that she's said too much to each one and is terrified of our meeting and comparing notes ...

Tom looks well and Eric and Georgie can, I think, look after themselves. G[eorgie] is pretty tough. E[ric] extremely intelligent ...

... What makes it more tricky ... is the brilliance of her [Dorothy's] analytical intuition. What is dangerous is the occult background. Collostrom and Robb are 'in the racket'. Howe [unknown] is 'putting over' Zen Buddhism and yoga. There is more than a hint of esotericism in Jung. Only the Freudians remain strictly 'scientific' but they are flirting heavily with drugs, shock treatment etc. Father Victor said the other night that the psyche and the soul seemed to him indistinguishable. Yet the psyche can be damaged, just as the body can, without ... injuring what some would call ... the soul ...

7 July   Since another and far more venemous [sic] letter came from D[orothy] this morning, I think it's a good idea to look back and see just how my connection with her started. I first heard of her from Kathleen Raine. This was probably in '45 or '46 – K[athleen]'s comment roughly 'You may think her phony: Graham [Greene] says she's sinister but I find her interesting. She walked out on her analyst because he didn't believe in God'.

Later she told me this woman had had a dream about me (something connected with the stage: I have never been told what this dream was). Eventually I was invited to lunch at Holland Park. We had a talk (she knew I had had trouble about writing): I liked her though I thought her cranky. She told me that, without meaning to, she found herself in the position of giving people advice and 'helping them' by interpreting dreams: she mentioned one or two cases of writers and painters. I think it was the second time she invited me there that she said she had read 'The Saint' [one of Antonia's short stories] and had had a wonderful intuition about my writing problem from it. I doubt if I went more than 3 times to her house, always by invitation and to lunch. I would have a drink and a talk with Hugh then lunch with the family and afterwards have a short talk alone with Dorothy ... The last time I went she said 'Do ring up and invite yourself to lunch any time you feel like it' As she had been complaining how rushed she was with 'patients' and a large family to cope with, I didn't like to bother her with suggesting she should feed me and she had given me the impression of being so awfully busy and rushed that I didn't like to ask her to come over here, so, though I would quite like to have seen her again, I lost sight of her. I used to hear of her sometimes from Kathleen [Raine] and I knew she had moved. It never occurred to me that there was any question of analysis at that time ... B[enedicta] seems to have been definitely told that I had been her patient at one time ... every time I refer to it and say 'I certainly never realised I was supposed to be a patient' she [Dorothy] purses her lips and says nothing.

I next met her, again through Kathleen, at one of Fr. Richard's lectures ... her manner to me was very cold ...

On March 20th [1947] I met her again after a lecture, with Kathleen and Leila and introduced her to Benedicta. The two got on well and did most of the talking. I invited D[orothy] to bring Edmée to a party on Easter Sunday ... D. came to the party. She sang and B[enedicta] accompanied her ...

In May, Tom wanted to send Lyndall to an analyst. I suggested ... D[orothy] ... I went to see D. to give the 'background' ... I went out to dinner with D. and I don't remember how it happened that we began to talk about B[enedicta] and I told her the whole story. She said she had found B. in a café looking very unhappy and she questioned her and knew there was a woman she was worried about and that someone had dreamt of her 'as a devil'. D. told her someone had 'contacted' her shadow side and was projecting *their* 'shadow' on to her. It was not till my long talk with D. over Lyndall that D. knew I was the woman. D. then told me that she could help both B. and myself if I was willing to submit to a rather painful ordeal. She said she and I would both be taking risks, as I had been in Bedlam and she was unqualified. She stressed the fact I could help B. .... She also said she would be able to release my writing ... Her reward, she said, would be the birth of 'the real Antonia'.

On May 25th B. rang me up and talked in a most extraordinary way. I was in great danger: had I any friends I could trust? She *must* see me. I went up in the afternoon and she talked wildly about plots to get her out of the tertiaries, threatening phone calls etc. All that I got clearly was that she seemed to feel it was dangerous for me to go to D. because D. was more of a Buddhist than a Catholic ... Not long after

B. rang again saying '... I've finished with the Kingsmill. No *discretion* there'. I said I knew what she meant but it didn't worry me ...

In ... August, I went through quite a bad analytical crisis but D. was ... ill with a sort of nervous breakdown. [William] Gerhardi [sic] said that he was accused by Hugh of bringing this on. He had had an argument with her about reincarnation ...

In January she took the cottage, her idea being that it was a very important part of my analysis that she should do so.

We had this extraordinary session down at the cottage in which she went so deep that I was babbling in a kind of trance. We both were frightened, she more than I ... I had a terribly depressed period for several weeks ... A few days later came a dream ... which D. said warned me of trouble with Sue. A few days later Sue came home with a kind of nervous breakdown and I sent her to Carroll ... I began to have dreams of and 'contacts' with Baba. I was remarkably well during the early summer of '48 ... It was then she asked me as a personal favour to come to all her group meetings ...

Shortly after that the cat fell out of the window. I am not sure when during this summer I had the severest of all crises, during which D. said she could do nothing but wait and warned the caretaker here that I might have an accident. I think I was in considerable danger during this summer. There were times when I really was not normal: I was in semi-cataleptic states and doing very peculiar things under the influence of Baba. I think what saved my sanity was Lyndall's coming here and my having to nurse her through tonsillitis.

I did finish the book [*The Lost Traveller*] during the autumn but it may well be as a result of a practical talk with Joan [Souter Robertson] and her standing over me that I got it done. Where D. *did* help, was in making me see my relation to my mother. And it was in December that *she* told me my analysis was over ...

She started on Tom and Eric, then Georgie and finally Lyndall were drawn in. I was partly responsible: I believed in her and when Tom was worried over Gerti last summer I suggested he should get in touch with D. Her original intention was to straighten things out for all of us. Immediate results were to drive Tom and Gerti further apart, to make Eric and Georgie on much worse terms, to provoke a violent attack on me from Georgie and to try and get Lyndall to go and live with Edmée in her flat ...

Since I have known her well (2 years) she has in turn rounded violently on Van Ryswick ... whom she greatly admired at one time. She has also had violent rows with patients and ex-patients such as Kathleen and Denis and Joyce Bonney [unknown]; also with her family: Edmée, her father and her sisters. She has also fulminated against Jalis [unknown], Douglas Jerrold,[†] Hesketh Pearson[†] and Malcolm Muggeridge ... not to mention Gerti and Georgie. This really does seem to add up to the fact that she is [in] no state to be taking patients at the moment or trying to manage other people's lives ...

7 July   Later ... Certainly I needed a friend: who doesn't? I was too weak to put up with human loneliness. Oh, the analyst, the analyst, the person who gives us their exclusive, undivided attention ...

8 July   I woke up this morning suddenly realising something so obvious that it is amazing I never spotted it before: the need of an audience. I would never have been expelled from Roehampton if I hadn't yielded to the temptation of letting someone read my book ... *Frost in May* written entirely because Tom listened ... Look at my desire to be an actress. In other words, exhibitionism. It seems odd neither of the analysts got on to this ...

Just now I am beginning to wonder if analysis is not very dangerous dynamite indeed. It is so difficult to stabilise, so much depends on the character of the analyst and the analyst himself is exposed to such dangers ...

4 Aug   I had an extraordinary conversation with B[enedicta] this morning. During the last week I've had a classic bad turn ... Dorothy's mention of 'depravity' obviously touched a very raw place: the sense I always have during a 'bad' turn of being a kind of leper ...

Now B. comes out with the very interesting idea that, in the famous book episode ... part of me thought my father judged rightly. Therefore, since he pronounced me guilty, I must remain under sentence for ever ...

What B. is trying to convince me of is that I am NOT GUILTY. This is a very difficult new idea to take in ...

... I suppose that, instead of properly 'forgiving' him I've gone on unconsciously trying to justify him all these years. Is that because a father can become such an idol, such a representative of God on earth, that the most painful things are more bearable than admitting he might be wrong? Because .. if one's father is fallible, there is no security anywhere. I have been pretty sure for a long time that if, during my childhood, even when I was very 'devout', my father had said he no longer believed in Catholicism, I would have left the Church at once with him.

Dorothy, of course, is doing exactly what an analyst shouldn't do. In trying to revenge herself for private unconscious grievances against me, she is trying to renew and reinforce my natural sense of guilt ...

... To be 'NOT GUILTY' in Benedicta's sense doesn't mean I have a beautiful nature or am not liable at any moment to behave disgracefully. It simply means that I am not responsible for the Fall of Man. My father was human and fallible, so am I, so is Dorothy, so is Susan. Susan judges me very severely ... Somehow the unconscious has to accept the 'NOT GUILTY' verdict. It seems to me that, humanly speaking, it can only be done by another human being whom one loves and trusts and who loves and trusts oneself. I need a friend far more than an analyst. And it is *that* that has been coming up so much this last week, the need for a friend. 'Without a friend, thou canst not well live' and, in my case, no one else can stand living with me either! ...

It really [is] time I grasped that my parents were dead and that I have no longer got to imitate them, defy them or obey them. I haven't any responsibility towards them except to pray for their souls. I can't go to them for comfort, advice, money, shelter or approval any more. But I haven't got to keep them, nurse them, worry about them or their approval or disapproval. My father can't judge me any more ... That menacing eye literally does not exist any more and never will ...

... Sometimes I think we are rather hard on Narcissus. He did not *know* he had fallen in love with his own image. His trouble was homosexuality and inability to let anyone, male (Apollo) or female (the water nymphs) love him. He wanted to do all the loving himself ... God is not too proud to be loved. Strange, this difficulty in accepting love when we are so frantically craving for it. God finds us lovable – *us*, not our notions of ourselves. But we prefer our notions of ourselves ...

The real ... thing is the having no pleasure in writing. Because one ought to enjoy using a talent. Writing is always a dreary duty ...

Always it goes back to the original book. Always something never gets released. What is the town I suddenly find I love but must leave tomorrow? Bells – the happy noise to hear – Bredon hill .. always the opposition between church and religion. And the girl died because she stayed with her lover on the hill instead of going to church.

So always the Church stands over against sex for me ... Two facts remain: I am religious: I am highly sexed. But I am always trying to castrate myself. The church condemns Benedicta and me to live without physical sex ... Probably this famous 'sex-appeal' of ones is nothing but vitality. She never seems to lose hers: I, of course, do and fall into this greyness ...

Never properly married: that's my trouble ... Under a curse: yes, yes, it does feel like that. The nuns, my father, Robin [early admirer] and in an odd way [Dorothy] Kingsmill. For she has cast me out very crudely and definitely. Something all wrong with me . . I am 'depraved', and she must 'withdraw from me and my situation'.

BUT who were all these people who cursed me? People consciously or unconsciously sexually attracted to me. Mother Bradshaw† etc. Men AND women. Evidently it is very dangerous for me if I attract people ...

My writing produces a strong effect on people. It must be sexually attractive. So I don't write.

But I *like* attracting people; so I want to write.

But I mustn't admit I like it so I mustn't like writing ...

8 Aug Oddly enough Sue brought up last night the fact that I do things in roundabout ways: in talk this time. I learnt a lot from that talk with Sue. She freezes up defensively the moment we get to the point of my *expecting* anything of her ...

... She admits that she will do things for Lyndall that she won't for me: she admitted that Lyndall complains of me to her but was obviously surprised to hear that L. complains of her to me, though she knows Lyndall is a chronic complainer. Lyndall is affectionate and treacherous; she is more subtly selfish than Sue.

Of course I'm horribly jealous too. I'm jealous that les Papas will produce money, holidays, clothes etc. for S. and L. but never dream of practical help for me. That is what makes me feel sore sometimes: that there is no one who concerns themselves about my welfare. I feel sometimes that I could die here and no one would even know . . .

25 Aug   D[orothy] K[ingsmill] has often said to me that there was too much sentimentality about the Baba people, that she herself did not believe him to be a Messiah . . . In her copy of *The Perfect Master* she writes the following –

'My Beloved Baba, not a day must pass without my giving thanks to Thee for having made Thy Life, for our sakes, a living sacrifice . . .'

1950

Antonia White's second novel, *The Lost Traveller*, was published in spring 1950.

26 Feb   . . . The extraordinary change that has come over me since the R[oyal] L[iterary] F[und] made me that grant and made it possible for me to pay all my most pressing debts. Among other things it must have symbolised a pardon of some kind: an official permission from Society to go on writing. Even my N[ew] S[tatesman] reviewing which was such a nightmare at first (mainly sense of incompetence) has become much more manageable.

During a lull I started up routine work again on the Tom–Eric book. Now it seems to me . . . that I am far from ready to write that book . . . It seems rather indecent to write about Tom and Eric so closely when they are married to other people. Also there are Susan's and Lyndall's feelings to be considered . . . Therefore I think now of writing a continuation of *The Lost Traveller*: there is no reason why I should not, like Proust and Duhamel continue with the same set of characters . . . One immediate difficulty – it must be related to *The Lost Traveller* which is not of course literally autobiographical. It *might* be possible to place the father's death in this book which would make the Archie [a fictional Reggie] marriage more convincing. But I think, by making Archie no longer rich, this could be avoided . . .

19 April (Tom's birthday) . . . In a way Tom destroyed my guilt about writing and then started it up again by his 'betrayal' . . .

22 April . . . One has friends who are nice to one only when one's 'down' and others only when one's 'up'. This book [*The Lost Traveller*] looks as if just possibly it might bring me money. In spite of the furious contradictions of the reviews it looks as if it may have 'established' me. I have quite forgotten what it feels like to be a success . . . Kathleen [Raine] is a wonderful 'failure' friend . . .

It's so silly; I can't help day dreaming about what I'd do if I had some money – after I'd paid my debts! It would cost literally hundreds to have the house done up which it badly needs . . .

12 July I had as usual no idea what my last entry had been. And I have just finished doing what I so much wanted to do . . doing up the house. I did a great deal of the work myself and got what I couldn't manage alone done cheaply. I have even got the stair carpet! . . . It cost £110 all told and the money from the book will pay it.

After the exertion of doing the house and writing some articles during it I was naturally very tired. But this tiredness prolonged itself into a long spell of lethargy of the old type. I think this was aggravated by my extraordinary conversation with Mother Bradshaw[†] on June 18 for after that I was certainly in a 'psychological' state, with a run of dreams etc. I find I have for the first time made a real success of a job, though it was sensible to resign from the N[ew] Statesman] when I did. Janet [Adam Smith] told B[arbara] Ward that I was 'irreplaceable.'

The real importance of my conversation with Mother Bradshaw was not that *she* had forgotten the whole thing but the conversation she had with my father. She swears that I was not expelled and that it was *he* who wanted me to leave. 'If this is how she is spending her time, the sooner she comes home and works with me the better'. That rings absolutely true: his very accents . . .

. . . He had wanted me to go to St Paul's a year before . . . What this boils down to is the revelation that my father was human and fallible, a fact the conscious knows but the unconscious still does not seem to *believe*. My cheerful dream about my father and the two French whores (the only cheerful dream I can ever remember having had about him) that followed so soon on the conversation seems a sign that the unconscious is beginning to grasp it! . .

Taking my father as human, his attitude to my writing was not unsympathetic. But he saw it as a *sideline*, a hobby . . . never to be thought of as *first*, either as profession or as moneymaker. He must have been jealous too of my talent: his behaviour in not letting me do English for the scholarship was quite crazy . . . and stopped me from getting one. Though he was interested in writing, he certainly saw it in some way as 'unrespectable' and I think this ties up with Wilde and his homosexual side. He actually wrote very well himself. What he absolutely *abhorred* my doing was not writing but *acting* and acting to me was of course the greatest *pleasure* of all.

So many complex things were touched off in the book episode that I will never be able to assess them all. There is Mother Bradshaw's side too. I must have affected *her* unconsciously and she got her own back by reducing me to that state. Someone must have crushed *her* most cruelly; it was touching, her confession of how terrified she was of *us*. Now, gradually, society is forgiving me and encouraging me to write. But *can* I accept forgiveness or – as so often – does something in me prefer to sulk and grieve and say 'No. It's too late – You see what you've done to me'. Enormously strong, this drive to the deathbed scene – the remorse of my friends who should have been kinder.

I am pleased that I have stood up quite well to many very 'misunderstanding' and even insulting notices of the book . . .

. . . [Eliot] Seabrooke believed that sex was essential to the artist. But then when I fell in love with Robert (and that was straight, simple sex) I think art would have gone completely. What I got was madness and out of that came art.

9 Sept   My present nagging preoccupation is Susan . . . She cannot bear to stick to any sort of plan or arrangement: it is as if she waited till I decided on something so as to decide the exact opposite . . . She hates living with me yet when I wanted to go away for four days she complained that she hated being left alone in the flat and I had to ask

Jan[et de Glanville, a Somerville friend of Susan] ... Though she very rarely consults my convenience, she makes a great show of consulting Sheila's and uses Sheila as a convenient excuse for getting out of things she doesn't want to do ... She has a genius for finding the most wounding phrase and the most contemptuous tone or expression ...

5 Nov ... This last week I have had quite an orgy of plays, films and listening to wireless plays. This was deliberate. Is something buzzing underneath? No idea turns up, however ... A faint possibility I may get offered a job in a publishers: alarm as to whether or not to accept it ... I do worry much too much about money but it's hard not to when I am always in debt and never know how to get through each quarter ... There may be good surprises (how childishly, how irrationally I have hoped for one these last 2 months) ... But the next few months are quite grim enough. Everything costs so much and it is hard to see where to cut down enough to make any serious difference ...

... Now I most certainly don't horde [sic] money. But I *do* horde [sic] and am most reluctant to part with the obvious means of making money: e.g. writing. I like *thinking* about writing: I like cutting: I like having written. But I find acute difficulty in getting down to getting it out.

During these weeks when I have been very worried about money and have made all sorts of unsuccessful attempts to get commissions, I have had anxiety dreams. Two of these were connected with packing at short notice for a journey and both had a sexual accompaniment. In one I *thought* I had packed everything and found that in reality I had packed practically nothing I needed ... The sexual accompaniment of the first was much more violent. It is rather difficult to know exactly what the right attitude to sex is. I always fight against orgasms in dreams. Sexual deprivation *is* difficult certainly. Deprivation of love and companionship much harder ... Psychologically, what could this sexual excitement, which adds a further difficulty to the packing mean? What causes the excitement, the journey or the packing? ...

... I broke off and added up all I received last year and this. It looks more than adequate on paper: in fact it is frightening to see how much I have spent with so little to show for it. In this year 1950 I have received several hundreds extra because of the book. Yet here I am in Nov. not knowing how to get to the end of the year and pay the rent, let alone my debts. We certainly don't seem to live extravagantly. This year I did up the house, bought some clothes and had a holiday. Yet I and house were so shabby it seemed a real necessity. It is fearfully hard to alter one's way of life: mine is very much lower in standard than before the war as it is . . .

. . . I need a net income of £2,500 a year. It sounds fantastic. I see no possibility of making anything like it . . . What can I do *now*? The story and the reviews. Give myself a week for that. Then start up on the book again. That must not be shirked. And simultaneously do a *N[ew] Y[orker]* piece. TRY by Nov 18th – 12 days from now to have finished the story, the reviews and the *N[ew Y[orker]* piece. That is *not* impossible.

FIVE

1951–1954

At the start of 1951 Antonia was working on her third novel, *The Sugar House*, to be published like her second, *The Lost Traveller*, by Eyre and Spottiswoode. Her fourth and last novel, *Beyond the Glass*, came out in 1954. Her editor at Eyre and Spottiswoode was Douglas Jerrold. In that year she also published *Strangers*, a collection of short stories.

Susan celebrated her twenty-first birthday at Binesfield but on her return to Oxford attempted suicide because of anxiety about her finals. She returned home after three months in hospital, but Antonia then expelled her from home. Susan married Thomas Chitty (Thomas Hinde),[†] an Oxford friend. Lyndall, in flight from Dicky Muir,[†] settled in Italy for life. With room to spare at Ashburn Gardens, Antonia took her first lodger, Daphne Borrett,[†] a friend of Lyndall's.

1951

14 Jan, Septuagesima   Odd. Turning out drawers today found this book and opened at packing dreams. Recently had another: this time that I started on journey to America. In train, realised that I had brought *empty suitcases*.

Work and money problems temp[orarily] solved by doing nothing but book which I have promised by June 30th This is terribly short time and already it looks impossible to *reduce* and *produce* it. I wanted 9 months and Jerrold only gave me 6 . . . Thought of shortage of material makes me rather nervously stock up on stationery etc. More than I could use in a year. *Watch this*. Must *write* on the stationery: not hoard blank blocks!

I think a tendency to identify *spending money* with work. When I am not working well, I begin to spend money – usually on account of course . . .

* * *

Antonia discussed her problems with Edward Thornton,† an amateur
psychologist, but analysis was not initiated. He was associated with
Dorothy Kingsmill and 'all this eastern stuff'.

* * *

22 Jan   Spent last evening with Edward Thornton. He seems very
anxious we should be friends. I like him and find him very easy to talk
to.

I told him a lot about the Kingsmill business. He was very
interesting about the animus, the unconscious male side of women
which can become diabolical . . . V. interesting too on the correspondence between parents and children in the unconscious. Quoted his
patient in the north whose son was put in an asylum. When the
woman faced her own unconscious difficulties, the boy got well. Also
interesting: when I told him about my father appearing dressed as a
monk the night I went out of my mind he said 'The monk would
represent the celibate: your father, with whom intercourse was
forbidden, would naturally appear like that.' I obviously represented
both son and daughter to my father: in a sense animus and anima. My
own trouble is obviously concerned with this animus, my male side
. . . Rather odd situation: a man is as it were forcing me to write this
new book. Jerrold in his letter used the very expression. 'I am sure
you have several good books in you'.

This book is being done in quite a new situation for me. 1) The
man 'driving' me is one who has a purely professional and unemotio-
nal relation with me 2) It is also a 'job': i.e. I am being supported
while I write it 3) Time element: I feel 6 months is too little. I . . .
certainly have feeling child will be unfinished: an abortion. On the
other hand I did begin and plan it some time ago . . .

After my conversation with E[dward] T[hornton] I had an odd
dream. I dreamt I was going to have a baby (Tom's) . . . A friendly but
strict nurse received me into the hospital . . . Suddenly I realised I had
made no preparations whatever for the baby: had bought not so
much as a vest. I was in a panic. Then I remembered I had some credit
at [John] Lewis and Harrods and if I went up there at once (I had not
begun labour) I could probably get what was necessary . . . The ward

seemed to be for men and women. At the last moment the nurse said 'What a pity Oliver could not come in' . . .

I associate this Oliver with Oliver Marlowe [a girlhood friend] whom I certainly never think of . . . My father rather despised Oliver M. because he was a socialist and a pacifist. My prig cousin Arnold's joke 'Libera nos a Marlowe' . . .

. . . The clothes I was wearing when I went into hospital were those of the period before Susan was born. The 'men' in my life have been, superficially at least, gentle types. Robert even, was gentle though far more typically masculine than any of the others . . .

1 Feb   Two dreams last night. This obviously C[ommunist] P[arty] inspired meeting to wh. I went with Tom at Pearl Binder's[†]: talk after in which I said a certain amount about D[orothy] K[ingsmill] and it was clear that Tom was considerably involved with her still (He has a certain reserved smile when I mention her) . . .

Dreams were

1. I was going to be hanged . . or rather to hang myself. Kathleen Raine was . . . very interested and excited about it . . . telling me how wonderful the corpses of the hanged were: tremendous experience etc. etc. Felt I would be letting her down . . . if I didn't hang myself . . .

2. I was going to be remarried to Tom . . .

I am obviously still terrified of being disapproved of. I hadn't the guts to say what I really thought at that meeting, feeling what a weight there would be against me . . fear of being branded right wing, reactionary, warmonger etc . . .

23 Feb   Conjunctivitis has stopped me working for a whole week. Looking at above entry makes me think I was right not to sign. Recent events make me surer than ever that the whole thing was a C[ommunist] P[arty] stunt. I think there *is* something fishy about this eye. It came on just after I'd been writing about Maidie [Trixie, actress from the 1920 tour] looking at Clara with accusing eye 'Thou God seest me'. Something about the male side of myself and destroying it. The death of Charles [Clara's charge in *The Lost Traveller*] must symbolise something. Clara feels guilty though it is not really her fault. I think the abortion of the first child: a son, is worrying me. Certainly I was responsible and committed a grave sin.

But I did suddenly see the other night that my father perhaps had a slight share in this. He wanted me to have the child; yes. But he wanted me to go abroad . . .

5 March   I am having severe trouble over Part II of the book . . . This morning nervous and restless: trying sitting in my father's chair at my desk. Can't decide whether to use it is (a) being too like him (b) using what I have no right to . . .

10 May   Since the last entry, everything bouleversé. Sue's increasingly bad state culminating in two attempts at suicide, the observation ward, the Maudsley. For three weeks I behaved with unnatural calm and efficiency. The real break did not come till last Saturday when I developed a state as bad as Sue's. The 2 of us obviously terribly tied together in this. She has this breakdown at the time most critical for her and for me: her finals: my book. She attempts to destroy herself and, in a sense, me too. Yet neither time does she succeed (she takes precautions not to) and she also inquires anxiously even when she is very remote, how my book is going.

E[dward] T[hornton] has been very helpful: he came round that awful last Saturday night. But I cannot quite dissociate him from D[orothy] K[ingsmill]. All this eastern stuff . . .

All the dreams I have had after talks to him are connected with men and marriage . . . The 'deep' one after Saturday crisis. Sue's doctor (Harris) has gone mad and Sue is in danger. A white-coated young doctor performs a delicate operation (at risk to himself) taking black object from the madman . . . Then I am given a black bag containing genital fluids from the madman. I have to kiss it, repelled though I am. Then I join a procession into a church, carrying the bag . . . I enter the church as they sing 'Adeste fideles': white foaming cleansing fluid is running down the right of the aisle.

He says this shows the true outcome: the creative force of the animus accepted and dedicated . . .

I feel very much that my next stage is as it were *marriage*. Actual marriage has of course been a hopeless failure for me. I can see that I am always after fathers or sons, not husbands . . . Already I catch myself out with E[dward] T[hornton] thinking 'Ah . . . here's someone who will look after me; take over all my burdens etc' Quite a shock when, on Sunday, he had a violent attack and *I* had to look after *him* . . .

Two things have of course produced severe shocks in last week, apart from Sue.

a. Eric nagging, almost blackmailing me into giving him the £50 I had put by from the Jerrold money for the rent. Certainly I owed it him. But the old Eric would never have behaved like that. He has repudiated me all right. Can't blame him: he is in a terrible state. But dangerous to me at the moment.

b. discovery that Tom and D[orothy] K[ingsmill] are lovers. This discovery I made on Saturday and Saturday was the worst turn I have had for a very long time . . .

Now must face fact *all* my three men have gone.
Eric: the intelligent, understanding 'good' father
Silas: the romantic
Tom: the companion; the fellow writer.

Well and truly divorced from all of them – Tom; the last thread gone now because writing which began the whole thing now deflected on to D[orothy] K[ingsmill].

E[dward] T[hornton] a *very* odd type for me. Shrewd business man of the save, buy and sell type . . . *He has the ready cash*. Exact opposite of everyone I know! But he has first class knowledge therefore he gets the best for his clients. Also actor and singer . . .

11 May   How would I describe my own character? . . .

As a child. Obstinate; self-willed: argumentative: impertinent: untidy.

As a grown-up. Touchy: irritable: unwilling to take responsibility: changeable; self-pitying; mischief-making; cruel . . . Hopelessly bad at all physical things: games etc. But if someone can give me confidence I can sometimes do better than I thought possible. Yet I am always looking for someone I can trust completely. Over and over again I think I have found this, only to be let down. Obviously – and for good reason. I don't trust myself. And I don't seem able to trust God. It is *so* difficult not to think of God as waiting to catch me out . . .

Taxation is now at cruelty level. This presses hard on the neurotic who hates having things *forced* from him. The fear to declare, unless what one has will be taken away. The old story of the ten shillings [debt to her father]. Certainly cut very deep. Extravagance does perhaps come partly from deprivation. My father was extravagant himself: my mother too. Both had been very much deprived in their youth. It is always difficult for people who have less than those they associate with. Reggie was deprived – Susan too . . .

14 May   a most peculiar dream . . .

Reggie, grotesquely tall, almost a giant, asked me to marry him again. I was slightly tempted to accept though actually I refused. He said 'I'm afraid I'm not very well off now'. Nevertheless I had the impression that he had some sort of income and the thought of the security and the easy adoring affection was very tempting . . .

I can see that one part of me is screaming madly for kind Daddy who will look after me and make everything easy. Other part is looking for a partner with whom I share responsibilities. Possible danger of trying to make Sue this partner? . . .

How much do I really know even about my feelings for Sue – that great 'interruption' and turning-point in my life. How difficult I find the intrusion of Sheila [Glossop] – so well-meaning, yet so tactless. In many ways Si and Sheila are my worst 'nag' over Sue. Partly I am just selfishly jealous. But partly I am up against their obstinate refusal to admit Sue's spiritual side and Sheila's incessant butting in to protect Silas from any discomfort or guilt. I know I am wrong in wanting Sue's affection to be too much focussed on me.

26 May   . . . my interview with Silas. This interview – the first I have had for about 4 years – has been an enormous relief. We managed to talk in a very natural and friendly way and I felt we agreed much more about Sue than I can ever feel when Sheila acts as the intermediary. It was with great hesitation that I asked him to see me alone: now I am very glad I did. It helped immensely to alleviate my ghost-like feeling . . . The great relief was to find that Silas . . . has not entirely suppressed his other side under the bowler-hat . . . It is really only a question of getting Sheila to 'pipe down' a little and let Silas and myself deal with certain things which concern us as Sue's parents . . .

I am much relieved that, by mutual consent, E[dward] T[hornton] and I are avoiding the analytical situation. I like him very much but I think a) he is rather too obsessed by all this Eastern business b) he is not quite balanced himself yet. I find that peculiar nervous laugh disconcerting. Also I think he goes too far in despising ... the intellect. He ... seems to base *everything* on 'eggsperience'.

... It is *awfully* hard not to feel a bit suspicious of these people who proclaim themselves as 'integrated' because one feels one would recognise a particular quality in them if they were. I *have* felt it in people. I did in that Reverend Mother, in some lay sisters ... It is interesting that I have only found it in ordinary 'Catholic' Catholics ... It is impossible to imagine any of these talking of themselves as 'integrated' or in some higher category of soul achieved by their own efforts. E[dward] T[hornton] talks v. contemptuously of the ordinary run of Catholic priests. But he says he's found one marvellous one who lets him 'pray' to his Indian spiritual teacher. Now what *exactly* does that mean? ...

5 June ... Incessant pressure inside head. This morning cried uncontrollably in the street ... I can see no way out of the impasse. I cannot work: the book is due on June 30th: ... I have been trying to think how I *have* lived during the last 5 years ...

1947 The M[oodys] left. Benedicta. Susan went to France. I started with D[orothy] K[ingsmill]. Have no recollection what work I did after I stopped on the book. Poems: poss[ibly] 'Rich Woman' – occasional articles.

1948 Sue at Oxford and her breakdown. Translation *Une Vie*. That autumn must have finished *Lost Traveller*

1949 Changed all end of book in summer after Hugh [Kingsmill]'s death and did that hack job for E[yre] and S[pottiswoode]. Ordination art[icle] for *Picture Post*]. Dec. did *Flair* article. *N[ew] S[tatesman]* and other reviewing. Big drop in cottage rent.

1950 Think got grant then. Continued to review till about May or June. Autumn: looking for work. 1 or 2 special reviews for *N[ew] S[tatesman]*. Story for *Everywoman*.

3 Aug Sue left here on Saturday. Chaos, insolence, lying ... Six weeks since she left the Maudsley. At first, gentle, melancholy, gradually becoming apathetic, lacking all confidence. Then switched to wild high spirits, assertiveness, tremendous energy, endless

starting of new and never-finished projects. Soon all attempts to help
in the least at home frankly abandoned. Then a crescendo of
insolence, extravagance, endless demands, crazy disorder until I said
if she could not behave reasonably she had better go off on her own
... endless trouble for me and Lyn. Incredible vanity and conceit: out
to exploit everyone. Her room which was put in apple-pie order only
6 weeks ago left in more dirt and disorder than I've ever known even
Sue create. Has behaved most oddly since ... Keeps ringing up here,
trying to be very grown-up and off hand ... immensely on the make
... She has worn me down till I am tired and trembling and can't
settle down or concentrate but this time I am not going to give in to
her. I am very quiet and cold: have made no scene nor written to her
nor appealed to her ... Any impulse she has to gratify *at once*.
Outwardly everyone impressed by how radiant she looks ... But any
moral sense seems to have gone quite completely. There are times
when it is extremely difficult to believe that the whole suicide and
Maudsley episodes were not quite consciously and coldly planned
and executed ... That look of hers in St Francis [Observation Ward,
Greenwich] which struck Si and me so much: the satisfied smile of a
child who has brought it off.

... I doubt if she really believed that I could let her go off and not
allow her to go on treating this place as a convenience. I think she still
believes she has only got to appear with a bottle or a bunch of flowers
to have me just where she wants me again. But this time . . No. And
this has never happened to Sue before. I'm not impervious. Dear me,
no. I've been reduced almost to pulp. But I think I am growing a
protective skin ... I find both her and Thomas [Chitty] a little
repulsive at the moment: it doesn't look quite so idyllic and romantic
when one knows the facts. At the moment they're busy petting each
other's vanity. The interesting time will come when there is a clash
between those two egoists and they want different things. Thomas
sponges on Sue quite considerably ... But what is going to happen
when she becomes a liability, instead of an asset. Thomas is mild and
gentle but he is, I think, every bit as selfish as she is and has more
staying power ... At the moment of course he seems absolutely
hypnotised by her and *looks* fathoms deep in love. But I think she is
more *dependent* on him than he is on her: I suspect, when she is not
spending money or at her job, she is completely lost and simply does

not know what to do with herself when he is not about. With no one to gossip with or rebel against she is going to miss her home quite considerably ... She found Oxford bad enough – the money of course is being quite fatal to her [£400 insurance policy, maturing when Susan became 21]. But how could we have known that? As long as it lasts she will probably continue in her inflated state ... Whenever I write about Sue, I am frightened. How much of her there is in me ...

6 Aug It is a queer thought that this is the first time for 22 years that Sue has not been costing me money. She has been a financial drain on me from the moment she was conceived ... She has always caused *unnecessary* trouble all her life ... The last four years she has been more demanding and less co-operative than ever. It will be interesting to see how long she does manage on her own. She is of course relying not on her pay but on the 21st birthday money and that of course came from the family so is indirect support from parents. She would have to manage very carefully indeed if she really lived on her £4 a week [from working as a zoo attendant at Battersea Fun Fair during the Festival of Britain], kept her £100 for dress and left her capital. But she could do it: if she and Thomas pooled their money they could have £8 a week leaving Thomas £2 a week for extras as she has. Their rent is £2.10 [shillings] and they could cater for £3.10 comfortably. Often I *have* resented this money burden: chiefly when Sue is so ungrateful and demanding ... never even trying to see ... that one just *can't* afford drinks, entertainments, restaurants etc. let alone holidays abroad. I think I really can have a clear conscience about Sue now. She has made her own choice, she has enough to live on and she has got to the age where she *should* be independent. That little wool episode gave me the measure of her graspingness. I must realise and she must realise too that she has no more claims on me than Lyndall has. Both are my daughters and Lyndall too should not be costing me anything ... though I am very willing she should live here paying only what it costs me to keep her ...

... it is silly ... to spend hours doing calculations, forecasts of expenses etc. when this time would be far better spent on writing. My attitude to money is too tense and nervous at the moment and with Sue here it was like a hole in one's bag ...

... I am living at the rate of £1500 a year: far in excess of my income ... My first duty is to finish the novel ... Every day, except in the most exceptional circumstances, when I do not do 4 hours work a day on it, I am CHEATING. I have got to try and average 50 pp a week. Ideally the rough draft sd be finished before I go on holiday ...

20 Aug   Have completely reorganised house: worked at it for days: everything now tidy and convenient. It really is a great revolution in my life ... It marks the end of the long and difficult time of Sue being here with me. It is I think impossible for her to live at home or in anyone else's house ... What Sue cannot bear is women in authority – me, nurse, Miss Darroch [Susan's housemistress at Godolphin School], college authorities, Oxford landladies etc. I, of course, submit to women. I suppose it goes by reverse. I can't submit to men's authority. Sue perhaps is the last of my dominating women ...

25 Aug   Just trying out lighting at night for work at cottage. This seems a possible arrangement. Question entirely of where shadow falls. Try and simplify it as much as possible. As long as shadow falls under hand, rest of page seems more or less all right Certain amount of juggling necessary ...

26 Aug   ... My writing used to be extremely legible but I cannot honestly say it is now ... Always at the end of the word, I tend to degenerate into a scribble. Yet nothing is more agreeable than a well-written M.S... Extraordinary, when one thinks how one learnt to write ... one was forced to make letters a certain way: upstrokes, downstrokes ... However, the only thing to do is to go on trying to break in this new and by no means unpromising pen otherwise there is going to be an awkward gap when my dear old Eversharp finally gives out. I can't remember ever having worn out a pen before! It still writes far more smoothly than any other: But why is this ink brown when marked 'Midnight Black' ! ! ! Now, having changed over to 'Quink', we seem to have turned dark grey, although bottle is marked 'Permanent blue'! Anyway the bath seems to have done my old pen good ... it certainly is exceedingly heavy going ...

Curious to be down at the cottage once more. Inevitably rather a restless state: being a furnished tenant of one's own house. One doesn't quite know what one is up to. But I think it will work all right. Very nice having Jessica [Entwhistle, the cleaning lady] here. Have fixed up quite a good corner to work in. Tremendous wind outside. 48 years now I have been coming here. Always find myself either trying to reconstruct the past – the house as it was, the people or mentally trying to reconstruct it in the future if it ever really became my home . . . this is an important visit for many reasons. It is the first time I have been here for some weeks on my own as if I were really living here. It also comes at the end of a time when much has changed and when a new period begins. The big change is, of course, Sue's going. I am still sore from that, yes. Funny how the pieces keep shifting. A few weeks ago I felt closer to Silas again because of Sue. But he and Sheila give me strong impression now of wanting to keep as far away as possible. Sue's obvious centre is now Thomas. Queer relationship. Marriage with something left out.

Just before I came away I had an extraordinary evening with Eric. Really the first that was like our old ones for years. His marriage and everything else is now approaching the crucial stage. Almost it seemed as if there were a possibility of things turning out as we used always to suppose before he knew Georgie. How odd it would be. Almost too neat, one would think. One thing seems to keep coming out: E's preoccupation with the Catholic Church.

Also Tom [Hopkinson]'s growing hatred of it. It came out tremendously in his *Critics* [radio discussion programme] broadcast this morning. One can feel D[orothy] K[ingsmill]'s influence behind everything he says in public these days. Odd she should have lived here at Binesfield. But I don't feel any trace of her here now. Only physical trace – the red paint on the linoleum, now all peeling off . . .

Of course the cottage is critical too because of finishing the book. Most critical of all for that, really, is the whole point of my coming down here. Well, I keep wandering from room to room: thinking which room I'd use for which purpose. I suppose I'm even wildly thinking, suppose Eric and I lived here. We'd want a bedroom each etc. etc. . . I have PLENTY to cope with in the present. Principally . . of course . . the book . . . There are things which seem as if they will never come to an end and the upheaval of the responsibility – physical responsibility of providing a home for Sue – is something I can't yet take in. For nearly 23 years Sue has altered the course of my life . . . If she had never been born, I suppose I would still be with Eric

... *Of course*, poor darling, things have been hard for her. But her game has been to wear me down. I can see why she should always be revenging herself ...

27 Aug Think I am settling in properly here. I began to work a little this morning. House is really very habitable now. If I lived here it wd. probably be possible to make some arrangement about the garden. Small details, like painting inside windows and modern doors white has already made enormous difference – Great thing is to get house as light as possible. Almost prepared to consider having beams white some day – It would make it *far* easier to furnish and make rooms look larger – Study would be enormously lightened and improved by having a window facing south in it. That wd. probably make it the nicest room of all to work in, with desk at the window. Lack of boxroom is a nuisance of course. But I really must stop thinking about houses – my mania! ... About the book, I would like to think of an ideal reader. It will of course be dedicated to Sue because I promised that. I do think even now she takes a sort of interest in it. Lyn of course takes none, though she is sweet about it as a job I have to do. I suppose families don't usually care about one's work as work. It *does* make one feel awfully isolated! Well, whom do I know personally who really is interested? Tom no longer, I think. Anyway, he is so strange now and so under the Kingsmill that his opinion good or bad doesn't affect me much ... Eric, Julien Green, Emily, Kathleen Judd [unknown], Elaine [Lingham][†] (but she mayn't read novels any more), Viola [Garvin][†], Enid [Starkie] (I think), Evelyn Waugh, Edwin Muir[†] (but the last are public rather than personal) Nina Beachcroft[†] and her parents, Katharine Gurley.[†] Funny about *The Lost Traveller* – Very few people liked the book as a whole (though Julien Green ..., Evelyn Waugh ... and Edwin Muir did) but ... people like ... particular parts of it – usually quite different parts. Thus Tom likes ... Charles's death ... other people like the Opera, the Patsy scenes ... Djuna loves the Isabel–Callaghan parting scene ... But very few have the funny passion for it as a whole which they have about *Frost* which has obviously got something the *Traveller* hasn't got. Useless *my* trying to analyse that something or attempt to reproduce it. It is one of those things a writer never understands. I think of all the prolonged labour and misery of *The*

Traveller and the extraordinary, to me suspicious, ease of *Frost*. I do of
course feel *The Traveller* hasn't the unity of the other. Yet I was
certainly trying to go deeper. A transition book, I suppose. A freak,
too. It began in that sudden queer way with Tom. Lots of it I had no
control over. A lot invented. Isabel and Callaghan. The odd intrusion
of Charles's death. Then all that trouble over the end. Oh yes, a very
rum, hybrid book. This one should be simpler; more of a piece. But
practically all I have done so far – about 50,000 words, has really been
undoing what I did in *The Traveller* and getting the marriage on again
... What I have got to face and interpret now is all that queer, horrid
Chelsea time leading up to the asylum – a time which seems
particularly unreal and fantastic. And I have to simplify it quite
brutally. However, of course, I am in a much better position to
understand it now: at the time I had not the least idea what it was all
about. The [Eliot] Seabrooke thing must be given something of its
true importance. It is a pity, I suppose to have left myself so little
space for its development. It is a great pity that I did not make *Lost
Traveller* a proper sequel to *Frost* ...

31 August   Yesterday I had two odd letters, carefully timed to arrive
after they had left England, from Thomas and Sue, announcing that
they had been married in a registry office. I don't even know on
which day. I supposed Lyndall and the Glossops knew. I rang up Lyn
and found she knew nothing about it. I rang up Sheila. She was
extremely brusque. She and Silas knew they had been married and
were 'absolutely delighted'. They had not been to the wedding ...
Sheila was absolutely triumphant ... Sue was so happy etc. Best thing
that could possibly have happened etc. I don't think it ever occurred
to her that it might have been a considerable shock to me ... I
suppose she simply cannot grasp what this gesture of Sue's means:
complete repudiation of her religion. Thomas writes 'as we neither of
us have any religion'. Only last Easter – 5 months ago, Sue came to all
the Holy Week ceremonies with me, going to Communion. On Low
Sunday she missed Mass but told Lyn how she had felt about it. Then
the attempted suicides, the Maudsley and all that has happened since,
culminating in this marriage. I can see how Sheila feels though she
can't see how I feel. Here for her is the 'happy ending', getting away
from me, Sue a normal cheerful girl etc. Such smug triumph in

Sheila's voice. No more nonsense: now she knows where she is and can bustle round and Si won't be worried and I'm out of the way – Sheila has a robust lack of tact which I ought to find amusing.

But, apart from the religious aspect, I wonder if it is quite as simple and rosy as all that. I still don't think Sue's behaviour lately entirely normal and nor does Lyndall. If it *is* entirely normal then what was the other Sue .. the Sue of the Kolbsheim letters? ... The way she has behaved to me lately has been really brutal ... I suppose she felt she just had to assert herself crudely like that ... There was one sweet sentence in her letter 'we both want our Mother back again'. But what – if anything – does that mean? I am not Thomas's mother and he has never shown any particular affection for me. Lately very much the reverse. I am pretty sure that he has always profoundly distrusted me and influenced Sue against me quite a lot ... When she was first ill at St Francis and the Maudsley, she had thrown over the religion but she clung to me in a way she has never done all her life ...

... At the moment his [Silas's] one concern to see her 'hearty, unneurotic etc'. Unfortunately I don't think she is un-neurotic at the moment. I still think there is something extremely forced and hysterical about her gaiety. And Lyndall says she was so dirty in herself and her clothes on Sunday that Dickie [Muir] could not bear to eat in the same room with her and went out ...

Meanwhile, on the purely practical side, I know where I stand. A huge cycle of my life is closed for the moment ... Lyndall, I feel I know where I am with her as far as one ever knows with a child. I *like* Lyn more and more. I don't suppose she can ever cause me as much agony or as much exquisite delight as Sue. But she is immensely lovable and attractive and there is something terribly sweet in her dogged little way of paying her way. My father once said to me 'You always foot the bill' and this is much truer of Lyndall ... Lyn and I will probably get on like two pussycats, knowing each other well enough to avoid upsetting each other and not attempting the impossible ...

I found myself enjoying writing about Eric today. Well, one person in one's life goes: another comes or comes back ... This month I must concentrate on the book. It is a heavensent interlude and must be used. Otherwise I have only myself to blame.

Antonia had arranged with her tenants that she should have the cottage for a few weeks each year.

* * *

12 Sept   I am really very glad to be going home on Friday. This is a difficult house to live and work in and would be, I think, even if I had all my own things here. More and more thankful that I didn't give in to D[orothy] K[ingsmill]'s idea. It simply wouldn't have worked. Delightful as a part-time house, yes. But it just doesn't quite fit me: it is so dark, decidedly damp and the small rooms and low ceilings are oppressive. If I could afford to spend a great deal on it, *and* have a gardener and cook, one could of course make it very nice. But even then I'd still want something in London, I think. If I could afford to build on a wing at the back with one really good sized room: at any rate high-ceilinged and light and possibly a bedroom and another bathroom it would be *very* nice. That would leave all the rest of the house as it is with 3 decent bedrooms.

However, this is all absurd as its future is determined for the next 6 years. I haven't, of course ever really examined the financial situation. Even if I were getting the full rent . . £110, I have to deduct at least £40 from that for rates, insurance, tax etc. At the utmost I should only clear £70. At the moment, I suppose I only get about £28 a year from it! If I sold it for £5000 and had interest at 2½% I could get an income of . . . £125. I guess there is *some* unconscious thing mixed up in all this: guilt about selling because of my father's wishes: *cramped* feeling about living in it: my parents' house. Funny how they found it perfect and I don't. But I think it's a place for the old and the young: not in-between. This year in particular I feel oddly detached from the place and don't even feel any special ties with it any more.

This morning I made a rather interesting misreading which rang a bell. All the last few days I have been unable to work, v. low-spirited, reading compulsively etc. Mis-reading was this: for 'the terrific *confidence* of the artist' I read 'the terrific *conscience* of the artist'.

Funny what one is confident about. Say fixing up a house. I always feel capable of doing that and love it. Or translation. But writing a book or even an article . . Oh, oh, oh! This house *does* give me claustrophobia. Badly. I long to be back at Ashburn G[ardens] . . . Awful how I have slacked on the book [*The Sugar House*] since last

Saturday. I did all right up to then: partly heavy, close damp weather: day after day of heavy clouded sky.

It is no sin not to be able to live just as one's parents did. Of course, my father never gave *his* a moment's anxiety. But then he just managed their lives. The best of sons, of course. But I'm perfectly sure they never controlled him in any way after he was, say 14 ... My father, however, could be awfully dominated by *men*. Old Gluckstein,[†] Bromley, even to some extent Baines [unknown]: certainly the two High Masters [of St Paul's]. Rather interesting this domination question. Dominating people can usually be dominated by someone ... My own confidence was *really* undermined by women: e.g. the nuns. But my father put the finishing touches. And women obviously can still 'get at me' in a peculiar way: e.g. Sheila Glossop; even Daisy G[reen] W[ilkinson, Reggie's mother]

... I am envious of Sue. Why, chiefly? Her height and slimness. Her 'getting away' with things – even to eating such a lot and remaining incredibly slender! Her distinguished look ... I'm afraid I get a bit sick of the 'beautiful daughter' stuff ... Lyndall is just as attractive and I *don't* feel this envy about her. But envy extends to lots of people besides Sue. People who are loved, who have a husband or an intimate friend to share their lives ...

17 Sept Again a dream about Noel Coward. Friendly. These 'partners' that keep turning up! Both writers. Have been thinking about the 'homework' line. That has always been my trouble. Ever since I left Roehampton. Could *never* organise working on my own though I am always a good worker in a class or with a private teacher. Sue must have had the same trouble at Oxford. This has got to be surmounted somehow. It was the same in all office jobs as well as at the A[cademy of] D[ramatic] A[rt] and St Paul's. Could never do that *extra*, though pretty efficient on what *had* to be done. The taking over on my own still seems – at 52 – a major trouble ...

16 Nov I have finished the book [*The Sugar House*]; something that a few months ago seemed impossible. The usual flatness afterwards. I doubt if it would have been possible but for the almost miraculous arrival of Elaine [Lingham] ... Sue. It is 3 months since I saw her. She refuses to see me; rings up L[yndall] under false names: is obviously hostile, continues to grab from me as in the case of the table etc. wh. I lent her and which she has calmly annexed, challenging me to 'come and get them' which she knows I won't do. It is impossible to know why she is behaving in this extraordinary way ... But otherwise things are better with me than I ever hoped possible. This marvellous help from Elaine. Lyndall being delightful. The new '2 flat' arrangement working admirably ... I *have* to admit that not having to live with and be responsible for Sue is a huge weight off my shoulders ... It almost . . fantastically, of course . . looks as if what had been the 'matter' with me for so many years . . simply . . Susan ...

17 Nov ... I felt Elaine slightly disapproved of my going in for this competition [*Observer* Short Story] and was trying to put me off ...

5 Dec I did go in for it. Story [unknown] came out better than I hoped. But with 6,600 entries it must be such a lottery. And in any case the subject of mine would be against it . . anyhow for first prize. A distressing dream about Sue and Thomas last night. Both very hostile, cruel and mocking ...

Well, this has been a strange year in every way. Odd that the Kingsmill said I 'should not really get going till 1952' and at the moment, that looks not impossible ...

So much has happened. Sue's breakdown in the spring and all these months of anxiety. The 'too good to be true' feeling when she got better. Then her marriage and the 'iron curtain' ever since. My last letter – the fourth saying I would like to see her – left unanswered ... If she rings up here for Lyn and hears my voice she rings off at once ... Christmas coming and only this cold silence ... She has moved and now I don't even know her address. But the reports I have from people who know her well aren't good. They say she seems brittle and artificial.

But if there is this one thing . . and it is like an open wound . . everywhere else life feels more hopeful. I am well, working hard (the translations are a nuisance but I need the money and they *can* be done) and gradually getting my affairs straightened out. It is wonderful to have Elaine and she and Sheila Lingham [Elaine's sister] and Kathleen [Raine] are almost like my own family. Lyn is sweet but completely absorbed in her own life. She was obviously bored, even terrified at the thought of my inviting Dickie and his mother for Christmas. I suppose it is silly to want so much my real family round me at Christmas. Anyway I am immensely grateful to the Bullingham Mansions one [the Linghams]. Otherwise I would have been quite alone . . .

Who would have thought at the beginning of this year that the end would find Sue married . . . Lyn practically engaged, Tom and Dorothy Kingsmill in love with each other, Elaine out of Carmel and working as my secretary and myself having written another novel? Very few years have brought as many changes as this one. What is astonishing to me is that though I have been through a very hard time over Sue, since the autumn and the appearance of Elaine in my life, though I continue to be very sad and worried and hurt about Sue, I have been able to work, been in excellent health and almost completely free from *angst* . . .

7 Dec   I brought myself to ring up Sheila this morning and ask for Sue's address. She answered with extreme coldness 'It's not up to me to give you her address. If she wanted you to know it, she would have told you herself'.

25 Dec   I had a card from Sue; a note thanking me for the nylons. Later, a present from them both and a note not refusing to come and see me after Christmas. This has made a great difference to Christmas. From the human side it has been a little *triste*. I am very glad to be going to the Linghams today but the flat feels very lonely with Lyn away and Daphne [lodger] too and the so obvious fact that one's children don't want to spend Christmas with one! I dined with Tom and Gerti last night and saw their children. It was almost like old times except that Gerti was so evidently sad. I have got to like her very much during the last months. She is at last natural with me. The day before I saw Eric and Georgie. It is odd how she [Georgie] seems to want to see me again nowadays and even comes rushing round here when she is worried. Yet she loses no opportunity of humiliating me. About Sue she is quite remarkably hard and tactless: rubbing it well in how marvellous it is to get away from one's parents and not showing the faintest touch of sympathy with the parents' feelings . . . Tom, of course, is like someone partly hypnotised. The time seems to have come for *me* to withdraw and 'free myself' a little from my family. I think there really is some limit to the amount of humiliation one should put up with. I suppose I'm very impulsive and like to express feelings at once ...

28 Dec   The year running out ... inevitably, one wonders what will happen in 1952. How lucky for us that we don't know ... If I had known all that was to happen about Sue in 1951, how wretched I would have been and how much easier it was to bear a little at a time. Yet in spite of all the suffering, some of the moments I had with Sue this year were among the best. Those happy days after she had run away from the Maudsley and I fought with the doctors for her. Later came the worst times I have ever had with her. Now that there is a *chance* of seeing her again, the relief is of course great. But I cannot feel a great looking forward. I don't suppose I shall be able to see her alone. I do not indeed know what Sue I *shall* see. I feel as if I had lost real contact with her for ever ...

A day or two ago I wrote to Eric saying I had decided to 'evaporate' for the time being. Georgie's resentment against me is once more becoming so obvious that I really think it is better to keep right away ... They both, separately and together, keep discussing things endlessly with me but nothing ever happens except fresh bickerings between them and nasty slaps from Georgie at me ...

It is awfully odd being handed one's own life back again. For years Sue has been an incessant preoccupation: practically as well as emotionally. Lyndall too, for some time until very recently, depended on me as housekeeper etc. Now I have only myself to housekeep for and I can't get used to having so much more leisure and so few daily practical worries. The house runs smoothly. Sometimes I'm astonished how smoothly when I think how I've had to learn these things from the beginning ...

Almost I hardly want to see her [Sue] now. I have had so many shocks about her that I feel numb ... I am relieved that she no longer seems quite so hostile but I can't say she feels friendly. A not-ill-disposed indifference on her part, I should say. A reluctant concession on the part of Thomas? From Si and Sheila, I should guess, an attitude of 'See her at your own risk. If you get involved with her, you're in for trouble'. My private opinion is that Sheila is responsible for a great deal of all this. If she [Sue] does not ring up, I shall wait at least a month before making any further move. No doubt Sheila has the best intentions. If only she had a little more intelligence . . . she's spoilt Si and she's busy spoiling Sue. The terrifying strength of determined mediocrity! Interesting which do more harm in the long run, détraqué but not mediocre people like Djuna and the Kingsmill or the well-meaning brisk efficient little Sheilas. What Silas once said of Jasmine [an earlier fianceé of his] rather applies to Georgie. 'A climber with no sense of direction'. Well Georgie has qualities all right. But what DOES that girl really want? The ONLY thing I've ever known her constantly and always take immense pains over is cooking. If she'd take half the trouble over writing! Provided she really wants to write. Funny how one always finds something rather sweet and forlorn and appealing about her though she is SUCH a little bitch! A baby, really, in spite of all these maddening grown-up airs. Eric is naughty really. He loves her in his way but doesn't give her anything she needs. I imagine they are much *more* babies than Tom [Thomas] and Sue. Marriages without children are really appalling.

29 Dec   A note from G[eorgie] which looks as if Eric hadn't got mine or, if he has, has not told her about it. I thought the other day that the difference between Sue and Lyndall is this. Both are absolutely determined to have their own way at all costs. But Sue rides roughshod over people's feelings or remains determinedly unaware of them whereas Lyn is acutely sensitive to them and suffers quite a lot when having her own way involves hurting people. Nothing however stops her from doing what she wants even if she feels sorry or guilty about it. She is very like Tom in this way. Sue has Si's capacity for simply not noticing . . or ignoring . . what other people feel. But Si is rarely positively cruel like Sue.

30 Dec   Eric rang up and asked me to go and have a drink yesterday. He had got my note but asked me not to 'evaporate' entirely so I said I wouldn't . . . Heavy and shivery: hope not flu. Suppose I was more disappointed than I admit not even to be a runner-up for *Observer* [Short Story Competition, won by Muriel Spark] though the chances against are so vast . . . I suppose I feel that only something like winning a competition would impress Sue and Lyndall.

1952

23 Jan   I wonder WHY I feel so hurt and resentful at the notion which nothing really dislodges: viz that Sue and Lyndall despise me . . . I *feel* as if I weren't asking very much – only a little real interest in what I am doing . . enough perhaps to ask to read the new book in proof. Or to ask me now and then to meet their friends . . . *Is* this a preposterous demand? . . . Lyndall seems to prefer any company – or none – to mine. She really, though quite politely, seems to treat me with the utmost contempt as if I knew nothing at all and were, indeed, a mother to be hidden away as much as possible . . .

   . . . I must try and be sensible about it all. I have to remember that Lyn is an *extra* secretive person.

26 Jan   Much under a cloud for 2 days: couldn't get myself to work on St Thomas [an article for the *Religious Review*] and felt thoroughly jammed up. The internal cloud lifted after I managed to 'have it out' with Lyn without any distressing scene. Elaine's advice was excellent in all this. Lyn told me – and I think she was telling the truth – that her real embarrassment was the Catholic thing. She likes my short stories – especially 'The Moment of Truth' – if there is no Catholic reference. But any passages about religion embarrass her horribly and she finds the same trouble with Graham Greene . . . I had a most curious and difficult-to-remember dream last night. I seemed to be . . . on trial for something: . . . which had some connection with impotence or a null marriage. Carroll appeared in the dream and I was in terror that I was to be examined and treated by him as a result of a court decision. I was afraid because I was quite sure that psychiatric treatment would be quite useless and only make things worse. He was lame in both legs and had to walk on sticks as if he had a very bad accident or suffered from infantile paralysis like Dougall [sic] . . .

   Dougall [sic]. The liar: the man who got me on false pretences. The first physical lover. I conceived a child at once and had an abortion. He got round my father too. Daddy would like us to have married. I was not in love with him. I enjoyed his company, was flattered, was sorry for him because of his lameness . . . it occurred [the dream] at a time when I was having an actual jam in writing, connected with a

Thomas . . . a contributory cause of this jam was *emotion* over Lyndall; thus my emotions tend to get out of hand and stop my mind from working . . . There is something which is the equivalent of emotional masturbation. Still another possibility . . . is a subfusc envy of Sue who *has* got an adoring husband called Thomas! Now Sue's case is rather interesting because she has sacrificed everything: ambition, religion, parental approval and the development of her own talents in order to get that husband. There were always things I wouldn't sacrifice . . .

12 March   A queer dream last night. I was with Tom on a train in open country. He was young and gay and as he used to be. He was talking excitedly about 'the impossible' having happened. The 'impossible' was that he was having a play produced in America . . . He got off the train and walked off through sunny meadows. I watched him. I saw him go to the edge of a river, hesitate, trying the water with his foot, then walk into it fully dressed and happily swim away. Then I was in a boat without rudder or oars. I got frightened, realising I could not control it. There was a heavy swell from passing big barges which nearly swamped me . . . I was carried helplessly to the left of these and thought I was still in midstream but to my relief found I was beached. A woman from the boathouse, wearing a white overall, questioned me . . . The questions were very odd: how old was I? Was I happily married? . . . I suspected a trap, something which would involve me in psychiatric treatment . . .

Today I had a sudden impulse to get some definite solution to the Si and Sheila thing. I rang up Sheila but she was out. Then I wrote to Si at his office. A short note saying it was only common courtesy to let me know *why* I was being treated as non-existent. At the back of my mind *is* a faint . . hope, perhaps . . that Sheila intercepted my 2 letters to Sloane Square. My hand shook as I wrote . . . If Sue takes no notice of my birthday, I shall be horribly tempted to write to *her*.

18 May   She took none. Later, I heard from Lyn that she had remembered it and wanted to send me a greetings telegram but when she told Thomas what the money was for he refused to give it her. He doles her out every penny. This shows that Thomas is definitely very hostile to me but it still does not show that Sue could not have made some sign if she had really wanted to. A postcard stamp is only 2d. Not a word ever came from Si. I hear Sheila is going to have a baby which is the best possible thing ... Sue quite often sees Eric and Georgie. Everyone seems to think it the most natural thing in the world ... But Lyndall has been very sweet lately, ever since her breaking off with Dicky. I suppose one's children only want one around when they're worried or unhappy ... I see quite a lot of Eric and Georgie. G. is being friendly at the moment ... I am too weak not to complain about the hurt and long for Sue to be friends with me again ... It is strange to find how difficult it is *really* to accept the fact that one is actively disliked by people one loves .. accept it and yet somehow to go on and not be paralysed and shrivelled up by it ... Perhaps all one can say is 'Lord, love for me since I am not capable of love'.

9 Aug Back at the cottage again and the atmosphere happier than it was last year. I have just read through the year's entries. The reception of *The Sugar House* has been the coldest and most hostile I have ever had. Only 4 good reviews; the rest ranging from tepid to real downright sneering and hatred. In some cases, most in fact, the point of the book has been completely missed and the contradictions are farcical. One says 'Sordid and squalid', one 'witty and gay' ... Many take the line that it is pure novelette or 'glossy magazine'. Yet some 'private' readers such as Barbara Ward, Katharine Gurley and Mrs Mure [Muir, Dicky's mother] are definitely enthusiastic ... After the really cruel and spiteful review in the *Observer* (Robert Kee) ... I felt so crushed and depressed, my nerve went again ... this suggestion – so universal – that with every book I was fast declining ... Kee's went deepest under the skin because he is a great friend of Thomas's and published Thomas's novel [*Mr Nicholas* by Thomas Hinde] ... I felt Sue was sniggering over it ... I felt I ought to stop any further attempt at serious writing. All the small pleasure and interest I had begun to feel in the next book was destroyed ... Eric said 'You can't stop even if you want to. You are bound to a fiery wheel' ... If one tries to be honest and write simply, they think it is just cheap and superficial. The *Catholic Herald* beat all for sheer vulgarity. Pritchett and Snow and John Raymond *did* get it .. but no critic has got it in the way that certain 'ordinary' readers have.

I suppose it has been an extra blow because of the amazingly good reviews Thomas's book had. I read the book twice with the utmost care and though feeling occasional admiration, was left with profound 'un-ease' and even a kind of horror . . . I have seldom seen such public acclaim for any first novel. It is not the book which frightens me: it is what it tells me about Thomas and the profundity of his hatred.

Queer, now Sue has won this competition [*Vogue* talent], to see a hideous caricature of a photo of her in *Vogue* with a caption 'daughter and wife of writers: mother Antonia White husband Thomas Hinde.'

I have pretty positive proof now that Thomas hates me. He certainly fears me. Yet I wish his book could have been one that I could wholeheartedly have admired. Viola [Garvin] calls it ' a cry of hatred'. I mind the hatred less than what I can only call a kind of meanness in it. No compassion for anyone but himself.

Charles Hodgson† said the other night that Thomas is terrified of me. He thinks I am responsible for Sue's illness. That is something no one can know. Unconsciously I may be. Consciously, I think not. So I am up against something really formidable. What is interesting is that he has always been bitterly critical of his father's illness on the grounds that it was due to his father's own egotism. Obviously he would never admit such a possibility in Sue's own case. Yet every effort from the time Sue was 5 has been precisely to try and avoid for her that illness to which she might be predisposed and she has always resisted and refused to co-operate. Si obviously agrees with Thomas . . .

14 Aug   A certain malaise and depression always settles on me at the cottage. I don't quite know what it's due to. This year is better than last. The weather has been good. I enjoy pottering in the garden . . . Perhaps, except for very early childhood, this house is associated for me with sadness and frustration though it is such an obvious setting for happiness. My happiest times here since the rebuilding were when my father was alive. But that was soon clouded by all the circumstances of Sue's birth. I can see how that must have distressed him: he must have felt as I do about her marriage. Yet I cannot imagine treating him as she has treated me. Tomorrow will be the seventh anniversary of her Baptism [15 August 1945]. That *was* a happy day and she was happy – really happy. We were like a real family that day. Si and Sheila too. Oh, my darling Sue – do you really want to cut out everything we had together ... I love to be gay and happy with people – I want to be at peace with the ones I love – Your being in love should make you kinder, not more cruel. If you had sat down and deliberately planned how to hurt me most, you could not have done it more successfully ... You are being dominated by someone inferior to you and who will never, I think, be able to grow to your level ... No, at the moment I cannot be just to Thomas. Certainly I don't begin to understand him. For I was never his enemy; I encouraged him, I did everything I could for him when you were ill. I would have been glad for you to marry him but for the one fact of your giving up your religion to do so. Now he is my bitter, and, I think, unreasonable enemy ... What I dislike in Thomas is his *narrowness*, something cramped and stunted. No doubt it is not his fault. Perhaps you will humanise him. Thomas sneers at everything he does not understand. I find him shallower than Dicky though more intelligent .. less human altogether. What I like in Thomas is that he *works*. He *may* turn out a good writer in the end. As writers I think we are fundamentally antipathetic. I am sorry about this. I would like to have admired his work ... I can usually be pretty objective about work and I fairly fastened on anything that struck me as really true or good in *Mr Nicholas* ... What worries me is that he ... assumes that what he sees is all there is. Out to give others away, to bring out all their pettiness, unreasonableness, hypocrisy etc. he makes his young man a kind of touchstone of truth and never puts *him* in the same perspective ... He's good about himself as an artist .. there he is honest and touching. But it's the priggishness I dislike so intensely. However, if he really feels something for Sue beyond a projection of his own self-pity on a girl whom he obviously loves for her beauty and charm he may come to be less suspicious of all feeling as sham. Yet, through all the hatred of his father, one perceives that he loves him ...

... Lyndall has gone. But the net result of that has been the opposite of Sue's going. In spite of all the cloud of deceptions, her letters to me from Rome are more real than any I have had from her. Eric and Georgie have gone to live in Brighton. Tom is now quite inaccessible with Dorothy. Almost the only 'hangover' of this complex family business is Gerti. If there is anything I can do about the divorce, to help her get her injunction, I shall have to do it . . .

* * *

Tom Hopkinson continued to live with Gerti and their daughter, Nicolette, at 26 Cheyne Row, but by the time his daughter Amanda was born he was deeply involved with Dorothy Kingsmill.

* * *

. . . I have done four translations in ten and a half months and the time has come to think about my new novel [*Beyond the Glass*].

I had a most interesting letter from Lyn yesterday. I had asked her to try and tell me what she felt to be the real root of her resentment against me. Her answer was unexpected: she felt, and had felt since childhood, that I was jealous of her. I went into this in a long letter to her. There are, of course, elements of truth in this but my jealousy of Lyn is trivial compared with my jealousy of Sue . . . To be . . . tall, slender and . . how can I put it? poetical . . has always been an absurd . . . private wish with me ever since I was a child. Lyn, apart from being *much* better-looking than I ever was has this odd 'sex-appeal' which I had too and which has very little to do with beauty. But Lyn is beautiful: since I began to write this, her photograph has come and one sees that her face is far more beautiful than Sue's. Nor has Sue got this 'sex-appeal' . . . But Sue's odd, distinguished beauty; that angular . . . Gothic figure that so enchanted Viola . . . her 'dream-inspiring' quality (Viola again) – those are what I should so immensely like to have had. And Sue herself often feels *she* would like to have been a little magazine-cover floozy, just as Eric would like to have been a stout man with a moustache or a guards officer . . .

Jealousy . . and envy too . . are certainly among my besetting sins . . .

Lyndall, who is very jealous by nature and, unlike Sue, knows it, says that I am the only person she has never been jealous of; not, as she charmingly adds, that she feels there is nothing to *be* jealous of . . .

I certainly never *felt* any jealousy of my mother. But I think it must have been there because of my father . . . She was the very last person I wanted to be like. I used to be furious if anyone saw any likeness between us. Yet, at her best, I greatly admired her looks and knew I should never be as good-looking, even in youth, as she was in middle-age. It even pleased me to go shopping with her and induce her to buy what suited her best and I remember vividly certain clothes, certain ways of doing her hair, certain moments at which she looked quite lovely and I felt immensely proud of her.

My simplest envy of my daughters is the recent one . . if you can call it recent since it began at least 17 years ago . . their not having to be responsible for keeping themselves . . .

8 Oct Seeing Alick Schepeler last night, with so little to live on, prices rising all the time and frankly, very doubtful prospects of getting half time work does bring it home how awfully difficult things are getting for this class . . . I have never attempted to make the least provision for my own old age . . .

. . . The world is full of women, divorced women. I am obviously a great deal luckier than most. The fact remains that I do find loneliness very hard to bear . . . Someone to share things with: someone to talk to in the evenings. It is surprising that my mother did not apparently suffer from loneliness at the cottage . . .

. . . Sue, yes, I miss her more than Lyn in a way yet in others I hardly *want* to see her. I feel very, very fond of Lyndall but we have never been exactly 'companions' in the way Sue and I have been at times . . .

What are my happiest positive memories, apart from Robert, after growing up? Many, many times with Eric. I think my years with him *were* the happiest. Yet there was the restlessness and the lovers and the fact of doing a silly job at Crawford's. The Silas time, except for a few ecstatic moments, certainly was not happy. I was far happier with Tom. I sometimes think that our Saturday afternoon walks were as happy as anything I've ever known. Yes, I have had very much with Tom . . .

Now, I really AM on my own in a way I never have been before. ALL gone – Tom, Eric, Silas, Susan, Lyndall. One's life almost as if one had never been married, as, in a sense, I never have. Two nullity suits and, the rest, in the eyes of the Church, illicit lovers and no more. So, the old dread came true in an odd way: never married.

And never, financial security . . . I can still remember the exquisite pleasure of being for a *very* short time (!) out of debt . . . That was in 1924 . . . nearly 30 years ago. And it was the ONLY time, apart from

childhood. Eric and I were always in a precarious state, anticipating
etc. after our first few months. Tom and I hadn't enough money. We
weren't so extravagant as E. and I were but we were incessantly
worried about money. Each time the marriage broke up, the ex-
husband became better off but I became worse off. In 1938 I got
almost straight. By working *very* hard at freelancing, I kept things
going but was beginning to feel the strain. The war reduced my
income to practically nothing. Of course in 'good' times I am
absurdly reckless – look at the Reitlinger cottage, the money I spent
on Ian, Benedicta, David etc . . .

18 Oct   I spend an enormous amount of time at the moment doing
little sums all over everything . . . I was lucky to sell the sewing
machine for £8 and some books for £5 . . . I am thankful to have
Daphne here for the winter. I wd. feel the house very lonely in the
evenings otherwise: at least one sees and hears someone about. Now
that Elaine will have Agga [Mrs Lingham] and her Russian [un-
known] filling all her time, I truly will be on my own . . . how much
easier I feel with her than with my own daughters though her mother
and I had not much in common . . .

   IF this tiredness is just 'psychological' what is causing it? It is very
marked, has gone on . . . for over 2 weeks and the hard work over *La
Chatte* [translation] and the strain over Lyn's running away does not
seem enough to account for it. I have had time to recover from both.
Is it 'resistance' to beginning the book [*Beyond the Glass*]? . . . I don't
think 'going away' would be a solution even if I could afford it.
Viola's is *always* tiring to me, though she's so sweet. Concentrating
on talk for 7 or 8 hours exhausts me.

   This departure of Lyn's possibly affects me more than I realise. Yet
now that I know she has a job and is less depressed, I feel all right
about her. For she did not really *live* here: her whole life was
outside . . .

   . . . Today I put *all* those children in St Joseph's care – Sue,
Lyndall, Nicolette, Amanda [Tom and Gerti's two], Sheila's new one
(I don't even know if it has arrived), the Kingsmill's small
Dorothy . . .

   . . . *The Sugar House* has produced more extremes of heat and cold
than anything I have hitherto done. Utter silence from Julien Green,

Graham Greene, Tom. The barest trivial word from Sue: meaningless ... The curious hush which surrounds the book makes me feel as
if it were somehow *inadmissible*.

I don't see how to work the next yet. Perhaps the only thing is to *see*
here and there a scene ... Robert now seems to me so 'flimsy' as to
make it very hard to use him. Yet I think the asylum is necessary. Of
course it really should have come into *S[ugar] H[ouse]*. Yet it *didn't*
come after the strain but after a quiet time. Obviously (?) we begin
with Clara coming home and taking up her ordinary life. But I want
lots about the father and mother. Actually asylum came only 3
months after I'd returned home ... The R[obert] three weeks could
be dramatic ...

Yes, yes, surely the time has come to take life quietly and sensibly
for a bit (... famous last words!) ... I am 53. I must grow up and do
my work. This is the last lap of my life ... A little fun everyone needs
but I don't need as much as I think I do. No need to hunt restlessly for
new things, new people, new stimuli ... Avoid getting deeper into
debt: do the best you can. Then if there is a crisis in January, some
way will be found ...

4 Nov Dear Daisy [Green-Wilkinson] sent me £50. It was *exactly*
the sum I needed to put me straight. I have not been well ... I am out
of debt very nearly now and MUST KEEP OUT OF DEBT.

I am beginning to come up after a bad spell lasting about 5 weeks. I
felt the old head pressure; inability ever to work again etc. [Dr]
Symes' [Antonia's GP] treatment worked, as it has done in these last
two years. Not quite right yet but much better than a fortnight ago.

Sue is near the surface still in spite of determined efforts. Talking to
[John] Rothenstein[†] yesterday, I lost my head and made a little scene.
He was sweet and I was sorry ...

Down at the Speaights [Robert and Bridget][†] this week-end, on
the night of All Saints, I had an extraordinary dream.

I saw a man like my father looking out of the window of a friend's
house. Then I went into the house and it *was* my father. We embraced
with such love and relief. I was so happy to see him and I said so.
Then I told him how for years I had dreamt he was not dead ... I still
could not realise that he had not died. I kept saying 'But I saw you
buried'. He said that he had had the plague and that it was always

done in such circumstances. The person was buried and then secretly exhumed . . . All he had to do was to give himself injections. By now I really was convinced. There was a young doctor with him, very modern . . .

. . . I was so happy, so relieved. I would not be lonely any more . . .

I longed for us to get home here and be quiet together. It was all so vivid. I thought of all the things that he'd be so surprised about – my being able to cook and so on. I thought of the endless things I'd have to tell him, all about Sue and Lyndall from their babyhood till now . . . then things got dim and unreal and I began to wake up. As I did so, I was aware of a very faint sexual tremor.

The dream had been so vivid that it was the most terrible disappointment to find it was only a dream . . . yet the happiness of the dream . . or rather a sense of peace, a sense that *something* . . . had changed persisted . . . I suppose it means I have truly 'forgiven' my father.

21 Nov   The anniversary of my First Communion: the 39th. I was at the Hammersmith convent this afternoon. The atmosphere of the chapel in any Sacred Heart convent is extraordinarily the same . . .

On the 17th anniversary of my father's death I made a 'token' beginning of my new book. Only one page . . . I am sick of the whole subject of Clara. Guilt, of course, at NOT working. The illusion of work produced by doing 4 translations at speed makes real work all the more difficult. Also there is some urge in me to *make* it difficult: to suspect anything which comes easily. Yet *Frost in May* came easily.

24 Nov   I was going to write in this but played the piano instead: a thing I have not done for years. Then Dicky [Muir]'s beautiful flowers arrived . . . I enjoyed playing the piano which I never dared do when Lyn was here.

25 Nov   . . . I was fearfully hurt by D[icky]'s saying Lyn had met Rosamond Lehmann, been immensely impressed by her and said 'I wish my mother were like that'. I wonder why I mind so terribly . . because R[osamond] L[ehmann] is tall, distinguished and handsome or because I feel that I am as good a writer as she . . . I can't help being disgusted by Lyn's going on seeing Silas and Sheila – quite frequently, according to Dicky ... Dicky says that Sheila gave Lyn advice as to whom to go and see about birth-control. I sincerely hope this is not true. I suppose it would seem quite all right to Sheila with the sort of views she holds ... how can one help feeling resentful when one feels one has been cruelly and unjustly treated? ...

I broke off here. The impulse to write one last appeal to Sue is terribly strong. Yet I think I must resist it. It has that blind compulsive feeling about it which is, always, I think, a danger sign ... It is as if when people remain deliberately unaware of me, I cease to exist, can make no decisions, do no work ...

26 Nov ... Symes says I work too hard when I do work and that I live on my nerves. This may be true. Certainly I feel so awfully guilty when I don't work that I won't let myself do anything else and so the vicious circle tightens. I see that playing the piano *was* quite a step. Maybe the time has come to take stock a little and see if I can't sit a trifle easier to life. This is the first moment for years when I could take things easy for a few weeks with no *real* reason for feeling guilty. No urgent work has to be done and I have worked very hard for the past two years. This terrible 'must' which takes all pleasure out of work surely could be got rid of somehow. For I *like* doing everything but writing! If I am lonely now, at least there are no critical daughters around making me feel guilty! I am no longer at school. I am no longer in an office. Why then this furtiveness about any activity which is not writing? Why automatically always sit at my desk, for example?

... Now that my dream seems to show that I really have forgiven and accepted my father, shouldn't I consider the corollary that my father has forgiven *me*? What about the 'suspect' elements in the dream? Fear .. about my novels. Slightly wrong love .. the sexual element. A touch obviously of wanting the father as a *husband* ... If my father *were* alive now, he would be a very old man. If we come down to facts, the only man with whom I have a right to live is Eric. Eric cannot possibly stand for me any longer as a father-figure. If anything, he is dependent on me: a sort of 'problem' brother ...

27 Nov ... How many other women on *Critics*? Rose Macaulay, Arnot Robertson, P. Hansford Johnson, Dilys Powell, Lejeune,

Elspeth Huxley, Veronica Wedgwood – i.e. 7. If I am on the roster, my turn wd. come roughly once a year.

Don't know what I'm hankering after quite. Perhaps some work in association with other people. Certainly I am too much alone. I wish I could do something to help Alick.

1 Dec   A rather horrid dream last night. I don't know whether it is this uncertainty about Christmas ... which is making me paralysed and depressed in spite of dope. First I dreamt I was going to cinema after cinema with Gerald Mitchell [unknown friend from Antonia's youth]. This was quite pleasant though I felt a little guilty about wasting time. Then I dreamt I was telling Sue and Lyndall about this. They exchanged glances and then I realised that Mitchell was dead and they must think I was mad. Then Sue was severe, contemptuous and mocking with me. I could not quite get her meaning. One seemed to be that I behaved much too youthfully for my age: the other which *might* have been mocking or *might* have been kind, that I was all right in my 'little check apron.' ... Today I am in an absurd panic at the prospect of spending Christmas alone.

2 Dec   ... Restless nights: queer dreams ... something is going on inside. Very near edge of tears especially at silly things like talk of families and Christmas. Old unwanted feeling, I expect ... Feel out of things, unrecognised, all the usual stuff. I am upset at Elaine's going to Germany ... it will certainly make a big gap ... A funny dream last night. I had a baby with me: a lively one, a boy, I think and mine. A young woman doctor said the baby was dangerously ill ... Maybe I was too ... As she went out she caught her fingers in the door. It was only a stage door ... so she did not really damage her fingers ... I thought when I woke up how terribly wrong it was of me to let Sue be with strangers, however kind, the first 18 months of her life. How can I wonder that she doesn't love me now? ... It isn't *quite* all my fault perhaps ... if my mother had looked after her it would have been better ... It all seemed so impossible at the time to have her with me. I suppose I was really too selfish and cowardly. I am paying for it now. I suppose it's only fair I should pay. But I tried so hard to make it up to her with years of love and concern after and they seem to have made no impression at all. It goes deep, deep, deep, her coldness and neglect however much I try to resign myself and even tell myself I deserve it. Hard not to feel Tom stole my children's love and that Silas and Sheila did the same later. Is that frightfully unfair? I tried so hard to play fairly by them. How ABSURDLY one longs for one's children's love ... Lyn is such a little enigma; there is something perverse in her, yet she is warm-hearted. BUT *so* fickle, *so* untruthful, *such* a double-dealer. Sue is like her father in simply ignoring what would be uncomfortable to know. Thomas is terrified of anything he can't understand ... Yet if every single human being I knew hated me, it would not prevent God from loving me. Why can't I realise this and be content? Why, I have many loving friends. So I cannot say I have no human consolation ...

5 Dec Still very stupefied. But heaven has been kind. Bridget [Speaight] rang up this morning, inviting me most warmly for Christmas. I can't say how touched and grateful I am ... There is a heavy fog outside which increases the fog inside ... I heard last night from Rupert Doone ... that the Glossops' baby has arrived ... and is a girl [Emma]. I had an anxious dream last night. I dreamt I had promised to look after someone's baby for a few days. One day to my horror I realised that I had forgotten all about it and it had been without food or attention for a whole day and night. I rushed and got some food and prepared some for it. The baby was wrapped up and quite hidden in a white napkin. I was in such an agony of terror that it was dead that I dared not undo the napkin ... then to my intense relief I heard it breathing ...

This morning I had an impulse to write to Si and Sheila just to say I was relieved and glad to know the baby had arrived safely. I suspected the impulse but prayed and it seemed all right to do it. My hand shook as I wrote the letter. I have not posted it yet ...

7 Dec ... nowadays ... the enormous split there is between people due to the lack of a common background of ... beliefs ... how very odd this century is ... No age ever felt so guilty about war yet it has produced the most destructive wars ever known. With the practical disappearance of belief in God, humanity has become the most important thing. Yet human beings have been slaughtered and 'liquidated' on a mass scale never conceived – and never practicable

... before ... All the things that have seemed stable in societies ... are now questioned: marriage, parent-child relation ... religion. In the West there are two operative religions. Christianity ... and Communism ...

9 Dec I went to 'Roehampton' for the 8th. The Junior School play was exquisite: the Procession as lovely as ever. I was interested to meet Antonia Quiñones de Leon [schoolfriend]'s daughter of 14, Tonita. Not beautiful like her mother, but striking and interesting to look at ... I was delighted to hear her mother remembered me. It was the first news I had had of Tony since 1914. She is married to the Marquis de San Carlos ... Isabel is dead ...

22 Dec ... last Saturday a paroxysm of nightmare blankness and terror when I feel I simply CANNOT go on. Only being a Catholic stops me from taking an overdose. I hang on simply by the skin of my teeth. On Saturday I rang round furiously to find someone who wd. let me take them out to dinner ... My list boiled down to Graham Greene (whom I hardly ever see but who might have understood) Alick Schepeler ... In the end I tried Beryl[†] and Anthony[†] Hope who came and were very sweet ... Anthony, meaning *very* kindly, insists on trying to find me a job 'with people' ... and I immediately interpret it as failure as a writer. I wrote a crazy letter to Lyn. I couldn't help it. No letters from 'distant admirers' appease the craving for my own children to like my work ... I shd. observe just as a matter of interest that no one likes *all* my work. *Frost* continues, except of course with the nuns, to become a kind of legend, the perfect thing I brought off once and never will again. Very disheartening ... I shall miss Elaine terribly ... because of her ... instinct about my work. When I made, as I thought, a better version of 'Ubi sunt gaudia?' [a poem about Susan and Lyndall singing carols] the poem I suddenly wrote last week after one of the worst paroxysms of depression, she assured me the original was better. But for her I should have destroyed it.

After I wrote this I had a long and very nice letter from Lyn and stopped to answer it at length. I was terribly grateful for it but even that only registers dimly through the fog. The writing horror has got very bad again ... It seems to focus on Sue and Lyn ... the note of many of the reviews. Also the complete silence from Graham Greene

and Julien Green ... I feel utterly abandoned; utterly impotent.
Christmas I suppose makes me enormously conscious of the family
thing and how I now belong *nowhere*. I have *always* longed for a
recognised place in a family ... It had much to do with my marrying
Tom. At the Latteys I remember how I longed to belong ...

30 Dec   I was very grateful to the Speaights for having me there for
Christmas. They couldn't have been friendlier. It was both painful
and delightful to be in a family ... I came back feeling some sort of
sense of reality again.

Bridget had seen Sue at a dress show and actually raised the subject
of me. She's the first person who's ever had the courage to ... Sue's
line seems to have been that she was determined to keep me out of her
life: that she and Thomas had their citadel and I mustn't be allowed to
cross its threshold. Nor would she come here: it was too full of
painful associations of the 'unhappiest time of her life'. She said that
she knew various people liked her mother but that they didn't know
her other side .. that I was destructive etc. ... I asked Bridget what
her impression of Sue was. She said 'Smart, pretty, hardboiled and ...
emotionally immature'. So there we are ... The *real* Sue, such as she
was at Kolbsheim and in the first year or two of her conversion seems
to have vanished. I can quite see that Silas and Sheila ... must be
delighted with this bright ... simulacrum ...

This year has not been so violent in happenings as last except for
Lyndall's running away from her marriage and going to Rome.

The first five months ... I was in many ways happier ... I had the
immense joy of having Elaine.

This year ends in a kind of desolation. Elaine about to go to
Germany: Eric in Brighton: Tom waiting to marry Dorothy
Kingsmill ...

1953

2 Jan   ... Since Bridget's conversation with Sue, that problem no
longer presses quite so acutely ... I'm not even watching posts to see
whether she thanks me for the 2 small Christmas cheques ... I am

even relieved that Dicky has not rung up since he went to Rome. Fond as I am of him, I feel I've had enough trouble with the younger generation and seeing him only reminds me of Sue and all that . . . In the past week I have had quite a spate of letters, some from total strangers, about my work. It looks as if I'm *meant* to go on with it. Today there were 2 advertisements of jobs at the BBC which might be 'up my street'. Yet my instinct is not to apply for them, much as, in some ways, I long to work among people . . . I certainly wish I could write *more* . . that I had more ideas: above all more confidence. The *confidence* of a person like Bobbie Speaight, the quick turning-out, the apparent lack of self-questioning is quite staggering to me. The only thing I have *confidence* about is translating. Once something is *suggested* to me, I can usually produce something . . . This *confidence* business is very queer. I don't know how one acquires it. There have been one or two people in my life who could give it me. Eric . . . Sue . . . Tom . . . Elaine most deeply perhaps in the sense of sustaining me when I felt I couldn't manage a thing by her absolute certainty that I *could* . . . The weakest part of my 'powers of soul' is undoubtedly the work . . especially when it comes to making a deliberate choice and holding to it . . . If I *do* choose, I am usually pretty sure I have chosen wrong. It works in the most trivial things . . . no one can say whether it is 'better' to wash up first or write a letter first, to tidy a room or go out and do the shopping. Yet such trivial alternatives can paralyse me to such a point that I am too wearied out to do either and am then weighed down with guilt . . .

. . . I don't know how to assert myself in the right way. I let myself be exploited and then feel resentful. Or I suddenly assert myself in a perfectly ridiculous way . . in a shop or something . . and can't stop myself though I *know* I'm behaving absurdly . . . I am *fearfully* irritable by nature yet I *hate* quarrels and can't bear malice for long. Such a bore always writing about myself. But at the beginning of a New Year, it's inevitable . . . to . . . try and cope with one's impossible character . . .

First part of 1952 went pretty well. I really did a lot of translations. Barrages, Bordeaux, Colette's *Bella Vista* and *La Chatte*. Also did 5 weeks session for *Critics*; and the St Thomas article for the *Month* and something for *XXth Century*: a few stray reviews too and the Auntie Bee story for radio ['Aunt Rose's Revenge', published in *Strangers*,

1954]. I had a week in Paris but was too tired to enjoy it to the full. Two bad spells: one in the spring and a really bad one from October to end of year. Both, looking back, were connected with crises in Lyndall's love affair . . . *The Sugar House* came out with an odd baffling mixed reception. Pleasantest part of year was having Elaine working here. Also there was a real deepening of my relation with Lyndall. At the end of the year I wrote a poem suddenly: the first for 3 years.

Looking back, a far better year than 1951 with all the terrible time of Sue's illness . . . REALLY I must learn to say BOO to all the Glossops, Sues, Toms, Kingsmills etc. WHY should I worry if they hate me, despise me, wish to destroy me? . . . All right, *let* them be afraid of me . . . I know more than any of them. This isn't conceit. It isolates me, knowing too much . . . Someone said to me the other day 'I'm afraid you're a writer'. Yes, I'm afraid so too. If I'd *known* what it meant! . . . Oh, I DID want to be happy as a woman . . . But I'm a monster and must accept being one. Not *all* writers are monsters. But my kind is.

I opened *Little Dorrit* at this point and read 'She was inspired to be something which was not what the rest were and to be that something, different and laborious, for the sake of the rest'.

* * *

Tom Hopkinson had now married Dorothy Kingsmill and Gerti had brought a case for the exclusive custody of their children, Nicolette and Amanda. Antonia and Lyndall both provided affidavits to support Gerti's case. In the end the court awarded Tom and Dorothy access for eight days each school holiday. Antonia's support for Gerti caused a considerable rift between her and Tom.

* * *

29 Jan   Spent the morning with Gerti's solicitor over the Kingsmill question. Got up from 'flu for the first time last Thursday. Am just using bi-focals for the first time and find them decidedly awkward . . . Must try sitting up a little higher and having my back supported as I write. Funny what a lot of readjustment one simple change needs. But I do believe I work in unnecessary discomfort . . . No wonder I get so tired and dread sitting down at my desk. Must definitely try to begin the novel [*Beyond the Glass*] PROPERLY on Monday. Now since very tired – . . . GO TO BED!!

* * *

A woman named Virginia Johnes now became obsessed by Antonia through her books. She took to writing to Antonia up to three letters a day besides telephoning and coming round in person. Antonia told Lyndall (in a letter to Rome) that Johnes was like 'a Catholic Kingsmill' without Dorothy's liveliness or good looks. 'She's bossy and fearfully, unnecessarily unattractive.'

* * *

31 Jan   Clearing up, sorting out ... I hope ... that I can tactfully break with this Virginia Johnes who has exploded into my life. I have received no less than 27 letters from her in just over a month: 23 since Jan 6th. Fr. Bartlett [unknown] ... says she is mad and 'has her breakdowns on other people' ...

... Gerti is very anti-Lyndall now: perhaps too much so. She says she double-crosses and deceives all of us. That is probably so.

2 Feb   Today is the Purification, one of my favourite feasts. I want to make it a new beginning – of work and everything else. Last night I sat staring and smoking for $\frac{3}{4}$ hour, wondering whether to write to Sue and Thomas or even ring up Sheila to ask for a concrete explanation of this treating me as a leper ... I wrote to Lyndall instead, saying I did not think it would be possible for me to go to Rome because of the expense. L.'s letters to me lately have been very kind and thoughtful. All the same, because of her naturally deceitful nature, I cannot entirely trust her. It is difficult not to believe that, if she really *wanted* to, she could not have done something to bridge the gap between me and Sue ... I suspect Sue can still dominate her, however much she may criticise Sue ...

... My father ... looked for security above all things. My mother ... wanted excitement and change ... suffered from ... not having enough demands made on her ...

Of course I have been 'spoilt' too ... Eric and I tried to do the impossible thing that Sue and Thomas are now attempting: have a completely pleasurable, selfish private life ... I have seen the complete breakdown of poor Eric in a world which is not run for his private convenience and ... which, having now very little money, he can no longer organise to his fancy ...

... What Tom [Hopkinson] cannot endure is moral discomfort.

He has to reason in a way which justifies him in the most preposterous behaviour and ... Dorothy ... provides him with a false backing. Tom wants to behave exactly as he feels like doing but to feel morally impregnable ... but what *is* my weakness? ... I myself would say ambition ... to excel and above all to be *recognised*. My fervent admiration from my earliest years of people who were good at things ... desire ... to 'cut a figure' ...

... I wrote three friendly lines to Sue this morning ... Some part of her probably needs to feel that she has not provoked me beyond endurance and that I am genuinely pleased at her success in the job [on *Vogue*].

5 Feb No reply from Sue who has had ample time ... I assume she and Thomas received their Christmas cheques ... No dealings with Sue henceforth. Try not even to inquire about her. Try not to *think* about her ... I have made a small start on the book and must concentrate on that.

Spent the morning going into my whole situation as regards money, the book etc. Not waste of time since I really have got to get some order ... into my life ...

Rome or any sort of holiday abroad seems an impossibility ... I suggest one dinner party a week or a theatre or cinema so as to keep in touch with people and not get too eccentric ... About £6 a month could be called 'entertainment allowance' ...

I think I must definitely aim at getting the book finished by the 3rd week in July: that is 23 weeks; 3 weeks short of 6 months. By the end of Feb. since I have ... this Newman talk to prepare [address to the Newman Association dinner in Birmingham], I should try to get 2 chapters finished. After that 1 chapter a week. The thing is to organise myself but not *too* rigidly so that I do not get so depressed that I break out wildly.

With the book, try to aim at 1000 words a day which *need* not be done in the morning (though this is best when possible) and no week-end work unless I have got *very* badly behind. Try and organise some little pleasure every week-end. *Always* get out after lunch for a walk and have a little rest before tea since that is the most 'depressive' part of my day ... Try and have *one* good, nourishing meal a day. Early bed when possible and try to go to early Mass twice in the week.

19 Feb   I began the new book on Feb 3. I knocked off on Feb 7th (having done just 7 pages) to start on this piece for the Newman Association. I did not finish it till the evening of Feb 15th, working really hard at the end and writing 7–8 hours on the last day. I did quite 20 pp of rough notes. All this to read to about 16 at most people in Birmingham who wd. have preferred a short 'impromptu' speech and practically said so. This was impossible because Martin Turnell[†] was reading a paper he had already written and mine had to have some relation to his . . .

I came back yesterday so exhausted that I could not even write my thank-you note to the Burnses [unknown] who very kindly put me up . . . went to bed at 6 . . .

When I got back from B[irmingha]m Cecil King rang me up to say Basil Nicholson died in Dublin on Feb 16th. He was 45. I knew he had cancer of the throat . . . When I last saw Cecil a week or two ago, he said that the nuns were of course hoping for his conversion. Cecil *certainly* didn't think they had any hope! . . . [He] told me he was received into the Church some days before he died. This will not appear in the *W[orld] P[ress] N[ews]* article by Bill Connor so I want to put it on record here. Basil . . . preserved his old, grim humour to the last, even when he could no longer speak, only write. Last Saturday (he died last Monday) he wanted to go for a drive. It was all arranged but he was too ill to go. He had no clothes: the suit he arrived in was in such a state it had to be burnt . . . Cecil paid for a suit etc. but he never wore them. Cecil's kindness has been very touching. He had an extraordinary affection, even devotion to Basil. Basil must have been one of the strangest English characters of this century. He might have been one of the big 'success boys' and for a time was. I remember how much I once disliked him. Cruel he certainly was. Yet in the few weeks that we were lovers, I knew an entirely different side of him. And, though he treated me cruelly . . . I never disliked him again . . .

22 Feb   It will be practically March before I get into a proper routine on the book . . . Recently . . . I feel a change in myself . . . I suppose it is the beginning of the realisation that I have probably had all the major happenings of my life . . . Sometimes it is a great effort to get through the day: put on my clothes, write a letter or . . . do the necessary daily

... chores. I think what a meaningless business it all is ... There is no one left who really needs me ...

'Fame' sounds so exciting. Yet what it would be in reality? A mere multiplication on a bigger scale of Newman dinners. More and more 'fan letters'. Envy and flattery: people wanting to 'cash in' in public and pull one down in private ... One's little moments of limelight are just that. Oneself impersonating 'the well-known novelist'. Down comes the curtain, the audience hurries home, the impersonator slinks out of the stage-door in his ordinary ... clothes, unrecognised ... One would feel a pig being so much richer than one's friends. One might even begin to suspect friends. One would be envied and harassed. Sue would probably 'come round' but it wouldn't be from love. And I should probably become very arrogant ...

... Art does not mean what it once did to me. I *don't* mean that I don't still delight in works of art or don't still feel I know the real thing when I see it. It is just not an idol any more ... I think with sorrow it is my fault if my children have 'gone wrong'. If I had not deserted God, I would have given them a proper childhood ... Yet, if I had not deserted God, *these* children would probably not have existed ... I could not say for myself where I first 'went wrong' and began that series of entanglements and sins and muddles and disasters which still affect my own and other people's lives. How appalled my father would be if he knew the results of that fifteenth birthday. Yet I often feel as if I had never been a 'whole' person since that day ... For then, with every sort and kind of fault, I did ... put God first. That is something I don't speak of in *Frost in May*. Too private But it falsifies the book ... the profoundest *change* in my life was becoming a Catholic when I was seven (and *no one* will ever know how deep that change was) and the deepest shock was that interview with my father on Easter Sunday 1914 ... Darling Daddy, he understands it all now. And he sees that I'm trying to understand it too. We will have such joy when we meet. I must ask *him* to pray for Sue. He will know that *I* know now something of what he must have gone through over me. I used to think lovers suffered most. Now I think parents do. Tom simply amazes me with his superficiality. He 'adores' his children but he only 'suffers' about them intellectually . . rather [one] might say sentimentally. They are ill . . poor pets, get a doctor. They are 'maladjusted' . . poor pets, get a psychiatrist. They love him and need a home. But, poor pets, Tom needs a new woman, so they must get along as best they can ... Poor Tom, the trouble with him is he isn't human ... That would mean sometimes admitting he is wrong ... Dorothy is exactly the same. Their paradise consists of being always in the right ...

5 March   ... I spent three days hard work on my affidavit for Gerti and was absolutely limp after the effort. Have done *nothing* on the book for many days. This morning a letter from Senhouse[†] about *La Chatte* literally sent a rush of blood to my head. Yet it is not an offensive letter and I am not bound to make the alterations he suggests. It is as if the mere hint of criticism threw me right out of gear ... It is like ... finding I've made a slip in an exercise for my father ... I suppose I wd. have welcomed a little praise for I really put all I knew into that translation. He *does* say 'on the whole I was delighted' ...

12 March   ... spring-cleaning and painting up house a little. Always enjoy this. The worst is that as soon as you start ... you realise how dirty and shabby everything is. One longs to have a grand redecorating and refurnishing ...

I suppose Lent is the time for spring-cleaning one's character ... What are the ingrained faults ... Impatience and irascibility. Vanity. Not so much the physical kind for there's practically nothing left to be vain about. I don't think it's wrong to try to look as decent as I can. People look so ugly and unkempt nowadays that the sight of them is depressing. Trying to look decent brings it home to one that one is a plain, fat ageing woman and buying a new dress is a salutary destroyer of any hopeful illusions ... But mental vanity .. oh, dear, oh dear. And even the illusion, so strong as to be a conviction, that I am rather a *good* person. It's funny .. the first thing I remember wanting to be as a child .. was *good*!! ... I would call myself honest ...

... There is not much of my life left and I have lived it so badly when I think of all the graces, all the opportunities I have had and thrown away ...

27 March   Spring cleaning .. really a huge and detailed one over and the flat redecorated quite a lot and everything organised. Only Lyn's room left to do and that can be done in a day. Daphne and Harry come tonight. *So* nice to have people about the place again. They thought it all looked lovely: it really does look nice and fresh. Now I MUST stop housework and get down to writing. I KEEP saying 'Tomorrow .. tomorrow' It was to have been today but I found my desk drawer was filthy so I did that and cleaned and filled all my pens. Today on my way to have my bad foot (which has been v. troublesome all the winter) treated, a woman tried to sell me white heather. I always refuse but I didn't, saying she must give it me and I'd give her something. I gave her a lot in the end – 15/-. She was a real gypsy and said God had given her the gift of second sight. She said my initial was E and that I had had great sorrow during the past 18 months. I couldn't help being impressed and since it is 18 months almost to a day since I heard of Sue's marriage ... Also that seven important things would happen to me this year and that one would happen soon ...

12 April   I feel happier since Easter. There is no solution to any of my problems but the true one; to put first things first. Nothing matters but doing what God wants, trying to know, love and serve Him. There is no slavery, no frustration, no unhappiness like that of serving one's own egoism. I do truly, truly want to know what humility is because humility is the beginning – So much envy in my life and envy is the most destructive thing there is.

15 April   Today I have begun to try to get down to the book. All odd jobs are cleared up. I have had delightful letters from Julien Green and Emily this week. These are real comforts. I have a lot of friends and well-wishers ...* There are over 60 ...

25 April   ... I saw Esther [Hopkinson, Tom's sister] this week. I have not seen her to speak to for twenty years and then we always found it hard to talk. Now that she is an Anglican nun, nothing could be easier or more delightful. I felt a genuine glow of affection and admiration for her. How easy, how delightful it is when one can mention God openly in a conversation. She seemed to me so good, so

---

* Antonia then wrote out a list of names.

warm and honest all through . . and a good deal more humble than many of our own nuns! She is bravely going to face Dorothy in Tom's flat. Dorothy has already been writing her famous letters to her . . . and signing herself 'your sister'.

Tom seems to be losing all touch with sense or sensibility. He gave his poor old father the proofs of *Love's Apprentice*. The poor man is so shocked and shattered by it that he has practically collapsed . . .

Sue has not answered my letter and I assume she won't . . . I have no choice in the matter of 'withdrawing' from Sue: the choice is entirely hers . . . I do not think that Sue could possibly feel that I have rejected her. No, it must satisfy some violent feeling in her that she has so utterly rejected *me* . . .

1 May   I keep thinking – and saying – I have done no work at all since last October. Yet in fact I have done bits and pieces . . . two articles for *Punch* (of which only one was taken), the revision and proof correcting of the Colette translation. Preparing my statement about D[orothy] K[ingsmill] took me a whole week. She is legally Mrs Hopkinson now – She and Tom were married on March 20th . . .

. . . I have been working on the book for nearly 2 weeks fairly regularly but all I have done so far is fearfully flat, dull and niggling. I haven't so far managed to get a vestige of life into it. Don't quite know why. Perhaps because I'm so DESPERATELY bored with Clara. Two chapters (2 and 3) have simply trailed off . . one into hopeless muddle . . the other into such flat triviality that it's simply useless to go on with it. I'm going to try a different angle: do a chapter through the parents' eyes and see if that has any effect in getting it going.

24 May Whit Sunday   I made a novena to the Holy Ghost before Pentecost. I love the Veni Sancte Spiritus. I am calmer and more solid than I have been for a long time . . .

13 June   I don't need to write about that encounter with Sheila Glossop in Harrods. I'm not likely to forget it. What I've got to do is try and forgive it. Nor about Tom's attempt through his solicitors to cut off my supplies . . . I wish I weren't so dreadfully . . . shaken up by any sudden blow. Better firmly count my . . . blessings . . .

A very nice home anyhow for next 3 months.

Publishers wanting my book and doing all they can to help me write it.

Possibility of translations turning up ... I have made a good reputation as a translator ...

No serious debts ...

A more important form of optimism concerns your attitude to your work. TRY to get interested in it: try to enjoy it as you do writing a letter or making notes . . thinking, learning as you go, trying to *understand* more, not worrying if very much that you do is poor and has to be scrapped. Try to get away from that 'succeed or fail' attitude ... get *absorbed* in it, as you are in a window box or an interesting conversation or re-decorating a room ...

STOP WORRYING as to whether Daisy will send you anything. If she does, it will, in NO way, affect your present spending situation. It must be put by and forgotten, preferably in the P[ost] O[ffice].

* * *

Emily Coleman, who had spent the war years in the USA, and was now a convert to Catholicism, returned to England to live at Rye, Sussex. Lyndall returned from Italy for a holiday. Susan's son Andrew was born.

* * *

28 June   ... So far, a mixture of uneventful and eventful and, on the surface, not a 'good' half-year

... For the last month I have done practically NOTHING . . only 8 pages I think ... Two nice surprises: Emily's coming to England and the prospect of Lyndall being home for a fortnight in August ...

Irritations: ... Virginia Johnes and also the libel action [see page 308] ... also this worry about the money I lent Eric ...

Now, though I am sure Virginia means kindly, I'm sure now that it would be fatal to let her come to my rescue ...

One of my main practical troubles over the book is the weaving in of 'recapitulation': the penalty of writing a serial novel. I write nervously and repetitively: far too *much* ...

1 July   ... the pleasure of spending money freely must be replaced by spending *myself* freely ... I have been 'extravagant' from infancy. Some of it *can* be put down under the heading of 'generosity' ...

Much is desire to impress, to emulate ... spending money can appear
to one as creative activity. Or consolation, as a woman buys a new hat
when she is depressed. Or a form of buying love. Notable that, when
in love, I always spend a lot of money on the man ... No man has ever
spent a great deal of money on me ...

9 July   Now Jessie [Entwhistle, cleaning lady]. Her simply walking
out on me was the fourth of the possible reasons for her not
appearing day after day. I rejected it as mean and uncharitable even as
a suspicion! It is really rather odd how everyone closely connected
with me has been removed ... I do respond too quickly perhaps to
any affection ... It is odd that the one person who has charged so
heavily into my life since Christmas, V[irginia] J[ohnes], should, alas,
be one I could well do without. But she is absolutely convinced that it
is the Lord's will as well as hers that she should be involved with me
... I'm afraid I find it hard to like her. It is a comfort that her feeling
for me doesn't seem to have anything to do with affection. It is ...
obviously something to do with a power mania on her part. She may
be thankful that I don't feel the least desire to exert any power over
her . . except to dry up this incessant stream of letters!
   It's probably a good thing about Jessie. I was very fond of her (she
was a real 'original') but she exploited me like anything. She was the
most shameless 'hinter' for presents I ever knew: a time-chiseller and
time-waster too. But so kind and friendly and amusing and often
exerting herself like anything on my behalf. Quick and intelligent
too: you never had to tell her anything twice. I shall miss her and her
vivid talk. 'Without a word of a lie' . . . 'That road' 'It was throwing it
down' (raining) 'Pensillian' ... her polite 'beggar' (in deference to
me) ...

27 July   The immediate money problem has been almost miraculously solved by an unexpected £35 for royalties and £50 from an
'anonymous donor' paid into my bank. Of course V[irginia] J[ohnes]
is the most obvious suspect but how could she know my bank? It is
unlike her usual methods. I cannot deny her extraordinary kindness
to me but it is rather alarming ...
   My last 'earthquake' was a week ago on the 20th: a terribly
distressed letter from Lyndall enclosing a horrid one Tom had

written to her ... Eric and Georgie return to London today. Things seem a little better with them as regards money ... But G[eorgie]'s plan to borrow money to pay the initial instalment on a house sounds pretty wild ... especially as her job is not even confirmed yet. E[ric] obviously isn't at all happy and she is worried about him. I must say I find it difficult to imagine him happy at Worthing ...

20 Aug   It is delightful to have Lyndall here. She seems to be genuinely pleased to see me and is being very sweet. She is quite startlingly attractive, both to look at and in the extraordinary magnetism she has for men.

Through her I have got a good deal of light on the Sue situation ... Lyndall *did* go to the wedding, as I suspected and so did Silas and Sheila as I did not. Thomas's parents, like myself, were not told till afterwards. It is very shabby behaviour on the part of Silas and Sheila. Silas, a little tight, wanted me and the other parents to be rung up and invited to join the lunch party. It is just all rather disgusting ... Lyndall saw Sue on Sunday. She said Sue asked quite affectionately after me ... Lyndall says Sue is completely dominated by Thomas and agrees that Thomas hates me ... The oddest thing is that she and Thomas see Tom and Dorothy quite often. Tom has got Thomas a job in Shell Mex and that has put him in the Glossops' good books ...

... I *must* remember that it is no longer possible to talk frankly and freely to Eric. He talks to or is pumped by Georgie who is *totally* unreliable and not to be trusted. This applies to anything connected with Susan, the Glossops, Lyndall, Tom, Gerti ... everyone ...

16 Nov, St Cecilia's Day   Today I rang up Sue after getting Tom's father's letter. I heard her voice for the first time for 22 months almost to a day. She was not angry about my ringing up. She said she was going to tell me after the baby was born ... I said she no doubt had her reasons for telling me nothing about the baby and so on. She said yes and I could probably guess what they were. I said I couldn't ... She said she would write to me and explain ... speaking to her took away some of the nightmare feeling. I shan't be surprised if she doesn't write.

20 Nov   Andrew Edward Willes Chitty born.

31 Dec   It certainly has been an extraordinary year, full of changes
and surprises. The most fantastic the appearance of the anonymous
donor ... Over Christmas I have been very extravagant ... It is
amazing the difference these 6 months of security have made ... A
nice blow to one's vanity to see *what* a difference enough to live on for
a few months can make ... I have practically lived on charity this
year. My goodness, I ought to be grateful to whoever it is ...

... My poor cat [Domina]'s death. Final disappearance of Tom –
Eric and Georgie going to Worthing. Sue's baby and the total
shutting-down there. Tom's break with Lyndall. Georgie's violence
against me ... Sue never wrote of course. I sent her a greetings
telegram when I saw *The Times* announcement. Not acknowledged.
No card even this Christmas ...

I think the *nicest* thing in 1953 was having Lyn at home for a
fortnight. The most painful Sue's not telling me about the baby. The
most upsetting that meeting with Sheila in Harrods. The most
alarming, Tom's solicitors threat. The luckiest, the donor. Most
comforting, Emily's return.

Spiritually, what can I say? I think nothing but an *enormous* need for
gratitude ... Our Lady has showered me with kindness all the year ...
even to the two kittens [Minka and Curdy] ...

1954

2 May   I can't believe that I am off to Italy tomorrow, that the book
[*Beyond the Glass*] is finished etc. Thanks to Virginia and the A.D. I
have got over 3 weeks lovely carefree holiday ahead and no
immediate worries to return to. I have managed to work really hard
all this spring and even feel result is good. Best of all, I have had no
depression. I have been quite extraordinarily blest and fortunate for
the past six months ... Except, of course, for Sue ... It struck me
today how remarkably like Silas she is. The way she won't commit
herself in words so that one has no idea what she really means. Also
the way she escapes from unpleasant situations by running away from
them or simply ignoring them. Also the way she can suppress a whole
side of herself. Her new 'part' is extraordinarily like Silas's since he

married Sheila – She is almost imitating him now ... Not one sign from Eric since he rang me up (January?) about Lel [Eric's younger brother]'s[†] attempted suicide. I do not even know whether L. survived or not. I think this is the longest period of total silence from Eric ...

7 June   I've been back from Italy a week and more and don't know where to begin. It was a wonderful holiday in spite of very bad weather. I saw so much and there were so many impressions to take in that ... ever since my return I've been exhausted: ... 'lead spectacles' etc. ...

The Villa Mora, where L[yndall] is living this summer is about 3 miles out of Rome (Porta S. Sebastiano) on the Via Appia Antica. It lies back from a drive with immensely tall stone pillars at the gate. Our room had a terrace outside with roses climbing over the parapet. In the wild garden, cypresses and ilexes (the typical Italian trees along with olives), and flowers like English ones. Nightingales sang all night and on one of the few fine evenings there were fireflies – little streaks of white light darting among the bushes. Through the bathroom window was a lovely view of Rome in the distance. It is built over the catacombs. All along the Via Appia are Roman ruins and inscriptions: they dig up fragments all the time. In the local garage, little ancient figures, broken inscriptions, pieces of statuary etc. are displayed along with the cans of oil and petrol ... There are *Trattorie* along the road, too; some unpretentious, some expensive, with tables set out under a trellis of vines. It is odd to see such signs as Ristorante dei Cesari: Dancing. A fast shaky little bus with wooden seats (like all the Roman buses) bumps you along quickly into Rome and deposits you by the Coliseum [sic]. It is so *like* the Coliseum that though I saw it every day for 12 days I never seemed to want to do more than look through into the arena. Opposite the Coliseum is the vast white modern rectangular block built by Mussolini where Lyndall works ... I didn't 'do' ancient Rome at all: i.e. I saw such things as the Forum, Coliseum, the little temples of Vesta ... One comes across these things lying about almost haphazard and ... they seem oddly unreal, like a stage set ... Noise unbelievable: incessant roar of Vespas and Lambrettas, grinding brakes, hooting of horns, clatter of buses dashing through the narrowest side streets.

13 June ... No point in making Italian notes a bugbear. But try to pin down some day the singing in S. Francesco ... the cat inlaid in the lectern at Monte Oliveto, the great square in Siena ... St Clare's body with the flesh withered and brown, shrivelled and revealing the teeth ... The pleated mountains outside Siena: the castle-crowned hills: the cream oxen with long horns ... The altar boy tucking his little brother under his arm. The great moths outside the window at Assisi ...

Lyndall showed me a snapshot of Sue with Andrew. He is nearly 7 months now. A charming baby with a well shaped head and eyes that look dark. Sue looked different. I wouldn't have known her. At that angle her face had an odd look of mine. The mystery is no nearer a solution ... No one will tell me the facts yet someone ... must know them ...

I wonder how the new book [*Beyond the Glass*] will go. E[yre] and S[pottiswoode] and even May Pritchett [Antonia's agent in the USA] are enthusiastic. I can't help feeling it's good myself ...

15 June Eicholz[†] [sic] has discovered that my father's will is so worded that it excludes Sue from inheriting anything under him [sic]. I know that he meant to do the exact opposite .. to make sure that she *did* inherit, in spite of her illegitimacy. By not naming her and merely referring to 'eldest grandson or granddaughter' he accidentally debarred her since, in law, any descendant unqualified is assumed to mean legitimate descendant ... She therefore loses both the cottage and the royalties. This is hard on her and I fear will be a severe blow, particularly psychologically since it brings up her illegitimacy and deprives her of the cottage which she counted on getting and which she almost looked on as hers already and felt decidedly possessive about ...

Sue's overbearing pride and ruthlessness makes it difficult to feel sorry for her as I wd. otherwise have done. I wonder if this *real* blow and grievance might not even have a good effect ... She was such a grabber in the old days, even to shamelessly grabbing things of mine on the pretext that they would automatically be hers one day (in which she was wrong since the cottage furniture was mine and not part of my father's estate) ... Thomas hates religion .. and the spirit. In Sue too. He has some honesty .. more than the rest of them. But there's something mean, narrow, a little *grubby* about him. But though I *like* him the least of the lot as a person, I respect him the most. I never realised that till this moment. He's cruel, but not, I think, dishonourable. And though immensely self-pitying, not cowardly ...

16 June   I quite enjoyed spending an evening with Benedicta. But a whole evening in a pub leaves me a wreck ... and ... it's more expensive ... than taking someone out to a civilized dinner. I found her admirable company ... but it is astonishing to look back and see what tremendous emotion an evening with her would have aroused 7 years ago. As usual she gave me several entirely new versions of things that happened then ... I don't think she is exactly a liar ... though on simple questions of *fact* she improvises wildly ... 'What *really* happened, darling' was etc. etc. ... . She still sticks to her theory that D[orothy] K[ingsmill] took drugs ... I believe that D. K. (I still can't remember to write D[orothy] H[opkinson] works entirely by psychic domination ...

I wonder *what* is happening to Eric. Sheed [Sheed and Ward, publishers] said there was no sign of the translation [*Clem* by Henry Muller]. That is what I feared ...

17 June   ... A 'hunch' that a novel is at last likely to be a real success is nonsense and I know it. All I know is that my publishers ... are very keen on the new one. Oddest of all, I'm rather 'in love' with it myself in retrospect. I keep thinking about it, still living in it. I don't remember ever having felt quite like this about any book of mine before and it may not be a good sign. Elaine likes it but not as much as *The Sugar House*. . . I also feel almost as if someone else had written it . . especially the asylum part where I worked with a speed and intensity that I've never known before so that it was almost like being possessed ... It is horrifying how selfish and unimaginative one can be when one is young. I keep reminding myself of that in Sue's case. It is obvious she never gave a thought to what I went through when she was in the Maudsley ... I *don't* believe my mother felt it in quite the same way ... Possibly because she was not in the least self-questioning ... She never *brooded* although she was subject to fits of depression ... I wonder just when I *did* get my nullity decree [from

Reggie]. I came out of Bethlem in August 1923. Perhaps the case was heard in that autumn? I married Eric in 1925 (April 15, I think) and I reckoned that it had taken 18 months to get it through the ecclesiastical courts. The Dougal thing must have happened in the early part of 1924. That is one of the most tangled parts of my life to look back on. I went to Crawford's, I think, in the summer of '24. All that Alan [Walker]† and Eric business must have been then. By the autumn of '24 I must have been engaged to Eric. I suppose we all went to Italy in May or June '24. It was '28 when I met Silas and '29 when Sue was born ... I married Tom in Nov 1930. When I look back at my life from '24 to '30 I can hardly believe anyone could have so messed and muddled it ... People suppose I led a wild sexual life but, in fact, that is not the case. I had sporadic 'affairs' while I was married to Eric. Yvon,† the Austrian boy [Edo], I[an] B[lack], B.H. [unknown] and then genuine affairs with Silas and afterwards Tom. Certainly I had no moral scruples about it then, nor did Eric. When I was with Tom I had two absurd infatuations – they were just *that* – but I did not, mercifully, sleep with either of those men. When Tom left me ... I did sleep once or twice with R[onald] and with J[ohn] S[ummerson] ... I would have slept with N[orman] C[ameron] if he had wanted to. I had a very brief affair (serious for *me*) with B[asil] N[icholson]. After that a real affair with I[an] which I broke off when I came back to the Church in 1940. For 14 years I have had no sexual life at all. And, except for Tom and I[an], no continuous sexual relations with anyone ... It is a very queer sexual record, even in these days ... I shall never understand the Tom thing which has at last so completely gone. My affection for him is always there and could be revived at any moment ... Love, never. Whereas, with Silas, though *unthinkable*, it is not unimaginable ... There was from the first something odd about my falling in love with Tom. For it was *not* instantaneous, as it was with Silas ... Tom, whom I had always rather disliked ... suddenly assumed this violent, almost compulsive importance soon after my father's death. Why? It had never occurred to me that *anyone* could be a rival to Silas for me. And my father had, reluctantly, accepted the fact that I should eventually marry Silas so there was almost 'paternal approval' there. Had he lived, should I have dared to take another lover? ... Why did Tom's conventionality make such tremendous appeal to me? Or was it just that accident of the drunken men trying to push him out of the window? ... *good at games*, gifted for writing? My father would like to have been that sort of young man, too ... I think there *is* some association in my mind between Tom and my father ...

18 June ... Last night I had one of those queer recurring 'Buckingham Palace' dreams. I am always a little apprehensive when I'm there. I know that I have a right there but am always nervous of its being challenged ... I know my way about the palace but am not quite sure if I have a right to be there ...

What do *these* dreams mean? ... The 'royal family' . . Julien Green and suchlike . . treat me as an equal. It is inferior literary people who patronise me ... Obviously some part of me . . longs for open recognition ... It hurt me that in an article on English Catholic novelists (by someone English I had never heard of) I was not even mentioned though Bruce Marshall was discussed at some length. I really can't help feeling that I'm better than Bruce Marshall ...

21 June I had a nice week-end at the Bertrams[†] [Anthony, author, and Barbara]. I always like going there. I doubt if I know any woman I like and admire more than Barbara. She's so absolutely good and honest right through like a ... new-baked loaf ... She's my opposite in every way and I'm more touched and flattered by her liking me than almost any woman I know ...

... I often wish there were some friend at hand really interested in what I write. Emily is of course . . and in anything one *has* written ... She is my opposite in writing. Writes all the time with passionate zeal and zest and complete confidence in her own genius. Practically all my other friends hardly mention my writing at all, beyond being pleased for my sake if I've finished a book. Elaine is different of course but I've slightly 'lost touch' with her though I'm as fond of her as ever. I absolutely *thirst* sometimes to be able to get down and talk shop with another writer as I used to with Tom. That has gone for ever ... we are now completely out of sympathy with each other's work ... When I think how I listen by the hour to Robert Speaight and Tony [Bertram] talking about theirs and never even pretending to be interested in mine. It's childish of me but there it is. The way they say with such superiority that they never read any novels except masterpieces etc. . . . HOW those boys patronise me. It is funny really when Julien Green treats me as an equal which I know I'm not. Even Virginia is only interested in what I write as part of her own mysterious 'game' . . . But I'm 55 now and would like a status . . to be mentioned when other novelists are being discussed in articles etc. I get so sick of people always talking about *Frost in May*. If I've learnt nothing as a person or a writer in 30 years, it's pretty disheartening . . . I can't see that *Frost in May* is all that wonderful. Yet the book's become a kind of legend . . . But I *do* feel the new one is an advance. Am I wrong? And I *know* that there is more truth in it than in *Sugar House*. I idealised Reggie in that. Not that it matters. He *was* good and simple. But it overbalanced it somehow . . . I think the new one is much better balanced because of the parents etc. and the tragedy being in the *situation*. The next one must be *much better still*.

22 June   What peevish complaining . . . What a light, almost negligible cross compared to what many people have to bear . . . I *do* find it hard to forgive my enemies though . . . It is a puzzling world to live in when all standards are arbitrary. The other day Kathleen McClean said to me of Peregrine 'the only thing that worries me is that there are no *girls*. I don't want him to stay virtuous too long or he'll become neurotic'. That is a devoted . . . 'modern' mother speaking . . . Yet *is* that assumption true, quite apart from any question of religion . . .? I can think of plenty of young men who have had mistresses and who are just as neurotic as the chaste ones. My own generation who took to 'free love' almost as a duty could hardly be *more* neurotic . . .

1 July   . . . trying to pretend I'm not wondering whether the A[nonymous] D[onor] is going on . . . who *can* it be? I don't think it *is* Eickholtz [sic], as Lyndall thinks . . . A week ago, I suddenly had a letter from Eric 'de profundis'. Asking if Elaine could do his typing, saying he was coming up 'very soon' and longed to see me . . . I answered by return. Not a word from him since, of course. Can't resist slight amused cynicism. After all these months, he breaks silence because he *wants* something. In spite of his horror of writing letters, ever since he got into this terrible state, he always manages to overcome the horror when *he* wants something. Never because *you* might like to hear from him . . . he *is* a little naughty.

Better think of my faults than other people's ... My tongue runs away with me ... 'Destructive' Ronald used to say and Basil too ... How terribly, terribly hard it is to know oneself even if one wants to. I *should* know from the sins that come up regularly in confession: discontent, pride, contempt, hasty judgement, jealousy, self-pity, anger.

27 July   Have done very little writing since I came back from Italy 2 months ago ... First 4–5 weeks too exhausted to do anything.

Tonight I am extraordinarily tired again. I saw Eric for the first time for 7 months: he spent whole day here. He did not seem too bad at all and has finished his translation. They both hate Worthing: Georgie ... is as fierce against me as ever. Yet she liked the short stories [*Strangers*, 1954] ... and – astonishingly – the 'Tantum dic verbo' poem. He says her changes of mood are violent. She is ... in her bitter, attacking mood against everyone. We both agreed that what she needs is a little success ... I'd certainly do anything I could to help her about work etc. I can't *like* her. Yet I can understand ... her ... frustrations ... she is such a little stinging nettle ... One cannot say that the subtle deterioration in Eric is due to her.

28 July   I had 2 vivid dreams during the last night or two ... One night I dreamt Sue and I and Lyndall were together again and ... happy.... It was sad to wake up ... Up till then she [Sue] has always been hostile in dreams ... I wonder if Eickholz [sic] has told her about Daddy's will ...

The other dream ... I was giving a party ... I was worried because I found it was my father who had made all the arrangements for the party and I was afraid that he would not realise how much drink people expected nowadays ... Cyril Connolly was there ... I went away to get dressed but could not decide whether to wear my ... black evening frock or fancy dress. The fancy dress was ... black velvet trousers, a red shirt and a big black Spanish hat ... realising the party was in 'full swing' ... I decided on the fancy dress. Then I couldn't find it ... the trousers were missing. I wandered over roof tops trying to find them. Eventually two women who looked like Lesbians found them for me. They were terribly dusty. The women said they would drive me back to the party. They were very kind. I knew they *had* been Lesbians but were now 'converted'. But I woke up before I ever got to the party or even got dressed ...

My power to attract. It operates mainly on women nowadays ... have not made a single man friend on my own ... for something like twenty years. There is Julien Green of course but I hardly ever see him ... Once or twice, men have appeared in the last few years, but almost at once, old as I am, they have wanted to make love to me and I have had to get rid of them ...

... I have spent all the morning writing these notes: doing only a page or two of my story. But dreams of that kind always prod me since they usually mean something is boiling up ... they seem to say that I am missing something through over-anxiety or the temptation to take a line which is not my true one ...

Later   At the hairdresser's, I looked at the magazine with the picture of E[ric] and G[eorgie]'s bungalow. Absurd reactions. Seeing things which used to be in Eric's and my place before Selwood [Place] and feeling resentful that G. should be able to refer to them now as 'mine' ... what pathos when you read between the lines of that article about 'Eric and Ursula Noble'. You would think they were blissfully happy ... She is gifted and pretty but she is gnawed by vague ambitions and never satisfied. She wanted to marry Tom, to have money, to be a famous writer – *Would* she have been happy with him? ... What satirist would ever have guessed that of all Tom's women . . me, Frances, Gerti, Georgie and the rest, the one who has completely swept him off his feet . . and apparently permanently . . should be Dorothy Kingsmill ... Georgie ... is a genuine human being and, compared to Dorothy, a paragon. And she was sweet and touching, even though she *was* a little Robber Girl, when she was in love with Tom ... Her shrewd and go-getting side never gets her anywhere though she is prepared to go to astonishing lengths ... Why do I go on talking about them? ... she can't destroy his [Eric's] feeling for me even if we never met again ... But she resents it bitterly ... [Her] whole compulsion is towards wanting something someone else has and trying to acquire it by force ... She wants to *be* everyone she envies ...

Later still   No, surely I must just get on with my own work since there is nothing I can do to bridge all these estrangements ...

16 Aug   On Saturday I ran into Joan Cochemé at the Tate. She had seen Sue and the baby the day before ... *her* impression is that Sue is very fond of me, asked after me etc. ... Cochemé [Jacques, Joan's husband[†]] felt Sue was brittle and tense: Joan didn't. It is extraordinary how difficult it is to get an authentic impression. Gerti's was different: that Sue asked after me but in an icy, nervous way ... I had been going to send her a small birthday present. Joan thinks much wiser not to ... when I last wrote to her . . a year ago last Good Friday, I said if she didn't answer that I would take it as meaning she never wanted to have anything to do with me again. And she didn't answer ...

... She only lives 10 minutes away [at 25, The Little Boltons]! Now they're moving to the country and I shan't even know her address. I could die without being able to get in touch with her. I wandered down their street and stared up at the windows. Curtains were still up so they can't have gone yet. But I think they were away. Joan says Andrew looks like me. He doesn't *at all* in Lyndall's snap.

She never answered Eicholz's [sic] letters. So like her! So she still doesn't know about Daddy's will ...

More and more, writing seems to be my only real function. I have odd recognition of a kind: very slow. *Frost in May* hangs round my neck like a withered wreath ... Critics are being polite about *Strangers*. Some even see the point I'm trying to get at. I'm getting more mature now: I see myself what I'm trying to do . . a little. Emily does see. But there aren't many Emilys. The fact is, people *are* very immature nowadays. I was interested that Gerti now sees the point of things like 'The Moment of Truth' because of experiences she's now had. If people haven't had them, they either don't believe what I write or think I'm faking. I am more and more struck by how people don't *listen* and don't *remember*. I am not in the least original or inventive but I *do* listen and remember. That is really all there is to it.

One's gift isn't one's own. I see that more and more. It is both a gift from God and a curious product of one's background. I could as easily say it is my parents' gift . . my father's formal clarity, my mother's oddness. The fact of being an only child: no distractions and being much alone. Drawbacks, of course, in being an only child: not so much being 'spoilt' which I wasn't, but being the only thing of its kind in the household. Tendency to think of oneself as odd and

unlike other people: also to feel oneself 'unique' in a conceited way
... What is hardest of all to realise is that one has a marked *personality*
... One can look back ... and there are people one *cannot* forget (they
may not be at all *likeable*) and far more agreeable ones whom one
cannot remember ... I obviously belong to the kind people remember ...

   ... One even moderately late night ... knocks me out the next day.
As today, after having had 3 people to dinner ... Work is restful
compared to entertaining and talking. I am waiting with absurd
apprehension to know what Emily thinks of *Beyond the Glass* ... I feel
that Emily's praise is immensely worth having (*far* more than that of
any professional critic) ... I love ... her so much: I wish to goodness I
could really see what she is getting at in these poems she writes ...

18 Aug   Sue's 25th birthday. The boy will be 9 months old on 20th.
Yesterday I overheard 2 small boys (say 8 and 7) talking in a bus.
A) (elder) Over there's that museum we went to. The one where they
had a little model of a fire. Remember?
B) *I* don't remember. What fire?
A) With all the houses burning and the roofs coming off the houses
... You *must* remember.
B) I *don't*. What else?
A) Well, costumes. All sorts of costumes ...
B) I can't remember *anything*.
A) Not even the rocking-horse?
B) I'm not sure about the rocking-horse. I think I *did* see a rocking-
horse. But p'rhaps it was only in a dream. Tell me some more we
saw ...
A) Well, there was a dog outside on a lead.
B) (interested) *Was* there? I wish I'd seen the dog. Do you think I *did*
see that dog?

21 Aug   After so many good reviews of *Strangers*, I suddenly got 3
attacking ones ... The cruellest of the reviews went back to *Frost* as
usual. The 2 novels dismissed as a great falling off. 'Traces of the old
quality apparent in the stories'. Might have hoped they were signs of
'rebirth' but alas, best of them ('Rich Woman', in this critic's
estimate) dated 1949. They talk of my 'early, possibly too early'

success. Hang it all, I was in my early thirties when I wrote *Frost*!

. . . *Frost* has now become a legend. I meet quite young people who know it and 'adore' it. They never read anything else of mine or even seem to know I've *written* anything else!

Once again the same extraordinary contradictions in the reviews. I'm too emotional or too cold and detached. The stories are straight from life or they 'creak mechanically'. I need to 'go into training' or I have 'brilliant technique'. I am constantly accused of inventing impossibilities, especially in stories which are, in fact, almost photographic reports of experience. I am said to have a 'hard, bright talent', a 'creepy' one, to be 'entertaining', to leave an indescribably nasty taste in the mouth. One critic dismisses 'The House of Clouds' as 'fantasy' having no relation to clinical madness! . . . What always hurts me is when I am accused of 'faking' . . . (they usually mean 'House of Clouds' and 'Moment of Truth' . . . the two most painfully acquired of the experiences). One critic mentions 'The Key' [poem]. Not *one* ever refers to 'Sed Tantum'.

It *is* disheartening sometimes, trying to be an honest writer . . which is what I try most of all to be. I wonder immensely how they will take *Beyond the Glass*. Not a word from Emily yet. Is that a bad sign? . . . Will *Beyond the Glass* re-establish me as having at last done something better than *Frost* or put another nail in my coffin? . . . I feel anything might happen to that book: complete failure, succès d'estime . . or a best-seller, attacked by the pundits. I've never felt so queer about any novel of mine.

11 Sept I really have to be on my guard all the time against an absurd touchiness and secret 'uppishness' about my writing. It happens automatically . . at the least touch of patronage, however well-meaning, or at neglect . . if people make no reference to it. It even happens with strangers who have no possible means of knowing that I am writer. It is idiotic . . .

I keep telling myself: 'If God wants you to have fame you will have it. If he doesn't, you won't.' And, oh, how wonderful it would be not to have serious money worries. All this is very wicked and ungrateful when I think how amazingly I've been 'looked after' this year; how good my health is; how amazingly happier my whole life has been, not only than it has for some 20 years, but almost than ever before for this past year. The quite *amazing* difference the 'anonymous donor' has made in every way. It is almost as if *that* were what were needed all the time ... I wonder if X will ever know the extraordinary good he has done me.

This may partly account for my anxiety over the new novel ...

In a way, it will be my 'coming of age' as a novelist: 21 years since *Frost* was published. I am still nervous and un-self-confident as a writer: frightened to launch out on anything new in case it fails ... So often things start promisingly – I mean in the way of commissions etc. then suddenly peter out, like the BBC *Critics* thing ... One would think the time had come for a reprint of *Lost Traveller* ... but, again, silence. It is queer. And I am 55. Translations earn me a little money. I am quite glad to do them ... No one offers me a cosy one book a week well-paid review ... It is rather awful to feel that one is better ... than most novelists in England ... Among the 'ancients' I feel a minnow. But among the moderns, in England, I have to admit that there are very few who are definitely 'better'. Graham and Evelyn Waugh are infinitely more brilliant: that is indisputable. Hartley at his best is very good indeed. Henry Green . . again, *far* more brilliant ... I'm NOT brilliant ... I only want to see straight and put it down *right*. Elizabeth Bowen[†] can do things I can't touch . . at her best which is VERY good. So can Anthony West. So can plenty of Americans: Eudora Welty, Martha Gellhorn . . and of course Djuna. But Djuna is a phenomenon. I belong to the French line and there I'm well outdistanced . . Mauriac, Colette, Julien Green. It is silly comparing oneself with other writers. Nearly as silly as the way critics compare me to others. I have been compared to George Eliot, Jane Austen, Galsworthy, Compton Mackenzie and (by Julien Green) even to Dostoievsky. However one nasty review of *Strangers* suggested the person whom I really ought to follow was Daphne du Maurier!

No critic, no friend, likes *all* my work ... Eric judges each thing on what *kind* of thing it is meant to be and has no prejudices. Tom presumably hates everything since *The Lost Traveller*.

What should encourage me is that the few serious critics such as Edwin Muir are always interested ...

* * *

The book Antonia now began to write as a successor to *Beyond the Glass* she at first called the Eric one (*Clara IV*, see *As Once in May*), since it was to cover the period of her marriage to Eric Earnshaw Smith (1925–1929).

* * *

12 Sep ... The E[nfants] de M[arie] meeting always tires me so much. I wish I got more out of such things. I am naturally resistant to anything 'congregational' ...

I begin to think what shall I do next after the translation [*The Wind Bloweth Where it Listeth*, Paul-André Lesort]. There is something to be got out of the convent story. But what long thing? If a novel, still another in the Clara sequence? Presumably the Eric one ... I think it shd. go to the father's death ...

What did actually happen?

After Sue was born, I went back to Eric. I was to have gone out at Christmas but Si changed his job and went to Mexico. My father died in November ...

10 Nov Finished *Le Vent* trans on Monday Nov. 1st 109000 words and took 3 months 'hard'.

19 Dec E[ric] says the second nullity suit is more than people will stand for. That is possible. But I rather think it is essential. It could be worked as a divorce but I think that would falsify the situation ...

31 Dec ... This year has been an extraordinary one ... V[irginia] J[ohnes] turns out, after all, to have been the 'anonymous' donor ... [She] has just fastened herself into my life and looks like staying in it. I have come to like her though I often find it extremely difficult to know how to deal with her ... I don't know whether I've done right or wrong in accepting this loan she's forced on me ... it is to be paid back out of a percentage on royalties ... I had, of course, a great spending bee on house and clothes ... All sorts of nice things have happened such as going to Italy and Lyndall's coming here for Christmas ... a whole year without the black depression.

Also *Beyond the Glass* has had some amazingly good reviews and *seems* to have exorcised – almost – the ghost of *Frost in May*. Anyhow, it has made a real *impact* . . .

I had Gerti to stay for several weeks. It is odd to think of Tom hating us both so much now . . .

My new cats are sweet. My new char is perfect. Altogether I am a very, very, *very* lucky woman.

I fear all my old faults are still there . . . Above all gratitude, gratitude . . . And *humility* . . . A little success . . . goes so to one's head . . .

SIX

1955–1957

After a five-year break, Antonia and Susan were reconciled and Antonia met her two grandchildren, Andrew and Cordelia, for the first time. In 1955 Lyndall married Lionel Birch† and returned to England for a year. She worked for Rediffusion Television, as a personal assistant on 'This Week'.

Antonia had already begun her twenty-five-year-long effort to complete a fifth novel, promised to Eyre and Spottiswoode for September 1956. She attempted the novel already mentioned, about Tom and Eric and provisionally entitled *Clara IV*. She went back to the subject of her first lover, Jim Dougal, provisionally entitled *My Father's House*, and when this was accidentally burned she attempted a book about Eric and Si, to be completed by June 1957. And she looked ahead to novels about her later adventures, taking her at least to the Second World War, when she and Eric almost perished together in the Blitz. But the block was insuperable, and there never was a fifth novel.

In the meanwhile she worked on *Happy Release*, a novelette aimed at the American market. Its subject was her relationship with Susan and Sheila Glossop and it ended with her owned imagined death. The story was too full of spleen to find a publisher. At this time Antonia also wrote the first of her two cat books for children, *Minka and Curdy*. Her career as a translator was now at its peak; in 1954 she translated four novels.

1955

Ash Wednesday   No excuse now for not getting down to the novel. As usual frittered away the morning in elaborate financial calculations and admonitions to myself. Amazing how much of my diary is devoted to these calculations ... it is time to stop self-indulgent spending and to produce ... I have to be careful not to become a *spoilt* child ... *Absurd* how I mind Bobbie Speaight's thin excuses for not reading *Beyond the Glass* ... I must get on ... with ... the current novel ... surely there is *interest* to be got out of writing this one ... The three interesting people in this one are Eric, Silas and my father. Clara, as usual, is a bore ... interesting only in her relationships. It is a

study of weakness, really. The character of Frank [Freeman] turns up
so much in Si's letters that I think I'll have to introduce him.

8 June   I am utterly and hopelessly stuck over the novel. Three
weeks on that first chapter has produced nothing but a meaningless
mess ... I had vague ideas of dropping the entire Clara sequence and
trying something completely new. But no theme presents itself ... Of
course it is always a difficulty, these introductory, recapitulating
chapters. But they are necessary ...

   Later   ... Since the only serious upheaval in my life lately has
been Lyndall's marriage, is there some connection? To see her so
radiantly happy truly does please me and she could not be sweeter to
me, nor could Bobbie [Lionel Birch] ... and this is not just maternal
pride, everyone admits it ... It may be, not Lyndall, but Bobbie that I
envy .. having this wonderful new beginning at 45. In a sense
Lyndall's happiness is built on the unhappiness of other women. But
she has stolen nothing. One could wish Bobbie's past were not what it
is ... But he has no religion to give him a reason for not taking what
he wants ... And, by being analysed, he is doing the best he can to
straighten himself out ... Lyndall is like me: she withers without
stimulus. I need *incessant* encouragement.

10 June   I need to keep constantly bringing my mind back to the real
thing .. viz what is God's will for me ... I want everything made easy
for me in an absurd fairy-tale way. Or I long to die, to give up the
incessant   struggle   against   insecurity,   loneliness,   boredom,
depression. I want things *my* way, not God's way ... The novel *seems*
a hopeless task yet I feel guilty at dropping it before I have made some
tiny beginning which is right. For 3 weeks I have nothing to show
but a pile of papers which are all wrong. Yet I know there were times
when *Beyond the Glass* seemed equally impossible. Yet I have the
excuse that in the next three months I have undertaken to translate
some 90,000 words ...

   ... I see from back notebooks that with *Beyond the Glass*, I scrapped
the entire beginning and began again in late June. BUT it took me
from then till April to finish it i.e. about 10 months.

12 June   I had a long talk to Elaine last night which helped clarify my mind about the book. Thank God for her! She thinks I really ought to drop it now for the translation ...

... I meant to go to the E[nfants] de M[arie] meeting but was so tired I went and lay down for over 2 hours. Not depressed .. just incapable of doing anything. I really thought I must be ill: such enormous lassitude for no apparent reason. I hope it goes by tomorrow and I can get back to normal work ...

... I read Anthony Powell's *The Acceptance World*. I don't think it amounts to much though extremely funny in parts. It's all scraps. I got it really to help me with the twenties atmosphere but he doesn't give one single date to help one fix things. Just a vague diffused sense of period. ...

I rather think this book is upheaving me somewhere. Obviously it cuts deeper than I realise ... it means going back to Sue's birth. AND facing and admitting how I shirked responsibility over that. How can I blame her for her behaviour now? ... By writing it for Elaine, it may make an impossible ... task easier.

23 June   *Astonishing* the relief of going back to translation ...

2 Aug   I have finished Colette. Also have revolutionary ideas about the next novel being one stage earlier than planned: i.e. Dougal ... It all started by a violent dream ... concerned with Basil Nicholson ... To *me*, of course, the Dougal episode is something I would like to rule right out since it is so trivial ... as well as being so shaming ... D.'s character is another snag. There is also the possibility of his being still alive. I broke off here and wandered about the room milling it over and finding myself jam up on this too.

Another nag of a different kind. May [Pritchett] has written to me saying what a pity I have to spend so much time on translations instead of doing more of my own ... She suggests my writing a short story ... for the American Magazines which she says are well paid. Have I an idea for one? Well, have I? Is there something in the Sue-Sheila situation?

* * *

Antonia went to Ireland with her American friend and admirer, Dr Katharine Gurley. It was to Dr Gurley that she had dedicated *Beyond the*

Glass – 'without whose encouragement this book might never have been written'. The two women went on a tour of the west coast of Ireland with Jim Twomey, a Cork taxi-driver and undertaker, and amongst Antonia's papers there is a notebook containing a typed account of the journey, with photographs, that Twomey made for the ladies.

* * *

20 Aug J[im] T[womey] ... When someone dies, undertaker comes at once, bringing appropriate shroud: white for unmarried girl, blue for child of Mary, brown for rest, unless a tertiary when he supplies the habit. Undertaker or nun lays out body ... Burying Jews is usually v. damaging to an undertaker's business: others will often not go to him if he is known to bury Jews. Jews have a coin put in their hand to pay ferry over Jordan ... In Limerick a firm has practically monopoly of funerals since it has horse-drawn hearses and carriages, now almost unprocurable and the people there prefer horse funerals. Only twice in our 1500 miles did J. take a wrong turning and once was because he was studying a 'hearse' with professional interest ...

... His father, also undertaker and car-driver (horse-drawn) did not want to go in for mechanisation ... Persuaded his father to let him and his sister reorganise business. Now has 4–5 cars and drivers ... we never had a cross word or even a sulk out of him in 8–9 days of incessant driving. He sings at the wheel ... Amazing repertoire from 'If I were a blackbird' ... to every kind of sentimental modern song ... On Sunday he sang all the Benediction hymns in Latin and we joined in ...

... He thought I could not be a Catholic because of my name ... He did not grasp that K[atharine] G[urley] was when he saw her 4 years ago ... Obviously adores K. and luckily took to me at once too.

K. 'Do many Irish writers come from Cork?

J. 'Hawse riders, is it?

... Favourite recreation, playing cards ... Takes rosary out of pocket when playing cards ... Gave a lift to a Jehovah's Witness on condition the man did not preach to him. The man did and J[im] gave him 'the bum's rush' and pushed him out of the car ...

... Even at the airport, the show case displays chalices, altar plate etc. ... The last lot of pilgrims were returning from Lough Derg, buying things from barrows ... one stall offered 'Relics of St

Anthony!' Pilgrimage lasts 3 days during which they fast except for black tea and biscuits. Once on the island they go barefoot. First night is spent in prayer ... It sounded *very* hard to me but K. as usual pooh-poohed it saying *she* often went without a night's sleep etc. etc. ...

Connemara, the endless green hills and dark lakes. The fuchsia hedges and palms ... The horse-drawn funeral in Limerick ... The tinkers in their gay hooded carts, surprisingly neat and tidy inside though the owners were in rags (J. says they are rich) ...

17 Sept Our family situation – one could almost call it our family curse – goes on and on. Already Lyndall and Bobbie are in trouble. Bobbie says the happiness lasted 8 days of marriage and 30 before. Lyndall is the discontented one ... Her old trouble – not wanting what she has got – being unable to *accept* love. He thinks analysis the only solution for her ... But how can they raise the money? They are already deep in debt ... I am very tired today after sitting up with them till 1 a.m. What began as a pleasant evening, my first meal with them in their own house, ended as a painful showdown ... The real trouble, of course, is that neither of them has any religion. Analysis cannot take the place of that but it *could* remove ... Lyndall's ... incessant compulsion to pursue something, get it, then not want it.

I had a nightmare after this evening. There was a wild party which seemed to have begun in my flat and ended in Kathleen Raine's ... The main feature (and this is new to any dream I have ever had) was that everywhere, on rugs, etc. was spilt semen ...

... obviously concerns Lyndall and Bobby in some way. The elegant house completely wrecked, the 'wasted' semen etc. Why Kathleen Raine? The poet, the frigid woman, the loving mother, the lapsed Catholic. One side of me probably ... Lyndall saying she does not *want* a child now: she would envy it, think it would have all the things she missed ...

Some nights ago I had another dream: a happy one. I loved a Siamese prince and he loved me. We were amazingly happy together. The only thing the matter with him, he had some crippling in one leg ... This is another version of the recurring 'marriage' dream in which there is so often some weakness or disability in the man. Not unnatural to be having them now because of the Dougal book ... the

curious one in Ireland about Twomey and 'Our Lady of Misery', the
picture he took me to see was a beautiful Polish primitive of the
Nativity ... 'Misery' . . it just occurs to me, might also = 'Miser — y'.
Am I still afraid of *real* giving in spite of my extravagance and so-
called 'generosity'? Those compulsive little daily calculations ... Am
I an unconscious miser?

The book ...

People angles ...

Clara ... She is *not* attracted to Dougal at first, simply amused and
flattered. It is fun to be with someone who works, someone on the
fringes of Fleet St. And she admires him for his supposed courage.
And is sorry for him, all the more because he never obviously asks for
pity. A touch of the old 'in it together'. 'We're both bad pickers'. He
talks chivalrously about his wife. As a lapsed Catholic, he married her
in a registry office: wartime marriage . . she was a V.A.D. Kind to him
after his accident. 'We don't talk the same language. She's found
another man who suits her better.' He's divorced her: no ill feelings.

... It is the father who asks him to stay the night. Clara does not
even know he is in the house because of her having to go to bed at ten.
So when he comes into her room, it is almost like a dream. He is
wearing a dressing-gown of her father's.

I think when she does see him next day there is a reaction; she
notices small things about him that are distasteful ... He sees he is
losing ground. Perhaps it is then he suggests the ride. They are going
past his cottage when the 'housekeeper' appears. He ... suggests they
call instead on Patsy [Marion Abrahams] and family ...

Then she has a scene with him and breaks the whole thing off ...
She throws herself into neglected Spanish classes ...

When she discovers the truth she is in a panic. Patsy is the first
person she confides in ...

She goes over to Chelsea in a wild state of mind ... with a vague
idea of seeing Clive [fictional Eric]. Clive is out and the person she
meets is Gundy [fictional Seabrooke]. Gundry gives her the address
[of an abortionist] ...

31 Dec   How little I have written in this notebook in 1955. But it has
been a year of hard work, even if mainly translations. I *did* do the
'novelette' ['Happy Release'] wh. took me 11 weeks really hard

going. Fearful temptations to publish it (or try to) in England but I really think this would be wrong for Sue's and Sheila's sake. I do not feel much hope of America ... particularly necessary to try and get out of V[irginia] J[ohnes]'s clutches. This last week I *have* managed to stop her writing to me or ringing me up ... nothing short of brutality seems to have any effect on V.J. Having forced this money on me she now does everything she can to make me feel guilty about it ... This imaginary drama is her whole life ... I really hope she is the last of my 'dominating women' ...

I hope 'Happy Release' is not too much of a cheap revenge on Sheila ...

A few weeks ago Tom's father wrote to me that both Sue's children were baptised on Dec 4th. The same letter revealed that Lyndall had lied to me: saying she had not seen Sue when she had. Last night I had a little scene with L. about it. In front of Bobbie .. but I never see her alone now. He said 'What else could she do?' ... I wrote to Sue for the first time for years; a cold, formal letter simply asking for the long-promised explanation of the ostracism ...

Alick has cancer and does not know it. I am appalled at the pain she has to suffer .. according to her doctor, she has only four months to live ... how awful *not* to know. What can one say to the dying who do not know and who do not believe? ...

1956

1 Jan Very interesting that in searching for a notebook, I found this scrap of 1952 [entries from 4 to 25 Nov 1952] I then re-read up to 1954. The Sue preoccupation, the marriage dreams – all the old stuff ... *Very* odd to see that 3 years ago I 'hoped I had broken with' V[irginia] J[ohnes]. Well, I don't want to be unfriendly. Merely to pay her back her money and get out of her psychological web ...

On the other hand ... she came to my rescue at a time when I was at my wit's end over money. And by the 'Anonymous Donor' thing she did completely hoodwink me ... because anonymity is so uncharacteristic of her! ...

The novel is the important thing to get down to ... I think the best approach to it is really as *private* as possible: a book written for Elaine. I have, in an odd way, my 'good' daughters – Elaine and

Gudrun [unknown]. Heaven knows I don't mean Lyndall is a 'bad' one. But she is a child still: too young and too unaware yet of the 'spirit' to understand many things. I must bring Elaine and Gudrun together ...

It is essential for me to preserve my balance vis-a-vis Lyndall and Bobbie. There is something slightly slick, slightly raffish about Bobbie. And yet he can shake me by his obvious good-natured concern that I should be better paid, do serials etc. ...

9 Jan   I am delighted that Elaine likes 'Happy Release'. Her father thinks it the best I have done so far ... Can't get over my resentment towards Sheila. I suppose though I *was* trying to see her point of view. Trouble is of course that the thing was a bit manufactured and so a little overdone ...

I had another of the 'reconciliation' dreams last night. They are curiously naturalistic. In them Sue is amiable to me again but they are always a bit of a muddle ... She keeps me waiting, invites me to a party but doesn't give me time to dress for it .. all vague, last minute and slapdash – just the way things always were with Sue. Emily writes to me that she's afraid 'Lyndall is not entirely to be depended on' which, I fear, is true ... She [Lyndall] rang up very sweetly the other night to thank me for her present ... But she's obviously avoiding being alone with me ... I wonder if I shall ever have a normal, happy relationship with those two daughters! ...

The beginning is terribly important ...

Well, we know her father's state of mind. Relief that she is decertified ... And an immense desire to make up to her .. give her presents etc. Unconscious delight that she is 'his' again ...

What about her? Sense of a totally blank future. But she is interested in the past and wants to talk about it and her father's one [aim] is to blot it right out of her mind and everyone else's ...

18 Jan   ... It is absurd how any change in routine upsets me. A week-end away, the fact that I've had nearly 2 weeks without Mrs L. [Lintrum, the cleaning lady] and I go all to pieces ...

How *does* one get properly humble? ...

... I am in a frenzy not having a word from May [Pritchett] – not even if she has received MS of 'Happy Release' which was posted on Dec 28th – 3 weeks ago.

I *must* keep looking on good side and not being discontented. I have just had nice surprise that Daddy's royalties will be not less, but a little more than last year ...

19 Jan ... What *is* this book about, anyway? And how far does it go? What really happened to me, anyway? After the Dougal thing and Paris, I got away with Eric and Alan [Walker] and then got my Crawford job. I think it must end with the possibility of her marrying Eric ... The impossible thing to explain to myself is the Dougal thing ... It wd. be possible to change D.'s character. If she is terribly sorry for him? He shouldn't be wicked. His attitude to his wife .. It's *so* difficult to get *interested* in this book!

20 Jan Have heard at last from May. Neither here nor there really, tho' it might have been worse. Obv. disappointed that it's about the stepmother [Sheila Glossop] not Vanessa [Sue]. No comment whatever on story *as* a story. Has sent it to L[adies] H[ome] J[ournal], editor of which is said to 'like my work' ...

... A quite horrifying description last night of the effect of the bomb on Hiroshima. One can't take it in – these horrors deliberately produced in this supposedly civilised, humanitarian age. Has there ever been cruelty on such a scale?

I am writing in this notebook as an excuse for not getting down to my book ... Every day I re-write what I have written – slower and slower – with no idea whether new version is better or worse ... Why? Is it because I hate the theme? ... What does it matter if the beginning is wrong? I can always correct it later ... The father's dilemma is a real one: not *quite* simple – dilemmas never are ... Remember what HIS idea was – she should go and have the child abroad – all by herself. So he wasn't worrying much about her health! Conventionality plays an *enormous* part in his mentality ...

He does not *seriously* attempt to dissuade her from the abortion: merely puts the responsibility on her ...

Paris [with her father] is definitely a sort of honeymoon. Yet in a way he wants to see her married. Why did he encourage D[ougal]? For he *did*. He certainly liked him ...

24 Jan   Même jeu day after day: rewrite the page or two I have done and it seems no better . . . I see I'm v. worried how to make D[ougal] convincing . . . Clara's story *is* such a mess anyway. And how is Clive reintroduced? Obviously Nell [fictional Dorothy, Robert's sister] rings him up and tells him she is better. What are all the strands doing? The court case, the church-etc. etc. It is NO good getting in a frenzy, though the book is sticking so badly . . . Some people just have to be pushed out of my mind *while* I'm writing – Emily is one of them, admirable as she is after it's finished. Gudrun is another –immensely intelligent as she is. Geniuses who haven't quite found themselves are dangerous to have around during the actual process. The only one right person to *keep* in mind is Elaine who knows how to judge without drying one up completely. This is, after all, Elaine's book since she is the one who is so convinced I ought to write it. K[atharine] Gurley was too. But now she isn't interested in me as a writer any more. I am simply someone to whom she can talk about Ireland – and still more Mr Twomey – who has become a kind of obsession with her . . . Maybe, having killed myself off as 'Leonora' [in 'Happy Release'], I feel like a ghost. I wish I could recover the passionate absorption I had in *that* odd piece . . . I suppose the real trouble . . . apart from all this silly, babyish 'temperament' is that it simply doesn't *excite* me in the least. It seems to me a very uninteresting subject . . .

   Remember Clara is extremely *gay* in this book (mem . . how like Sue!) She is almost a 'good-time-girl' for the first time in her life. I really think I must resist the temptation of using this notebook when I get in a jam with the novel . . . Just try and remember:
1) E[yre] and S[pottiswoode] expect SOME novel from you in Sept.
2) This novel is the only logical bridge if you're going on with the series.
3) Elaine is genuinely interested in it, if you aren't . . .
   I suggest you have a really good go at it from now until end of March. Then you can stop and think. But a really good go. NOT these niggles.

26 Jan   A DISINTOXICATING THOUGHT OR TWO
1) If you haven't heard by Feb 1st this almost certainly means L[adies] H[ome] J[ournal] haven't taken 'Happy Release'.

2) If they don't take it, it's practically certain no one else will ...

29 Jan   Must try and get in better heart about this novel. Have just received German translation of *Lost Traveller*. Astonishing to read all the handsome things English critics said about it ... apparently this stuff, so dull to me, *does* interest someone.

This has been rather a bad month: interrupted a lot and, from work point of view, quite unproductive. At least there's nothing to *show* though most days I've sat down and scratched away, even if I've destroyed it the next. Today Sunday I haven't even started on my pile of letters. No word from Lyn. Just a month. I feel something is wrong ... Already in the position where I daren't write to Lyn or ring her up for fear of annoying her ...

1 Feb   Lyndall rang up last night. A great relief. I think I worked myself up about nothing. The whole of January was just sticking as regards the book. Yesterday I destroyed everything I had done last week. Over and over again I tried to work a scene, this time with the grandmother [Cecil's mother] as an opening. Of course the recap. is always a problem with these books. I must be very careful not to let V[irginia] J[ohnes] interfere. The letters have started up again; it is highly necessary not to let myself get fussed with them and all her sinister implications – the whole thing is hooey. V.J. is an unfortunate, slightly crazy woman whom I have very stupidly allowed to lend me money and that is that. The only possible way to deal with her is stonewalling and refusing to let myself be drawn into discussions ... I have just sent her a short, sharp note with my cheque ... If I'd realised she was the Anonymous Donor I'd have put a stop to that. I went wrong in accepting the £500 loan. That was a temptation I should have resisted ... Mercifully, all this hooey she talks about the sacraments shows that religion for her is so much (poor thing) mixed up with superstition that one can't think of her as being quite sane on this point ... Under the guise of 'helping' (with fantastic generosity) she is simply trying to 'make herself important' and exercise power ... She probably spent about £1000 on me ... The £500 was a loan. She suggested 10% of my royalties as repayment. I insisted on 20% and have kept to it ... But V.J. has

certainly not spent the whole of her inheritance on me, as some of her
wild letters imply . . .

. . . Instead of working, I've spent the whole morning writing a
long letter to Father Victor. I feel a certain relief after doing so. I'd
put it off for a long time, but after V.J.'s last wild letter, I feel
something has to be done. I've written him a full statement of the
money side – which is the only intelligible one.

3 Feb   Last night, another long letter from Virginia Johnes. More
unintelligible than ever. It SEEMS to be back on the Joan Fletcher
obsession now. Saying she didn't want to frighten me but that for 2
years Joan Fletcher (whom I've never met) has been 'getting at' V.
and myself in some sinister way. And that V. has somehow 'saved' me
and Lyndall by sacrificing herself . . . She asked how I was and I
resolutely said 'fine'. Heaven knows what she would make of it if I
told her that for the whole of January I had made no progress on
the book, that I had no news of my American story, that poor Alick
had cancer, that my libel action was coming to a head, that Lyndall
had lied to me about Sue and hadn't rung me up for a month. Even
the freeze-up of my pipes would be grist to her mysterious mill. What
is amazing is . . . the ingenuity with which she makes it impossible
for me not to answer some point cleverly inserted in one of these
crazy letters without being openly rude or leaving her under a
complete misapprehension or about to do something which at all
costs I want to prevent her doing – such as pestering Lyn or Fr.
Victor . . .

Can I find *any* coherent pattern in her behaviour over 3 years.
Roughly certain things always emerge.
1) An attempt to force gifts, usually money.
2) When I refuse, agonised imploring that if I don't take it she will be
dreadfully unhappy . . .
3) Then comes a series of requests for prayers for herself, for people I
don't know, for 'special intentions' etc.
4) Then one gets a lot about my past sins and hers, expiation,
penitence etc. My books always bulk large in this. They are not 'my
books' but *her* books.
5) Then she starts to frighten me, give me a bad conscience about
everything, including writing. She also draws horrifying pictures of

herself on the verge of bankruptcy . . .

9) Then she usually climbs down and says she has been hysterical and that all is going fine and I've helped her enormously . . . Will I come and dine to 'celebrate' something or other?

This is a very crude simplification. In her sane spells she is a very nice person, generous, amusing, intelligent. Perfectly straightforward and businesslike too . . .

How wonderful, after all this mess, to hear Fr. [Thomas] Gilby [a theologian] talking on the wireless about St Thomas Aquinas. I have the wisest of all counsellors as my patron saint . . and I ignore him for months at a time . . .

4 Feb   What a creature of habit I am. Mere fact of not being able to have a bath because of the freeze-up is enough to throw me out of gear. Indecision about what to do first – niggling little jobs, letters etc. piling up. I sit smoking, composing imaginary letters to Gudrun etc. (rather cross ones!) instead of getting on with something . . . However my real weakness at the moment is post-watching for news of 'Happy Release' . . . Of course I am 'tender' about this story. It is such an obvious piece of wishful thinking about my *hopes* about Sue. I must remember that they are *in no way* justified as things are. She does NOT love me. She does not want to have anything to do with me. She does not even care enough to spend a few minutes telling me why she treats me like this. Even my death would probably not produce the faintest qualm of remorse, any more than the death of Georgie's father produced on her. It would simply be 'good riddance' . . .

It is true I really did *not* know that she [Virginia Johnes] was the Anonymous Donor. I know that from my feelings and behaviour when I went to see Eicholz [sic]. And I did make a stand about that £500 loan and only gave in when she said she had talked to Father Victor about it. BUT there are certain facts I must face . . .

. . . The odd thing is that the other 'no-remorse' character is Tom – who is *not* Sue's father. It never struck me before how like Tom Sue is in that way. Did she imitate him? I know now that he was far more important to her than I realised. *Did* his bland sense of being justified in breaking up the marriage influence her in some way?

I have not thought enough about Sue's relation to Tom. I think in

some way Tom's devotion to Nicolette must have been a relief to her
– seeing Lyndall's nose put out of joint. She was always unconsciously jealous of Lyndall, though Lyndall is also one of the few
people of whom she is genuinely fond ...

... Sue again is like Tom – self-approval is *essential* to her. She has
always been able to detach herself completely from her own actions as
if they simply did not concern her ... Actually, my promise to Lyn
not to mention Sue again may have quite a healthy effect on the
situation. I am not at all sure that Sue for all her haughtiness may not
be a little shaken by it ... Total silence, from now on.

6 Feb   A note from Virginia Johnes this morning announces that
'the case of the Catholic Novel v. J.C. Fletcher' has now been opened
... She says it seems to her 'a very ugly story' and that this Miss
Fletcher is a medium.

What DOES she mean by all this stuff? 'The Catholic Novel'
presumably means my novels which she regards as *hers*. Nothing will
induce V.J. to admit that my books have nothing to do with her ...
Not knowing anything about this Fletcher woman who sounds to me
a type like [Group Captain] Cheshire, one of these self-willed 'saints'
I cannot see why she should be dragged in ... these psychic ladies
who muscle in on me are becoming quite a feature of my life. They all
have one thing in common – to try and make me feel guilty ... What
she wants me to concentrate on is not my work, but herself and her
fantasies. I've just remembered Fr. Bartlett's acute remark: 'She has
her breakdowns on other people'.

The only answer is to ... hope that Fr. O'Malley tells her to stop all
this nonsense ...

Is this new novel a particularly critical one for me? Invitation to
come out of the nursery? to assert my more masculine side as a writer?
... It is ... the story of the girl really getting away from her father ...
poss titles 'My Father's House' 'The New Leaf' ... 'The Easy Way
Out'? 'Deception'

And stop thinking about V.J. ...

... I have to 'forgive' my father but not to 'appease' him. He must
have suffered very much on my account ...

... My reaction to his death was to do the thing he would have
disapproved of more than anything else hitherto – fall in love with

Tom and marry him instead of Silas ... I hadn't even *liked* Tom before.

... Does Sue feel about me as I felt about *him*? Very probably. It never stopped *her* defying me, either ...

Then there is all this sex-writing complex. Tom had a prodigious effect on my writing. And losing Tom dried me up for something like 15 years ...

Well, I've struggled on and produced 3 more novels. But with immense difficulty, no pleasure in writing etc. Now I *did* get some pleasure out of 'H[appy] R[elease]' but I feel guilt over that because of Sheila and the wishful thinking over Sue ...

... I am pretty well committed to this task and can't very well drop it in the middle. As I see it it's got to go on through several more – up to the point of her return to the Church anyway and that scene with E[ric] during the bombing ...

It's no good my saying what *I'd* like. Here I am, unable to do anything else BUT write about my own life. No good hunting nervously for 'precedents'. I'm 'for' it . . and I'm getting old ...

8 Feb   It is extraordinary how I stick on this first chapter ...

The time that goes by is astonishing e.g. this morning. I was as usual trying to get that opening right. I did nothing else and was not distracted. All I did was revise the opening paragraph – 3 sentences – which I eventually scrapped. I then started another opening paragraph on different lines. Wrote about $\frac{3}{4}$ of a page – When I looked at the time, I had taken $2\frac{1}{2}$ hours over this ...

Again, a letter from Virginia Johnes ... asking me to ring her. Will I see Fr. O'Malley if he wants me to? Of course, I can hardly refuse. From what she said on the phone, she *sounds* as if she had managed to convince this priest that there was something wrong with this woman Joan Fletcher's set-up ... I went suddenly cold and shakey when I'd put the receiver down ... I know I *am* sometimes susceptible to these 'influences' ...

10 Feb   Last night got to a point of lockjaw on the novel. 4–5 hours work produced only a few lines – to be scrapped today. Wondered if to give up would be better ... But I think it better to peg on, at least till one chapter is written, then go to translation ...

I was considerably relieved to get a letter from Fr. Victor this morning. I have now what I am sure is the true version of her conversation with him about the loan. It confirms my suspicions that V.J. will twist anything to fit it into *her* plans ...

... I can't help feeling that if anyone is 'persecuting' me it is V.J. not some person I don't know. The usual letter again today ... Someone has had a stillborn child (due to J[oan] F[letcher] of course) ...

... It is an awful pity I don't *like* writing. That is my curse. My poor Papa destroyed my natural pleasure in it ...

I almost feel like sitting down and deliberately trying to write a best-seller. I said that as a joke – But it mightn't be a bad idea!

But what could it be about?

My mother?

What fun it wd. be to write a book that WAS fun to write – Something with real characters but a situation entirely diff from anything in my own life ...

Well there's nothing wrong with the idea – except that I haven't got one. This lack of invention is a serious handicap.

Oh I *am* in a state ...

14 Feb   Virginia Johnes's last letter quite hysterical. In despair I wrote to Raymond [Johnes, Virginia's husband] ... She talked of 'suicide as only honourable alternative to bankruptcy'. This morning she returned me the letter unopened. She must have intercepted it .. They *cannot* be on the verge of bankruptcy ...

... She said her capital was £8000, so she *cannot* say it has all gone on me ... I must remember this when she starts up all this stuff about being 'ruined' and implying *I've* ruined her ...

... I was, I suppose, a fool not to guess she was the 'Anonymous Donor'. But it was *so* unlike her methods and Lyndall's suggestion of Eickholz [sic] convinced me ...

15 Feb   Yesterday the unbelievable happened. The Carmelite Prioress, putting it in a way I simply could not refuse, sent me a cheque for £300 so that I could pay off Virginia Johnes at once and owe it to them ... I felt I oughtn't to take it but Elaine said I should ...

Most of all, I must stop fussing about material wants, the house etc. I have much more than most people have anyway. And – for all practical purposes – at the moment, no debts ...

I had a sleepless night and violent dreams. Once again a marriage dream. The 'husband' was a quite new figure. Very vital, immensely attractive physically to me, intelligent, but *working class*. Some of his 'little ways' disturbed me a little – but only snobbishly – there was nothing vulgar about *him*. He had a passion for George Eliot and we kept comparing notes about passages we particularly loved.

Yesterday I managed for the first time for weeks to write $5\frac{1}{2}$ pp. Elaine insisted on reading them and said the first ones were *right*. She was an enormous help, as usual.

16 Feb ... the amount of neurosis about these days is alarming. Last night poor Margot King was here – *very* bad indeed. Cecil now wants a divorce so that he can marry some new love. Her loyalty to him is a kind of idolatry. 'I love every breath that comes out of his body' she said weeping. Accuses herself as usual. Impossible to reason with her. Says he is one of the great men of this century. And a SAINT! Yet he has been always unfaithful to her, at times cruel, and now won't even allow her in her own house. He is a very rich man and allows her a mere pittance and now talks of buying back some of the jewellery he gave her so as to give it to his mistress. Her delusions still range from thinking herself an appalling sinner to pathetic belief in her enormous capacities and brain. Why must such innocent creatures as Margot suffer so?

... Was there *ever* a period of so many breakdowns, bouts of insanity, neurosis, drink or drug addicts, as this century – so much homosexuality, so many sex-murders? Yet we are more sensitive to cruelty and injustice, less 'worldly', more conscientious in many ways than preceding ages. What is the matter with this age? It cannot all be put down to decay of religion for these neuroses and breakdowns occur among very religious people. Look at Fr. White, Fr. Kehoe ...

17 Feb I still make no progress with this book though I have worked at it every day. The same thing happening – it spreads and spreads – then I chop, start again and the same thing happens ... I may be starting *too* early. C[lara]'s situation being so extraordinary that it is difficult to convey at once. Yet another of those queer marriage dreams last night. This time it was, of all people, Eickholz [sic]. I knew him of course to be very rich but he was very shabbily and oddly dressed – gay and amusing about it ...

18 Feb ... I have just had a letter from a bookseller, reminding me that my biog. will appear in the 1956 *Who's Who*. I am, of course, very glad to be in at last. There are over 30,000 'distinguished men and women' in it! ... Nothing to be so conceited about, after all! ...

In spite of feeling absolutely nothing has happened to me this year ... quite a lot has. First of all, the dramatic release last week from the V.J. loan ...

... this 'dominating women' period started in 1947 – 9 years ago – A break from 1949 to 1953, between D[orothy] and V[irginia].

I ... have always been very susceptible to authority, yet rebellious too. Part of me longs to be ordered about, told what to do, finds pleasure in exact obedience, makes me a 'good pupil'. But I also, at some point, resent being interfered with and ordered about 'for my good'. And part of me likes ordering others about – I am a good teacher. I've enjoyed my power in the past over men who were in love with me. But I think I can honestly say that men have treated me worse in the long run than I've treated men. I think Margaret Walter [a convent friend] was the only person in love with me whom I *exploited* – *that* was my cruel side, all right. No good pretending there's nothing sadistic in my nature, there is. My childish fantasies were of torturing people and then being sweetly kind and tender to them. Horrible. In love, I provoked scenes. Felt bored when nothing dramatic was happening. Bored – and insecure – Lyndall is like that. Poor Sue needs peace and quiet. I never gave it her ... It may be a slight hangover from an excessively monotonous, though not unhappy, very early childhood. Boredom, suspense and monotony are my 'natural' bugbears ...

20 Feb ... Very glad to hear from John Coleman [Emily's son] that my letter about cost of living in London *had* been a help to him. A confused script from Gudrun she asks me to send on to BBC. Rather worried about her – Her work is always the same – never finished properly and monotonously about herself though some fine things in it.

... Amazingly, nothing from Virginia Johnes ... Suspect

Carmelites wrote to her and told her to leave me in peace. She wrote to L[yndall] that she and I 'were at daggers drawn' ...

21 Feb　Heard yesterday that *L[adies] H[ome] J[ournal]* have turned down 'Happy Release'. A disappointment, but at least it ends the suspense and post-watching of the last month ...

... The Carmelites have taken over my burden. *Naturally* I want to relieve them of it. But God has a hand in this as in everything. He will find a way for me to pay them back when it's time ... Stop fuss, fuss, fussing. A little humiliation is jolly good for me. And NOT meant to be *discouraging*.

23 Feb　Much cheered and stimulated by Emily's visit. She blows away the Virginia Johnes cobwebs. Also she's convinced too that I ought to write this particular book. I've given her 'H[appy R[elease']] to read. Longing, if apprehensively, to know what she thinks of it. I've certainly got a slight weakness for that book ...

25 Feb　... Have been reading some American reviews of *Beyond the Glass*; mainly pretty contemptuous ...

... I got landed with a lot of foreshortenings and invented stuff via *Lost Traveller* which have hung round my neck. But this cd. be a new beginning in a way because I can now discard those ...

I don't wonder the Americans are puzzled by Clara and dislike her. I can hardly blame them. But I'm glad one of them likes Claude [Cecil] anyway. Most of them fairly impressed by the madness ...

3 March　A relief to have heard from Emily because I've been post-watching. She couldn't stand Lou's language in 'Happy Release' and really that finished it for her ...

Anyway her letter has had one good effect. It's removed my 'obsessive' feeling about 'Happy Release' and put it into a normal perspective ...

5 March　The book goes worse and worse ... The fact is I am bored to tears with Clara and her family and everything to do with them.

13 March　Still same trouble ...

14 March   ... After 3 weeks of peace Virginia Johnes exploded with more than usual violence. The occasion was my paying off the last £48 of the loan. One of her craziest threatening letters: *all* the themes .. threats of suicide, implying that if I didn't 'back her up' I'd have her death on my hands. Saying that my refusal to annul my *two* marriages (!) was doing untold harm to her and everyone else ...

The next day came a mild, patronising letter returning £45 of the £48 saying that I 'perfectly well knew' that she needed it much less than I did ...

I wrote back promptly sending back the cheque. A very sharp letter. I have also sent back her mother's statue. My hand shook as I wrote the letter ...

... She's doing her best to get hold of Lyndall now. It's no good blinking the fact she is *very* dangerous ... It is not a SIN to drop the book for a little since I am making no headway whatever ... For the time being I will 'chore' quietly on with Arnothy [translation, *Those Who Wait*].

15 March   Always a trying time of year for me. Lucky not to have flu or anything. But always a chilled sense physically and mentally, reinforced by weeks of cold weather ...

20 March   ... Virginia still not over. Raymond rang up for a long talk today. He says she's in a very bad way: drinking too much etc. ... Her idea now is to communicate only through him. She's told him she intercepted my letter. the idea of not communicating with me at all doesn't *still* seem to occur to her ...

I saw Barbara [Ward] and her baby. Nice to see something good and happy and straightforward for a change. The baby is exquisite – tiny but perfectly made ... B. looked so happy ...

I am really only pottering on with translations at moment. Endless letters. Small requests to be dealt with, people turning up all the time ...

24 March   Shall be relieved once Virginia Johnes returns that statue. I wanted her to keep it but she won't and suggests giving it to Fr. O'Malley to 'dispose of'. Naturally I'd rather have it back than that! ...

Later   Raymond rang up again. Now V.'s idea is to 'lend' the statue to Fr. O'Malley. Should have thought it wd. be simpler to send it back to me, if she doesn't want to keep it. She had written a letter to me – all the usual stuff about the statue being 'used' in an occult way but I asked R[aymond] not to send it . . .

With Emily and Mother Prioress and Mother Benedict praying for my book, something ought to happen . . .

13 May   A year today since Lyndall married. She has just rung me to say that Bobbie has resigned from *Picture Post* and is leaving at end of June. This means that, except for her small salary, she is destitute. Bobbie talks of going abroad and 'making his living by writing'. It is true Lyn was thinking of going away for a year or so herself as a last faint hope of restoring the marriage. This sudden move of Bobbie's is quite crazily irresponsible, with all his commitments. He talks of selling the house – which is on 'hire-purchase' like all their furniture nearly. Poor Lyndall! I feel it would be wiser of her, instead of rushing abroad . . . to keep on in T.V. and camp out here until she can make other plans. I think we can manage somehow . . . It seems wrong having this party on May 24th in these circumstances . . . But she might meet someone useful and I have asked John McMillan who is now a director of her firm . . . She could have the dining-room as her sitting-room . . .

17 May   In the window boxes I have
  3 varieties geraniums
  6 varieties pinks
  pansies
  heliotrope
  African daisies
  nasturtiums
  creeping Jenny

15 July   . . . Poor Lyndall still in a state of complete uncertainty about her future. I can't – and daren't – advise her. But the marriage looks definitely over . . .

. . . Things at least are no worse with the book. But progress is so slow that I daren't do any Colette as well. Colette [*Claudine in Paris*] is about 64,000: cd. be done in 6 weeks hard. But the MAXIMUM I can expect is £75 balance, and *that* wd. keep me 2 months ...

7 Aug ... Last night for first time Lyn gave me a faint hope about Sue. Said she feels Sue would secretly like to show me the children but dreads emotional tie-ups and references to the past ...

11 Aug Lyndall left for Rome this morning, looking enchanting. I *hope* this will be a real new beginning for her after the worry and anxiety she has had these last months. I suppose I superstitiously tie up a 'new beginning' for myself with it ...

[She] managed to have a few words with Sue. Not the long conversation she had hoped for because Thomas returned unexpectedly and made it impossible. She said Sue never meant it to be permanent, but ... says I must NOT make the first move, not even send her a birthday present. Sue still has a phobia about coming here to Ashburn Gardens ...

Lyndall had a drink with Tom [Hopkinson] before she left ... She said she simply found nothing to say to him: they just sat on the edge of their chairs talking about nothing ... What a lot of extraordinary things began with the irruption of Benedicta into my life and Sue's. Nearly 10 years ago and it's not all worked out yet by any means ... Carmelites and Dominicans all so strangely mixed up in this tangle .. for good and, in some ways, bad. I don't mean *they're* to blame for the bad. Yet HOW good religious have to be. In some way, I think Father Victor failed Sue. His own conflicts are too acute to make him able to be a Père Maydieu ...

9 Aug [sic] Virginia Johnes blew up again. I tore up the crazy letter ... The next morning ... a card asking ... when Fr. Victor returned? The good old trap of the definite question it would be uncivil [not] to answer ... I rang her up. For 25 minutes she talked incoherently almost inaudibly about all the old themes. In the end I gently said I had to work and she rang off. She is drinking again. It was impossible to make *any* connected sense .. Just all the old stuff .. my books .. people dropping dead .. prostitutes .. Joan Fletcher ...

As a matter of interest, taking this year since last August ... I have actually produced 2 translations, Colette [*Claudine at School*] and

Arnothy [*Those who Wait*] . . both very long . . . and 'Happy Release'.
And I must have produced them in about 7 months for I have spent
nearly 5 on abortive attempts at the Dougal book . . .

. . . Mrs L[intrum]'s holiday only means that for 10 days you will
have to [do] the chores. These can easily be done in 1½–2 hours.

14 Aug   There is one thing I really must try and learn from all the
money worries of the past years, that is the misery extravagance
brings on. The delicious pleasure of 'blueing' – and no one enjoys it
more than I do simply isn't worth all the misery of months of
worrying how to make ends meet . . . One becomes an abject slave of
preoccupation with money. I have poor E[ric] and G[eorgie] as
terrible object lessons . . .

Later   Absurd how restless I am. Is it this spring-like weather,
blustery and sunny . . March, not August? Almost a mania, wandering and looking at houses, wondering what it would be like to live in
them. Yet I love my flat and don't want anything better . . . Even
starting up crazy dreams of building on to the cottage or putting up a
little house for Mr and Mrs Lintrum . . . I believe the thing I like
doing best in the world is furnishing or redecorating houses . .
planning impossibles! I really *love* that kind of creating . . .

. . . I ought to be grateful instead of whimpering. I am crazy. When
the daughter in *Mrs Dale's Diary* told her mother she was off to Wales
with her husband, I nearly wept. Lyndall's going, I suppose, which I
haven't really had time to take in yet. Such a lot of partings.
Something a little inhuman about E. and G. . . especially G. Must
remember they've never had children . . .

21 Sept   Naturally the fire in my study [see biographical sketch for
Eric Siepmann] on Sept 15th has dislocated me. I must try and be
sensible. I have now done all I can about replacements except small
things like book-rest and lampshades . . .

Once their fire-assessor has been, I can

1) move desk back into position
2) get tallboy out
3) move damaged bookcase and put a chair there . . .

The only necessary thing at once is the *N[ew] S[tatesman]* article.

* * *

In 1953 a libel action concerning *The Sugar House* had been brought against Antonia by an actress, June Sylvaine, who claimed that a minor and rather silly character in the novel not only bore her name but physically resembled her. The sixteen lines referring to this character, she declared, were defamatory. All copies of the book had been withdrawn at the time, but the case was not brought until now. Antonia had Peter Carter-Ruck as her solicitor.

The action became part of legal history because it was the first to which the 1952 Defamation Act applied. Part of this Act had been specifically intended to *prevent* actions arising from an accidental co-incidence of name.

* * *

1 Oct　I did somehow get the *N[ew] S[tatesman]* article off. It took 4 days hard work plus 2 for the reading and a morning for cutting. A full week in fact for reviewing 2 books in a 1000 word article.

I shd. like to get Chapter II properly roughed out before getting down to Colette [*Claudine in Paris*]. But next week I shall have to begin on that again, come what may . . . There will be interruptions in any case: the law-suit, Brighton etc. . . . a *min* of 4 days, I shd. say and 1 at least for straightening things out. Rows have of course been infuriating: delays, lies etc. . . . But at least I am now in direct touch with Sawyer [insurance agent] . . .

. . . having Siepmann here for 10 days is dislocating but in some ways stimulating, once one has recovered from the shock and the nervous exhaustion. For dear S. produced those as well as the fire! When *he* wants to sit up till all hours drinking and talking, all his promises to respect my routine – *and* sleep – are forgotten. When *he* was tired, he went to bed at 8 or 9. But it was touching how, since he became a Catholic on Aug. 26th he made obviously heroic efforts to be considerate and control his natural violence. He *can't* drink moderately: he just has to go on till he gets to the truculent, bullying stage. Half-way he's the best, most stimulating companion imaginable. Mary [Siepmann's wife, the novelist Mary Wesley] is a wonder.

I looked up my old notebooks and read them to him. They astonished both of us. Since then I've glanced at the Basil Nicholson. Extraordinary to think what has happened in 20 years. Who would have thought when I was in such a state over Siepmann, Basil, and, to a lesser degree, Norman Cameron that they would all become Catholics? Norman became one about a year before his death, Basil on his deathbed ... And then Emily and Phyllis too ...

... in the end (only as usual *patience* is so hard!) the study may be nicer than ever. I rescued the khelim [rug] cut off the burnt parts, turned it over and now it is almost the chief ornament of the room! And the battered Georgian desk I am buying ...

Seeing symbols everywhere as I do, I see 'good out of evil' in all this ... Not a break with the past but a slight relegation of it . . like putting Daddy's beautiful desk in 'honourable retirement' and having one of my own . . moreover one which has had a bad time, been put to wrong uses and is now being reconditioned and will be used and cherished. Also I have found myself reconditioning old things and buying a few new ones (*must* be careful not to be extravagant) and it gives me a little confidence (must not become presumption!) that this writing jam will loosen up.

In a fortnight I should have ready in hand: or lined up anyway – rug: new desk: little shades: pelmet: curtains: BUT nothing can be assembled until Sawyer has got going. AND if that is done in a fortnight, I shall be VERY lucky indeed. And a fortnight today THAT CASE [the libel case] is due. *Wouldn't* it be nice to be able to make a fresh start in a tidy remodelled study ...

Clothes new dress and hat should be here this week.

order bedjacket and slippers

Possibly get a top or stole knitted.

Not a word from Lyndall though I wrote to her a day or two after the fire. Does this mean she is absorbed in some new love affair?

7 Oct Of course I have been rather extravagant again ...

Elaine likes the first chapter. I saw all sorts of horrors in it of course when I read it aloud ... I have got stiff and awkward in writing. This book has at last to be adult: none of the others are really. Clara is more or less formed now.

I do not think it is *just* relief of pressure that makes me feel calmer. What I *do* have to watch carefully is not to get too excited over material things (forced by the fire to be conscious of them) and get myself tied up in financial knots ... The next 'stretch' must run from now till end of March. NOT think of a deadline for book. Colette must

be finished by end of November. Do Xmas presents in bits, calmly . . .
My private deadline for book next June perhaps . . .

9 Oct   . . . For the study I have only to keep track of
  1) Lampshades
  2) Desk
  3) Carpets
and, I suppose, SAWYER.
  NO KNOWING WHEN THAT MAJOR INTERRUPTION WILL BE . . .
  I get into far more confusion and mess than is necessary when I
work. I would *feel* less hurried and also *do* more if I didn't rush at
everything, litter my desk and so have to waste time hunting for
things . . . Look at the mess after *one morning* of letters, etc! LAZY!

14 Oct   Have been sitting by phone for ¾ hour waiting for Carter-
Ruck to ring. Case comes on tomorrow. The whole week-end has
been taken up with an entirely unexpected and rather alarming rush
of developments. Apparently June Sylvaine's lawyers are now going
all out and calling 9 witnesses. I had to try and get Graham Greene.
By a miracle I found him and he sweetly came over and saw my
solicitor. But he leaves for the West Indies tomorrow afternoon and
unless they let him 'interpose' his evidence (and this depends not on
the judge but on the opposing counsel Gerald Gardener) there will
not be time for him to be called. They think the case will take at least
two days. Sir Compton Mackenzie (again, caught by a miracle just as
he was leaving London) has angelically promised to be a witness for
me. Fearnley Whittingstall is defending me. It seems fantastic that
because, by pure chance or rather mischance, I invented a name
which happened to be the stage name of a real person, we should have
been landed in all this. This case – always delayed by the other side,
has now dragged on for three and a half years . . . the things her
counsel said then were completely untrue . . that she was the
'principal character' in *The Sugar House*. Actually she is such a tiny and
utterly unimportant character in it that she is only referred to in 16
lines out of over 250 pp. . . . This will be the first case to be heard to
which the new Defamation Act . . . applies so legally it will be
interesting. This act is supposed to stop these frivolous actions about
a pure coincidence of name . . .
  It's a queer, unsettling feeling to be suddenly thrust into court in

what may be a publicised case . . . There *might* be repercussions after . .
if I win. If it means *The Sugar House* or some of the older ones sell . . .
Mary Siepmann has sweetly offered to come to the Courts with me . . .
one of those strange menstrual dreams – the second I have had
recently. What do they mean? In each I refuse to believe it . . I am
much too old. Do they just mean a hope of reviving the creative side?
I certainly wish that were so. I *don't* think they are sexual . . .

28 Oct   The case *was* horrible and took nearly all of a week for me to
get over it. It was like Kafka – the cross-examination . . perpetually
trying to trap me, asking apparently irrelevant questions, formulat-
ing them in such a way there was [no] clear . . . answer, twisting one's
meaning, trying to confuse one, make one break down or lose one's
temper. Fantastic suggestions that I had deliberately inserted June
Sylvaine's name to blacken the Sylvaine family – as a 'Catholic plot' –
bc. Vernon Sylvaine – it came out in court – is a lapsed Catholic. They
kept asking me why I had destroyed the MS of *The Sugar House* – and
when. Suggestion, of course, that I had originally used another name
and deliberately substituted J[une] S[ylvaine] . . . My solicitor was
wringing his hands. Fearnly [sic] Whittingstall was obviously feeling
ill and missed several points. Obviously, too, he hadn't got the case
up properly. Well, thank goodness it's all over. I *did* get a great many
letters of sympathy . . . a letter from Rebecca West. Lots from friends,
some from total strangers . . .

I was not allowed on Tuesday to speak, even outside the court to
solicitor, counsel, other defendants and had to go and sit alone in
court like an 'untouchable'. This was bc. I was still under
cross-examination.

They produced extraordinary red-herrings. My E[yre] and S[pot-
tiswoode] contract (trying to make out it was fishy the title was
different from the one in the contract). E. and S. Sales Sheet (wh. of
course I'd never seen and which meant nothing to me). They'd even
dug up the Lee Play Agency and the fact I'd written a play . .
goodness knows what that was meant to prove!

When all the witnesses etc on both sides have been heard, each
counsel makes a closing speech, trying to discredit the other side.
Then the judge sums up and gives his verdict. We lost. £200 damages
for June and costs (£1000). I broke down for a minute outside the

court. The publishers and everyone were very sweet . . .

Mary Siepmann was an angel and came to court the whole time each day.

Not a word from Sue . . .

. . . Georgie's account of that birthday party to wh. Sue so surprisingly invited her and Eric (and to which, from my point of view they rather surprisingly went) made me pretty sure things were as unpromising as ever. Apparently Si and Eric had a tremendous get-together. I don't imagine, from what G. said, that E. said one word for me . . . I'm probably prejudiced in thinking it would have been more 'delicate' not to go to the party. They could have got out without offending Sue in the least on the score of transport difficulties. As it was, they had to take 2 people Sue doesn't know so as to be able to go in a car . . . I expect it of Georgie . . . but not of Eric. Still, to do her justice, I don't think she actually backbit me. She couldn't help telling me about it in the most tactless possible way . . the one designed to hurt most! . . .

V[irginia] J[ohnes] is starting up all over again about Joan Fletcher, my statue and all the rest of it. Proposes to write to Fr. Victor . . . I simply didn't answer . . . Of course the case has started her right off again . . because she knows someone called ROSS and some woman who knows someone she knows and was called JUNE committed suicide recently . . . Oh dear, oh dear, oh dear! Lucky she doesn't know about my fire or my having destroyed months of work on the novel! . . .

What is the matter with this pen? It is suddenly sticking after behaving perfectly all the week! Probably protest at having just written a NINTH letter . . a carefull [sic] guarded one to Vivian Burbury – *another* result of that case! . . .

My new desk is sober, but workmanlike and easy to write at. I am still waiting for Row's builders to come and do window, walls and ceiling though it is 8 weeks since the fire. Fin[ancial] sit[uation] is extremely bad, even with this new translation . . .

16 Nov I saw Fr. Victor yesterday. He said Virginia Johnes is definitely paranoiac. I could not decently get out of seeing Raymond last night. I made my position very clear: that I would have nothing to do with this Fletcher business . . . also told him that I would not answer any more of V.'s letters and he said he would try to stop her writing them. Within 24 hours .. by this afternoon's post .. I got one of the usual ones ...

1 Dec   May Pritchett is retiring. *Some thoughts on agents.*

Has one, either here or in America, ever *placed* a novel for me? NO.

Has one, either here or in America, ever placed a short story for me? NO.

Has one ever obtained a commission for work for me? NO.

What, in practice, *has* any agent ever done for me? Placed novels for translation, on wh. they collect 20% ...

18 Dec   ... Only a fortnight more of 1956. What an odd year .. the fire, the case, Siepmann and now Lel [Leslie Earnshaw Smith] staying here till he can get a room. The financial crisis .. miraculously .. solved by *dear* Phyllis, Emily, Daisy [Green-Wilkinson], so that, with care, I can manage till April.

From the work point of view, bad. Months of work on the novel destroyed and still very un-confident about the new one, barely begun. I am trying to relax and forget it for the moment. I have really nothing to 'show' for a whole year but the Arnothy translation and the Colette ...

This year has seen what seems the final collapse of Lyndall's marriage. She is in Rome now: talks of going to America in the spring.

Looking back quickly through this notebook it is striking how much ... is taken up with V[irginia] J[ohnes]. She permeates it ...

... Of course there have been wonderful surprises this year. Spiritually, the Siepmanns' conversion ... Materially, the Carmelites' heroic 'rescue' and the recent 'rescue' by friends ... The Sue situation at least no worse ... Lyndall very sweet to me after all her private storms.

... Appreciation from France and Germany very nice ...

... I must definitely accept no more translations after June ...

27 Dec   ... With care, even without the £40, I shd. have just enough coming in to manage ...

MEM ... stains ... Coffee and wine ½ ounce borax to one part warm water.

1957

Antonia was now threatened with a huge rise in her rent at 13 Ashburn Gardens and was considering moving. In March she contributed to a symposium on Christian art at Downside, the Catholic public school, with a lecture entitled 'The Novelist'.

30 Jan   No use worrying too much over this alarming new possibility of a doubling of the rent. In any case can only wait till Dow [the tenant in the flat below] gives us a hint of what his mother means to do. It is not practical for me to go and live at Binesfield. By selling it, I might get £5000 wh. invested at 3½% would bring in ... £175 ... But Lyn doesn't want me to sell and I would, in any case, prefer not to sell yet. I see no poss. hope of getting another flat in London at a reasonable rent ...

St Thomas says a man can be a good artist without necessarily being a good man. Aristotle makes art 1 of the intellectual virtues ...

1 Feb   I have really had to drive myself through Thomas's new novel [*Happy as Larry*]. Even so, I skipped a good deal. The monotony of these drunks, unpaid bills, dirty rooms, vomit and violence, all revolving round a search for an obscene photograph (with no apparent reason for the photograph's existence) simply exhaust one. What *is* it all about except the permanent hang-over of a tiresome, self-pitying young man? Thomas *has* a very good eye for physical details and a good ear for talk. He can be very funny. But what *does* the book add up to? I find him completely puzzling, both as a person and a writer. His obsession with dirt is amazing.

4 Feb   It is inevitable I shd. be in something of a 'state' over the likely rent-increase and also over the poss. of L[el] as permanent. I see I have already put down pages of wild calculation. I have asked L. to stay till Easter. Conscience comes into this: it seems awful not to offer him a home ... Of course I *do* value my privacy ...

... I do *not* think it practical for me to ... live at Binesfield. In that case, the only possibility wd. be .. to have both S[hirley, lodger] and L. here. I wd. have to raise Shirley to £3 minimum ...

... possibilities are:

1) S[hirley] and L.

2) Sell cottage (this would probably only raise another £100 [p.a.] at most.

3) Raise cottage rent ... If I raised it to £130, this for me wd. only mean £40 a year and all the liabilities ...

What do I *know* L. costs.

Milk	1.0
Butter	2.8
Bread	1.4
Eggs	2.0
Papers	1.7
Tea and marm	2.6
Laundry	3.0
	14.1

And with heating etc. at least £1.5.0

18 Feb ... It is strange this L[el] situation: a very odd change in my life. In some ways I quite like it. As a permanency, a little alarming ...

... The present translation [*Claudine in Paris*] is a chore, but mercifully short ... The other [*The Stories of Colette*] should be begun in July.

19 Feb ... I suspect the novel is secretly worrying me more than money. If only I cd. write it with the zest with which I wrote the little cat book! [*Minka and Curdy*, 1957] My slightly cramped feeling is due perhaps a little to Lel who, bless him, is *not* a stimulating person ... It is not Lel's fault but my own if I feel dull-witted. The real stimulus I need can only come from myself and envisaging, being *interest* in the novel ... The important people are Eric, Si, the parents ... I must definitely resolve to get that novel finished this year .. if poss., apart from revision, by June ...

20 Feb ... I find I do love stimulus and excitement. I *must* learn to do without these ...

... 'What would I do if I had heaps of money – say £50,000?' ... A lump sum for redecorating etc. £500 wd. be *ample* for this. And £1500 a year for life apart from any earnings. Oh and of course £5000 'behind me'! What a hope! And HOW SILLY . . indeed rather wicked . . I am!

22 Feb   I do not think poor Alick can live more than a few days. It was pitifull [sic] to see her yesterday, drugged and shrunken. It is cancer of the spine. I lay awake an hour in the night thinking of her, trying to pray for her. Also, I fear, oppressed by the thought of L[el] staying on more or less indefinitely . . . Poor man, he is fighting for his life. And he seemed to think it was nice for me getting an extra 10/- a week (and this is the maximum I *do* get, for he gets all sorts of little 'perks' . . wine, bits of food I buy etc.) . . . He *has* plenty to grumble about . . indeed he has . . but it would be nice if he sometimes stopped . . .

26 Feb   Alick died on Friday. Surprising how much I have thought of her, apart from praying for her. Maybe we all feel her loss more than we realised we should. It is touching to find how fond of us she was, in spite of her critical ways with us all. She was incredibly brave through all those months of pain − 18 months at least. There was something noble about her, Sylvia [perhaps Sylvio, young Italian author] and I agreed. That uncompromising pride and honour . . it's rare nowadays. Strange how little we knew about her after 30 years. She hardly ever spoke of her childhood and her parents.

I still find myself fussing mentally . . over money . . over Lel . . .

2 March   The Lord is so *kind*. Just as I was making that complaining entry, John Coleman rang up, asking me to dinner. I had a lovely evening. And there is Eva [unknown] tonight, Siepmann next week, the Freemans [Frank Freeman had remarried] etc. Just when I felt a little suffocated, God, knowing my weakness, opened the window . . .

Have now bought what clothes I need: I *think* sensibly − and need only hat and foundation [corset]. No urgency about these: try and wait till a cheque comes in. This was a madly expensive week but now, apart from perm, shd. revert to normal. And must get down to work next week. Bound to feel a little eye strain till new glasses come . . .

20 March   A week ago last Tuesday I heard from Sue for the first time for 5 years. It is awful that I cannot even be properly thankful yet: the shock has been so great. It has affected me exactly like the fire and the libel case: a week of restlessness, bad sleeping, inertia and extreme tiredness. I have done no work: only revision and letters. I will be seeing Sue and the grandchildren on April 13th or May 4th. It will be, in a way, 'on sufferance' and, for me, rather artificial. I am told I must make no reference to the past as 'our two versions of what happened will never agree'. She does not say what her version is, of course. Sylvio is the only person who understood at once what I feel. Of course it is beyond anything I could have hoped. And I see that now I *had* at last given up hope. The restoration of it is almost more painful than what I had grown used to. They say that restoring circulation after nearly freezing or drowning is agonisingly painful. I feel *dreadfully* ungrateful to God . . but I *am* thankful underneath. It means much patience and humility on my part and I do implore grace for that. I know it is the cool, hard, casual Sue I am going to see, not the other. I need so much grace and strength for it. It is silly, the last 2 days I have been reading *Little Women* and crying over it. Perhaps NOT so silly for the sentiment in the book is *not* false. Amazing how it wears after nearly a century.

21 March The shock feeling persists. I don't know if it is Sue or not: tension in head and eyes; tired, dull irritable. Not a word from Sue, after a week to tell me which day! . . . Everything frightens me . . .

29 March Still tired and restless. My eyes are a nuisance, giving more trouble than before the new glasses. What small beginning I made on the novel I have destroyed but I *do* think I now have the right idea for the first chapter . . . Downside next Saturday: waiting today for Alick's mirror to be delivered: tired from late night with Raymond to dinner. Can't get to grips with him over V[irginia] but he seemed touchingly grateful for his evening here. The night before, John Coleman and *his* problems. He was so sweet and grateful too . . . I heard from Sue yesterday that it is to be 13th April, for which I am very grateful. I begin to take it in. It has all got to be kept as light and casual as possible. I don't suppose I'll see her alone, even for a minute. But her notes, though casual, are not unfriendly . . .

. . . This seeing of people and trying to see their problems is a little tiring but seems to be part of my 'job'. The Downside thing will probably be tiring: the [other lecture] papers look heavy going.

6 May   More than a month since the last entry. All I have to show of the novel is some 15 pages of the most brutish rough salvaged from the usual pages of divagations (mostly destroyed) To be frank: not ONE page. On June 13th I go to Ireland . . . It seems absurd to be able to write nothing about April 13th and that wonderful visit to Sue and the grandchildren. It means too much. I don't need notes to remember it.

The novel is becoming a nightmare again. Why? *What* is it that seems to make me unable to select or control any more? . . . This is the 4th attempt to do this wretched 'next'. There was

(1) beginning in Paris [with her father]: weeks spent on opening scene. Hopeless. Destroyed.

(2) deciding it must be the Dougal thing [see p. 287]. About 7 months in all spent on doing 1st chapter from different angles. Hopeless. Destroyed . . .

(3) Decided the E[ric] book. Began with the marriage. Weeks of work produced 1 bad chapter − ½ another infinitely worse . . .

(4) the present one on which I have done 2−3 weeks hard on 1st chapter. Not one *page* right yet.

It is no good getting in a frenzy.

25 Sept   My father's birthday. He would have been 87. Hard to realise: harder still to realise that next year I shall be the age he was when he died . . 59.

A long time since I wrote anything here: I have worked v. hard but only at translations . . . Not having touched my own novel, the angst about that is temporarily allayed. But Jerrold said there was 'a new note of confidence' when I said he wd. get it next year and *he* at any rate believes he will! . . .

Meum [Stewart, a woman friend of Antonia]† died last week. I had an extraordinary sense of her nearness to God during those last weeks of her dreadful illness. Her gaiety, serenity and humility were wonderful.

I have quite accepted the 'permanency' of Lel. It is one of the most unforeseeable things in my queer life, that he should be here as an accepted part of my life. He is touchingly grateful ... My hopes that he would come back to the Church have received the most definite check ... Yet ... if he is willing to accept any form of Christianity it may be something ...

It has been an extraordinary year. I cannot expect any of the old intimacy with Sue but it is wonderful to feel that I am accepted enough to be 'the other Grandmother'. I have seen her and Thomas once by themselves and twice with the children. And, by heaven's mercy, I have managed to 'keep it light'. Elaine's impression of her was interesting: that she was 'hard' and 'polished' but that she had a warm, spontaneous feeling for me. She *has* been friendly these times I have seen her. We have not exchanged one word in private yet I do have the impression that, in some way, she is glad that the 'ban' she put on me is lifted.

Lyndall I worry about, for she can't be anything but unhappy and restless till she is free of this wretched marriage. It is a year since I saw her and have no prospect of seeing her for a long time ...

29 Sept A week-end absolutely alone in the flat. A long time since I had that. I have spent it generally clearing up, sorting, tidying ...

I had meant to toy in this spare hour or two a little with the book. But I am tired and it is difficult to switch the mind on to it. V[irginia] J[ohnes] involved me in a long letter to the poor Carmelites. She is on the warpath again: enemies, persecution, lapsed Catholics, my books: all the stuff. Some young woman called Ann White has been shot by an antique dealer and that started her up again ...

14 Oct It is difficult not to worry about the housing situation ...

The cottage, all by myself does not seem practical. If it were possible to share it with Phyllis that would be different. Regent's Park would not really be cheaper because I should be losing Shirley and it would cost more for hot water etc...

I am sorry to open this new book with accounts but finances *are* a constant worry ... The thing I must remember is that there is a year before they can evict me ...

26 Oct ... I have been in bed since Tues. with this year's version of 'flu. Not quite well yet but risking sitting in workroom for a little while as it less depressing. It is v. uncomfortable trying to write in bed . . . A nuisance because I'm behindhand with Tortures.

Of course, these last days I've squirrel-caged a lot about the housing situation. In fact the real reason for wanting to sit up is to try to clear my head a little about it. Bc. I think the good old unconscious is involved in this too. Of course the rent act is a very real and rather alarming menace. But I am *not* called to deal with it at once . . .

Yet there is some kind of problem and I wd. like to try for a clue. I wd. 'guess' that I am simultaneously wanting a complete change, brand new beginning (and I see it always as lovely clean new rooms, esp. kitchen and bathroom). AND to keep everything exactly as it is: i.e. stay on indef. at Ashburn G. Now when one wants 2 mutually exclusive things at the same time, one is NOT being realistic . . .

But house qua house does seem to be something special. Look at my Sunday afternoon 'house game' wh. has gone on for so long: my dreams of new flats (so often 'old' flats rediscovered but all new and nice) of 'extra rooms' etc. And my passionate interest in other people's houses, always comparing to adv. or disadv. over my own. Of course this is an old mania of mine: I shd. say it began with 38 Glebe Place! And then there is always Binesfield at the back of everything: the house I *possess* and don't want to live in.

Take Regents Park. I lie in bed speculating and trying to reconstruct a place I haven't even seen properly and don't really, from the human angle, want to live in and, from the practical point of view, can't afford . . .

. . . In 18 months I shall be 60 . . .

I don't suppose I ever *have* what is called a 'clear objective'. My life really has been a set of muddles, blunders, mishaps etc. in which – looking at it from a purely earthly and practical point of view, most of my time has been spent getting through or out of some predicament in which I have involved myself – usually through my own fault, coping with the consequences of same and, if ever getting straight, usually just in time for another predicament . . .

My twenties. Reggie – the asylum . . exactly *3* years of comparative peace with Eric – then Silas, Susan and all the consequences of that.

My thirties. Tom: about 2 years of comparative peace but none too secure: then chaos and misery, breakdown, analysis, divorce.

My forties. In 1938 Dec. *Just* started 'a new life'. The new flat –

children there – beginning to earn just enough to keep it going. 9 months later: the war: all gone: back to the very beginning. Six years of 'managing somehow', war jobs, blitz, moving around ...

My fifties: I did get some books written, yes. Severe financial troubles: severe trouble over Sue ending in 5 years total silence from her. Honestly never time to stop and plan, took all one's time and energy – to keep where one was ...

27 Oct   Up for first time: not too bad but very weak in the head. Less depressing than being in bed, anyway. The Sunday papers depress me: have noticed this for several weeks! And not only the fantastic rents and premiums for flats which go up week by week ...
Later   Perfectly mad ideas. If I had the money! Do up: kitchen, dining-room, bathroom, my room, Shirley's ceiling and wall

And all this is wicked crazy speculation because I am lucky if I HAVE the flat, let alone renovate it!

Think about WORK, my good woman, not fancy WHIMS.

Biographical Sketches

Abrahams, Marion St Paul's schoolfriend of Antonia, Patsy in *The Lost Traveller*. A charming, frivolous girl who introduced Antonia to the forbidden joys of cosmetics.

Baba, Meher Indian holy man of whom Dorothy Kingsmill was a follower. Claimed to be the 'Ancient One, come again to redeem man from his bondage of ignorance'. Antonia put his photo beside that of Padre Pio on her bedside table in 1948 when she was being analysed by Dorothy. Baba had taken a vow of silence many years earlier but his followers believed they received messages from him. According to Lyndall he once ordered Antonia to eat a turd from the cats' scratch tray by way of a penance. She disobeyed. In 1953 Tom and Dorothy paid their respects to Baba when he visited England and many years later, accompanied by Lyndall, they visited the ashram of the now deceased Master. Tom and Dorothy collaborated on a book about him, *Much Silence*.

Barker, George Author of slim volumes of verse including *Thirty Preliminary Poems* (1933) and *The True Confession of George Barker* (1950). He was twenty-three but already married to Jessica when Antonia met him. His later affair with Elizabeth Smart was the basis of her novel, *By Grand Central Station I Sat Down and Wept* and of his *The Dead Seagull*. T.S. Eliot said of him, 'He's a very peculiar fellow.'

Barnes, Djuna American author of the surrealist novel *Nightwood*, 1936. Had worked as a journalist in Paris, where she fell in love with the woman called Robin in *Nightwood*. She also met Emily Coleman there. Emily once asked her if she was 'really Lesbian' and she said 'I might be anything. If a horse loved me, I might be that.' Silas Glossop was one of her admirers.

Beachcroft, Nina Only child of Tom and Marjorie Beachcroft. Friend of Lyndall Passerini at Headington School, Oxford.

Beachcroft, Tom Novelist and contributor of critical pieces to publications all over the world. Chief Overseas Publicity Officer for BBC (1941–61). Father of Nina.

Bernfeld, Corin Journalist, of Irish-Jewish descent. She worked on *Vogue*. Antonia met her through Silas's sister, Elspeth, who also worked there. Just before the war, she went to China and was never heard of again.

Bertram, Anthony Author of many books on art history including *Life of Rubens* (1928) and *A Century of British Painting* (1951). Fought in both World Wars and awarded Legion of Honour. Married Barbara Randolph. Their son, Jerome, now a priest, is Antonia's godson. Antonia used to stay with them at Coates Castle, Fittleworth, Sussex.

Bezer, Benedicta de Religious painter, formerly jazz pianist, living in Belsize Park with an actress friend, Dorothy Truman-Trumpington. Benedicta (real name Kathleen) was dark and handsome and she always wore trousers except when she wore a monk's habit. She developed a passion for Antonia with strong religious overtones in January 1947, but it ended in tears when Antonia chose to be received as a Dominican tertiary in Paris, instead of at Haverstock Hill, Benedicta's local priory.

Binder, Pearl Caricaturist who also wrote and lectured on Communism in the 'thirties. Her 'Chalking Squad', showing a band of furtive revolutionaries scrawling '*Workers unite against Fascism*' on a wall, appeared in *Left Review* (May 1935). She lent it, with others, to the *Thirties* exhibition at the Hayward Gallery (1980).

Birch, Lionel Known as Bobbie. Journalist, protegé of Tom Hopkinson on *Picture Post*. Himself became editor of *Picture Post* in 1950s. Lyndall became his fifth wife in 1955, but the marriage only lasted a year.

Black, Ian Scottish businessman with a liking for beautiful women, the arts and France. He was briefly Antonia's lover in the 'thirties and let her have a room in his house in Linden Gardens, Notting Hill, early in the War. At that time, too, he published his book *A Friend of France* (1940).

Bloy, Léon French Catholic writer who bitterly castigated political and social institutions and had a strong devotion to the weeping Madonna at La Salette – a manifestation that appeared before a peasant boy and girl in the Alps in 1846. There has been a revival of interest in Bloy's work since 1940. His *Le Désespéré* (1886) and *La Femme Pauvre* (1897) are autobiographical.

Borrett, Daphne Friend of Lyndall's who moved into 13 Ashburn Gardens as a lodger after Susan's departure in 1951. She left to marry a boy called Harry, but many other lodgers followed.

Botting, Cecil Father of Antonia White, married to Christine. Brilliant child of Sussex shopkeeper, who taught himself Latin and Greek at the age of four. Educated at Dulwich College and Cambridge, he then taught at St Paul's School where he rose to be the senior classics master and was the co-author of the well-known Hillard and Botting text books from which Antonia received royalties until 1979. Convert to Catholicism. Retired early and died in 1929 soon after the birth of Susan, his first grandchild. Antonia was his only child. Private tutor to such famous names as Victor Gollancz and Compton Mackenzie.

Botting, Christine Wife of Cecil and mother of Antonia White. One of six children of Henry White, a city businessman living in Upper Norwood. Governess in Hamburg for four years (1889–93), then married young.

Bowen, Elizabeth Anglo-Irish author of *The Hotel*, 1927 and *The Heat of the Day*, 1949. Lived in shabby splendour at Bowen's Court, County Cork. When Antonia stayed with her in 1956 the guests drew up in front of the house in horsedrawn conveyances, and a retainer swept up the droppings of each horse. Antonia was so enchanted by

Ireland that she was tempted to buy a Georgian house on the coast which was going for £100. Bowen wrote an introduction for the 1948 edition of *Frost in May* which included the much-quoted sentence 'In the biting crystal air of the book, the children and the nuns stand out like early morning mountains.' The last book Antonia read was Victoria Glendinning's biography of Bowen (1979). She said of Bowen: 'She was not a Lesbian, she was just ... strange'.

Bradshaw, Mother A nun at the Convent of the Sacred Heart, Roehampton. Years later, after Antonia had returned to the Church, Mother Bradshaw told Antonia, at a meeting of 'The Children of Mary' (Roehampton old girls) that she had *not* been expelled from the convent by Rev. Mother Archer-Shee. It was her own father who had removed her from the school in order that she could attend the sixth form at St Paul's. Appears as Mother Radcliffe in *Frost in May*.

Braybrooke, June Wife of Neville, writer and critic. Novelist as Isobel English. Her works include *Every Eye* (1956) and *4 voices* (1961).

Brown, Dr William Psychotherapist famous for his work on shell-shocked soldiers after the First World War. Now forgotten, even by professionals, Brown published half-a-dozen books, was the Wilde reader in mental philosophy at Oxford and a consultant at Bethlem Royal Hospital. He relied partly on hypnosis in treating his patients. Antonia first went to see him in December 1934.

Cameron, Norman Tall, thin Scottish poet, Oxford contemporary of Auden and Day Lewis. Cameron's poetic style was sardonic and meticulous and his 60 poems were not published until after his death of alcoholism in 1953 when he was 48. Robert Graves admired his early work, *The Winter House*, and in 1932 Cameron started to build a house near Graves on Majorca. He was deeply under Laura Riding's spell, but, before the year was out, he had developed a horror of her and left, although he remained her 'Protocol Secretary' until he resigned the post in 1938.

Antonia met him when they were copywriters at J. Walter Thompson in 1937. On a disappointing holiday in Germany together she concluded that he was impotent. In fact he preferred German girls. He married three in the next ten years, but only the last, the Austrian Gretl, brought him any degree of happiness.

Chitty, Sir Thomas, Bart Novelist (Thomas Hinde). Author of *Mr Nicholas* (1952) and many other novels and historical works. Public relations for the Shell Petroleum Co. in the 1950s, visiting Professor, Boston University, 1969–70. Married Susan, 1951. Father of four children, Andrew, Cordelia, Miranda and Jessica.

Cochemé, Jacques Meteorologist, descended from a distinguished French family in Mauritius. Joan Souter Robertson, the painter, was affected by his considerable charm and they married just before the War. He served with the RAF and afterwards with the World Health Organization in the Middle East, Rome and Kenya. His hobbies were pursuing giraffes on horseback, gliding and doing anything else that was dangerous.

Cochemé, Joan Painter under name of Joan Souter Robertson. Married first Frank Freeman, then Jacques Cochemé. She was one of Antonia's oldest friends and Susan was the subject of one of her first child portraits, a field in which she subsequently excelled. She travelled extensively after the War in connection with her husband's work. Friend of Frances Partridge. Has lived in Oakley St, Chelsea for as long as anyone can remember.

Coleman, Emily Holmes American writer whom Antonia met in 1933 with Peggy Guggenheim and Djuna Barnes. Daughter of Connecticut businessman, Emily was tall passionate and blond. She married Deke Coleman and had a son, John. In 1930, published *The Shutter of Snow*, a novel about a period of insanity. Returned to USA during the War where she married a cowboy, Jake Scarborough. Was converted to Catholicism by Jacques Maritain. Back in England from 1953 to 1968, she developed religious mania. From then till her death in 1974 lived on a Catholic Worker Farm in New York State. Antonia considered Emily her best friend.

Cowan, Hélène, see Moody, Hélène.

Davenport, Clement Handsome, boyish blond, married to John Davenport (see below). Clement was a painter who flirted with surrealism but after the War made her mark as the head of the scenery painting team at Covent Garden. By then she was married to William Glock (see below). Her life was cut short tragically by a brain tumour.

Davenport, John Distinguished book critic for the *Observer*. Gifted amateur pianist. Owner of The Malting House, Marshfield, Wiltshire where Antonia and her daughters stayed in the early part of the War. Married to painter, Clement but soon afterwards divorced.

d'Erlanger, Charlotte Convent schoolfriend of Antonia at Roehampton. Original of Léonie de Wesseldorf in *Frost in May*.

Devine, George Devine was partner to Michel St Denis at the London Theatre Studio, where he taught and directed in the 1930s. After the War he became one of the founders of the English Stage Company at the Royal Court Theatre. It was he who selected Osborne's *Look Back in Anger* for production, thus leading the way to a revolution in British theatre.

Doone, Rupert Creator of the progressive Group Theatre in the 'thirties, famous for its production of Auden and Isherwood's *The Ascent of F.6*. A homosexual with a partner, Robert.

Dougal, Jim A very minor journalist and Antonia's first lover. They spent one night together in 1924 under her parents' roof. Dougal was a considerable liar. He persuaded Antonia's father that his shortened leg was the result of a war wound (and not polio) and he did not mention the existence of a wife. One night he came into Antonia's bedroom wearing her father's dressing gown. The result was a pregnancy and an abortion.

Eicholtz Partner in a city-based firm of Jewish solicitors now known as Adlers. He was the trustee of Cecil Botting's estate, taking the place of one of his ex-pupils. It was he who discovered, soon after Susan's break with Antonia in 1951, that Susan could not inherit the cottage in Sussex, Binesfield, because she was illegitimate. On his death in 1958 it was discovered that Eicholtz had embezzled half a million pounds of his clients' money.

Fenby, Charles Friend of Tom Hopkinson at Oxford in the early 'twenties. Worked on the *Westminster Gazette* with Tom and then launched and edited the *Oxford Mail* until he became assistant editor to Tom on *Picture Post* in 1940. Returned to the Westminster Press and stayed there, editing the *Birmingham Gazette* for a time. A lean, poetic man with a dry sense of humour, he also wrote books, including *Anatomy of Oxford* with C.Day Lewis.

Freeman, Frank Freeman studied mining with Silas Glossop but spent most of his life trying to be a painter. It was he who introduced Antonia to Silas, when she was still married to Eric Earnshaw Smith. He was married first to the painter Joan Souter Robertson (see Cochemé, Joan), then to Pamela, who, with his encouragement, became a painter of flowers. They had three children. Those who knew him describe him as an unpleasant little man who wore the wrong kind of yellow shoes, a mixed up kid.

Garvin, Viola Widow of James Garvin, famous editor of the *Observer* (1908–42). She lived in North Oxford and Antonia used to stay with her when visiting Susan at Somerville.

Gascoyne, David Bright young poet of the 'thirties, except that David did not seem bright and young, even at nineteen, but pale, melancholy and rather beautiful. He described himself as 'a noctambule, drugged and vicious, with an androgynous face, enormous eyes and a sensual mouth'. In reality he seemed rather less alarming. He usually seemed to be in search of a cup of tea. Gascoyne formed a group with Dylan Thomas, George Barker and Humphrey Jennings, who published poems in Geoffrey Grigson's *New Verse*, and who had all been to the Surrealist Exhibition. Antonia fell in love with David in 1936, unaware (as, indeed, was he) that he was homosexual. Gascoyne, after a life of wandering, now lives with his wife on the Isle of Wight. He has published a diary of the period when he knew Antonia.

Gathorne-Hardy, Hon Robert Son of 3rd Earl of Cranbrook, but without dynastic ambitions, the young Bob became the literary collaborator and friend of Logan Pearsall Smith from the late 'twenties. He supplied, for example, such useful addenda as the bibliography for *The Golden Grove*, Logan's book on the sermons of Jeremy Taylor (1930). On his own he wrote a memoir of Logan (1949) and *Ottoline, Memoirs of Lady Ottoline Morrell*, 1963. He was a fine amateur botanist and a Fellow of the Linnaean Society (1960). He lived for many years at the Mill House, Stanford Dingley, near Reading, setting of his *3 Acres and a Mill*, 1939. Antonia saw little of him after the War, when Logan was gone.

Gill, Colin and Betty Friends of Antonia's; a well-known Chelsea couple. Betty used to do a dance dressed in a muff.

Glock, William Chief music critic on the *Observer* throughout the War, had studied the piano under Schnabel. He was knighted in 1970, probably in recognition of his work as the BBC Controller of Music. He married Clement Davenport after courting her secretly at night in the kitchen of her husband's house. Antonia was required to act as chaperone on these occasions.

Glossop, Rudolph Known always as Silas, a mining engineer from Derbyshire, educated at Cheltenham College and the Royal School of Mines in London. Worked in Canada and on the Gold Coast. Met Antonia in Chelsea in 1928, and father of Susan. He attempted to persuade Antonia to leave Eric Earnshaw Smith and marry him, but while he was in Canada earning enough money to support her and Susan, Antonia became involved with Tom Hopkinson. During the War Silas married Sheila and joined John Mowlem, civil engineering company, rising to be a managing director. By Sheila, he had a daughter, Emma.

Gluckstein, Isidore Montague Gluckstein was president of J. Lyons and Co (1961–8) and an active member of the Flyfisher's Club. He was educated at St. Paul's and was a pupil and later a venerated friend of Cecil Botting. He married a Miss Adler and it was possibly because of him that the Bottings became clients of the firm of solicitors now known as Adlers. The notorious Eicholtz was a partner.

Green, Julien French Catholic novelist and diarist. His parents were from the deep south of America but he was born in France and has lived in Paris all his life apart from a spell as a student in the United States and another during the War. On his return to Paris in 1946, with his sister Anne, he became a friend of Antonia, who found in his guilt-tormented diaries an echo of her own difficulties. Novels include *Minuit* (1936) and *Moïra* (1950).

Green-Wilkinson, Reginald Reggie was married to Antonia in 1921, and separated from her the same year. He was the gentle, gangling, ne'er do well son of a wealthy and aristocratic family, his uncle being Tom Sopwith, the designer of the Sopwith Pup. Antonia was sorry for Reggie, and she shared his passion for the theatre and toy soldiers. They lived in a tiny house on the corner of Glebe Place, Chelsea, described in the novel *The Sugar House*, but his drinking and homosexuality drove her to despair. He died young, in South Africa, but his mother, Daisy, widow of the impossible Fred, remained a friend and benefactor to Antonia for many years.

Greenwood, John Ormerod Greenwood combined Quakerism (which he chose in place of Methodism at the age of 14) with a passion for advanced drama. He was 28 when Antonia met him at a camp of the Group Theatre of which he was secretary. He was at that time in a confused emotional state.

He later married Jessica and continued an active and outspoken Quaker for the rest of his long life. (He once let drop a four-letter word at an Easter Settlement.) His interest in the theatre world also continued and he wrote a libretto for John Gardner's *The Visitors* (Aldeburgh, 1972).

Grigson, Frances A tall, dark, boyish American, Frances Galt married Geoffrey Grigson in 1927. The Grigsons, with other literary figures, were frequent guests at the Sunday tea parties given by Tom and Antonia at Cecil Court, off the Fulham Road. Frances became Tom's mistress in the summer of 1934. She died of TB in 1937.

Grunelius, Lexi and Antoinette, Catholic owners of the Château de Kolbsheim, Alsace, to whom Antonia was introduced by Robert Speaight and with whom she became good friends. They were believers in the apparition of Our Lady weeping at La Salette. They passionately admired the works of Léon Bloy and Jacques Maritain. When Maritain's wife died they provided him with a home and after his death opened a study centre in his memory.

Guggenheim, Peggy Wealthy American collector of modern art, later famous for her gallery in Venice. She was a niece of Solomon Guggenheim of the Guggenheim Museum, but was in revolt against her family. Peggy was generous to artists; if they were writers she made them allowances, if they were painters she exhibited their work (at 'Guggenheim Jeune'), if they were male she sometimes slept with them. Her lover in 1933 was a literary Englishman, John Holms. She rented Hayford Hall on Dartmoor as a suitable background for him and invited Djuna Barnes (see above), Emily Coleman (see above) and Antonia to stay.

Gumbley, Father Walter, OP Dominican writer and lecturer. Author of the popular Catholic Truth Society's booklet on St Dominic.

Gurdjieff G.I. Leader of a spiritual movement, fashionable in the 'twenties and 'thirties. He established his 'Institute for the Harmonious Development of Man' in the Château du Prieuré at Fontainebleau-Avon. It was here that Katherine Mansfield died. Gurdjieff attempted to describe his system in his book, *All and Everything, or Beelzebub's Tales to his Grandson*. His most famous disciple and interpretor was P.D. Ouspensky.

Gurley, Katharine, MD Dr Gurley, of Jersey City, presumably came to admire Antonia through her books. *Beyond the Glass* (1954) was dedicated to her, 'without whose encouragement this book might never have been written'. The two went on a tour of County Cork the following year in Jim Twomey's taxi.

Havinden, Margaret Red-headed director of W.S. Crawford Ltd and wife of Ashley, famous designer and typographer. Antonia counted her among the powerful Margarets in her life but the two women were on good terms and Margaret tried to prevent Antonia from being sacked from Crawford's in 1930 (probably for laziness and not for the last time). The Havindens had two children, Michael and Venice, and Antonia took her own children to play with them occasionally. The taxi usually got lost in the sumptuous suburb where they lived and Antonia invariably insulted the driver.

Henderson, Ian Older son of Wyn Henderson. Educated at Stowe and Cambridge, he was preparing for the Civil Service examination, possibly at the suggestion of Eric Earnshaw Smith, when Antonia fell in love with him. He appeared a rather solid, unimaginative person, but their physical partnership was successful for longer than most of Antonia's, although (perhaps because) they never shared a home. It ended when Ian went abroad with the RAF at the beginning of the War.

Henderson, Nigel Younger son of Wyn Henderson. Sensitive, ambivalent and at times hysterical. Antonia became his lover late in 1937, referring to him as an '*âme bien née*'. She eventually abandoned him for his brother Ian, advising him to seek help with his homosexual problem from her psychologist, Dr Carroll. Nigel and David Gascoyne had a relationship in Paris at about this time.

Henderson, Wyn Wyn was the mother of Ian and Nigel. Originally a dancer, she at one time managed Peggy Guggenheim's London gallery, Guggenheim Jeune. She recommended *Frost in May* to Desmond Harmsworth, its first publisher.

Hoare, Sir Samuel Known to his friends as Peter, a distinguished civil servant who had risen to be head of the international division of the Home Office. He led a double life, being a member of the Oakley Street set of writers and poets during the mid 1930s (George Barker, David Gascoyne, Dylan Thomas). He even published an essay on Rimbaud. Emily Coleman pursued him passionately for years but he preferred the privacy of his Chelsea flat. He was a close friend of Silas Glossop.

Hodgson, Charles Actor, broadcaster and business man. Undergraduate friend of Thomas and Susan.

Holms, Dorothy Estranged wife of John Holms. Amateur astrologer.

Holms, John A 'bearded and ethereal' English gentleman, supposed to be a writer and a sage. Emily Coleman had discovered him in the South of France but Peggy Guggenheim fought for him and won (at the cost of a black eye). He was the guest of honour at her house, Hayford Hall in the summer of 1933, but was dead within the year, never regaining consciousness from an anaesthetic administered on Peggy's kitchen table after a minor riding accident.

Hope, Lieutenant-Colonel C.E.G. Known to his friends as Anthony, formerly cavalry officer in India. Writer of books on equitation and editor of magazine *Light Horse* and *Pony*. Antonia's neighbour in South Kensington.

Hope, Beryl Wife of Anthony Hope. Convent schoolfriend of Antonia and, later, neighbour in South Kensington.

Hopkinson, Gerti Viennese photographer who came to London before the War and met Tom Hopkinson when he worked on *Weekly Illustrated*. Married Tom in 1939 and had two daughters by him, Nicolette and Amanda.

Hopkinson, Lyndall see Passerini, Lyndall.

Hopkinson, Sir Tom Author and journalist, editor of *Picture Post* during the War. He was the second son of Henry, an archdeacon living at Cockermouth. His brothers were Jack, Paul and Stephan; Esther was his only sister. Antonia met Tom, a fellow copywriter, at W.S. Crawford's advertising agency in the late 'twenties, when she was already involved with Silas Glossop. Hopkinson was some years younger than Antonia. They were married in 1930 and divorced in 1938, during which period Tom worked on *Weekly Illustrated*. Lyndall was Tom's daughter by Antonia. Nicolette and Amanda were the children of his second wife, Gerti Deutsch. His third wife was Dorothy Kingsmill, widow of Hugh Kingsmill (see below). Tom later edited *Drum* in Johannesburg and returned to become professor of journalism at Cardiff. He and Antonia remained virtually estranged from the time of his marriage to Dorothy. His early novels included *The Wise Man Foolish* and *The Man Below*. His short stories were his most imaginative work. He died in 1990.

Horley, Georgina see Smith, Georgina Earnshaw.

Jackson, Lady (Barbara Ward) Originally writer on foreign affairs on *The Economist*. Became a close friend of Antonia in 1943 after giving a speech to members of the Catholic Society, Sword of the Spirit. Antonia wrote an article about Barbara for *Picture Post*, and asked her to be Susan's godmother when she entered the Catholic Church in 1945. She married the international economist, Robert Jackson (1950) and had a son by him. She became Professor of International Economic Development at Columbia University (1968). Latterly she was one of the first to champion the cause of the environment. Her many books include *Only One World; the care and maintenance of a small planet* (1972).

Jennings, Humphrey Poet, described by Antonia as one of 'the young revolutionaries' of the 'thirties. David Gascoyne and George Barker were his co-revolutionaries. Established Mass-Observation with Charles Madge (1938). (It was soon taken over by the sociologist, Tom Harrisson). Became a film director and died by walking backwards off a cliff in Japan while planning a take.

Jerrold, Douglas Managing editor at Catholic publisher, Eyre and Spottiswoode, of which Graham Greene was a director. It is probable that Hugh Kingsmill encouraged Antonia to become one of Jerrold's authors.

Jepson, Selwyn Thriller writer who also produced scripts for the cinema and television. Held high positions in Military Intelligence and SOE, during the War. He was a businesslike man who helped his fellow authors. For instance he arranged for the sale of some of

Robert Graves's manuscripts in 1969. His many books include *Golden Eyes* (1924) and *Letter to a Dead Girl* (1971). Antonia disliked him.

Jones, Phyllis One of Emily Coleman's closest English friends. A lean, handsome redhead whose dry comments conceal a great deal of kindness. 'Send for Phyllis', was the constant cry of those with domestic problems. Though much pursued, she never married. She farmed in Sussex during the War and devoted many years to looking after her mother, eventually moving down to Buckfastleigh in Devon. She typed all Antonia's later manuscripts at absurdly low rates.

Jouve, Pierre Jean Surrealist French poet and reader aloud. Translated Shakespeare. Author of *Mozart's Don Juan* (1942), a psychological study, translated by Eric Earnshaw Smith in 1957. Knew David Gascoyne in Paris just before the War.

Kehoe, Father Richard, O.P. Golden-haired Dominican theologian whose lectures in London were well attended by women.

Keiller, Alexander Antonia was introduced to Keiller, the 'Marmelade King' by Wyn Henderson, his mistress, early in 1934. He had been excavating Avebury Ring (which he owned) for nine years, but he lived at Charles Street, Mayfair, behind drawn curtains. It was here that he suggested to Antonia that, clad only in a mackintosh, she should get into a laundry basket and permit him to poke her through the wickerwork with an umbrella. She declined. In 1966 the Alexander Keiller Museum at Avebury was presented to the nation by his widow, Gabrielle.

King, Cecil Harmsworth Director of the *Daily Mirror* from 1929 and subsequently chairman of the *Daily Mirror* and *Sunday Pictorial* Group and then of the International Publishing Corporation (1963–8). Married to Margaret Cooke, who remained a close friend of Antonia after the Kings' divorce. They had four children: Michael, Francis, Colin and Priscilla.

Kingsmill, Dorothy Wife of the writer, Hugh. She was an attractive blond from the North Country, originally engaged to a young officer called John. He took her down to one of his family homes where his uncle showed her round the flower garden and afterwards told the boy never to bring 'that w----' there again. She never recovered from this rebuff. She then became involved with the Russian novelist, William Gerhardie, who introduced her to Hugh Kingsmill, by whom she had four children, Tony, Edmée, Brook and Dorothy.

Dorothy set up as a psychologist after the War, handing her prospectus round. Tom, Gerti and Antonia were among her patients, but Antonia's analysis, commenced in 1948, was suspended before it had been completed. To add to the complications, Hugh and Dorothy were by now living in Antonia's cottage, Binesfield, where Hugh contracted the gastric trouble that killed him in 1949. Dorothy then married Tom Hopkinson. With him she met Meher Baba, the Indian holy man when he visited England in 1953, and together they later wrote a book about Baba, *Much Silence*.

Kingsmill, Hugh Novelist, biographer and wit. Friend of Hesketh Pearson and Malcolm Muggeridge. Dorothy was his second wife. Books include *Blondel* (1927) and *The Progress of a Biographer* (1949). Kingsmill died in 1949 while he and Dorothy were renting Binesfield, Antonia's Sussex cottage. Antonia dedicated *The Lost Traveller* (1950) to his memory.

Lee, Vernon Real name of Violet Paget. Aesthetic philosopher, author of *The Beautiful* (1913), one of the best known expositions of the 'empathy' theory of art. Also wrote on the Italian Renaissance. Lived in Florence.

Legg, Robert Officer in the King's Own Scottish Borderers. When he was on leave from Ireland Antonia fell ecstatically in love with him for three weeks in 1923, between the collapse of her marriage to Reggie Green-Wilkinson and her own collapse into insanity. Robert had a sister, Dorothy, who was an artist in Chelsea. In *Beyond the Glass* they became Richard and Nell Crayshaw.

Lingham, Elaine Elaine Lingham was the daughter of Agga Lingham, a Catholic friend of Antonia. She had abandoned her

Carmelite vocation shortly before taking her final vows as a nun and worked as an unpaid secretary to Antonia for a time. Later she left to go to Germany.

McClean, Douglas Medical research scientist with strong left wing sympathies. Keenly interested in wine and for many years on the committee of the Wine Society.

McClean, Kathleen (Hale) Artist and author (as Kathleen Hale) of children's books, especially the 'Orlando the Marmalade Cat' series, first of which published in 1938. She was married to Douglas McClean. They had two sons, Peregrine and Nicholas, and lived at Rabley Willows. Eric Earnshaw Smith featured in her books as Mr Buttermeadow.

McMillan, Brigadier John An Australian, Antonia's boss at SOE (Special Operations Executive). Later director of Rediffusion Television (1955–68) where Lyndall worked as a producer's assistant on 'This Week'. A cultured man with an interest in history and the theatre, he lived not too far from Antonia in Kinnerton St.

Madge, Kathleen see Raine, Kathleen.

Malinowsky, Arno A painter whose works are now much sought after. Antonia had known him when she was married to Eric Earnshaw Smith and doing the rounds of the Chelsea studios. Perhaps encouraged by rumours of her many lovers, Malinowsky had suggested she should include him among them.

Maritain, Jacques Neo-Thomist philosopher, author of *Art and Scholasticism*, follower of the prophet Léon Bloy. Lexi and Antoinette Grunelius were close friends and have established a study centre at their home in his memory.

Mathew, Father Gervase OP Dominican brother of David, Catholic Archbishop of Westminster. Lecturer on Theology.

Maydieu, OP, Père Augustin-Jean French Dominican, member of the seminal community in the rue de La Tour-Maubourg which published a revue, *La Vie Spirituelle*, relating religion to the arts. Antonia contributed to this, and was invited to lecture (in French) on Graham Greene's *The Power and the Glory* in 1946. Maydieu had all the warmth and vitality of a true Gascon, having been in the Resistance and survived imprisonment by the Germans (with the aid of his pipe). He invited Antonia and Susan to stay at this family home at Arcachon, on the coast near Bordeaux. His death at a comparatively early age prevented this.

Minka and Curdy Two kittens entered Antonia's life in 1954. Minka was a Siamese and Curdy a common marmalade. Antonia wrote two children's books about them. They survived the move to 42D Courtfield Gardens and lived to a ripe old age, sleeping one on either side of Antonia's head at night and frequently fighting over it.

Moody, Hélène Came of a wealthy Jewish furniture manufacturing family. Ronald Moody married her just before the War, when he was living in Paris. The Moodys later shared flats with Antonia at 29 Thurloe Street and 13 Ashburn Gardens, until 1947. Hélène was a dark, handsome, strong-featured woman with a pile of grey hair on top of her head. She worked as a secretary to support Ronald. Terry-Thomas, the gap-toothed comedian, was one of her employers.

Moody, Ronald Jamaican sculptor who came to London in 1923 to study dentistry. Influenced by Indian and Chinese philosophy. Produced fine works in wood of male figures with Buddha-like faces. One of these, John the Baptist (1936), was recently exhibited at the Hayward Gallery. Married Hélène Cowan who predeceased him.

Mortimer, Raymond Distinguished and well decorated literary critic, four years older than Antonia. A Bloomsberry, he attempted to achieve immortality by writing a few books late in life, including a biography of Duncan Grant (1944). In spite of this he is now largely forgotten. He lived at Long Crichel House in Dorset.

Muir, Edwin Scottish poet, son of a crofter. His poems had an archetypal quality, but his landscape was always that of Orkney. 'The

Horses' is a much anthologised example. Appointed head of the British Institute, Rome (1948) and Professor of Poetry, Harvard (1955). Published eight slim volumes of verse and some critical works.

Muir, Richard Temple, Known to friends as Dicky. Businessman. Graduate of King's College, Cambridge. Engaged to Lyndall in 1948. Publisher of magazine *Autocourse*. Proprietor of London restaurant, La Popotte. Married Patricia, ex-wife of Humphrey Lyttelton.

Neill, Alexander Sutherland Author and child psychologist from Forfar. In 1924 he founded Summerhill School at Leiston in Suffolk, where the children could do what they liked (and did). He wrote *The Problem Parent* (1932) among many books. Antonia met Neill when he leased Summerhill to Rupert Doone for the Group Theatre Summer School.

Nicholson, Basil Journalist, working on the *Daily Mirror* for Cecil King, who said of him 'He was among the half dozen most brilliant men I ever met. He threw off ideas like a catherine wheel.' Also a copywriter, said to have invented the strip cartoon with his Horlicks series. He wrote a novel, *Business is Business*, and was an amateur ornithologist.

Passerini, Count Lorenzo Civil engineer who worked for many years in Africa. Inherited Il Palazzone, Cortona, Tuscany, but gave it to the University of Pisa. Met Lyndall while she was working in Rome and married her when the Italian law allowed him to divorce the former wife from whom he had been long separated. He was some twenty-five years older than Lyndall.

Passerini, Lyndall Antonia's daughter by Tom Hopkinson, two years younger than her half-sister. Educated at Headington School, Oxford, followed by a secretarial course in Cambridge and a production course at the Old Vic Theatre School. She fled from her fiancé, Dicky Muir, to Rome on 16th September, 1952 to join Willy Mostyn-Owen, the art historian. For years fitted a brilliant social life round a job with the Food and Agriculture Organisation of the United Nations. Briefly married Lionel Birch, her father's successor on *Picture Post*; now the widow of Count Lorenzo Passerini. She lives in Tuscany and is the author of *Nothing to Forgive; a Daughter's Life of Antonia White*, 1988.

Pearson, Hesketh Writer of many perceptive and witty biographies in the 'thirties and early 'forties, including *Bernard Shaw* (1942) and *Oscar Wilde* (1946).

Perlès, Alfred Czech poet and diarist, born in Vienna but lived mostly in Paris. Edited the bilingual review, *Delta*, with Henry Miller and Lawrence Durrell. Accepted three of Antonia's poems, 'Epitaph' (on the death of a friend), 'The Crest' and 'The Double Man' (about Ian Henderson) in 1938, and also reprinted 'The House of Clouds', her short story about madness. Wrote a poem about Antonia when she was close to suicide in Paris in 1938.

In 1940, at the age of forty, he joined the British Pioneer Corps. Among his publications are *Sentiments Limitrophes* (1935) and *Round Trip* (1946) a war diary wittily observant of the British.

Pius, Father ODC Prior of the Carmelites in Kensington Church Street. When Kathleen Raine, the poet, required instruction, Antonia persuaded Father Pius to undertake the task.

Raine, Kathleen Author of several volumes of verse, including *Stone and Flower*, 1943 and *Collected Poems*, 1956. Also of two-volume *Blake and Tradition*, 1968. Kathleen was the daughter of a school-teacher and spent part of her childhood in the wilds of Scotland. She has something of the beauty but also the severity of the northern hills. Her years at Girton College added to this severity. Antonia met her in 1943 when they were both working for SOE (Special Operations Executive). Kathleen, almost ten years her junior, later declared 'in a dark year [she] was to me a light-bearer'. Through Antonia, Kathleen became a Catholic. The two women quarrelled violently (Antonia always insisting that it was Kathleen who turned on her) but ended 'fellow traveller[s] for so many years' as Kathleen put it. She lives in Chelsea at 47 Paulton's Square, divorced from Charles Madge (founder of Mass-Observation) and has two children, James and Anna. She is also a translator from the French.

Reitlinger, Gerald Robert Started life as a painter, but, after supervising an Oxford University expedition to Hira in Iraq, became more interested in writing books about art and *objets d'art*, moving ever further East. He was ugly, resembling (as he well knew) the grotesque porcelain dragon's head on the dustjacket of one of his books. He did, however, have the advantage of a private income and a cottage in the grounds of his house near Rye, which he rented out to Antonia.

Riding, Laura American poet. Close collaborator with Robert Graves from 1926, both in London and Majorca. Believed herself to have mystical powers and inspired Graves's *The White Goddess*, 1948, a book about women as Muse, both cruel and kind. She was a small woman with a big personality, sometimes referring to herself as 'Laura Riding on a White Horse', although those who suffered under her preferred to call her 'Laura Riding Roughshod'. Married Schuyler B. Jackson (1941) and moved to Wabasso, Florida. Books include *Anarchism is Not Enough*, 1928, *Collected Poems*, 1938, and *Selected Poems*, 1970.

Robb, James Psychologist involved with the Arcane Society whom Antonia consulted in 1934. She did not undergo a complete analysis with him because she feared its effect on her writing. At an earlier period she had had a brief affair with him.

Rothenstein, Sir John Art historian and director of Tate Gallery (1938–1964). Son of famous portrait painter, Sir William Rothenstein. Author of many books on twentieth-century British artists and a three-volume book about himself that told all.

Russell, Bertrand, 3rd Earl Russell One of the greatest logicians of all time, involved in political controversy until his death at the age of almost a hundred. Antonia caught his eye at a lecture when she was twenty-seven, and Russell started an affair with her. She said he once got down on his knees in a taxi and bleated like a sheep to try and persuade her to go away with him for a weekend. The friendship ended when Russell divorced his wife, Dora, and Antonia refused to give evidence that Russell was Susan's 'pagan godfather'.

St Denis, Michel St Denis was the French director of a group of acrobatic actors known as the *Compagnie des Quinze*. He later opened a drama school in Islington called the London Theatre Studio, where the Motley Sisters made their reputation. Antonia became excited by his work when she was drama critic for *Time and Tide* in 1934. She lectured to his students (very competently) on Greek drama and wrote a play for them, *Alcibiades*, now lost. It will be recalled that this Athenian statesman was somewhat cheeky as a youth. After a good dinner he attempted to roll Socrates up with him in his blanket. The talented Vera Poliakov was St Denis's mistress.

During the War he made daily broadcasts to Occupied France on the BBC European Service under the alias of Jacques Duchesne. He then returned to France.

Schepeler, Alick A beautiful, rather tragic woman who had been a model (and therefore mistress) of Augustus John. She attended Tom and Antonia's Sunday tea parties at Cecil Court, when she was working on *Vogue*. She died of cancer, old, alone and poor, but left Antonia a fine gilt mirror which Susan Chitty inherited.

Seabrooke, Eliot Bohemian Chelsea painter and talented actor who had escorted Antonia round the Chelsea parties in the early 'twenties. He was nearly twice her age, and in *The Sugar House*, under the name of Marcus Gundry, made an unsuccessful attempt on her virginity. After her night with Jim Dougal, in 1924, Seabrooke introduced her to Wyn Henderson who arranged an abortion for her.

Senhouse, Roger Literary critic, adored young friend of Lytton Strachey. He abandoned his ancestral northern home at Maryport (it fell down shortly afterwards) to join dubious friends in the south. His translation of Colette's *Gigi* appeared in the same volume as Antonia's of *The Cat*. He was a director of Secker and Warburg, who published it.

Siepmann, Eric Diplomat of German origin, subsequently author and journalist. Antonia became involved with him in the 'thirties and went to stay at a villa he was renting in Spain, but did not have an affair with him. It seems probable that she was more in love with him than he was with her. After the War he married the novelist, Mary Wesley and in 1956 he set fire (unintentionally) to Antonia's sitting-room-cum-study by throwing a lighted cigarette end into the waste-paper basket before going down to dinner. All her work on the Dougal book was destroyed (somewhat to her relief).

Smith, Eric Earnshaw Antonia met Earnshaw Smith, her second husband, in 1919 while she was still at the Academy of Dramatic Art, and married him in 1925. He was a homosexual and considerably older than herself, having been wounded in the First World War. He was a senior civil servant for the rest of his working life, keeping his interest in the arts and philosophy for outside office hours. His older brother Harold was Vicar of All Souls, Langham Place. Eric talked Antonia out of the Catholic Church but shared her interest in cats. During the Second World War he married Georgina Horley, but remained a close friend and adviser to Antonia. When he was in financial difficulty after his retirement, she handed on two books for him to translate from the French, one of them Pierre Jean Jouve's *Mozart's Don Juan* (1957) and the other Henry Muller's *Clem* (1962). Both caused him exquisite agony, as he was not in the habit of putting pen to paper.

Smith, Georgina Earnshaw Wrote under the name Georgina Horley and known to her friends as Georgie. Real name Elizabeth Essex. Author of the novel, *Bus Stop* (1955), of which Eric was the hero and of the Penguin Handbook, *Good Food on a Budget* (1969). Close friend of Tom Hopkinson is his *Picture Post* days. During the war she married Eric Earnshaw Smith, Antonia's second husband, and returned with him to her home town, Worthing.

Smith, Leslie Earnshaw Eric's younger brother, always referred to as 'dear little Lel', appears to have suffered most in the unhappy home at Cambridge where his father died of alcoholism. Never achieved much in life; became Antonia's lodger briefly before retiring to 'a very nice home for old gentlemen on the River'.

Smith, Logan Pearsall Ageing American pederast and man of letters, living in Chelsea. Son of Hannah Whitall Smith, a Quaker writer, whose pamphlet, 'How Little Logan came to Jesus', he reprinted. From his mother, also, he inherited a fortune. Antonia met Logan in her twenties, through Eric, and won a boasting game at one of his parties by declaring that her virginity had been certified by the Pope. He encouraged her to parody the works of other writers, particularly Henry James and Flaubert, by way of training. He himself could only write in the periods between depressions, but he is still remembered for *Trivia*, *On Reading Shakespeare* and his prose selections. Bob Gathorne-Hardy was his friend and collaborator.

Speaight, Bridget Wife of Robert. Oxford graduate, painter and pianist. They met at Aldeburgh in 1949, where she lived; he was lecturing at the Festival and observed a young woman 'several decades further from the grave than the rest of the audience'. They were married with the consent of the Vatican (both had been married before) and Bridget bought Campion House, a fine but cold six-teenth-century residence in Kent, without consulting Robert. There she kept things (including Robert) in a high degree of 'shipshapeli-ness' for the rest of Robert's life. She has grown-up children from her previous marriage.

Speaight, Robert Distinguished Catholic actor who made his name preaching Becket's sermon in *Murder in the Cathedral* and was condemned thereafter to clerical roles ('sealed in the tomb of St Eliot'). He became a friend of Antonia during the War after his first marriage had collapsed but confined his sensual enjoyments to good wine and cigars. He consented to be Susan's godfather. Published biographies of modern Catholics on both sides of the channel, and his own autobiography, *The Property Basket* (1968). Introduced Antonia to many Catholics, religious and lay, in France and the USA.

Starkie, Dr Enid Irish writer of books on the nineteenth-century French poets, including Rimbaud. A colourful member of the senior common room at Somerville College, Oxford, and the keeper of the cellar key. Antonia probably met her through such Oxford friends as Lord David Cecil and Viola Garvin. She used to invite Susan to her Chinese red rooms when she was an undergraduate at Somerville and quiz her with bright blue eyes made bluer by her (dyed) red hair.

Stewart, Meum Writer. Shared Antonia's youthful experience of 'talk over studio fires' in the 'twenties but probably did not meet her until she included Antonia's poem 'Epitaph' in *The Distaff Muse: An Anthology of Poetry Written by Women* (1949). By this time Meum, an elegant creature, was living in Hampstead. Her collaborator on the book was Clifford Bax, brother of the composer.

Summerson, John Readable writer on architecture and eventually curator of the John Soames Museum. He gave Antonia a copy of his *John Nash: Architect to George IV* (1935) during their brief love affair.

Thornton, Edward A Catholic businessman with more than a foot in the Eastern-mysticism camp along with Dorothy Kingsmill and others. Antonia almost agreed to be analysed by him in 1951, but fortunately withdrew on the brink because his nervous laugh suggested that he was not himself fully 'integrated'. He was an amateur actor and singer; Antonia implied that he was unmarried.

Thornton, Margaret Possibly sister of Edward – certainly shared his spiritual interests.

Thorp, Peter Peter Thorp (real name Joseph) was the recipient of the letters published under the title *The Hound and the Falcon*. These letters concerned Antonia's return to the Catholic Church. Peter had trained as a Jesuit, had worked in advertising and had originally written to Antonia as a stranger about *Frost in May*. The couple exchanged increasingly warm letters during the War but the correspondence ceased when Antonia visited him (and his wife) in Wales. She declared, as was her wont, that his wife was much nicer than he was.

Turnell, Martin Somewhat academic writer on French literature, and contributor to *Horizon* and *The Life of the Spirit* (Dominican). Published *The Novel in France* (1950). Two of the seven great novelists he selected for this book, Laclos and Benjamin Constant, wrote only one novel apiece, yet, he declared, these were not just 'superb flukes', which was satisfactory for Antonia. His life of Baudelaire came out in 1953.

Tyrrell, George A Catholic Modernist theologian, friend of Baron von Hügel, the Continental Modernist. He was expelled from their society by the Jesuits and finally, in 1907, from the Catholic Church, for championing the cause of living faith against dead theology. In his posthumously published book, *Christianity at the Cross-Roads* (1909) he suggested a universal religion of which Christianity was only the germ. Antonia had originally been given an earlier book of his, *Nova et Vetera*, 1897 by Peter Thorp, but this was not questioned by Church authorities. It was strongly influenced by Newman, as were most of Tyrrell's books. His tragic life story was written first kindly by his friend, Maud Petre (1912), and now unkindly by Nicholas Sagovsky (1991.)

Walker, Alan Alan Walker had been a friend of Eric Earnshaw Smith at Cambridge. He was briefly engaged to Antonia in 1924. On a pre-marital tour of France in his open car that year, his glasses flew off shortly after leaving Calais and were never seen again. He made such a fuss that Antonia decided there and then that she would rather marry Eric, who was of the party. Alan entered the Diplomatic Service and later married into the Bute family. For some years he was *Daily Telegraph* correspondent in Madrid.

Ward, Barbara *see* Jackson, Lady.

White, Father Victor OP Dominican friar from Blackfriars at Oxford. Victor White lectured on St Thomas Aquinas, and was an expert on Jung whom he visited regularly in Switzerland. A small man in a shabby black suit with false teeth that clicked when he was enthusiastic (which he usually was), he soon became a family friend. His books included *Soul and Psyche* (1960).

Yvon (surname unknown) French-speaking lover of Antonia's from Martinique. She met him on a holiday in the South of France in 1927 while she was still married to Eric Earnshaw Smith. She described him as 'slender and small boned, having a body like a very young girl'. This, her first real love affair, gave rise to her first short story, 'Mon Pays c'est la Martinique', first published in *As Once in May* (1983).

Index